American cup measures – Dry ingredients

(Using the eight liquid ounce cup—Cups should be lightly packed)

1 cup flour	4 oz.
1 cup cornflour	4½ oz.
1 cup sugar (granulated or superfine)	8 oz.
1 cup confectioners' sugar (free from lumps)	5 oz.
1 cup shortening (butter, margarine, etc.)	8 oz.
1 cup brown sugar	5 oz.
1 cup soft breadcrumbs	2 oz.
1 cup dry breadcrumbs (made from fresh breadcrumbs)	3 oz.
1 cup packet dry breadcrumbs	4 oz.
1 cup rice (uncooked)	6 oz.
1 cup rice (cooked)	3 oz.
1 cup mixed fruit or individual fruit such as sultanas, etc.	6 oz.
1 cup grated cheese	4 oz.
1 cup nuts (chopped)	4 oz.
1 cup almonds (whole)	4 oz.
1 cup almonds (ground)	6 oz.
1 cup cocoa	4 oz.
1 cup minced raw meat	8 oz.

American liquid measures

(Using the eight liquid ounce cup measure)

1 cup liquid	8 fluid oz.
1 gill liquid (½ cup)	4 fluid oz.
1 liquid pint (2 cups)	16 fluid oz.

Oven temperatures

When you buy a gas or electric cooker the manufacturer will provide you with a chart giving his recommendations for the oven settings. There is often a slight variance between different makes of cookers and also between gas and electric temperatures. The chart which follows, therefore, can only be a guide but if you follow it carefully, whatever type of cooker you use, you will not go far wrong.

	Temperature ° Fahrenheit
Very cool or very slow	225°—275°
Cool or slow	275°—300°
Very moderate	325°—350°
Moderate	350°—375°
Moderately hot	375°—400°
Hot	425°—450°
Very hot	450°—500°

COOKING for every occasion

Edited by MARION HOWELLS

CHARTWELL
BOOKS INC.

Jacket illustrations
Front: Tournedos. See recipe on page 54.
Cream puff. See recipe on page 206. Cheese soufflé. See recipe on page 32.

Front Flap: Canapés. See pages 10, 12.

Back: Chicken in a basket. See recipe on page 81.
Ginger cake, patty cakes and easy Dundee cake. See recipes on pages 152 and 156.

Back flap: Chicken salad with lychees and oregano-tomato salad.
See recipes on pages 117 and 118.

Frontispiece: Australian apple charlotte. See recipe on page 217. Apple pie (at rear).
See recipe on page 214.

Published by Chartwell Books Inc.,
a division of Book Sales Inc.,
110 Enterprise Avenue
Secaucus, N.J. 07094

This edition © Octopus Books Limited 1971

ISBN 7064 0003 8

Produced by Mandarin Publishers Limited
22A Westlands Road, Quarry Bay, Hong Kong

Printed in Hong Kong

Contents

Weights and measures

If you are to get consistently good results when cooking it is necessary to weigh or measure the ingredients very accurately. All the recipes in this book are based on the Imperial weights and measures with American equivalents given in parenthesis (see inside front cover). Dry ingredients are given in ounces or spoonfuls and the measuring spoon designed by the British Standard Institute has been used to ensure accurate measurements.

All spoons should be filled level. This is most important.

The B.S.I. measuring jug is used to measure liquids. The one illustrated holds 10 fluid oz. or ½ pint. A larger one holding 1 pint or 20 fluid oz. is also available. (The American 1 pint is 16 fluid oz.)

NOTE: The standard measuring cup shown on this page measures up to 250 millilitres; this is equivalent to quarter of a litre.

For those who may prefer to use the American method of measuring in cups, a conversion of some of the basic ingredients is given inside the front and back covers. Cups should be lightly packed unless the recipe states otherwise.

For those who wish to adopt the Metric system of measuring, we give below the exact conversion and also the agreed working equivalent.

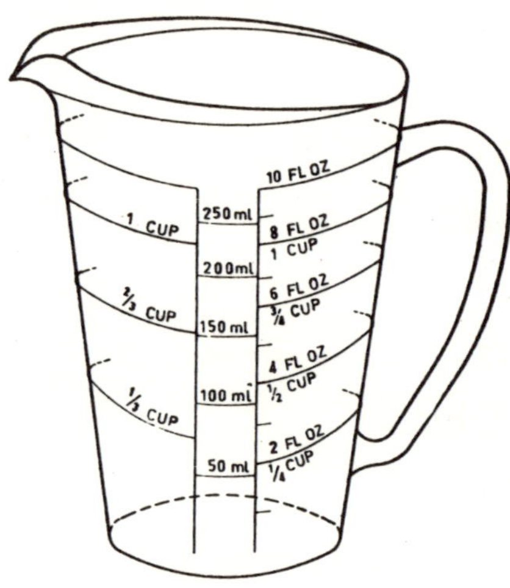

Standard Imperial ½-pint measure

Oven temperatures

When you buy a gas or electric cooker the manufacturer will provide you with a chart giving his recommendations for the oven settings. There is often a slight variance between different makes of cookers and also between gas and electric temperatures. The chart which follows, therefore, can only be a guide but if you follow it carefully, whatever type of cooker you use, you will not go far wrong.

	Mark	Temperature ° Fahrenheit
Very cool or very slow	¼—1	225°—275°
Cool or slow	1—2	275°—300°
Very moderate	3—4	325°—350°
Moderate	4—5	350°—375°
Moderately hot	5—6	375°—400°
Hot	7—8	425°—450°
Very hot	8—10	450°—500°

Temperature conversion

Measurements of heat used in Britain at present are given in degrees Fahrenheit or Centigrade. When the metrication programme has reached a more advanced stage, it is possible that a change will be made.

The unit at present known as the degree Centigrade will be replaced by degrees Celsius. The reason is to avoid confusion with a unit in some other countries having the same name, but used to denote fractions of a right angle.

IN THIS BOOK DEGREES FAHRENHEIT ARE USED THROUGHOUT
—but for future reference we give a conversion chart.

	Fahrenheit	Celsius
Very cool or very slow	275 F.	135 C.
Cool or slow	300 F.	149 C.
Very moderate	325 F.	163 C.
Moderate	350 F.	177 C.
Moderately hot	375 F.	190 C.
Fairly hot	400 F.	204 C.
Hot	425 F.	218 C.
Very hot	450 F.	238 C.

Metric measures

When the Metric system comes into operation, although many people will continue to use their well tried recipe books the new weights will be in grams instead of ounces and kilograms instead of pounds.

The exact conversion would not be practicable from the cook's point of view, and we have therefore given a working equivalent.

Imperial oz.	Metric grams	Working Equivalent grams
1	28·35	25
2	56·7	50
4	113·4	100
8	226·8	200
12	340·2	300
1·0 lb.	453	400
1·1 lb.	½ Kilo	
2·2 lb.	1 Kilo	

Liquid measures

	millilitres	millilitres
¼ pint (1 gill)	142 ml	150 ml
½ pint	284 ml	300 ml
1 pint	568 ml	600 ml
1¾ pints	994 ml	1 litre

Linear measures for cake tins

1 inch	2½ cm
2 inch	5 cm
3 inch	7½ cm
6 inch	15 cm
12 inch	30 cm

Appetizers

In this section we give a tempting selection of hors d'oeuvre, canapés, savouries and dips.

Hors d'oeuvre make a tasty, colourful beginning. They should have a distinct, sharp taste to clear the palate for the next course. They should be light, so that the appetite for the next course is not dulled.

Canapés are savoury pieces, generally bite-sized, to offer with drinks. They are small rounds, squares, triangles or fingers of fresh bread, toast or crisply fried bread, or savoury biscuits. They're topped, simply, with a pâté or spread, or they can have an irresistible selection of good things to top them. The word 'canapés' is derived from the French, meaning 'sofa'; it was considered the small bases acted as a 'seat' for the delicacies which topped them.

Savouries are another popular accompaniment to party drinks; these are savoury bites such as Angels on Horseback.

Hors d'Oeuvre

A selection of any of the following would look appetizing and colourful.

Sliced continental sausages: salami, liver sausage, etc.

Vegetables, both fresh and canned: artichoke hearts, beans, asparagus, tiny champignons (mushrooms), mixed vegetables, cauliflower, carrot, broccoli, beetroot, etc. When using fresh vegetables, cook them lightly, drain well, toss in a little French dressing.

Fish of all types: smoked salmon, herrings made into roll mops, oysters—fresh and smoked—crab, prawns, lobster, etc.

Salads of various types: potato, mushroom, etc.

Chicken Liver Pâté

This superb Chicken Liver Pâté makes the perfect first course for a dinner party; or use it as a spread, on small toast squares, to serve with drinks.

1½ teaspoons gelatine	¼ teaspoon thyme
2 tablespoons cold water	1 bayleaf
¼ pint (½ cup) chicken stock	2 tablespoons dry sherry
1 lb. chicken livers	4 tablespoons cream
2 tablespoons brandy	2 tablespoons chopped parsley
2 oz. (¼ cup) butter	salt, pepper
2 small onions	3 oz. (good ¼ cup) butter, extra
4 rashers bacon	

Soften gelatine in cold water, add to boiling stock, stir until dissolved. Pour into a lightly oiled mould or loaf tin, refrigerate until set.

Chop chicken livers roughly, place in basin with brandy and marinate 1½ hours. Drain livers, heat 1 oz. (2 tablespoons) butter in frying pan, add livers and sauté just long enough to brown on all sides.

In separate pan, melt remaining butter and cook the chopped onion, chopped bacon, thyme and bayleaf. Add the semi-cooked chicken livers, cook further 5 minutes. Remove from heat, remove bayleaf.

Blend mixture until smooth in electric blender or pound to a paste, then rub through sieve. Stir in any brandy left from marinade, sherry, cream, parsley, and salt and pepper to taste. Melt extra butter and fold through. Spread over gelatine in mould, pressing mixture in gently and evenly; refrigerate until firm. Unmould on to serving plate. Serve with triangles of toast.

Serves 4 to 5.

Liver Pâté

1 lb. calves liver	3 dessertspoons medium cream
2 oz. (¼ cup) butter	1 beaten egg
4 oz. belly of pork	salt, black pepper
1 tablespoon parsley	2 oz. chicken livers
pinch thyme	1½ tablespoons brandy
1 clove garlic	4 oz. streaky bacon
lemon juice	4 bay leaves

Brown liver in butter, put through a mincer with the pork. Add finely chopped parsley, thyme, crushed garlic, lemon juice to taste, cream, egg and seasoning.

Trim chicken livers and fry in remaining butter. Remove from the pan, add brandy and flame. Stir up the sediment and add to the liver mixture.

Line a terrine with the bacon rashers, half fill with the liver mixture, spread chicken livers on top and cover with remaining liver. Fold ends of bacon over the top and add the bay leaves.

Cover tightly with the lid or buttered foil and

stand in a baking tin with about ½ in. water.

Cook in a very moderate oven, Mark 3, 325°F., for 2 hours.

Put a light weight on top while cooling and serve when completely cold with hot toast.

Brandied Liverwurst Pâté

2 oz. (¼ cup) butter	2 teaspoons grated
1 lb. liverwurst	onion
2 tablespoons chopped	2 tablespoons medium
parsley	cream
½ teaspoon dried thyme	2 tablespoons brandy
pinch nutmeg	

Beat together butter and liverwurst until smooth. Add remaining ingredients, beat again. Place in a greased mould, refrigerate several hours or overnight.

Serves 5 to 6.

Ham Rolls

4 oz. (⅔ cup) rice	4 tablespoons single
1 bay leaf	(light) cream
pinch saffron	grated rind of 1 lemon
1 tablespoon oil	2 tablespoons lemon
2 oz. onion (½ small	juice
onion)	1 oz. (2 tablespoons)
2 oz. apple (½ apple)	chopped ham
1 oz. (2 tablespoons)	1 tablespoon chopped
butter	red pepper
1½ teaspoons curry	8 slices ham
powder	

Cook the rice with bay leaf and saffron, drain, rinse and add the oil. Sauté the peeled and chopped onion and apple in the butter for 5 minutes. Remove from heat, add cream, lemon rind, lemon juice, ham and red pepper. Season carefully and set aside in a cool place for 1 hour. Roll in slices of ham and garnish with black olives and red pepper.

Serves 8.

Smoked Haddock Pâté

¼ lb. cooked smoked	¼ teaspoon freshly
haddock	ground pepper
4 oz. (½ cup) butter	1 teaspoon lemon juice
1½ tablespoons finely	¼ teaspoon curry
chopped onion or	powder
shallot	chopped parsley

Skin and bone fish. Pound butter and fish together until well blended. Add onion or shallot, pepper, lemon juice and curry powder, beat well. Sprinkle with a little chopped parsley.

Serves 4.

Tchinin

A tasty fish-flavoured hors d'oeuvre.

7 oz. can sardines	1 teaspoon
5 hard boiled eggs	Worcestershire sauce
2 tablespoons mayon-	salt, pepper
naise	2 tablespoons whipped
1 tablespoon lemon	cream
juice	

Drain oil from sardines and remove bones. Chop eggs roughly. Emulsify all the ingredients except the cream. Correct the seasoning then add cream. Put the mixture into a forcing bag and decorate the lettuce hearts, dust with paprika and sprinkle with finely chopped nuts or chives.

Serves 5 to 6.

Avocado Creams

2 avocado pears	2 teaspoons sugar
1 tablespoon wine	salt, cayenne
vinegar	1 teaspoon paprika
4 anchovies very finely	¼ pint (½ cup) whipped
chopped	cream
1 teaspoon very finely	
chopped onion	

Remove the stone and flesh from the pears and mash the flesh to a soft cream. Add all the other ingredients, mix well and correct the seasoning. Pile back into the avocado cases and garnish with lemon.

Serves 4.

Mushrooms à la Grecque

2 tablespoons oil	1 clove garlic
juice of 1 lemon	pepper, salt
2 tablespoons tomato	8 oz. (2 cups) button
purée	mushrooms
bouquet garni	

Put the oil, lemon juice, tomato purée, bouquet garni and crushed garlic into a small pan, cover and cook for a few minutes. Season with pepper and salt. Wash mushrooms, drain and add to sauce. Cover and cook for 7 minutes. Serve cold.

Serves 4.

Cauliflower with Aioli

1 cauliflower	2 egg yolks
2 cloves garlic	½ pint (1 cup) oil

Divide the cauliflower into small sprigs. Pound the garlic, stir in the egg yolks. Add the oil very gradually at first, as if for mayonnaise. When all the oil has been added, put the aioli into a bowl standing on a flat dish. Arrange the sprigs of cauliflower round.

Savoury Pancakes

2 eggs
1 oz. (2 tablespoons) butter
8 oz. (2 cups) plain flour
salt, pepper
1 teaspoon dry mustard
approx. 1 pint (1¾ cups) milk
4 oz. (1 cup) grated cheese (Cheddar or similar)
parsley

Separate eggs, melt butter. Sift together dry ingredients. Make well in centre, add egg-yolks and melted butter to flour mixture. Gradually add milk, stirring constantly until mixture is smooth. Lastly fold in stiffly beaten egg-whites.

Heat a little oil in small frying pan. Pour sufficient batter into frying pan to make thin pancakes, cook over medium heat until lightly browned, turn and cook other side. Turn on to a board, spread with desired filling and roll up. Put on to dish and keep hot while rest of pancakes are being cooked. Sprinkle with cheese and put under grill to brown. Serve garnished with parsley.

Makes 10 to 12 pancakes.

A choice of 3 fillings is given below. If the main course is to be fish, meat or poultry, you can choose a filling for the pancake entrée that will contrast with the main dish.

Red Salmon

7½ oz. can red salmon
2 dessertspoons chopped mint
4 oz. (½ cup or 1 package) cream cheese
2 oz. (½ cup) grated cheese (Cheddar or similar)
1 teaspoon curry powder
½ teaspoon sugar
2 dessertspoons lemon juice
salt, pepper

Drain salmon and remove bones. Combine salmon with remaining ingredients; mix well. Season to taste with salt and pepper.

Asparagus

10 oz. can green asparagus tips
2 oz. (¼ cup) butter
2 oz. (½ cup) flour
2 egg-yolks
2 sticks finely chopped celery
2 oz. (½ cup) grated cheese (Cheddar or similar)
4 rashers bacon
salt, pepper

Drain asparagus, make liquid up to ¾ pint (1 cup) with water. Melt butter in saucepan, stir in flour, cook few minutes. Gradually add reserved liquid. Bring to boil, stirring; simmer 3 minutes. Remove from heat, add egg-yolks, celery, grated cheese and asparagus.

Chop bacon, cook in frying pan until crisp, add to asparagus mixture. Season to taste.

Chicken

½ lb. cooked chicken
3 oz. (1 cup) mushrooms
1 stick celery
2 medium potatoes
1 oz. (2 tablespoons) butter
¼ pint (½ cup) milk
2 chives or spring onions chopped
2 egg-yolks
2 teaspoons curry powder
2 tablespoons port wine
1½ teaspoons salt
pinch pepper
½ teaspoon nutmeg

Finely chop chicken meat, mushrooms and celery. Rub peeled boiled potatoes through sieve.

Melt butter in saucepan, sauté mushrooms until soft. Add sieved potato and milk, stir over low heat until mixture is heated and thoroughly combined. Remove from heat, add chopped chives or spring onions, celery, egg-yolks and chicken. Stir in curry powder and wine. Season to taste with salt, pepper and nutmeg; mix well.

Serves 6.

Stuffed Peaches

Use 2 large ripe peaches or 4 halves of canned peaches.

6 oz. (¾ cup) cream cheese
1 oz. (2 tablespoons) seedless raisins (plumped in boiling water)
1 oz. (2 tablespoons) walnuts
endive
watercress

Mix the cheese, raisins and chopped nuts and shape into 12 small balls. If the mixture is too soft refrigerate for a short while before shaping.

Arrange the peaches on a little endive, put 3 balls of cheese in each and garnish with watercress.

Serves 4.

A tempting selection of canapés; use any of these toppings; smoked salmon with scrambled eggs; lettuce, camembert cheese, sliced radish; asparagus and rare roast beef; prawns, shrimps, lettuce, mayonnaise (see page 121); lettuce, sardines, lemon; creamed blue cheese with stuffed olives; smoked salmon, asparagus, cucumber; liver pâté, beetroot, gherkins; egg slices with anchovies; cucumber, prawns, mayonnaise (see page 121); cucumber, rare roast beef and cocktail onions.

Grilled Chicken Livers

2 oz. (¼ cup) butter	2 oz. (½ cup) fine dry
1 lb. chicken livers	breadcrumbs

Sauce

1 oz. (2 tablespoons) butter	2 tablespoons water
1 tablespoon prepared mustard	1 dessertspoon grated onion
2 tablespoons tomato paste	pinch cayenne
	2 teaspoons Worcestershire sauce

Melt butter, dip cleaned chicken livers into butter, then coat firmly with breadcrumbs. Thread on to 3 or 4 skewers. Place on greased grilling tray and grill about 3 minutes on each side or until chicken livers are tender. Serve with sauce for spooning over or dripping.

Serves 3 to 4.

Sauce   Melt butter in saucepan, add remaining ingredients, stir over heat until boiling.

NOTE: In their uncooked state, chicken livers are very tender; if too thick skewers are used, the livers may break. The fine bamboo skewers are ideal. They can be bought in some speciality shops, or shops which sell oriental goods.

Dutch Bitterballs

3 oz. (½ cup) chopped raw veal	1 teaspoon chopped parsley
1 teaspoon gelatine	salt, pepper
1 oz. (2 tablespoons) butter	nutmeg
2 tablespoons flour	dried breadcrumbs
3 oz. (½ cup) chopped ham	1 egg
1 oz. (¼ cup) grated cheese (Cheddar or similar)	oil

Cover veal with water and simmer until tender. Drain, reserve ½ pint (1 cup) stock. Dissolve gelatine in hot veal stock.

Melt butter, add flour, cook 1 minute. Remove from heat. Gradually add stock. Return to heat, bring to boil, simmer until smooth and thickened, stirring constantly. Add chopped veal and ham, grated cheese and parsley. Season well, turn into bowl, refrigerate overnight.

Using teaspoon, form mixture into small balls. Roll in dried breadcrumbs, dip in beaten egg, roll again in breadcrumbs to give firm coating. Deep fry in hot oil—till golden, drain on absorbent paper.

These are the famous Dutch savoury snack and drink accompaniment. They are traditionally served with a mild mustard, into which the balls are dipped before eating. It is the mustard accompaniment which gives them their name.

Makes approx. 2 dozen.

Crunchy Cheese Croutons

1½ oz. (3 tablespoons) butter	2 tablespoons chopped parsley
2 oz. (½ cup) Cheddar cheese	salt, pepper
	French bread

Combine butter, grated cheese and parsley in bowl; blend well until creamy and smooth. Season to taste. Place slices of French bread on baking tray; cover surface with cheese mixture. Bake in very hot oven, Mark 8, 450°F., 8 to 10 minutes or until lightly golden brown and crisp.

Sufficient covering for approx. 12 slices of French bread.

NOTE: For a more crunchy top, press tops of croutons in finely chopped nuts before baking.

These are a quick-and-easy, delightfully savoury snack to eat just as they are, hot from the oven. Or serve them as an accompaniment to soup or grills.

Ham Savouries

3 teaspoons gelatine	pinch dry mustard
8 oz. cooked ham	pinch nutmeg
2 oz. (¼ cup) butter	salt, pepper
2 oz. (½ cup) flour	beaten egg
½ pint (1 cup) milk	breadcrumbs
1½ tablespoons chopped parsley	

Soften gelatine in 1½ tablespoons water. Mince or chop ham finely. Melt butter, add flour and cook, stirring, 1 minute. Remove from heat, gradually add milk. Return to heat, cook until thickened, stirring constantly.

Dissolve gelatine over hot water. Add ham, parsley and gelatine to sauce, add mustard and nutmeg; season to taste. Spread on tray, refrigerate until set.

Form into balls, about the size of large walnut. Dip in beaten egg, then in breadcrumbs; do this twice. Deep fry until golden brown.

Makes approx. 3½ dozen.

Cheese Twists

4 oz. (½ cup or 1 stick) butter	7 oz. (2 cups) grated Cheddar cheese
6 oz. (1½ cups) plain flour	1 egg
	salt

Rub butter into sifted flour. Add ⅔ of the grated cheese, stir in egg; mix well. Roll out dough to

$\frac{1}{8}$ in. thickness on floured board. Cut out $\frac{1}{4}$ in. × $4\frac{1}{2}$ in. strips. Twist 2 strips together, place on greased oven tray, sprinkle with remaining cheese. Bake in hot oven, Mark 7, 425°F., 10 to 12 minutes or until golden brown. Sprinkle with salt while still hot. Loosen and allow to cool on trays. Makes approx. 5 dozen.

Savoury Bread Cases

sliced bread   melted butter

To Make Cases   Remove crust from bread slices. If using one-day-old bread, brush slices lightly with melted butter; for fresh bread, this is not necessary. Press into deep, greased patty pans. Bake in moderate oven, Mark 4, 350°F., approximately 20 minutes or until golden and crisp.

Spoon hot filling in just before serving, or they can be filled 30 minutes ahead, then reheated in moderate oven, Mark 4, 350°F., 5 to 7 minutes; they can also be made days ahead and stored, unfilled, in air-tight tin.

Fillings
Basic Sauce

1 oz. (2 tablespoons) $\frac{1}{2}$ pint (1 cup) milk
  butter   salt, pepper
2 tablespoons flour

Melt butter in saucepan, stir in flour, cook 1 minute. Remove from heat, gradually add milk, blend well. Return to heat, bring to boil, reduce heat, simmer until smooth and thickened, stirring constantly. Season well.

Canned salmon, seasoned with lemon juice, with chopped parsley added, can be mixed into the basic sauce; or stir in drained asparagus pieces with chopped hard-boiled eggs and a little curry powder; or drained whole kernel corn, little grated cheese, chopped parsley makes a good combination.

Makes enough filling for approx. 12.

Little Italian Pizzas

Quick Pizza Dough

$\frac{1}{2}$ lb. (2 cups) self-   1 oz. (2 tablespoons)
  raising (all purpose)   butter
  flour   about 6 fl. oz. milk
pinch salt   oil

Sift dry ingredients into basin, rub in butter. Add milk nearly all at once, keeping a little back to be used only if dough seems too dry. Knead lightly on floured board and roll out thinly. Cut into squares or rounds, place on oiled tray. Brush dough over lightly with oil. Bake in hot oven, Mark 7, 425°F., 5 to 8 minutes. Remove from oven.

Arrange toppings on partly cooked scone dough, return to oven and continue cooking until golden brown (approximately further 10 to 15 minutes). For flavour and colour sprinkle a little chopped parsley on top of each pizza after cooking.

Ideas for Toppings

1. Rounds of salami, slices of tomato, salt, pepper, cheese slices, and, if desired, sliced stuffed olives.
2. Bacon and onion chopped finely and cooked lightly, slices of tomato, salt, pepper, grated cheese.

Stuffed Eggs

Eggs, hard-boiled and halved, with yolks removed and combined with savoury ingredients, make a delicious hot weather snack. Serve on a bed of crisp lettuce, or with sticks of young celery or asparagus spears.

To make stuffed eggs, hard-boil eggs, cool and shell. Cut in halves lengthwise, remove yolks. Rub yolks through sieve, using wooden spoon, then mix in any of the following well-blended combinations and spoon or pipe back into egg-halves. Quantities given are sufficient for 6 eggs.

1 can sardines, drained and mashed, 1 teaspoon chopped capers, 1 teaspoon lemon juice, salt, pepper.
2 tablespoons finely chopped ham, 2 chopped gherkins, salt, pepper. Add sufficient mayonnaise (see page 121) to make a creamy mixture.
2 tablespoons pâté, 1 tablespoon chopped parsley, salt and pepper.
2 tablespoons cream cheese, 1 teaspoon anchovy paste, salt and pepper. Add mayonnaise (see page 121) to make a creamy mixture.
1 small can tuna, 1 teaspoon prepared mustard, salt and pepper, mayonnaise (see page 121) to bind. Decorate platter with black olives.
1 small can anchovies. Chop finely, add to eggs with sufficient mayonnaise (see page 121) to bind.

Devils on Horseback

prunes   small rounds of bread
port wine   oil
short ends of bacon
  rashers

Stone prunes, soak overnight in port wine. Prunes can be stuffed with a little chutney. Roll each prune in slice of bacon, secure with small wooden stick. Grill gently, turning once. Serve on round of bread which has been fried in oil or hot bacon fat until crisp.

Hot Crab Savouries

½ oz. (1 tablespoon) butter	2 tablespoons heavy cream
1½ tablespoons flour	1 dessertspoon chopped parsley
¼ pint (½ cup) chicken stock	salt, pepper
7½ to 8 oz. can crab meat	seasoned flour
2 tablespoons chopped mushrooms	oil for deep drying
2 tablespoons mayonnaise (see page 121)	

Melt butter, blend in flour, cook 1 minute. Remove from heat, blend in chicken stock; return to heat and cook, stirring, until sauce boils and thickens. Drain crab well, sauté mushrooms in a little butter, add to sauce with mayonnaise, cream, parsley, salt and pepper. Refrigerate mixture until firm; roll into balls, toss in seasoned flour.

Fry in hot deep oil until golden brown.

Makes approx. 1½ dozen.

Savoury Celery Stick

celery sticks, approx. 2½ in. long	1 tablespoon chopped gherkin
4 oz. (1 packet or ½ cup) cream cheese	2 slices ham (about 3 oz.)
	salt, pepper

Wash celery sticks, cut into required length. Beat cheese in bowl until smooth. Stir in chopped gherkin and finely chopped ham; blend well. Season to taste with salt and pepper. Fill cheese mixture into celery sticks.

Two ounces blue cheese can replace 2 oz. of the cream cheese in above ingredients.

Garlic Crisps

3 oz. (⅜ cup) butter	3 to 4 oz. (about 1 cup) grated Parmesan cheese
2 cloves garlic	
12 slices bread	

Place butter and crushed garlic in saucepan; heat gently, stirring, until butter has melted. Remove from heat, let stand several hours so butter absorbs the full garlic flavour. Remove crusts from bread. Brush bread slices generously with garlic butter on one side, sprinkle generously with grated cheese. Cut bread into fingers or triangles (or, with sharp cutter, cut out 2 in. rounds of bread before brushing with butter). Place on lightly greased baking tray, bake in moderate oven, Mark 4, 350°F., 15 to 20 minutes.

Makes approx. 12 circles or approx. 4 dozen triangles or fingers.

Hot Steak Titbits

1 lb. rump steak	¼ pint (½ cup) water
1 green pepper	¼ pint (½ cup) red wine
1 onion	1 teaspoon salt
2 cloves garlic	½ teaspoon mixed spice
8 tablespoons oil	2 oz. (¼ cup) butter
8 tablespoons wine vinegar or white vinegar	

Cut steak into 1 in. squares. Combine in a bowl sliced pepper and onion, add crushed garlic with remaining ingredients, except butter. Marinate steak in mixture. Leave in refrigerator several hours or overnight. Drain, reserve liquid and vegetables.

Melt butter in frying pan, add meat. Sauté quickly until well done. Add onions, green pepper, and 8 tablespoons of reserved liquid. Sauté further 2 to 3 minutes.

Serve hot, in a bowl, accompanied by cocktail sticks and toast squares.

Serves 4 to 5.

Crab Tartlets

8 oz. shortcrust pastry (made with 2 cups flour)	approx. ¼ pint (½ cup) heavy cream
2 oz. gruyère cheese	2 eggs
4 oz. can crab meat	1 tablespoon finely chopped parsley
¼ pint (½ cup) sour cream	½ teaspoon salt
1 tablespoon mayonnaise (see page 121)	pepper

Roll out pastry to ¼ in. thickness, cut into rounds with 2½ in. cutter; line 24 tartlet tins. Dice cheese very finely, flake crab meat. Put into pastry cases.

Combine sour cream with mayonnaise, add cream to measure ½ pint (1 cup) of liquid. Blend in lightly beaten egg, chopped parsley and seasoning. Pour into pastry shells. Bake in moderately hot oven, Mark 5, 375°F., 25 minutes.

Makes 2 dozen tartlets.

DIPS

Creamy mixtures, almost endless in their variety. Serve them with a surround of small cracker biscuits; or have crisp sticks of celery or young carrot, or potato chips for dunking. Dips can also be used as savoury spreads for canapés.

Cheese Dip

½ small red pepper
4 to 6 stuffed olives
2 to 3 gherkins
1 teaspoon capers
8 oz. (1 cup) cottage cheese
salt, cayenne pepper

Slice red pepper very thinly, slice olives thinly, chop capers and gherkins.

Mix all ingredients together, season carefully, chill and leave to stand for at least 1 hour before use.

Serve with biscuits, crisp bread or potato crisps.

Cheese and Cucumber Dip

4 oz. (1 package or ½ cup) cream cheese
1½ tablespoons sour cream
1½ tablespoons grated onion
3 tablespoons finely chopped cucumber
¼ teaspoon salt, pinch pepper

Blend all ingredients in a small bowl.
Makes approx. ¾ pint.

Avocado Dip

1 large, ripe avocado
4 oz. (1 package or ½ cup) cream cheese
1 tablespoon mayonnaise (see page 121)
1 tablespoon lemon juice
salt, pepper
1 teaspoon grated onion

Cut avocado in half, remove stone, scoop all the flesh into a bowl, add the softened cheese and mayonnaise. Blend together well. Add lemon juice salt, pepper and grated onion, mix well. Use as a dip or savoury spread for toast and biscuits.

Asparagus Dip

1 small can asparagus pieces
4 oz. (1 package or ½ cup) cream cheese
salt, pepper
lemon juice

Drain asparagus, reserve liquid, mash asparagus pieces with a fork. Place cream cheese in a basin, beat until smooth and softened, then gradually beat in asparagus pulp, mixing to a soft consistency; add a little asparagus liquid, if necessary. Season with salt, pepper, flavour with lemon juice.
Makes approx. ½ pint.

Brandied Blue Dip

4 oz. Danish blue cheese
½ oz. (1 tablespoon) butter
2 tablespoons mayonnaise (see page 121)
1 egg-yolk
1 tablespoon brandy
1 tablespoon light cream or milk
½ clove garlic

Cream cheese and butter in bowl until smooth. Add mayonnaise, egg-yolk, brandy and cream or milk. Blend well to make a soft consistency. Add crushed garlic.
Makes approx. ¾ pint.

Tuna Dip

7½ oz. can tuna
2 hard boiled eggs
2 oz. (¼ cup) softened butter
1 dessertspoon chopped parsley
1 teaspoon chopped chives or spring onion (scallions)
salt, pepper
lemon juice

Drain tuna, rub through fine sieve or blend in electric blender with eggs until well combined and smooth. Add softened butter, parsley, chives or spring onion. Blend on low speed or mix until well combined. Season to taste with salt, pepper and a little lemon juice.
Makes approx. ½ pint.

Devilled Ham Dip

1 teaspoon gelatine
8 tablespoons tomato juice
6 oz. liverwurst
1 small can devilled ham paste
1 very small onion
1 teaspoon lemon juice
salt, pepper

Soften gelatine in tomato juice, stir over very low heat until gelatine dissolves. Blend liverwurst, ham paste, finely chopped onion, lemon juice, salt and pepper together in a basin; gradually stir in tomato juice mixture. Spoon into small bowl, refrigerate until required.

Serve with triangles of toast.
Makes approx. ¾ pint.

Soups

Hot Soups

The family will hurry home for these hot, hearty soups. A small bowl or cup of soup is a good start to a meal; a generous steaming mug of soup, served with hot cheese or bacon sandwiches, is a satisfying meal in itself.

French Onion Soup

2 large onions
1 oz. (2 tablespoons) butter
pinch sugar
1 dessertspoon flour
3 pints (6 cups) beef or chicken stock
salt, pepper
French bread
grated cheese

Peel onions, cut into thick slices. Heat butter in pan (you may need a little more butter); add onions and sugar and cook, stirring, until golden and transparent; they should not be dark in colour. Stir in flour, gradually stir in stock. Season to taste with salt and pepper. Cover, cook gently 20 minutes. Spoon into hot bowls.

Take some slices of French bread, toast them, and sprinkle well with grated cheese. Place under grill until cheese melts and is golden. Put one toasted cheese slice on top of each bowl of steaming soup.

Or place a toasted round of French bread in base of soup plate, sprinkle with grated cheese, and gradually pour in soup. As toast floats to top, sprinkle with extra grated cheese.

(For easier eating, some people prefer to cut the crusts from toast before putting into bowl.)

On a cold winter's night, put 1 dessertspoon of brandy into each bowl before pouring in the hot onion soup.

Serves 6 to 8.

Scotch Broth

2 carrots
2 onions
2 leeks
3 sticks celery
4 oz. ($\frac{2}{3}$ cup) barley
bouquet garni
1½ lb. neck of mutton
2 quarts of water or stock
chopped parsley
salt, pepper

Prepare vegetables, chop finely. Wash barley, put into pot with vegetables, bouquet garni, meat and stock or water. Bring slowly to the boil, skim well, then reduce heat, simmer, covered, 2 to 3 hours. Remove bones from meat, chop meat, return to saucepan, add chopped parsley; season to taste.

Serves 8.

Celery Soup with Rice

2 oz. ham
1 small onion
½ oz. (1 tablespoon) butter
¼ lb. (1 cup) finely chopped celery
2 tablespoons rice
3 pints (6 cups) water
4 chicken stock cubes
salt, pepper
chopped parsley

Cut ham in strips, finely chop onion. Melt butter, fry ham and onion 2 minutes. Add celery and rice, fry further 2 minutes. Add water, crumbled stock cubes and seasonings; stir well. Cover, cook approximately 20 minutes, stirring occasionally. Serve sprinkled with chopped parsley.

Serves 6 to 8.

Lentil Soup

6 oz. (1 cup) dried lentils
2½ pints (5 cups) beef stock
ham or bacon bones
2 potatoes
1 oz. (2 tablespoons) butter
1 tablespoon flour
freshly ground black pepper

Wash lentils and drain. Cover with cold water and leave to stand at least 2 hours. Strain. Place in a large saucepan, with stock and bones, cover, bring to boil, reduce heat and simmer for half an hour, or until lentils are tender. Add potatoes and simmer a further 20 minutes. Cream together butter and flour gradually mix into soup, then cook for a few minutes longer. Add pepper to taste. Serve with lots of hot buttered toast, or hot rolls.

Serves 6.

French Onion Soup—so easy to make, so very good to eat. Hot cheese-toast can top each serving.

Pea Soup

½ lb. (1¼ cups) split peas
1 chopped onion
1 carrot
few bacon pieces and
  ham bones

2½ pints (5 cups) stock
  or water
salt, pepper

Wash peas well. Put into saucepan with onion, carrot, bacon bones and pieces and stock or water. Bring slowly to boil, skim well. Cover, cook gently until peas are tender (about 2 hours). Rub through coarse sieve, return to saucepan; taste, and season if necessary. A little finely chopped mint can be added to the soup before serving.

Top with small croutons or sippets made by sautéing small cubes of bread in bacon fat, butter or hot oil until golden; drain well before using.

Serves 6.

Curried Pea Soup

1 lb. quick-frozen peas
hot water
2 oz. (¼ cup) butter
2 tablespoons flour
3 chicken stock cubes

2 pints (4 cups) water
1 to 2 dessertspoons
  curry powder
scant ½ pint (¾ cup) milk
salt, pepper

Cover peas with hot water, bring to boil, boil until tender. Drain. Rub through a fine sieve or purée in electric blender.

Melt butter in saucepan, stir in flour, mix well. Cook over low heat 2 minutes. Remove from heat, gradually add chicken stock (made with stock cubes and water). Return to heat, simmer 2 minutes stirring constantly.

Stir puréed peas, curry powder, and milk into sauce. Season with salt and pepper. Bring to boil, stirring, reduce heat, simmer 2 minutes.

Serves 6 to 8.

Minestrone

½ lb. (1¼ cups) haricot
  beans*
1 clove garlic
1 onion
6 shallots
3 sticks celery
2 carrots
2 potatoes
1 dessertspoon oil
1 teaspoon chopped
  parsley

¾ teaspoon basil
1 tablespoon tomato
  paste
1 cup elbow macaroni
2 pints (4 cups) chicken
  stock
salt, pepper
extra parsley
grated parmesan cheese

* Green beans could be used instead of haricot, but would not require overnight soaking.

Soak beans overnight in cold water; drain. Boil in salted water about 1 hour or until tender; drain and reserve.

Prepare vegetables: crush garlic, chop onion and shallots, peel, seed, and chop tomatoes, chop celery and 1 carrot, slice the other carrot, peel and chop potatoes.

Heat oil in large saucepan, sauté garlic, onion, shallots, parsley and basil until lightly browned. Add tomato paste and cook, stirring, 5 minutes. Add tomatoes, celery, carrots, potatoes and stock. Bring to the boil; reduce heat, simmer gently 45 minutes to 1 hour or until vegetables are tender; add the beans. Add macaroni and cook 10 minutes or until tender.

Season to taste with salt and pepper. Serve sprinkled with chopped parsley and grated parmesan.

Serves 6 to 8.

Chinese Long Soup

½ lb. lean pork
8 chives or spring
  onions
¼ head cabbage
1 tablespoon oil
3 pints (6 cups) chicken
  stock

1½ tablespoons soy
  sauce
salt
4 oz. (1 cup) egg noodles
4 tablespoons finely
  chopped chives or
  spring onions

Cut pork in shreds. Wash chives and cabbage, slice finely. Heat oil in large saucepan, add pork and cabbage, fry quickly a few minutes, stirring constantly. Add stock and seasonings. Bring slowly to boil, reduce heat, add chives, simmer 10 to 15 minutes.

Meanwhile, cook noodles until tender in boiling salted water (5 to 6 minutes); drain well. To serve, place a spoonful of noodles in the base of each soup bowl. Pour over the hot soup, sprinkle a few extra chopped chives on top.

Serves 8.

Cream of Cauliflower Soup

¼ large cauliflower
1 pint (1¾ cups) milk
1 pint (1¾ cups) water
2 oz. (¼ cup) butter
1½ oz. (3 tablespoons)
  flour

1 chicken stock cube
½ teaspoon nutmeg
salt, pepper
2 to 3 tablespoons
  medium cream

Trim cauliflower, cut into large flowerets. Wash well. Place in saucepan with milk and water. Bring to boil, reduce heat, simmer slowly, covered, until just tender. Remove from heat; drain, reserve liquid. Melt butter in saucepan, stir in flour, cook 1 minute. Remove from heat, gradually stir in reserved liquid. Return to heat, bring to boil, stirring; stir until smooth and thickened. Reduce heat, stir in crumbled stock cube, nutmeg and salt and pepper to taste. Stir in cream. Cut cauliflower into small flowerets, return to soup. Heat through gently.

Serves 4 to 6.

Crab Chowder

1 pint (2 cups) fish or chicken stock	1 large potato
6½ oz. can crab meat	1 teaspoon Worcestershire sauce
½ pint (1 cup) milk	salt, pepper
½ oz. (1 tablespoon) butter	¼ pint (½ cup) medium cream
1 large chopped onion	3 oz. (⅔ cup) grated firm cheese (Cheddar or similar)
2 oz. bacon	
1½ tablespoons flour	chopped parsley

Combine in saucepan the stock, liquor from the can of crab, and milk. Bring to boil; remove from heat. Melt butter in separate saucepan; add onion and chopped bacon, brown lightly. Stir in flour, cook 1 minute. Gradually add hot stock. Bring to boil, stirring; simmer 5 minutes. Peel and cut potato into small cubes; cover and simmer further 20 minutes.

Season to taste with Worcestershire sauce, salt and pepper. Add crab meat, flaked into large pieces. Just before serving, pour in cream, heat through gently. Top each serving with grated cheese and parsley.

Serves 4 to 6.

Cream of Asparagus

2 oz. (¼ cup) butter	3 chicken stock cubes
1 medium onion	10 oz. can asparagus spears
2 sticks celery	
1½ oz. (3 tablespoons) flour	¼ pint (½ cup) medium cream
1½ pints (3 cups) boiling water	salt, pepper

Melt butter in pan, fry chopped onion and celery until soft but not brown. Stir in flour, cook 1 minute. Remove from heat, gradually stir in water, in which stock cubes have been dissolved. Return to heat, bring to boil, stirring. Add asparagus and liquor from can. Simmer for 30 to 40 minutes.

Purée in blender or rub through a sieve, return to pan, reheat gently. Add cream; season with salt and pepper, if necessary.

Serves 4 to 6.

Potato and Marjoram Soup

2 potatoes	¼ pint (½ cup) water, extra
½ pint (1 cup) water	
½ pint (1 cup) milk	¼ pint (½ cup) milk, extra
1 oz. (2 tablespoons) butter	
	salt
1 tablespoon flour	chopped marjoram

Peel potatoes, cut into small pieces. Simmer uncovered in combined water and milk until soft.

When completely soft, purée or rub through a sieve with the liquid.

In another pan, melt butter, stir in flour, cook 1 minute. Remove from heat. Gradually add ¼ pint (½ cup) milk and ¼ pint (½ cup) water. Return to heat. Bring to boil, simmer until smooth and thickened, stirring constantly. Add potato purée and finely chopped marjoram. Reheat gently.

Serves 4.

Mulligatawny Soup

3 oz. (⅜ cup) butter	1 lb. uncooked chicken
1 onion	4 oz. (⅔ cup) lentils
2 teaspoons garam masala	2 tablespoons flour
2 cloves	3 to 4 tablespoons tomato purée
2 bayleaves	4 pints (8 cups) stock
2 teaspoons curry powder	3 oz. (1 cup) cooked rice

Garam masala is a mixture of spices obtainable from some speciality or continental shops. If not available add ⅛ teaspoon cumin and ⅛ teaspoon cardamom with the other spices.

Melt butter, fry chopped onion until golden, add spices and cook 1 minute. Add chicken, fry 5 minutes. Add remaining ingredients, bring to boil, reduce heat and simmer, covered 1½ to 2 hours. After 30 minutes of cooking remove chicken, allow to cool, cut meat into dice. Set aside.

At serving time, strain soup through a sieve, reheat. Put a little diced chicken and a little boiled rice in base of each serving dish, pour over the hot soup.

Serves 6.

Shrimp Soup

1 lb. potatoes	2 egg-yolks
2 oz. (½ cup) leek (white part only)	¼ pint (½ cup) medium cream
2 pints (4 cups) fish stock (or milk)	2 to 3 oz. (½ cup) shrimps
little chopped fennel	croutons
1 oz. (2 tablespoons) butter	salt

Peel and quarter potatoes, slice the leek and put into a pan with the stock and fennel. Cover and simmer 20 minutes. Rub through a sieve, return to the pan and bring slowly to boiling point stirring in the butter in small pieces.

Mix the egg-yolks and cream, add 3 to 4 tablespoons of the soup then stir into the rest of the soup. Add the shrimps, season carefully and reheat without boiling.

Serve with croutons.

Serves 5 to 6.

Cold Soups

These are superb soups you'll be proud to serve. They're light, subtly flavoured—the perfect start to a summer meal.

Tomato Soup

10½ oz. can condensed tomato soup
¾ pint (1½ cups) chicken stock
1 medium onion
pinch of dill or oregano
1 dessertspoon tomato paste
¼ pint (½ cup) medium cream
chopped parsley

Place tomato soup, chicken stock, chopped onion, dill and tomato paste into saucepan, heat gently, stirring constantly, until soup begins to boil; remove from heat, strain through sieve; stir in cream. Refrigerate. Garnish with chopped parsley.

Serves 4 to 6.

Fresh Tomato Soup

3 lb. ripe tomatoes
juice of 1 orange
juice of ½ lemon
sugar
black pepper
salt
brown bread and butter

Scald the tomatoes, skin, cut in half and remove seeds. Strain through a fine strainer pressing gently to extract all juice.

Sieve the flesh of the tomatoes, mix with the tomato juice, orange and lemon juice. Add sugar; pepper and salt to taste. If too thick, dilute with a little white wine and water.

Serve very cold with rolls of brown bread and butter.

A little grated orange rind mixed with the butter before spreading on the bread, gives a distinctive touch.

Serves 5 to 6.

Cold Curry Soup

6 spring onions
1 oz. (2 tablespoons) butter
2 teaspoons curry powder
2 tablespoons flour
2 pints (4 cups) vegetable or chicken stock
1 piece lemon rind
salt, pepper
1 egg-yolk
2 tablespoons medium cream
chopped chives

Chop spring onions, cook gently in butter until golden brown; add curry powder, cook another 5 minutes. Stir in flour; add stock and lemon rind. Bring to the boil, reduce heat, simmer 15 minutes, stirring occasionally.

Purée or rub through a sieve. Return to saucepan, season to taste. Add 2 tablespoons of hot soup to egg-yolk and cream combined, then add this slowly to the soup, beating constantly. Reheat without boiling until soup thickens. Cool, then refrigerate. Serve topped with chopped chives.

Serves 4 to 6.

Gazpacho

¾ lb. ripe tomatoes
1 small cucumber
1 small onion
½ green pepper
2 sticks celery
1 small clove garlic
½ pint (1 cup) tomato juice
2½ tablespoons oil
1½ tablespoons wine vinegar
salt, pepper
few drops tabasco sauce

Prepare and coarsely cube all vegetables; reserve about ¼ of vegetable mixture to use for garnish. Place remaining vegetables in blender with tomato juice, oil, vinegar, salt, pepper and tabasco sauce; blend 40 seconds on high speed. Pour into bowl, refrigerate. Place vegetable mixture reserved for garnish into blender. Blend 10 seconds on low speed. Spoon into soup bowls, pour chilled puréed mixture on top.

Serves 4 to 5.

Vichyssoise

4 leeks
1 medium onion
2 oz. (¼ cup) butter
5 medium potatoes
2 pints (4 cups) chicken stock
1 tablespoon salt
¾ pint (1½ cups) milk
½ pint (1 cup) medium cream
chopped chives or parsley

Slice leeks and onions and fry in butter until just turning golden. Add peeled and sliced potatoes, chicken stock and salt. Bring to boil; reduce heat, cook 35 to 40 minutes; cool. Place about half the cooled mixture in blender, blend on high speed 1 minute, repeat with remaining half. Pour mixture back into saucepan, add milk and half the cream.

Season to taste, bring to boil; cool. Put quarter of mixture into blender. Blend on high speed 30 seconds. Repeat until all mixture is blended. When cold, stir in remaining cream; refrigerate.

Serve sprinkled with chopped chives or parsley.
Serves 8.

Superbly flavoured cold soups for hot days. 1. Tomato Soup; 2. Borsch; 3. Vichyssoise; 4. Cream of Broccoli (also in tureen); 5. Gazpacho; 6. Curry.

Green Vichyssoise

6 oz. (1 cup) peeled
  and chopped raw
  potato
4 chopped spring
  onions (scallions)
  (green tops included)
¾ pint (1½ cups) chicken
  stock

¼ lb. (½ cup) fresh or
  frozen green peas
salt
¼ pint (½ cup) medium
  cream
extra cream for topping

Simmer vegetables with stock and salt for 10 minutes, or until barely is tender. Rub through sieve or purée in electric blender. Return to saucepan, add cream, heat gently without boiling. Cool, then refrigerate. Top each serving with a spoonful of whipped cream.

  Serves 4.

Iced Cucumber Soup

3 cucumbers
1 leek (white part only)
1 oz. (2 tablespoons)
  butter
1 bayleaf
1 dessertspoon flour
¾ pint (1½ cups) chicken
  stock

1 teaspoon salt
¼ pint (½ cup) medium
  cream
juice ½ lemon
salt, pepper
1 teaspoon finely
  chopped mint
sour cream or whipped
  cream

Peel and halve 2 cucumbers, remove seeds, cut into ½ in. dice, slice leek. Melt butter in saucepan, add cucumber, leek and bayleaf; sauté 10 minutes until tender but not brown. Stir in flour, cook over low heat 1 minute; gradually add chicken stock. Cook, stirring constantly until thickened. Add salt, simmer gently 30 minutes. Remove from heat, cool.

  Rub through fine sieve or blend in electric blender; refrigerate. Peel, seed and grate remaining cucumber, add to soup with medium cream and lemon juice, mix well. Adjust seasoning with salt and pepper, stir in mint; refrigerate. Serve icy cold, topped with a spoonful of sour cream or whipped cream.

  Serves 6.

Cream of Broccoli Soup

1 onion
1 carrot
1 stick celery
salt, pepper
9 oz. packet frozen
  broccoli

1 clove garlic
½ pint (1 cup) chicken
  stock
¼ pint (½ cup) medium
  cream

Peel and chop onion and carrot and place in small saucepan, with chopped celery. Add ¼ pint (1 cup) boiling water and a good pinch of salt. Cover, cook until tender; set aside. Cook frozen broccoli in boiling water until tender. Drain and cool.

  Purée drained broccoli with vegetables and liquid in which vegetables were cooked, crushed garlic and chicken stock in electric blender, or rub through a fine sieve. Stir in cream, season to taste. Refrigerate until well chilled. If desired, top each serving with a little whipped cream.

  Serves 4 to 5.

Iced Avocado Soup

2 large ripe avocados
little lemon juice
2 10½ oz. cans beef
  consommé or
  consommé madrilene

¼ pint (½ cup) sour
  cream
salt, pepper
1 teaspoon grated onion
chopped parsley

Halve avocados, scoop out flesh. Mash with lemon juice, or purée in electric blender approximately 12 seconds on low speed. Warm soup slightly, remove from heat, combine with avocado and sour cream. Season with salt, pepper and onion; refrigerate.

  Top each serving with a little parsley.

  Serves 6 to 8.

Cream of Carrot Soup

4 carrots
1 onion
1 stick celery
1½ pints (3 cups)
  chicken stock

salt, pepper
1½ oz. (½ cup) cooked
  rice
¼ pint (½ cup) medium
  cream

Slice carrots, onion and celery; place in saucepan with half the stock. Bring to boil; reduce heat, cover, simmer 15 minutes. Remove from heat, add salt, pepper and rice. Purée in electric blender or rub through a fine sieve. Beat in remaining stock and cream; chill. Garnish each serving with a little chopped parsley.

  Serves 4 to 6.

Cold Borsch

1 lb. fresh beetroot
1 small onion
1½ pints (3 cups)
  chicken stock
1 tablespoon sugar

1 teaspoon salt
1 tablespoon lemon
  juice
sour cream

Peel beetroot and onion, cut into ½ in. dice; cover and cook in chicken stock until tender. Drain the vegetables, reserving the liquid. Cool a little. Place vegetables with a little liquid into electric blender, or rub through a fine seive. Add remaining liquid, sugar, salt and lemon juice to the vegetable purée. Refrigerate until well chilled. Top each serving with a spoonful of sour cream.

  Serves 6 to 8.

Eggs are one of the few foods we can eat, in one form or the other, each day—and enjoy them every time. Omelets, souffles, vegetarian curries—eggs play an essential part in all types of sweet and savoury dishes.

When buying eggs it is obviously wise to obtain the freshest possible. The water trial is a reliable test for freshness. To make this test, place the egg in sufficient cold water to cover it. Fresh eggs will lie flat in water. Slightly stale eggs will tilt a little. They can be used for frying or scrambling without ill effect. Stale eggs will sit upright in water.

Eggs should be stored in refrigerator or cool cupboard, with ends pointing down; when the yolk rises, the air space protects it from touching the shell. If storing in cupboard, ensure there is good circulation of air. Eggshells are porous and should not be washed before storing, because this removes the fine covering film. They tend to absorb strong odours, and should not be stored near strong-smelling foods.

Storage of left-over eggs

Yolks Store in refrigerator, covered with cold water.
Whites or *Whole Eggs out of shell* Store in covered container in refrigerator.

Basic Cooking Methods

Eggs are coagulated by heat, and are best cooked slowly at low temperature. High cooking temperatures toughen coagulated protein contained in eggs, and over-cooking results in a tough, dry dish or, if any liquid has been added, curdling.

There are five basic ways of cooking eggs—boiling, poaching, steaming, baking, frying.

1. Place eggs in saucepan, add cold water to cover them by 1 in. Bring rapidly to boil. Start timing from when water boils. (Cooking times are given below.) Once water boils, reduce heat to simmering, cook for required time.

2. Bring to the boil sufficient water to cover eggs. Gently spoon eggs into saucepan. Keep at full heat until water boils again and start timing from this moment. Reduce heat to simmering for rest of cooking.

For this method it is important the eggs should be at room temperature before lowering into water, otherwise the shell could crack. A simple way to bring them quickly to room temperature is to hold eggs for a few minutes under warm running water.

3. For hard-boiled eggs use Methods 1 or 2. Cook eggs for 8 to 10 minutes. Do not over-cook eggs or the smell can be unpleasant. When eggs are cooked, run cold water over them. Crack each shell gently. Eggs will shell easier if cracked and peeled from broad end.

Cooking Times

Times given are for a standard-sized 2 to 2½ oz. egg. Adjust cooking times slightly for smaller or larger eggs.
Soft—3 minutes.
Medium—4 minutes.
Hard—8 to 10 minutes.

Boiled Eggs

There are several methods of boiling eggs—we set them out below. You might like to try each method to see which one gives the best results for your family's taste.

In each case, choose a saucepan of suitable size. Don't have a big saucepan if you're cooking only one or two eggs, but don't overcrowd a number of eggs into a small saucepan.

Coddled Eggs

This cooks the eggs with a soft white, and is the method recommended for young children or invalids. Lower eggs into boiling water, as for Boiled Eggs, Method 2. Remove saucepan from heat, cover, and allow eggs to stand in hot water for 8 to 10 minutes. If a slightly firmer white is required, let egg boil for 1 minute only before removing from heat and covering to let stand.

Fried Eggs

Butter or bacon fat adds a rich flavour when used to fry eggs, or they can be cooked without fat in non-stick pans. Here's how to get best results from both methods.

1. Melt small amount of butter or bacon fat in frying pan. Break eggs into pan one at a time—or break into saucer first, then slip into the melted butter. Cook slowly, basting yolk occasionally with the butter. Remove from pan with a flat perforated spoon.

If you like fried eggs to be perfectly round use egg-rings, or plain pastry cutters. These are quite cheap from hardware stores or kitchen sections of departmental stores.

Place egg-rings in hot butter, then turn over so that both sides are well greased—this will keep eggs from sticking to the rings. Use tongs or a fork for turning rings. Or use rings with non-stick coating.

Break an egg carefully into each ring. Baste the yolk occasionally until cooked. Remove rings before lifting eggs from pan with egg-slice. If rings stick, run a knife carefully around inside of ring to separate it from egg.

2. For health reasons—or because it saves time in the busy breakfast period—many people prefer to fry eggs in a non-stick pan, without butter. Just brushing the pan with butter will make all the difference to flavour and finished result. Without butter the white is apt to cook long before the yolk, and the white of the finished egg can be tough and somewhat indigestible.

However, if you prefer to fry eggs without fat, here's how to get the best results. Break eggs into pan, then quickly sprinkle about 3 tablespoons of hot water around eggs. Cover with lid. Cook gently about 3 minutes. This will partially steam the egg-yolk and hasten cooking time.

Poached Eggs

Place approximately 1 in. of water in frying pan of suitable size. Add ½ teaspoon salt or 1 dessertspoon lemon juice to help eggs set and add flavour. Bring water to simmering point only; fast-boiling water tends to break up egg-whites.

Gently break in eggs. Hold eggs as close as possible to surface of water; this will help prevent them breaking, as they might if dropped from a height of a few inches. Occasionally, spoon some of the hot water over yolks. Simmer gently until cooked.

Cooking time will vary according to whether you like a soft or firmly poached egg, but it is

around 3 to 5 minutes. Lift carefully with egg-slice, hold above pan for a few seconds to drain well.

Steamed Eggs This is a variation of the poached egg. Take a shallow pan with lid. Half-fill it with water, bring to the boil. Break eggs into the boiling water. Then place close-fitting lid on top, remove pan from heat. Let stand for 3½ to 4 minutes.

Baked Eggs

Also known as *Eggs en Cocotte*. Grease one small ramekin or 'cocotte' dish per person. Break an egg into each dish, season with salt and pepper; spoon cream over to cover egg. Bake in moderate oven, Mark 4, 350°F., 15 minutes, or until egg has set.

Some finely chopped cheese can be sprinkled into the dish before adding the egg and cream, and extra grated cheese sprinkled on the cream before baking.

Scrambled Eggs

Allow 2 to 3 eggs per person. Add 1 tablespoon of water or milk or cream for each egg; water will make the scrambled eggs lighter in texture but milk or cream gives more flavour. Season with salt and pepper. Beat together lightly.

Melt ½ oz. (1 tablespoon) butter in pan, add egg mixture; cook, stirring, until eggs are just set; don't have the heat too high, or eggs will be tough. Spoon on to hot toast.

Some grated cheese, chopped chives or spring onions, curry powder, chopped parsley, canned whole kernel corn can be mixed in with the beaten eggs.

Creamy Scrambled Eggs

2 oz. (1 package or ½ cup) cream cheese	salt, pepper
1 oz. (2 tablespoons) butter	2 tablespoons finely chopped spring onions (scallions)
2 tablespoons medium cream	
3 eggs	

Combine cream cheese, butter and cream in frying pan, stir over low heat until creamy. Break eggs into mixture, cook gently until egg whites are barely set, add salt, pepper and spring onions, stir mixture well with a fork until eggs are cooked. Serve on hot buttered toast.

Serves 2.

Omelets—mixed and cooked in minutes—make a delicious light meal.

Omelet-Batchelor
2 Eggs. 2 oz. Butter. 1 Teaspoon-
ful of Flour & tea cup of Milk.
Mode. Make a thin cream of the
Flour & Milk, then beat up the
Eggs. Mix all together, and add
a pinch of salt & a few grains
of cayenne pepper. Melt
the Butter in a small frying
pan, & when very hot pour in
the batter. Let the pan remain for a few minutes over a
clear fire, then sprinkle upon
the Omelet some chopped
herbs & a few shreds of ver

Citron = Omelette
10 Æggeblommer røres hvide med ½ pd. hvid Sukker
og med Saft af 3 Citroner/ reven Skal af 1/ og tilsidst
røres de pidskede Hvider i.

Omelets

An omelet is quick to make, inexpensive, and most versatile. Plain, or with varying fillings, it can be served for breakfast, lunch, or a light main course for dinner. And sweet dessert omelets make a perfect light ending to a meal.

Flavourings, such as those for scrambled eggs, can be mixed into the savoury omelet. Asparagus; chopped, cooked bacon; fried tomato slices; chopped, cooked chicken; sautéed mushrooms, are other popular fillings or additions.

The Omelet Pan

It is best to keep a special pan just for omelets. A new omelet pan should be 'seasoned' before use. To do this, pour oil into the pan to cover the base and come a little way up sides. Warm this slowly over heat, and turn or gently shake pan occasionally so that the oil coats the sides. When the pan and oil are hot, remove from heat and allow to cool. Do this once more, and let the oil stand in the pan overnight. Next day, warm the pan and oil again, pour off the oil and wipe the pan dry. The pan is now ready for the cooking of omelets.

If possible, do not wash the omelet pan after use. Simply rub it clean with paper towelling or a clean cloth. This helps prevent omelets sticking to the pan. If you have to wash the pan, then season it again with oil, as above, before using it again.

Types of Omelet

There are three basic types of omelet—the classic French omelet, the Spanish omelet and the Soufflé, or 'puffy' omelet.

French Omelet

3 eggs	1 dessertspoon water
salt, pepper	½ oz. (1 tablespoon) butter

Break eggs into bowl, season with salt and pepper; add water. Beat eggs briskly with fork until well mixed. Heat pan, add butter; it should sizzle and foam almost immediately. Pour in egg mixture, and, using a fork, draw the eggs from the side of the pan into the centre; do this quickly, shaking the pan constantly. Continue lifting the eggs with a fork until all the liquid is cooked. With spatula or fork fold omelet and roll on to warmed serving plate. Serve immediately.

Serves 1.

Spanish Omelet

Unlike the French or Soufflé omelet, the Spanish omelet is not folded or rolled, but is served flat. When the omelet is golden brown underneath, turn with spatula and cook the other side until just set, or place under grill to set the top; do not over-cook, or the omelet will toughen.

2 oz. (¼ cup) butter	4 eggs
2 oz. (½ cup) finely diced mixed vegetables	salt, pepper

Heat 1 oz. (2 tablespoons) butter in saucepan, add vegetables, sauté over gentle heat until tender but not brown. Break eggs into bowl, beat lightly with fork, season with salt and pepper, add cooked vegetables. Melt remaining butter in large omelet pan, when sizzling pour in egg mixture. Stir gently to distribute mixture evenly, then allow to set over low heat. When golden underneath, turn with spatula and allow to set on other side, or place under grill to set top. Serve immediately.

Serves 2.

Vegetables can include chopped cooked onions; tomatoes; cooked green peas; cooked potatoes; a light touch of crushed garlic and chopped parsley can also be added.

Soufflé Omelet

The soufflé (or 'puffy') omelet, as its name indicates, puffs up like a small soufflé while cooking. After base of omelet is cooked, the pan is placed under grill or into moderate oven, Mark 5, 375°F., for a few minutes to set top lightly.

4 eggs	1 tablespoon milk
½ teaspoon salt	½ oz. (1 tablespoon) butter
pinch pepper	

Separate eggs, beat yolks until thick. Add salt, pepper and milk. Beat egg-whites until soft peaks form. Fold whites into yolks.

Heat pan, add butter, turn pan to allow butter to flow evenly over base and around sides of pan. Spread egg mixture evenly into pan, cook over medium heat until omelet puffs and under-part is lightly golden. Bake in moderate oven, Mark 5, 375°F., 5 minutes or place under hot grill until top is firm and springs back when pressed lightly with fingertips. Fold over, serve immediately.

Serves 2.

For a savoury topping, sprinkle finely grated cheese over before placing under grill.

Dessert Omelets

These are a version of the soufflé omelet; omit salt and pepper from the soufflé omelet recipe, add $\frac{1}{4}$ teaspoon sugar per egg before mixing omelet.

Individual dessert omelets can be made with 2 eggs in 6 in. pan.

Here are some suggested fillings:

Apricot   Spoon hot, sieved apricot jam over half of omelet, turn on to warm serving plate. A spoonful of rum can be added to the jam when heating, or a little rum can be warmed in a separate saucepan, poured over the omelet and set aflame. Serve a bowl of whipped cream separately.

Strawberries and Cream   Sweeten sliced fresh strawberries to taste, or use warmed canned strawberries. Fill omelet with 1 dessertspoon berries for each egg used. Fold over, decorate with whole fresh strawberries, or another spoonful of the canned strawberries. Serve with cream.

Caramel Cream   Do not fold omelet. Spread with fresh or canned peach slices marinaded in brandy or rum. Spread sour cream over, sprinkle with castor sugar. Place, unfolded, under grill just long enough to set cream and lightly caramelize the sugar.

Sweet French Omelet   For a sweet French omelet, add a small pinch salt and 1 dessertspoon sugar to the eggs before beating together; omit the pepper. Make the omelet, and after folding sprinkle with an extra dessertspoon of sugar; place under very hot grill for a few minutes or until sugar melts and glazes the omelet. Place on warmed serving plate. Alternately, fill with a sweet filling as for Soufflé Omelet.

Egg and Bacon Pie

Cheese Pastry

6 oz. (1½ cups) plain flour
½ teaspoon salt
1 teaspoon baking powder
3 oz. (⅜ cup) butter
3 oz. (¾ cup) grated firm Cheddar cheese
approx. 1 tablespoon water

Filling

1 oz. (2 tablespoons) butter
3 onions
4 to 6 rashers bacon
1 teaspoon salt
¼ teaspoon pepper
½ teaspoon dry mustard
3 eggs
1 pint (2 cups) milk
1 dessertspoon chopped parsley

Pastry Sift flour, salt and baking powder into basin. Rub in butter, add grated cheese. Mix to dry dough with a little water. Knead lightly on floured board. Roll pastry out to line base and sides of 11 in. × 7 in. or deep pie plate.

Filling Melt butter in saucepan, add sliced onions and chopped bacon; fry 4 minutes. Add salt, pepper and mustard, mix thoroughly. Beat eggs in basin, add warmed milk, drained onion-and-bacon mixture, and parsley. Spoon mixture into pastry case. Bake in moderate oven, Mark 4, 350°F., 35 to 40 minutes or until pie has set and browned.

Serves 6.

Quiche Lorraine

Pastry

4 oz. (½ cup or 1 stick) butter
4 oz. (1 package or ½ cup) cream cheese
4 oz. (1 cup) plain flour

Filling

6 oz. gruyère cheese
4 rashers bacon
1 small onion
3 eggs
2 to 3 tablespoons thin cream
¼ teaspoon nutmeg
salt, pepper

Pastry Cream butter and cheese together. Add sifted flour, and blend with a fork. Wrap in waxed paper, refrigerate for 1 hour. Roll out to fit 8 or 9 in. pie plate. Refrigerate while preparing filling.

Filling Slice cheese thinly (or use packaged cheese slices), cut into 2 in. strips. Cut bacon into small pieces, fry until crisp, drain. Arrange alternate layers of bacon and cheese in pie case; sprinkle with chopped onion. Beat eggs lightly, combine with cream and seasonings, pour over bacon and cheese.

Bake in hot oven, Mark 7, 425°F. for 10 minutes,
reduce heat to moderate, Mark 4, 350°F., cook further 30 minutes or until set.

Serves 6.

Malayan Egg Curry

1½ lb. onions
1 or 2 small green chillies
1 clove garlic
¾ pint (1½ cups) chicken stock
1 teaspoon turmeric
1 tablespoon curry powder
1 teaspoon salt
6 hard boiled eggs

Slice onions, green chillies and garlic. Combine all ingredients, except salt and eggs in saucepan, simmer uncovered 30 minutes. Halve eggs, add with salt to curry mixture, heat well, serve over hot boiled rice.

Serves 4.

Egg Nog

1 egg
1 tablespoon sugar
1 tablespoon brandy
1 tablespoon rum
½ pint (1 cup) milk
grated nutmeg

Whisk all ingredients together, except nutmeg, until well blended. Pour into glass and sprinkle top with nutmeg.

Serves 1.

Indian Egg Curry

4 medium onions
2 cloves garlic
4 medium tomatoes
4 oz. (½ cup or 1 stick) butter
2 teaspoons coriander
1 teaspoon turmeric
1 teaspoon ground ginger
2 teaspoons cumin
2 teaspoons paprika
1 teaspoon salt
¼ teaspoon chilli powder
2 teaspoons garam masala*
6 hard boiled eggs
*See note on page 21

Slice two onions, finely chop remaining onions and garlic. Peel and chop tomatoes. Heat butter in a saucepan, add sliced onion, sauté until golden brown, add remaining onion, garlic and tomatoes, sauté 3 minutes. Add remaining ingredients, except garam masala and eggs, simmer uncovered, until some of the liquid has evaporated (approximately 30 minutes), stir occasionally.

Halve eggs, add with garam masala to curry mixture, heat well, serve over hot boiled rice.

Serves 4.

Cheese Soufflé—tall, tempting, feather-light in texture. The soufflé mixture can be refrigerated—even frozen—in advance.

Soufflés

In the past, soufflés have been temperamental—you had to mix, cook, serve them without a moment's delay. But these special recipes allow you to prepare the mixture well ahead of time, refrigerate it overnight—or even freeze it for up to five days—and when baked it will rise as tall and as tempting as ever before.

Preparing the Dish

Each recipe in this section will make one large or four individual soufflés. For large soufflé, 7 in. (approximately 2½ pint capacity) soufflé dish is used; individual soufflé dishes have about ½ pint capacity. Grease dish or dishes; tie collar of greased greaseproof paper or aluminium foil round outside of dish; this will help soufflé to rise straight.

Cheese Soufflé

4 eggs	pepper
4 oz. (½ cup or 1 stick) butter	¼ teaspoon dry mustard
4 tablespoons plain flour	1½ gills (½ cup) milk
1 teaspoon salt	4 oz. Cheddar cheese

Separate eggs; allow to stand, covered, while preparing sauce. Melt butter in top part of double saucepan over hot water; remove from heat, stir in flour and seasonings, stirring until smooth and free from lumps. Stir in milk all at once, return to heat; stir over hot water until smooth and thick. Remove from heat; stir in grated cheese while still hot, stirring until melted. Allow to cool slightly. Beat egg-yolks until pale and fluffy, gradually stir into cheese mixture, using thin-edged metal spoon or rubber spatula.

Using clean bowl and beaters, beat egg-whites until short, moist peaks form. Add half the whites to sauce, folding through carefully with flat spatula; then fold in remaining whites. (Adding whites in two portions like this makes it easier to fold them through the mixture; it also makes sure you do not over-beat mixture; thus breaking down the aeration). Pour soufflé mixture over back of spoon or over spatula into prepared dish. This prevents mixture dropping hard on to base of dish, so bursting some of the air bubbles. Fill soufflé dish to within ½ in. of top. Place on oven tray.

Serve cooked soufflé with a green salad.

Directions for Baking

To bake at once Bake in moderate oven, Mark 4, 350°F. Allow 40 to 45 minutes for one large soufflé; 25 to 30 minutes for individual soufflés.

To refrigerate overnight (or up to 24 hours) Refrigerate uncovered. Next day, place in moderate oven, Mark 4, 350°F. Allow 55 to 60 minutes cooking time for large soufflé; 30 minutes for individual soufflés.

To freeze Cover top of soufflé dish, or dishes, with plastic food wrap or aluminium foil; this will prevent hard skin forming on top of mixture during freezing time. When ready to bake, remove plastic wrap or foil. Soufflés can go direct from freezer to oven; do it this way. Place soufflés in cold, unlit oven; then light oven and set temperature at moderate, Mark 4, 350°F. Allow approximately 60 minutes cooking time for large soufflés; approximately 40 minutes cooking time for individual soufflés.

Crab and Chive Soufflé

4 eggs	1½ gills (½ cup) milk
4 oz. (½ cup or 1 stick) butter	6½ oz. crab meat
4 tablespoons plain flour	2 tablespoons chopped chives or spring onions (scallions)
1 teaspoon salt	(including green
¼ teaspoon mustard	tops)

Separate eggs; allow to stand, covered, while preparing sauce. Melt butter in top part of double saucepan over hot water; remove from heat, stir in flour and seasonings, stirring until smooth and free from lumps. Stir in milk all at once, return to heat; stir over hot water until smooth and thick. Remove from heat; stir in crab and chives. Allow to cool slightly.

Then proceed as for Cheese Soufflé. Baking times are the same as for Cheese Soufflé.

Vanilla Soufflé

4 eggs	½ teaspoon salt
4 oz. (½ cup or 1 stick) butter	1½ gills (½ cup) milk
4 tablespoons plain flour	1 tablespoon castor (superfine) sugar
	1 teaspoon vanilla

Separate eggs, allow to stand, covered, while preparing sauce. Melt butter in top part of double saucepan over hot water; remove from heat, stir in flour and salt, stirring until smooth and free from lumps. Stir in milk, all at once, add sugar; return to heat; stir over hot water until smooth and thick. Remove from heat, allow to cool slightly, stir in vanilla.

Then proceed as for Cheese Soufflé. Baking times are the same as for Cheese Soufflé.

Chocolate Soufflé

4 eggs
4 oz. ($\frac{1}{2}$ cup or 1 stick)
   butter
4 tablespoons plain
   flour
$\frac{1}{2}$ teaspoon salt

1$\frac{1}{2}$ gills ($\frac{1}{2}$ cup) milk
6 oz. (6 squares) plain
   chocolate
2 oz. ($\frac{1}{4}$ cup) castor
   (superfine) sugar

Separate eggs; allow to stand, covered, while preparing sauce. Melt butter in top part of double saucepan over hot water; remove from heat, stir in flour and salt, stirring until smooth and free from lumps. Stir in milk all at once, return to heat; stir over hot water until smooth and thick. Remove from heat; stir in grated chocolate and sugar while still hot, stirring until dissolved.

Then proceed as for Cheese Soufflé. Baking times are the same as for Cheese Soufflé.

Other Hot Soufflés

The following two soufflés—Chestnut and Apricot cannot be refrigerated or frozen. They should be mixed, baked and served at once.

Apricot Soufflé

4 oz. (1 cup) dried
   apricots
4 egg-whites

2 oz. ($\frac{1}{4}$ cup) castor
   (superfine) sugar
extra castor (superfine)
   sugar

Place apricots in bowl, cover with hot water, leave until well plumped; then purée in electric blender or rub through sieve. Place egg-whites and 1 tablespoon of the sugar in large mixing bowl, beat until thick and of meringue consistency. Gradually beat in remaining sugar and apricot purée. Grease soufflé or ovenproof dish, dust lightly with extra castor sugar. Pour in soufflé mixture gently so air bubbles will not be broken down (a good way to do this is to pour it over back of spoon). Bake in moderate oven, Mark 4, 350°F., 30 minutes.

Chestnut Soufflé

1 large can (about 1 lb.)
   unsweetened
   chestnut purée
6 oz. ($\frac{3}{4}$ cup or 1$\frac{1}{2}$ sticks)
   butter
5$\frac{1}{2}$ oz. ($\frac{2}{3}$ cup) castor
   (superfine) sugar

1 teaspoon vanilla
8 egg-yolks
6 egg-whites
extra castor (superfine)
   sugar

Prepare 8 in. soufflé dish, by greasing and dusting lightly with extra sugar; place a greased paper collar around outside of dish, secure firmly with string.

Rub chestnut purée through sieve, place in saucepan with butter and sugar. Stir constantly over low heat until butter is melted and sugar dissolved; add vanilla. Remove from heat, cool slightly. Beat egg-yolks until thick and creamy, gradually add chestnut mixture, beating constantly. Beat egg-whites until soft peaks form. Lightly fold half the egg-whites into chestnut mixture, then remaining egg-whites. Pour mixture carefully into prepared dish, sprinkle top lightly with extra castor sugar. Bake in moderate oven, Mark 4, 350°F. 50 to 60 minutes. Serve at once with cream.

NOTE: There are two types of canned chestnuts; one is puréed chestnuts flavoured with sugar, glucose and vanilla. The other is pure chestnuts puréed; this is the type to use for this recipe. Check ingredients on can.

Cold Soufflés

The cold soufflé can be made in endless variations. Simply prepared, it stands above the rim of the dish in distinguished imitation of the baked soufflé.

Lemon Soufflé

3 eggs
4 oz. ($\frac{1}{2}$ cup) castor
   (superfine) sugar
grated rind and juice
   3 lemons

1$\frac{1}{2}$ dessertspoons
   gelatine
5 tablespoons water
$\frac{1}{2}$ pint (1 cup) whipping
   cream

Prepare a 6 in. soufflé case or straight-sided container, by tying double band of greased greaseproof paper round dish on the outside with string, extending paper 2 in. above the edge.

Separate eggs. Place yolks, sugar, lemon juice and rind in the top of double saucepan, cook over hot water, stirring constantly, until mixture thickens slightly, approximately 10 minutes.

Soak gelatine in the water, dissolve over hot water, add to slightly cooled custard mixture. Allow to cool, stirring occasionally to prevent mixture setting at the bottom. When mixture is beginning to set, fold in gently the whipped cream and stiffly beaten egg-whites. Pour into prepared soufflé dish, refrigerate until set. Decorate with whipped cream and a sprinkling of grated lemon rind.

Orange Soufflé

As for Lemon Soufflé, but substitute the grated rind of 2 oranges and the juice of 1 orange for the lemon rind and juice.

Cheese

There are so many varieties in cheeses, it is difficult to imagine that they all begin in much the same fashion. Most cheese is made from cows' milk, although cheese can be made from the milk of any milk-giving animal. Simply defined, cheese is the solid portion of milk separated from the whey. The many different cheeses which result from this similar beginning are the product of variations in the manufacture and curing of each variety.

A wide variety of cheese is available. Apart from that made in this country cheese is imported from France and many other countries.

Cheese can be divided broadly into three categories, hard, medium and soft. Below are some of the most popular.

French Cheeses

Brie   One of the world's great cheeses. A creamy, flat round cheese of delicate flavour. It does not keep very well, and should be served at room temperature.

Camembert   At its best when soft and served at room temperature. Also available from Denmark, Sweden and Ireland.

Port Salut   A soft creamy cheese, full of little holes and of good flavour.

Roquefort   Made from ewe's milk, has a creamy but crumbly texture and a rich pungent flavour.

Tome or Grape Cheese   Has a white buttery texture, mild in flavour and the outside is covered closely with grape pips taken from the wine press.

English Cheeses

Caerphilly   A medium hard cheese made in Wales. White in colour and with a mild flavour.

Cheddar   Close textured, ranging from semi-soft to firm, creamy in colour and has a unique nutty flavour. It is much used in cooking. This cheese is also imported from Australia, New Zealand and Canada. In America it is usually considered best crumbly, pungent and well-aged.

Cheshire   Stronger in flavour than Cheddar and more crumbly. It can be white or a rich golden colour, or, in America, blue.

Cottage Cheese   A crumbly, low caloried cheese, generally served in salads.

Double Gloucester   Very smooth in texture and similar to Cheddar in flavour.

Dunlop   A Scottish cheese similar to Cheddar.

Lancashire   White in colour and with a rather strong flavour. Its loose texture makes it ideal for crumbling over soups and hot-pots and it toasts well.

Leicester   Deep in colour with a mild flavour, often served with fresh fruit.

Stilton   A rich blue veined cheese. White Stilton is a younger version, milder in flavour.

Wensleydale   Semi creamy-textured cheese, white and slightly veined with green. Often served with apple pie.

Italian Cheeses

Bel Paese   A soft cheese, full of flavour.

Gorgonzola   A strong cheese veined with blue.

Mozzarella   Has a mild flavour and usually sold in pear shaped bags. Excellent for pizzas.

Parmesan   A very hard pungent cheese used only for cooking.

Provolone   Firm, smoked cheese cured while hung from ceiling.

Ricotta   Soft, unsalted and unripened cheese. Extremely perishable but used extensively in Italian cooking.

Neapolitan Pizza has a topping of quick-melting Mozzarella cheese; it's an excellent supper dish, and popular with all teenagers.

Swiss Cheeses

Gruyère   A firm pale yellow cheese with large holes, often mixed with Parmesan for cooking.

Emmenthal   A little softer than Gruyère with large and irregular holes. An all-purpose cheese.

Swiss Cheese   The American name for Emmenthal.

Dutch Cheeses

Edam   A round decorative cheese with red skin, mild in flavour, primarily for appetisers or snacks.

Gouda   Mild flavour, golden in colour with a white skin. Richer in butterfat than Edam.

Danish Cheeses

Crema Danica   Soft white dessert cheese, high in butterfat.

Danish Blue   Has a creamy texture and a well developed piquant flavour.

Samsoe   From the island of Samsoe—pale yellow in colour with a few large shiny holes and has a mild nutty flavour.

American Cheeses

American   Pasteurized, golden cheese mild in flavour.

Coon   New York State Cheddar.

Liederkranz   Soft, pungent cheese resembles a mild Limburger (creamy, smelly).

Muenster   Mild, semifirm with small holes.

Cream or Mild Cheeses

Demi-sel   A soft milk cheese.

Petit Gervaise and Petit Suisse   Made from cream.

Cooking with Cheese

When cheese is to be melted during the cooking process, make sure it is grated, or the pieces cut in similar size, so they will melt evenly at the same time. In all cheese cookery, it is important to remember cheese must be cooked slowly, over gentle heat. If cooked too quickly, the protein in cheese toughens, and the cheese becomes stringy.

Keeping Qualities and Storage

The moisture content of cheese—whether it is a hard cheese or soft—is a guide to its keeping quality. Very hard cheese, such as parmesan has excellent keeping quality. Parmesan can be bought grated in packets. If this is to be kept, once the packet has been opened, transfer it to a screw-top jar; this will ensure that it keeps fresh and retains its flavour. Wrap firm cheeses, such as cheddar, in plastic food wrap or aluminium foil, and store in a cool place, or refrigerate. For best flavour, let cheese return to room temperature before using.

Soft cheeses, such as cream or cottage cheese, have a high moisture content. Wrap them well in plastic food wrap or aluminium foil, or place in plastic food container, and keep refrigerated. They should be used within 3 or 4 days of purchase and again with the exception of cream or cottage cheese should be served at room temperature.

Cheese-Topped Vegetable Pie

Rice Pie Shell

1 oz. (2 tablespoons) butter	6 oz. (2 cups) cooked rice
1 small onion	1 egg

Filling

1 oz. (2 tablespoons) butter	1 carrot
4 small zucchini (courgettes)	1 teaspoon salt
2 onions	$\frac{1}{4}$ teaspoon pepper
3 sticks celery	1 teaspoon curry powder
$\frac{1}{4}$ lb. (2 cups) mushrooms	

Cheese Sauce

2 oz. ($\frac{1}{4}$ cup) butter	4 oz. (1 cup) grated cheese
4 tablespoons flour	2 tablespoons medium cream
$\frac{1}{2}$ teaspoon salt	
pinch pepper	
$\frac{1}{2}$ teaspoon dry mustard	1 dessertspoon chopped parsley
$1\frac{1}{2}$ gills ($\frac{1}{2}$ cup) milk	

Pie Case   Melt butter in saucepan, sauté chopped onion. Add to rice; mix well. Beat egg, stir into rice mixture. Press into 8 in. pie plate, covering base and sides.
Filling   Melt butter in saucepan, add sliced

zucchini, chopped onion, sliced celery, halved mushrooms and thinly sliced carrot; sauté 3 minutes. Add salt, pepper and curry powder; mix thoroughly. Place vegetables into rice case. Pour sauce over vegetables, bake in moderate oven, Mark 4, 350°F. for 35 to 40 minutes.

Cheese Sauce Melt butter in saucepan, stir in flour, and cook 1 minute; remove from heat. Add salt, pepper, mustard and milk; blend well. Return to heat, stirring constantly until mixture boils and thickens. Stir in grated cheese, cream and parsley.

Serves 5 to 6.

Neapolitan Pizza

Yeast Dough

4 tablespoons milk
½ oz. (1 package) compressed yeast
1 egg
6 oz. (1½ cups) plain flour

½ teaspoon salt
½ teaspoon sugar
1 oz. (2 tablespoons) butter

Filling

1 dessertspoon oil
14 oz. can tomatoes
1 clove garlic
2 small cans (2½ oz.) tomato paste (¼ cup tomato purée)
1 teaspoon sugar

salt, pepper
2 oz. salami
8 oz. mozzarella cheese
sliced olives
1 teaspoon basil or oregano
chopped parsley

Yeast Dough Warm milk, add crumbled yeast, stir until dissolved, add beaten egg. Add yeast mixture to well in centre of sifted dry ingredients, blend well. Cream butter, work into the dough. Cover bowl, stand in warm place 40 minutes, or until doubled in bulk.

Press dough into oiled 9 in. pie plate, or pizza pan, brush dough lightly with oil. Arrange filling ingredients except olives over dough, and bake in hot oven, Mark 7, 425°F. for 15 to 20 minutes, or until golden brown. Sprinkle with sliced black or green olives.

Filling Heat oil in saucepan, add undrained can of tomatoes, crushed garlic, tomato paste, sugar, salt and pepper, simmer uncovered until mixture is thick, and some of the liquid has evaporated; cool.

Spread over dough, top with slices of salami and Mozzarella cheese. Sprinkle with basil or oregano and parsley.

Ham and Cheese Squares

½ lb. (2 cups) self-raising (all-purpose) flour
½ teaspoon salt
2 oz. (¼ cup) butter

¾ gill (6 tablespoons) milk
3 tablespoons mayonnaise (see page 121)

Filling

½ lb. smoked ham sausage
1 onion chopped
4 oz. (1 cup) grated cheddar cheese
¼ teaspoon dry mustard

2 tablespoons chopped parsley
salt, pepper
milk
extra grated cheese

Sift flour and salt into basin, rub in butter. Combine milk and mayonnaise, cut into dry ingredients with knife until all liquid is absorbed. Turn on to floured board and knead lightly. Divide in half, roll out one portion to fit base of greased 11 in. × 7 in. tin.

Sprinkle over chopped ham sausage. Combine onion, cheese, mustard and parsley, season to taste and sprinkle over ham. Roll out remaining pastry and place over filling. Glaze with milk and sprinkle with extra grated cheese. Bake in hot oven, Mark 7, 425°F. for 20 minutes. Cut into squares while still warm.

Makes approx. 15 squares.

Swiss Cheese Tart

Pastry

7 oz. (1¾ cups) plain flour
pinch salt
pinch paprika
5 oz. (good ½ cup) butter

4 oz. (1 cup) grated cheese (preferably parmesan and gruyère mixed)
1 egg
egg-white for glazing

Filling

1 teaspoon cornflour
1 teaspoon flour
1½ gills (½ cup) milk
4 oz. (1 cup) grated cheese (preferably parmesan and gruyère mixed)

2 egg-yolks
4 tablespoons sour cream
salt
paprika

Pastry Sift dry ingredients, rub in the butter. Add grated cheese, mix to a dry dough with beaten egg; chill 30 minutes.

Roll out, line 8 in. pie plate. Brush surface of pastry with a little beaten egg-white.

Filling Blend flours with cold milk. Add cheese, egg-yolks, cream, salt and paprika. Beat together spoon into pie case. Bake in moderate oven, Mark 4, 350°F., 40 minutes to 1 hour.

Fish should be a permanent part of the weekly family menu, not only for its high protein value, but for its good taste and the interesting variety it can add to family and party meals.

Sole Véronique

1½ to 2 lb. sole filleted	1½ oz. (3 tablespoons)
½ small onion	butter
1 bayleaf	1½ oz. (3 tablespoons)
few peppercorns	flour
juice ½ lemon	1 pint (2 cups) milk
water	salt, pepper
	½ lb. white grapes

Fold fillets or roll up and secure with small wooden sticks. Place fillets in greased ovenproof dish. Put in sliced onion, bayleaf, peppercorns and lemon juice, add sufficient water to half-cover fillets. Cover with greased paper, poach in moderate oven, Mark 4, 350°F. for 15 to 20 minutes or until cooked.

Transfer fish to hot serving dish; keep warm. Reserve ¼ pint (½ cup) liquid in which fish was cooked. Melt butter in saucepan, add flour, cook 1 minute. Remove from heat, gradually add milk and reserved liquid which has been reduced to half the quantity by fast boiling. Return to heat, bring to boil, simmer until smooth and thickened, stirring constantly. Season to taste with salt and pepper; spoon over fish. Simmer peeled grapes in a little boiling water few minutes; drain. Arrange grapes at side of dish. Serve immediately.

Serves 4.

Sole and Asparagus with Wine Sauce

1 lb. sole fillets	1 small can asparagus
approx. ¼ pint (½ cup)	tips
white wine	

Sauce

1½ oz. (3 tablespoons)	1½ gills (scant cup) milk
butter	salt, pepper
2 tablespoons flour	

Place skinned and boned fillets in ovenproof dish. Pour wine over, fish should be barely covered, poach in moderately hot oven, Mark 4, 350°F. for 20 minutes. Drain, reserve liquid for sauce. Place poached fillets on to warm individual dishes, arrange on top few drained asparagus tips, which have heated in their own liquor. Spoon sauce over.

Sauce Melt butter in saucepan. Stir in flour, cook 1 minute. Remove from heat, gradually add milk and ½ gill (4 tablespoons) of reserved liquid from fish. Return to heat, bring to boil; reduce heat, simmer until smooth and thickened, stirring constantly. Season to taste with salt and pepper.

Serves 4 as an entrée.

Trout in Butter Sauce with Almonds

4 cleaned trout	freshly ground pepper
salt	2 oz. (¼ cup) toasted
flour	almonds
4 oz. (½ cup or 1 stick)	parsley
butter	lemon slices
1 teaspoon lemon juice	

Select trout from 8 in. to 10 in. long; sprinkle inside and outside with salt, toss in flour. Heat half the butter in heavy frying pan, put in fish, cook until well browned on both sides.

Transfer to hot serving dish; keep warm. Add remaining butter to pan with lemon juice, pepper and toasted almonds; simmer a few minutes; pour over fish.

Serve immediately, garnished with lemon slices and parsley.

Serves 4.

Fish Meunière

1½ lb. fillets of white	1½ tablespoons lemon
fish	juice
seasoned flour	chopped parsley
4 oz. (½ cup or 1 stick)	
butter	

Skin the fillets if this has not been done by the fishmonger, toss lightly in seasoned flour. Melt ¾ of the butter in pan, fry fillets until brown on both sides; remove. Melt remaining butter in pan; add lemon juice, spoon over fish, sprinkle with parsley.

Serves 4.

Trout with Almonds is served with lemon-flavoured hot butter sauce. This method of cooking can also be used for other fish, in place of trout.

Sole Bonne Femme

2 oz. (¼ cup) butter
1 large onion
4 oz. mushrooms
1½ lb. sole fillets
salt, pepper

2 tablespoons chopped
   parsley
½ pint (1 cup) dry white
   wine

Sauce

2 oz. (¼ cup) butter
1 oz. (2 tablespoons)
   flour
1 egg-yolk

6 tablespoons light
   cream
salt, pepper

Melt butter in shallow pan. Add chopped onions and half the sliced mushrooms. Arrange fish fillets over vegetables, season with salt and pepper. Spread remaining sliced mushrooms over fish, sprinkle with parsley; pour wine over. Cover fillets with piece of greaseproof paper the size of pan, with small hole in centre. Bring to boil, cover pan, reduce heat, simmer 10 to 15 minutes. Using large spatula, remove fish and vegetables to warm serving dish, reserving liquid. Keep fish warm.

Sauce Melt butter in saucepan. Stir in flour, cook 1 minute. Remove from heat, gradually stir in reserved liquid; return to heat. Bring to boil, stirring; reduce heat, simmer until smooth and thickened, stirring constantly. Combine beaten egg-yolk and cream, stir into sauce; re-heat few seconds, stirring, season to taste with salt and pepper, if necessary. Spoon over fish.

Serves 4.

Fish Fillets Florentine

1 lb. spinach
1 oz. (2 tablespoons)
   butter
2 tablespoons water
1 to 1½ lb. fresh or
   quick-frozen
   flounder fillets

salt, pepper
nutmeg
1 tablespoon lemon
   juice
lemon slices
chopped parsley

Mornay Sauce

1 oz. (2 tablespoons)
   butter
2 tablespoons flour
½ pint (1 cup) milk
1 oz. (¼ cup) grated

Parmesan cheese
1 oz. (¼ cup) grated firm
   Cheddar cheese
salt, pepper
nutmeg

Wash spinach, chop and place in saucepan with butter and water. Steam gently over low heat until spinach is just wilted (approximately 2 minutes). Place drained spinach in greased, shallow oven-proof dish. Arrange thawed fish fillets on top, sprinkle with salt, pepper and nutmeg, pour over lemon juice. Cover with greased aluminium foil and bake in moderate oven, Mark 4, 350°F. 20 to 30 minutes or until fish is tender.

Remove foil and spoon over hot Mornay Sauce. Serve as entrée or main course, garnish with lemon slices and chopped parsley.

Mornay Sauce Melt butter in saucepan, add flour, cook 1 minute. Remove from heat, gradually add milk. Return to heat, bring to boil, stirring; simmer until smooth and thickened, stirring constantly.

Remove from heat, add grated cheese and seasonings, stir until cheese has completely melted.

Serves 4 to 6.

Sole Bercy

1½ lb. sole fillets (or
   other fillets)
½ pint (1 cup) fish stock
2 small shallots,
   chopped
½ pint (1 cup) white
   wine
3 oz. (⅜ cup) butter

salt, pepper
juice ½ lemon
2 tablespoons chopped
   parsley
4 to 5 tablespoons
   medium cream
1 tablespoon dry
   breadcrumbs

Place fillets in buttered shallow ovenproof dish, add stock; cover with sheet of greaseproof paper, poach in moderate oven, Mark 4, 350°F. 10 to 15 minutes or until tender. Sauté shallots in ½ oz. (1 tablespoon) butter. Add wine, bring to boil; boil over high heat until liquid is reduced by half. Strain liquid from fish into saucepan with shallots and wine; add salt, pepper, lemon juice and chopped parsley. Bring to boil, add remainder of butter, stir until melted.

Remove from heat, stir in cream. Spoon sauce over fish fillets, sprinkle with breadcrumbs. Place under hot grill or in hot oven, Mark 7, 425°F. until top is lightly brown.

Serves 4.

Grilled Whitefish or Mullet

1 medium sized
   whitefish or mullet
salt, pepper

1 lemon
1 to 2 oz. (about ¼ cup)
   melted butter

NOTE: Use this quantity for each serving.
Wash and dry fish, make several slashes across each side. Rub well with salt and pepper, sprinkle with lemon juice; insert slices of lemon in slashes on one side. Brush with melted butter, cook under pre-heated grill, allowing 7 to 10 minutes for each side, depending on size of fish. Turn fish once, brush liberally with melted butter.

Serve at once with lemon wedges.

Butter-Fried Whitefish

6 fillets whitefish, mullet or bream	seasoned flour butter

Egg Butter

3 oz. ($\frac{3}{8}$ cup) butter	parsley
2 hard boiled eggs	

Lemony Butter

3 oz. ($\frac{3}{8}$ cup) butter	lemon slices
lemon juice to taste	parsley

Skin and bone fillets, if not done by fishmonger, dip in seasoned flour. Melt butter in frying pan; fry fillets until cooked on one side, turn and cook on the other side. Serve with Egg Butter or Lemony Butter, or with Sauce Remoulade. (See page 149.)
    Serves 6.

Egg Butter Melt butter in pan. Add finely chopped eggs. Pour over fish and garnish with parsley.

Lemony Butter Melt butter in pan, add lemon juice to taste. Pour over fish, garnish with lemon slices, and fried parsley sprigs. Or lemon slices can be sautéed in hot butter and used as garnish.

Baked Fresh Haddock

1 fresh haddock ($2\frac{1}{2}$ to 3 lb.)

Stuffing

4 tablespoons soft white breadcrumbs	1 large orange
	1 egg
2 tablespoons chopped herbs (parsley, thyme, marjoram)	salt, pepper
	extra orange juice if needed
2 tablespoons finely chopped onion	$1\frac{1}{2}$ oz. (3 tablespoons) butter

Put the breadcrumbs into a basin with the herbs and season well. Soften the onion in the butter for a few minutes without colouring then add to the mixture with the grated rind and juice of the orange. Bind with the egg and add a little extra orange juice if too dry.

Stuff the fish with this mixture and sew up securely. Put into a buttered dish, brush well with melted butter and bake in a moderate oven, Mark 4, 350°F., for about 40 minutes. Serve with wedges of orange.
    Serves 4.

Sautéed Whitefish or Mullet with Capers

1 lb. Whitefish or mullet (filleted)	1 dessertspoon grated lemon rind
salt, pepper	2 tablespoons capers, drained
lemon juice	
flour	1 tablespoon chopped parsley
2 oz. ($\frac{1}{4}$ cup) butter	
1 tablespoon lemon juice, extra	

Rub fillets with salt and pepper, sprinkle with lemon juice; roll in flour. Melt half the butter in frying-pan, add fish, fry until golden brown on both sides.

Transfer cooked fillets to hot dish. Wipe out pan, add remaining butter. Cook until light brown, add extra lemon juice and rind, capers and parsley. Pour over fish.
    Serves 2.

Baked Minted Whitefish or Mullet

1 medium sized whitefish or mullet	2 or 3 sprigs of mint
	lemon juice
1 lemon	butter
salt, pepper	

NOTE: Use this quantity for each serving.
Wash and dry fish. Rub body cavity with lemon, sprinkle with salt and pepper; place mint sprigs inside. Cut 3 gashes on each side of fish, insert small slices of lemon. Sprinkle over a little more lemon juice and about 1 teaspoon of grated lemon rind. Sprinkle with salt and pepper, dot with butter, wrap in greased aluminium foil.

Bake in moderate oven, Mark 4, 350°F. 30 minutes; serve with lemon slices.

Whiting with Noodles

6 oz. (1 cup) ribbon noodles	4 oz. ($\frac{1}{2}$ cup or 1 package) cream cheese
1 oz. (2 tablespoons) butter	lemon juice
4 fillets whiting	4 oz. mushrooms
salt, pepper	4 oz. (1 cup) cooked peas
	2 oz. prawns (shrimp)

Cook the noodles in boiling salted water. Butter the grid of the grill, arrange the fish on the grid, season and spread with the cream cheese, sprinkle with lemon juice. Cook for about 8 minutes.

Cook the mushrooms in a little milk or water with salt, pepper and lemon juice. Drain, mix with the strained noodles, add peas and prawns. Toss all in a little butter and put into a hot serving dish. Arrange the fish on top. Serve hot.
Serves 4.

Escabache

1½ to 2 lb. thick fillet of cod or haddock	1 egg
seasoned flour	2 tablespoons milk
	oil for frying

Vegetable Pickle

½ lb. small carrots	1 small red pepper
½ lb. small turnips	1 to 1½ pints (2 to 3 cups) white wine vinegar
2 sticks celery	
½ lb. small white onions	2 oz. (¼ cup) sugar
1 small green pepper	1 teaspoon celery seed

Dressing

4 tablespoons salad oil	2 tablespoons dry white wine
2 tablespoons white wine vinegar	½ teaspoon dry mustard
salt, pepper	

Prepare fish and cut into large bite-size pieces. Coat with seasoned flour, brush with beaten egg and milk, coat again with flour. Fry in hot oil till well browned then drain on absorbent paper and place in serving dish.

To make the pickle—prepare carrot, turnip and celery and cut into 2 in. lengths. Peel onions and keep whole. Remove pith and seeds from the peppers, cut into strips. Put carrot, turnip and onion into pan and just cover with vinegar. Add sugar and celery seed and bring to the boil, reduce heat and simmer 15 minutes. Add celery and peppers and a little more vinegar if required. Cook for 3 minutes, then drain off the vinegar.

To make the dressing—mix all ingredients well together, pour over vegetables, toss lightly and pour all over the fish.

Serves 5 to 6.

Sweet and Sour Fish

2 lb. cod or other thick fish fillets	1 pint prawns (shrimp)
½ pint (1 cup) chicken stock	2 medium onions
	4 sticks celery
1 tablespoon tomato paste	3 to 4 chives
	1 red pepper
1 tablespoon soy sauce	cornflour
3 tablespoons white wine	oil for frying
	salt, pepper
1 teaspoon ground ginger	

Cut fish into bite-size pieces. Mix half the stock, tomato paste, soy sauce, wine and ginger. Place fish and prawns in this marinade and leave for 1 hour.

Peel and slice onions, chop celery and chives, remove seeds from the pepper and cut into thin strips.

Drain the fish and reserve the marinade.

Coat the fish and prawns with cornflour and fry in hot oil until golden. Keep hot. Fry onion until transparent, add celery, chives and peppers and cook for 3 minutes. Add fish, pour the sauce over, reheat, stirring well and serve with fluffy rice.

For the Sauce   Blend 1 dessertspoon cornflour with remaining stock, add to reserved marinade, stir over low heat until boiling and correct seasoning.

Serves 6.

Indian Curried Fish

2 lb. fish fillets	1 teaspoon turmeric
juice 1 large lemon	2 teaspoons curry powder
salt, pepper	oil for deep frying

Wash fish fillets, dry well. Cut into 2 or 3 pieces, according to size. Sprinkle on both sides with lemon juice, salt and pepper, place into a dish with remaining lemon juice. Allow to stand for a few minutes, then sprinkle with turmeric and curry powder. Move fish around in this mixture to coat well.

Fry in hot, deep oil a few minutes until cooked. Delicious with fried rice.

Serves 4.

Haddock Kedgeree

3 oz. (½ cup) rice	salt, pepper
1 lb. smoked haddock	1 dessertspoon lemon juice
2 hard-boiled eggs	
3 oz. (⅜ cup) butter	2 tablespoons chopped parsley

Cook rice in large quantity of boiling water until tender, 12 to 15 minutes; drain. Poach fish until tender. Shell and chop eggs.

Melt butter in saucepan, add boned, flaked fish and rice. Season to taste with salt and pepper. Stir in chopped eggs, heat thoroughly. Add lemon juice and half the parsley; reserve remainder for garnish.

Serves 4 as an entrée, or 3 as main dish.

Salmon Kedgeree   Substitute 7½ oz. can of salmon for the haddock; drain and add with rice, to melted butter in pan, as above.

Escabache—golden-fried fish pieces topped with a colourful vegetable pickle—makes an excellent buffet or barbecue dish; nice, too, for a light summer meal.

Fish Mornay

1 lb. fillet of cod or haddock
¼ pint (½ cup) milk
¼ pint (½ cup) water
1 bayleaf
1 small onion
few shrimps
1½ oz. (3 tablespoons) butter
2 tablespoons flour
salt, pepper
2 oz. (½ cup) grated cheese (parmesan or cheddar)
2 tablespoons breadcrumbs
1 oz. (2 tablespoons) butter extra

Wipe the fish. Combine milk, water, bayleaf and half the chopped onion in saucepan. Poach fish in this liquid until tender, drain, reserving liquid. Flake fish coarsely. Remove bayleaf from liquid. Combine fish and shrimps.

Melt butter in saucepan, sauté remaining chopped onion for 1 minute, stir in flour, cook 1 minute. Remove from heat. Gradually add reserved liquid. Return to heat, stir until sauce boils and thickens; cook 5 minutes, stirring constantly. Season to taste, stir in cheese, leaving approximately 2 tablespoons for topping. Fold in fish mixture, spoon mixture into greased ovenproof dish. Sprinkle with mixture of breadcrumbs and remaining cheese. Dot with extra butter; brown under hot grill or in oven, Mark 7, 425°F. Serve with hot rice.

Serves 4 to 5 as an entrée or 3 as a main dish.

Salmon Mornay Make up Mornay Sauce, as for Fish Mornay, omitting the fish and shrimps. Add 1 large can salmon, with bones removed, to the sauce, stir in 1 teaspoon lemon juice. Then spoon into casserole, top with breadcrumbs and cheese, dot with butter and brown.

Salmon Croquettes

7½ oz. can salmon
8 oz. (1½ cups) mashed potato
1 teaspoon curry powder
1 small onion
1 dessertspoon chopped parsley
1 dessertspoon lemon juice
1 egg-yolk
salt, pepper
2 eggs for glazing
dry breadcrumbs
oil for frying

Drain salmon, remove bones and flake. In a bowl combine salmon, potato, curry powder, onion, parsley and lemon juice; add egg-yolk, salt and pepper, mix thoroughly. Refrigerate until firm. Mould mixture into croquette shapes approximately 1 in. thick by 2 in. long.

Dip in beaten eggs, press breadcrumbs on firmly. Refrigerate 1 hour. Fry in hot oil until golden brown, drain on absorbent paper.

Makes approx. 1 dozen.

Tuna Mousse

1 tablespoon gelatine
2 tablespoons water
2 6½ oz. cans tuna
4 oz. (½ cup or 1 stick) softened butter
1 egg-white
1 tablespoon lemon juice
salt, pepper
1 tablespoon French dressing (see page 121)
2 oz. (½ cup) diced cucumber
4 to 5 finely chopped spring onions or chives (scallions)
¼ pint (½ cup) whipping cream

Cucumber Sauce

2 teaspoons finely chopped chives
1 oz. (¼ cup) finely diced cucumber
¼ pint (½ cup) sour cream
2 finely chopped spring onions (scallions)
salt, pepper

Soften gelatine in the water, dissolve over boiling water. Place tuna in bowl with liquid from cans, and beat well. Fish can be beaten in an electric mixer. Gradually beat in softened butter. Then add egg-white, lemon juice, pepper, salt and dressing; beat thoroughly.

Fold in dissolved gelatine, cucumber, spring onions and chives. Whip cream until thick, and fold into tuna mixture. Pour mixture into oiled mould, refrigerate until firm. Unmould; serve with Cucumber Sauce and a green salad.

Serves 4 to 5.

Cucumber Sauce Combine all ingredients, mix thoroughly.

Grilled Cutlets of Hake or Cod

3 to 4 oz. (about ½ cup) butter
4 steaks of hake or cod
salt, pepper
4 oz. small button mushrooms
1 oz. (¼ cup) grated Parmesan cheese
3 oz. (½ cup) blanched almonds

Brush the fish on one side with butter and season lightly with salt and pepper. Put under a hot grill and cook until golden brown. Turn over, brush with butter, season lightly and sprinkle with cheese. Continue cooking until brown and tender. Meanwhile, fry the almonds and mushrooms in the remaining butter.

Put the fish on to a hot serving dish and arrange the nuts and mushrooms round. Garnish with tomato slices and sprigs of parsley.

Serves 4.

Fish Cocktail

1 lb. fish fillets	mayonnaise (see page
1 large onion	121)
white vinegar	salt, pepper
juice 2 lemons	lettuce
2 oz. ($\frac{1}{2}$ cup) cooked	$\frac{1}{4}$ red pepper
green peas	$\frac{1}{4}$ green pepper

Prepare the fish, cut into small pieces. Peel onion, cut into thin slices. Put the fish and onion into glass or china bowl, pour over enough white vinegar to cover, stir in lemon juice. Cover, let stand to marinate overnight. Next day drain liquid from fish.

Combine fish and onion with peas and enough mayonnaise to hold mixture together; season to taste. Shred a little lettuce into the bottom of four cocktail glasses and place spoonful of the fish mixture on top. Sprinkle over the finely chopped or sliced peppers.

Serves 4.

NOTE: The fish in this cocktail is not actually cooked; the acid action of the vinegar and lemon juice, as the fish stands overnight, simulates the cooking process.

Halibut Portuguese

Sauce

1 tablespoon oil	
1 small onion	2 steaks halibut
$\frac{1}{4}$ green pepper	($1\frac{1}{4}$ to $1\frac{1}{2}$ lb.)
4 tomatoes	1 tablespoon flour
$\frac{1}{3}$ pint (5 tablespoons)	salt, pepper
white wine	1 tablespoon oil
12 stuffed olives	2 oz. ($\frac{1}{4}$ cup) butter

To make the sauce—heat oil in small pan, add finely chopped onion and cook until transparent, add thinly sliced pepper and cook a few minutes. Skin, quarter and remove pips from tomatoes, slice and put with onion and peppers. Add wine and olives. Cut fish steaks in half and coat with seasoned flour. Heat oil and butter in frying pan, put in the fish and cook on both sides until golden brown and tender.

To serve—reheat the sauce and pour a little into serving dish. Arrange the fish on top and serve the rest of the sauce separately.

Serves 4.

Cod's Roe Pâté

6 oz. smoked cod's roe	1 clove garlic
4 slices white bread	6 tablespoons oil
$\frac{1}{2}$ small onion	juice of 1 lemon
	chopped parsley

Put cod's roe into a mortar or basin. Trim crusts from bread, soak the bread in water then squeeze well and put with the roe. Pound to a smooth paste. Add grated onion and crushed garlic. Gradually stir in oil and lemon juice alternately until mixture is smooth. Put through a blender or rub through a fine sieve.

Put into a bowl and sprinkle with parsley. Chill, and serve with hot toast.

Serves 4.

Soused Herring

4 herrings	2 teaspoons finely
black pepper, salt	chopped shallot
1 teaspoon chopped	1 bay leaf
tarragon	vinegar

Clean and scale herrings, split down the front and remove backbone.

Sprinkle each with salt, pepper, tarragon and shallot. Roll up and put into a fireproof dish. Place a small piece of bay leaf on each.

Cover with equal parts of vinegar and water and bake in a moderate oven, Mark 3, 350°F. for $\frac{3}{4}$ to 1 hour.

Leave to get quite cold then serve in the liquor. Serves 4.

Mackerel with Cider Sauce

4 mackerel	juice of $\frac{1}{2}$ lemon
$\frac{1}{4}$ pint ($\frac{1}{2}$ cup) cider	bouquet garni
2 tablespoons tarragon	salt, pepper
vinegar	lemon or orange for
1 bay leaf	garnish

Remove heads of fish, clean and remove backbone. Put into a fireproof dish with cider, vinegar, bay leaf, lemon juice and bouquet garni. Sprinkle lightly with salt and pepper. Cover and cook in a moderate oven, Mark 4, 350°F. for 25 to 30 minutes.

Cider Sauce

1 oz. (2 tablespoons)	1 lb. cooking apples
butter	$\frac{1}{4}$ pint ($\frac{1}{2}$ cup) cider
$1\frac{1}{2}$ oz. (scant $\frac{1}{4}$ cup)	
sugar	

Melt the butter, add sugar, peeled and sliced apples and cider. Simmer until reduced to a thick purée. Beat until smooth.

Garnish the fish with slices or 'butterflies' of orange or lemon and serve with the sauce.

To Cook Fresh Lobster

Most people prefer to buy lobsters already cooked although there is quite a difference between freshly caught lobster cooked at home to exactly the right degree and the cooked lobster bought in shops, but it is often the killing of the fish that deters the inexperienced. There are two methods. The lobster may be plunged into a large pan of fast boiling water or court-bouillon—but if the latter is used, the minimum amount of vinegar should be used or the colour of the shell will be spoiled.

Simmer the fish for 10 to 15 minutes to the pound, then put into cold water to cool quickly. Ideally, use part court-bouillon and part sea water.

It is considered by some to be more humane to put the lobster into cold water and bring it gradually to boiling point.

A lobster should be heavy in weight in proportion to its size and the smaller hen lobsters are more tender and delicate in flavour. A good 2 lb. lobster will yield about ¾ lb. meat.

Lobster Mayonnaise

2 small lobsters, cooked	salt, pepper
½ pint (1 cup) mayonnaise (see page 121)	2 tablespoons finely chopped parsley
2 to 3 tablespoons heavy cream	juice ½ lemon
	lemon wedges

Split lobsters in half. Remove meat from lobster shells, cut in large dice. Combine mayonnaise, whipped cream, salt, pepper, parsley and lemon juice; mix well. Combine most of the mayonnaise with the diced lobster. Mix thoroughly, fill into lobster shells. Spoon over remaining mayonnaise mixture. Serve with lemon wedges.

Serves 4.

Lobster Thermidor

2 1½ lb. lobsters, cooked	2 spring onions (scallions) or chives
½ pint (1 cup) milk	¼ pint (½ cup) white wine
1 small onion	¼ pint (½ cup) medium cream
few cloves	salt, pepper
1 bayleaf	½ teaspoon prepared mustard
1 oz. (2 tablespoons) butter	4 oz. (1 cup) gruyère cheese
2 tablespoons plain flour	
extra 1 oz. (2 tablespoons) butter	

Cut lobsters in half; remove meat, reserve shells, combine milk with sliced onion, cloves and bayleaf. Bring to boil; strain, reserve liquid. Melt butter in pan, stir in flour and cook a few minutes without browning. Gradually stir in hot milk. Cook, stirring, until mixture boils and thickens; set aside. Melt extra butter in pan, add spring onion, chopped, and cook a few minutes. Add wine, reduce over high heat to half quantity; add the white sauce and cream. Season to taste with salt, pepper and mustard. Cook gently, stirring, about 5 to 8 minutes.

Stir in ¾ of the grated cheese. Stir until melted, add chopped lobster meat. Fill mixture into lobster shells, sprinkle with remaining cheese, and brown under hot grill, or in hot oven, Mark 7, 425°F.

Lobster Newburg

2 1½ lb. lobsters, cooked	¼ pint (½ cup) medium cream
2 oz. (¼ cup) butter	salt, pepper
3 tablespoons brandy	2 egg-yolks
¼ pint (½ cup) madeira	

Cut lobsters in half; remove flesh, cut into pieces. Melt butter in pan, add lobster meat, and sauté a few minutes; add brandy, set alight. Allow flame to die out, add madeira. Simmer a few minutes, then add cream, reserving 2 tablespoons. Simmer until reduced slightly. Season with salt and pepper, remove from heat and add beaten egg-yolks mixed with reserved cream. Heat gently, stirring, until mixture thickens slightly (do not allow to boil). Serve with triangles of hot buttered toast.

Serves 4.

Prawn Cocktail

1 to 1½ pints prawns	lemon slices
lettuce	

Cocktail Sauce

2 tablespoons tomato sauce	few drops tabasco sauce
1 dessertspoon Worcestershire sauce	salt to taste
1 dessertspoon white vinegar	½ teaspoon mustard
	2 tablespoons lightly whipped cream

Shell prawns, reserving 6 large ones for garnishing. Shred lettuce; arrange layer of lettuce in each serving dish. Top with prawns, spoon over cocktail sauce. Garnish side of each dish with lemon slice and reserved prawns.

Cocktail Sauce Combine all ingredients except whipped cream, mix well. Fold in whipped cream.

Serves 6.

Prawn Cocktail, topped with a well-seasoned sauce, makes an excellent first course.

Curried Prawns (Shrimp)

1 pint (2 cups) chicken
   stock
4 oz. (¾ cup) coconut
3 onions
4 sticks celery
1 apple
3 tomatoes
2 tablespoons oil
1 tablespoon curry
   powder
½ teaspoon ground
   ginger
½ teaspoon turmeric
¼ teaspoon cayenne

pepper
pinch cinnamon
½ teaspoon salt
6 peppercorns
2 bayleaves
½ pint (1 cup) white
   wine
juice ½ lemon
1 tablespoon red
   currant jelly
1 dessertspoon corn-
   flour (cornstarch)
3 tablespoons water
1 pint prawns (shrimp)

Bring stock to boil, pour over coconut, cover and stand for 15 minutes. Then drain, reserving liquid. Slice onions and celery, dice apple, chop tomatoes.

Heat oil, fry onions until lightly brown. Add celery, apple and tomatoes, cook further 5 minutes. Add curry powder, spices, salt, peppercorns and bayleaves. Pour on reserved coconut stock and wine. Cover, simmer 45 minutes. Sieve curry sauce, pressing as much of the vegetables through as possible. Add lemon juice and red currant jelly.

Blend cornflour with water, add to sauce. Bring to boil, stirring constantly; boil 2 minutes. Add shelled prawns, heat through. Serve with hot rice.

Serves 4.

Oysters Natural

'Nature' oysters are an expensive delicacy. Most people prefer to eat them uncooked.

'Sauce' oysters are smaller and less expensive.

Oysters should be closed when purchased; the liquid should be clear and have no unpleasant odour. They are seasonal from September to April.

In most of the recipes given below, canned or bottled oysters are used but fresh ones can of course be substituted if preferred.

A can or bottle of oysters usually contains about 12 oysters.

To serve oysters 'au naturel'—open them only just before they are required, serve in the deep half of the shell, embedded in crushed ice and accompanied by wedges of lemon, cayenne pepper and brown bread and butter.

Oyster Savoury

1 clove garlic
1½ oz. (3 tablespoons)
   butter
4 tablespoons fresh
   breadcrumbs

salt, pepper
1 jar or can oysters
4 rashers streaky
   bacon

Crush the garlic with a little salt and cook for 1 to 2 minutes in the butter. Add breadcrumbs, salt and pepper and brown lightly. Drain the oysters, put into a shallow fireproof dish and cover with the breadcrumbs. Arrange thin strips of bacon on top and put into a hot oven, Mark 7, 425°F. until crisp and brown.

Serves 4 as an appetizer.

Fried Oysters

1 jar or can of oysters
1 egg
1 dessertspoon milk

breadcrumbs
seasoned flour
oil

Beat egg with milk. Dip oysters in seasoned flour, egg mixture, then in breadcrumbs. Drop into hot oil and cook for few minutes until golden brown; drain well. Garnish with fried parsley and serve with tartare sauce (see page 149).

Fried Parsley

Choose good-sized sprigs of parsley. Wash and dry thoroughly. (If the parsley is at all damp, the oil will splutter.) Place sprigs in frying-basket, lower slowly into hot oil. When sizzling noise from parsley ceases, remove basket and drain parsley on absorbent paper. If parsley is fried too long it will lose its colour.

Oyster Cocktail

1 jar or can of oysters
4 tablespoons tomato
   sauce
1 tablespoon lemon
   juice

1 dessertspoon
   Worcestershire sauce
1 teaspoon white wine
   vinegar

Arrange oysters in 4 small, stemmed glasses. Combine all remaining ingredients, spoon over oysters. Serve with lemon wedges.

Scalloped Oysters

Fine white bread-
   crumbs
1 jar oysters
2 sticks celery
pepper, salt, mace

½ pint (1 cup) white
   sauce (see page 146)
butter
parsley
brown bread and butter

Put a layer of breadcrumbs into a buttered gratin dish. Drain the oysters and arrange on top. Add the finely chopped celery and season with pepper, salt and a pinch mace. Pour over the white sauce and sprinkle with more breadcrumbs. Dot with butter. Bake in a hot oven, Mark 7, 425°F. for 15 to 20 minutes. Garnish with parsley and serve with brown bread and butter.

Serves 4.

Scallops

These are usually prepared for cooking by the fishmonger, and sold shelled and washed. They are highly perishable and should be eaten the day they are purchased. The beard and any black part should be removed and the scallops well washed until free from grit. Always ask for the deep shell as these are more convenient for most methods of serving. Generally allow 1 or 2 scallops per person.

In America the small bays or cape scallops are more tender and delicate than the larger sea scallops. One pound or 1 pint sautéed or fried serves 4 where 1 lb. of sea scallops would serve 3.

Fried Scallops

4 tablespoons lemon juice
1 tablespoon oil
1 teaspoon salt
½ teaspoon paprika
2 tablespoons finely chopped parsley
8 scallops
2 eggs
2 oz. (½ cup) dry breadcrumbs
2 tablespoons grated parmesan cheese
oil for frying
lemon wedges

Combine lemon juice, oil, salt, paprika and parsley in bowl. Add scallops, let stand 1 hour; turn several times while marinating; drain. Beat eggs well. Toss breadcrumbs with grated cheese. Dip each scallop first in beaten eggs, then in crumb mixture. Deep fry in hot oil 4 minutes, or until golden brown. Drain on absorbent paper, serve immediately; garnish with lemon wedges.

Serves 4.

Scallops in Cream Sauce

4 to 6 scallops
½ pint (1 cup) dry white wine
2 oz. (¼ cup) butter
3 to 4 chives
2 oz. mushrooms
2 teaspoons chopped parsley
salt, pepper
1 teaspoon curry powder
2 tablespoons flour
3 to 4 tablespoons medium cream
fresh breadcrumbs
extra butter

Remove scallops from shells. Bring wine to boil in saucepan, drop in scallops; reduce heat, simmer 3 minutes. Set aside, reserving liquid. Melt butter in separate saucepan, add chopped chives and sliced mushrooms; sauté 5 minutes. Then add parsley, salt and pepper. Remove from heat, stir in combined curry powder and flour, cook a few minutes; off heat, gradually add ½ pint (1 cup) of the liquid in which scallops were cooked. Return to heat, stir sauce until it boils and thickens. Add scallops and cream to pan.

Spoon into greased scallop shells or small dishes. Melt a little butter in saucepan, add breadcrumbs, sauté ½ minute. Sprinkle breadcrumbs over filled dishes. Brown 5 to 8 minutes in moderately hot oven, Mark 4, 350°F., or under moderate grill.

Serves 4.

To Prepare Mussels

Mussels must be absolutely fresh with the shells tightly closed and need to be thoroughly washed and scrubbed before being cooked.

Scrape the joint of the shell with a short, strong knife to remove the filament, scraping away any foreign body attached to the shell. As each is prepared, put it into a bowl of cold water and when all are prepared, wash well with the hands, changing the water several times.

Mussels Marinière

1 quart mussels
2 shallots
¼ pint (½ cup) dry white wine
2 oz. (¼ cup) butter
1½ tablespoons flour
1 tablespoon chopped parsley
salt, pepper
3 to 4 tablespoons medium cream

Prepare mussels as described above. Place in saucepan with finely chopped shallots and white wine. Cover, boil gently 5 to 6 minutes or until mussels open; drain, reserving liquid. Remove one shell from each mussel, leaving the meat attached to the other shell. Divide mussels between two deep soup plates and keep hot.

Reduce liquid in pan by half over high heat. Cream together butter and flour, add to liquid in pan. Simmer until butter has melted, stirring constantly. Add chopped parsley; season to taste with salt and pepper. Stir in cream, heat through. Spoon over mussels.

Serves 2.

Mussels with Lemon

2 quarts mussels
2½ oz. (5 tablespoons) butter
2 oz. (¼ cup) carrot, finely chopped
1 tablespoon chopped shallot
salt, pepper, grated nutmeg
juice of 4 lemons
½ oz. (1 tablespoon) flour

Wash and clean mussels thoroughly. Put 1 oz. (2 tablespoons) butter into a large pan, add carrot and shallot, salt, pepper and nutmeg to taste. Cook gently until soft. Add lemon juice and mussels, cook quickly, shaking the pan until the shells open. Keep hot. In another pan, brown flour lightly in ½ oz. (1 tablespoon) butter, add strained liquor from mussels and boil for a few minutes. Add rest of butter in small pieces. Serve mussels in half shells and pour the sauce over.

Serves 4.

Meat

Beef

Varies in quality more than other meat. The lean should be bright red with a brownish tinge. A dark colour and dry appearance indicates that the meat has been cut and exposed to the air for some time or that it is from an old animal. The meat should have a marbled appearance, that is, it should contain small flecks of fat. The fat should be creamy in colour—although sometimes it is much more yellow due to certain breeding and feeding.

There are many different ways of cutting a carcass. They vary, not only between one country and another but also in different parts of one country. The cuts given below are the most commonly used. All prime cuts are usually tender and have a good flavour, medium and coarse cuts need slower cooking to produce these qualities.

The recipes which follow include many of the classic beef dishes of the world.

Cuts of Beef

Aitch-Bone   A medium cut from between the top rump and topside or sirloin usually reasonably priced as there is a large proportion of bone. It can be roasted or pot roasted or pickled and boiled.

Bladebone and Chuck   A coarse cut from the shoulder of the animal. It is fairly lean and needs long slow cooking either by stewing, braising or pot roasting.

Brisket   A coarse cut from the breast or belly with a fair amount of bone and fat. It can be roasted slowly, pot roasted, braised or boiled. It is often pickled and boiled.

Clod and Sticking   A coarse cut from the neck end of the animal. It can be used for stewing or is excellent used for gravy beef to make stock for soups, etc.

Entrecote   Prime cut from the top part of the sirloin—an expensive but very tender cut. Usually cut about $\frac{3}{4}$ in. in thickness and is grilled or fried.

Fillet   A prime cut from the undercut of sirloin. Like the entrecôte, it is expensive but generally considered the most tender cut. It can be roasted whole or cut into steaks across the grain of the meat in $\frac{1}{2}$ to 1 in. slices and grilled or fried under the following names—Fillet steak, Fillet mignon, Chateaubriand, Tournedos.

Flank or plate   A coarse cut from the belly of the animal and varies in thickness. Thick flank is suitable for slow roasting, thin flank should be braised, pot roasted or stewed. Short ribs come from the top of the short plate or thin flank and should be similarly cooked. It can be pickled and boiled and makes good stock for soup.

Leg of Mutton Cut or Chunk   A coarse cut from the shoulder of the animal and needs long slow cooking either by roasting, stewing or braising.

Leg and Shin or Shank   These are coarse cuts, the leg is the hind leg, shin or shank is the fore leg. Both contain a large proportion of gristle and connective tissue but are lean and give excellent gravy. It makes good stews and can be cooked quickly in a pressure cooker.

Ribs   These can be top rib, fore rib, or back rib. They are similar and classed as medium cuts. The difference is in the length of the rib bone, the fore rib having the longest bone. They can all be roasted on the bone as standing rib roasts or boned and rolled and can also be used for pot roasting or braising.

Round   A medium somewhat tough cut from the top part of the leg and divided into top side and silverside (top round and bottom round). Both may be slow roasted but silverside (or bottom round) is more suitable for salting or pickling and boiling.

Rump   A medium cut from the tail end of the animal. It is usually cut into steaks but may also be rolled and roasted.

Beef. Bourguignonne—rich-tasting beef casserole with wine and mushrooms.

Sirloin   A prime cut from the lower part of the back next to the rump. It has a short bone and in shape looks like a large mutton chop. The meat on top of the bone is the upper cut, and that under the bone, the under cut, tenderloin, or fillet. It can be roasted on the bone or boned and rolled.

Steaks cut from the upper part of the sirloin are grilled as entrecôte or Porterhouse steaks.

Silverside   See Round.

Skirt   A coarse cut, a thin lean steak from around the diaphragm. It gives a good rich gravy and is good for pies, puddings and stews.

Wing Rib   A prime cut. This is sirloin cut but without the fillet. Suitable for roasting.

Offal or Variety Meats

Oxtail   Excellent for stewing or braising or for stock.

Liver   Can be fried or braised.

Kidney   Used for stewing and in Steak and Kidney Pie and Steak and Kidney Pudding.

Tongue   Boiled and pressed and often salted.

Suet   Hard internal fat, used in puddings and for suet pastry.

Roast Beef with Red Wine

Wipe the meat and put into a baking dish. Grind some fresh pepper over the top. Dot with about 2 oz. ($\frac{1}{4}$ cup) butter, and put another 2 oz. ($\frac{1}{4}$ cup) butter into the dish with 2 tablespoons red wine or water.

Bake in moderately hot oven, Mark 6, 400°F., 15 minutes, reduce temperature to moderate, Mark 4, 350°F., for remainder of cooking time. Turn roast over once during cooking time. Allow approximately 15 to 20 minutes per lb. and 15 minutes over for cooking time, depending on thickness of roast and whether you like beef rare, medium or well done. When roast is cooked, remove to warm serving plate; let stand 10 minutes to set juices.

Season pan juices with salt and pepper. For a greater amount of gravy, add 1 or 2 tablespoons of red wine and water. Stir over low heat to incorporate all the crusty pieces from the pan. Add the juices which run off the roast while it is standing. Strain, serve over the carved beef slices.

Some cooks add $\frac{1}{2}$ lb. skirt steak, cut very finely, to the baking dish when cooking roast beef. This steak adds excellent flavour to the pan juices.

Horseradish sauce or mustard are traditional accompaniments. So, too, is a light Yorkshire Pudding.

Roast Fillet of Beef

1 whole fillet of beef (2 to 3 lb.)
4 oz. ($\frac{1}{2}$ cup) melted butter
freshly ground pepper
salt
little water

Trim any excess fat from meat, sprinkle with pepper. Place in baking dish, pour over melted butter. Roast in hot oven, Mark 7, 425°F., for the first 5 minutes, then reduce heat to moderate, Mark 4, 350°F., continue cooking until done to taste. Allow 10 minutes per lb. for rare meat and 20 minutes per lb. for medium; allow a little longer for well done. Remove cooked fillet to serving dish; keep warm. Boil up pan juices, adding little water, salt and pepper. Slice meat thickly, spoon over pan juices.

Serves 4 to 6.

Beef Wellington

2$\frac{1}{2}$ lb. fillet of beef
4 oz. ($\frac{1}{2}$ cup or 1 stick) butter
1 small onion
$\frac{1}{4}$ lb. mushrooms
2 oz. pâté de foie gras
salt, pepper
1 lb. puff pastry (see page 201-2)
1 egg-yolk

Spread beef with 1 oz. (2 tablespoons) of the softened butter, bake in hot oven, Mark 7, 425°F., 10 to 15 minutes, or until the fillet is browned well all over. Remove from oven, allow to cool completely; reserve pan juices.

Chop onion finely, slice mushrooms. Sauté in 1 oz. (2 tablespoons) butter until tender.

Combine remaining softened butter with the pâté, season lightly with salt and pepper. Spread over top of the beef fillet, top with cooled onion and mushroom mixture.

Roll out puff pastry very thinly. Place beef fillet in centre and wrap pastry round it; press edges neatly and firmly together. Make sure any overlapping edges of pastry are not too thick, or pastry will not rise well and will not cook through. Place pastry-wrapped fillet in baking dish, brush with beaten egg-yolk. Bake in very hot, Mark 8, 450°F., oven 10 minutes; reduce heat to hot, Mark 7, 425°F., cook further 10 to 15 minutes, or until pastry is rich golden brown.

To the reserved pan juices add $\frac{1}{2}$ pint (1 cup) stock (or $\frac{1}{2}$ pint (1 cup) water and 1 crumbled beef-stock cube) and 1 tablespoon red wine. Cook over high heat until sauce is slightly reduced; strain. Cut fillet into thick slices, spoon sauce over.

NOTE: Pâté de foie gras can be bought in small cans, or loose in bulk from delicatessen shops or counters of most large department stores.

Steak with Red Wine

4 thick pieces fillet steak	salt, pepper
butter	extra 2 oz. ($\frac{1}{4}$ cup) butter
$\frac{1}{2}$ pint (1 cup) red wine	juice $\frac{1}{2}$ lemon
4 chives	parsley

Sauté steaks in hot butter until cooked according to taste. Meanwhile, combine in saucepan the wine and the finely chopped chives; cook over high heat until reduced by half, add pinch salt, some freshly ground pepper, extra butter, lemon juice, finely chopped parsley, and pan juices from the steaks. Cook over high heat, whisking all the time, until the sauce is hot and bubbling. Arrange steaks on heated serving dish, pour over the wine sauce. Serve with hot baked potato and green salad.

Serves 4.

Steak Diane

10 to 12 oz. fillet steak	little crushed garlic
freshly ground pepper	1 tablespoon Worcestershire sauce
3 oz. ($\frac{3}{8}$ cup) butter	
1 tablespoon chopped parsley	

Ask butcher to cut steak 1 in. thick, then pound steak until it is quite thin. Season each side lightly with freshly ground pepper. Put butter into pan; when sizzling, add steak. While cooking on one side, rub garlic into top of steak with wooden spoon; turn steak over. Add Worcestershire sauce to pan, swirl steak round in the pan juices. When cooked to desired doneness, sprinkle with chopped parsley, transfer to heated plate.

A tablespoon of cream can be stirred into the sauce to soften the characteristic 'sharpness' of the sauce.

Serves 2.

Carpetbag Steak

1 piece rump steak	1 jar or can oysters
salt, pepper	butter

Ask butcher to cut the steak about $2\frac{1}{2}$ in. thick, weighing about 2 lb. Make pocket in steak with sharp knife, dust pocket with salt and pepper. Stuff oysters into the pocket (a little lemon juice can be squeezed over them first, if desired); fasten pocket together with small skewers.

Grill steak to desired doneness, or pan-fry in butter. Cut into serving pieces. Transfer to hot dish, season with salt and pepper, dot with butter.

Serves 4 to 5.

Steak Kebabs

2 lb. rump steak	1 green pepper
2 medium onions	4 medium mushrooms
1 red pepper	marinade

Remove fat from meat, cut into $1\frac{1}{2}$ in. cubes. Combine ingredients for marinade, add steak, and stir until well mixed. Cover and refrigerate overnight; stir occasionally to mix thoroughly.

Peel onions, cut in halves; remove centre portion. Wash peppers, slice in half, remove seeds, and cut flesh into $1\frac{1}{2}$ in. squares. Remove stalks from mushrooms and peel if necessary or just wipe.

Thread vegetables and meat on skewers as follows: First, onion, then meat, green pepper, meat, red pepper, meat. Lastly, top with mushroom cap. Cook under heated grill, turning frequently and brushing with remaining marinade or melted butter until done to taste. Serve on hot Saffron Rice, and accompany with broccoli or other green vegetable.

Serves 4.

Soy Sauce Marinade

1 tablespoon oil	pinch mustard
3 tablespoons red wine	pinch ground thyme
1 tablespoon lemon juice	1 small chopped onion
1 tablespoon soy sauce	salt, pepper
1 clove crushed garlic	

Combine all ingredients, add the cubed steak, cover, and let stand overnight.

Steak au Poivre

2 tablespoons black peppercorns	$1\frac{1}{2}$ gills (5 to 6 tablespoons) dry white wine
4 pieces rump, sirloin or fillet steak	1 dessertspoon brandy or sherry
2 oz. ($\frac{1}{4}$ cup) butter	1 dessertspoon butter
1 dessertspoon oil	

Coarsely crush the peppercorns, using rolling pin or mortar and pestle. You may need more peppercorns, depending on size of steaks. Press the crushed pepper into the steak, on both sides, or pound in with flat side of cleaver. Let stand 1 hour to absorb the pepper flavour.

Heat butter and oil in pan, add steaks, cook quickly on both sides to seal in juices. Then cook to desired doneness. Remove steaks to hot serving plates. Stir into pan the wine and brandy. Bring to boil, scraping the pan. Remove from heat, stir in extra butter. Strain over steaks.

Serves 4.

Tournedos

Tournedos are small, uniform slices of fillet, about 1 to 1½ in. thick. There are nearly 500 different versions; each is named according to the individual garnishings which accompany it.

Simple rules for cooking tournedos:

If necessary, trim or shape tournedos into a round, then tie or secure with small cocktail stick.

If they are to be grilled, brush them generously with melted butter or oil.

If they are to be sautéed, add enough butter to cover the base of a heavy pan; when melted, add 1 tablespoon of oil.

Start cooking over high heat, then reduce heat to moderate and cook to desired degree of doneness.

Remove cocktail stick. Serve at once on hot plate, accompanied by the chosen garnishing.

The tournedos is often raised up on the plate by means of a toasted or fried bread round; or hot pilaf rice can be used beneath the steak. These are to absorb the rich steak juices.

Tournedos Chasseur

4 thick slices fillet
   steak
	oil and butter for
	   frying

4 thick slices white bread	

Sauce

¼ pint (½ cup) stock	2 spring onions
1 tablespoon tomato paste	(scallions) or chives salt, pepper

1 oz. (2 tablespoons)
   butter
	1 dessertspoon corn-
	   flour

1 tablespoon oil	2 tablespoons madeira
½ lb. mushrooms	1 tablespoon chopped parsley

Trim steaks, remove crusts from bread, and cut into rounds. Heat some oil and butter in pan, fry bread until crisp and lightly browned on both sides. Keep warm in oven.

Sauté steaks in oil and butter until brown on both sides, lower heat, and continue cooking until done as desired. Remove steaks from pan, season with salt and pepper. Place on top of fried bread, keep warm in oven until sauce is made.

Pour off excess fat from frying pan, pour in stock and tomato paste. Boil rapidly, stirring in all the brownings and pan juices. In another pan heat butter and oil, sauté the sliced mushrooms 5 minutes over low heat. Add finely chopped spring onions, season, and cook further 1 minute; set aside. Blend cornflour with madeira, stir into sauce, boil 1 minute. Add mushroom mixture, cook

a few minutes more. Taste and adjust seasonings. Pour sauce over tournedos, sprinkle with chopped parsley.

Serves 4.

Tournedos Niçoise Prepare and cook steaks as above, top with Tomato Concassé (see page 114-15).

Chateaubriand

This is a thick slice of steak cut from choicest part of fillet of beef—the 'eye' of the fillet. It is at its best when underdone, and is cooked in one piece, then sliced for serving.

Here is a simple but delicious way to serve Chateaubriand.

Chateaubriand steak	2 oz. (¼ cup) butter
½ pint (1 cup) dry white wine	pepper Sauce Chateaubriand

Steak should weigh about 1½ to 2 lb. Heat butter in pan. Season meat with pepper, add to pan and brown quickly on all sides. Allow approximately 10 minutes cooking time per lb. for rare meat, slightly more for medium-rare. Cooking time, of course, depends on thickness of steak.

When done, remove from pan, keep warm. Drain butter from pan, pour in the wine. Boil rapidly until reduced by ⅔, stirring to collect any pan juices. Also add any juice which may have run from the fillet while being kept hot. This liquid forms the basis of the Sauce Chateaubriand.

To Serve Slice Chateaubriand thickly, place on hot serving dish. Spoon prepared Sauce Chateaubriand over. Serve with Pommes Parisienne.

Sauce Chateaubriand

2 shallots	1 teaspoon chopped
1 oz. (2 tablespoons) butter	fresh tarragon prepared pan juices
1 teaspoon chopped parsley	

Chop shallots finely. Melt half the butter in small saucepan, add shallots. Cook until softened, then add prepared pan juices. Cook few minutes, remove from heat, swirl in remaining butter. Stir gently; as butter melts, the sauce will thicken. Add tarragon and parsley.

Pommes Parisienne

Press potato baller into raw potato, twist, turn, scoop out potato ball. Parboil 3 minutes, drain well. Fry in hot butter, shaking pan occasionally, until golden. Alternatively, the parboiled potato balls can be deep-fried.

Tournedos are small pieces of fillet steak topped with a rich sauce; shown here are Tournedos Niçoise and, at back, Tournedos Chasseur.

Beef Stroganoff

2 lb. rump or fillet steak	1 teaspoon salt
½ lb. mushrooms	pepper
1 onion	1 oz. (2 tablespoons) butter
¼ pint (½ cup) sour cream	

Cut meat into thinnest possible strips, about ½ in. by 2 in. Melt butter in pan and fry chopped onion, add meat, and continue to cook until almost done. Add the sliced mushrooms, and fry until meat is tender. Pour in sour cream, season to taste, and heat through gently.

Serves 5 to 6.

Beef Goulash

1½ lb. topside (round steak)	3 teaspoons paprika
1 onion	2 oz. (½ cup) flour seasoned with salt and pepper
½ red pepper	
3 tomatoes	¾ pint (1¼ cups) water
1 tablespoon oil	2 beef stock cubes
	salt, pepper

Trim meat, cut into 1 in. cubes, chop onion, seed and slice pepper, peel and chop tomatoes.

Heat oil in large saucepan, add onion and pepper, sauté until tender, add paprika. Toss meat in seasoned flour, add gradually to pan, cook until well browned. Drain off any surplus fat. Add tomatoes and water in which stock cubes have been dissolved, season with salt and pepper, bring to boil, cover, reduce heat, simmer 1½ hours, or until meat is tender.

Serves 4.

Steak Saté

¼ pint (½ cup) oil	1 teaspoon cumin
4 tablespoons soy sauce	2 lb. rump steak
2 large onions	1 tablespoon sesame seeds or coriander
1 clove garlic	
1 dessertspoon lemon juice	

In bowl combine oil, soy sauce, grated onion, crushed garlic, lemon juice and cumin. Cut steak into 1 in. cubes and add to marinade; stir well and marinate approximately 1 hour. Using rolling pin, crush sesame or coriander seeds to a pulp; add to meat and marinade, leave to stand further 1 hour. Thread meat on skewers and grill lightly, turning occasionally and brushing with marinade.

Serves 5 to 6.

Beef Steak Tartare

4 to 6 oz. fillet steak	1 dessertspoon finely chopped or grated onion
1 egg-yolk	
	1 dessertspoon capers

Scrape or mince meat, removing any fat. Shape into patty shape, top with egg-yolk. Place onion and capers at side of steak (or they can be mixed into the meat). Have a pepper grinder so that fresh pepper can be ground over the meat. Serve with hot buttered toast or pumpernickel bread.

Gherkins, anchovy fillets, horseradish can be additional seasonings.

Serves 1.

NOTE: Steak Tartare also makes a good, unusual appetizer. Combine all the ingredients, spread on buttered toast, top with a little caviar.

Steak Normandy

2 lb. chuck steak	2 tablespoons tomato sauce or purée
1 dessertspoon sugar	
2 tablespoons flour	2 tablespoons vinegar
3 onions	¼ pint (½ cup) stock
1 clove garlic	2 to 3 rashers bacon
1 tablespoon Worcestershire sauce	salt, pepper
	bouquet garni

Cut steak into 1 in. squares, coat with mixture of combined sugar and flour. Line ovenproof dish with 2 of the peeled and sliced onions, sprinkle with finely chopped garlic. Place meat on top, pour sauces, vinegar and stock over. Let stand several hours. Top with bacon strips (with rind removed) and remaining onion cut into rings. Season with salt and pepper, add bouquet garni. Cover, bake in moderate oven, Mark 4, 350°F., 2 to 2½ hours. Remove cover for last 20 minutes of cooking time to crisp bacon and onion topping.

Serves 4 to 6.

Boeuf à la Bourguignonne

2 to 3 lb. topside (round steak)	½ pint (1 cup) dry red wine
2 oz. (¼ cup) butter	stock
12 baby onions	salt, freshly ground black pepper
2 oz. bacon	
¼ lb. mushrooms	bouquet garni
pinch sugar	chopped parsley
2 teaspoons flour	

Cut meat into large cubes, brown on all sides in heated butter. Remove meat, add onions, diced bacon and quartered mushrooms, to remaining fat together with sugar, brown slowly. Remove vegetables and bacon, sprinkle in flour, cook slowly until brown. Pour wine into flour mixture, bring to boil, stirring constantly. Put in browned meat; add sufficient stock to cover. Season to taste, add bouquet garni.

Cover tightly, cook in slow oven, Mark 2, 300°F., or on top of stove approximately 1 hour. Then add onions, mushrooms and bacon, continue cooking until meat is tender. Thicken, if necessary, with a little blended flour. Sprinkle with chopped parsley before serving.

Serves 6 to 8.

Steak and Kidney Pie

2 sheep's kidneys or piece of ox kidney	½ bayleaf
1½ lb. stewing steak	2 small onions
1 pint (2 cups) beef stock or water	½ lb. flaky or puff pastry (see page 201-2)
	egg-yolk for glazing

Skin, core and dice kidneys, cut steak into 1 in. cubes. Put into saucepan. Add stock, just enough to barely cover meat, bayleaf and chopped onions, and simmer, covered, 1 to 1½ hours or until meat is tender. Adjust seasoning. Thicken with a little blended flour. Pour into pie dish.

If you want a rich dark colour in the gravy, add 1 teaspoon soy sauce.

Roll out pastry to an oblong just larger than pie dish. Cut thin strips from ends and fit round moistened edge of dish. Brush pastry rim with water and place remaining pastry on top of pie. Press edges together, trim off excess pastry, using sharp knife. Make 2 slits in centre to allow steam to escape. Glaze with beaten egg-yolk. Stand dish on baking tray, bake in hot oven, Mark 7, 425°F., 10 to 15 minutes. Reduce heat to moderately hot, Mark 5, 375°F., bake further 25 to 30 minutes or until pastry is golden brown.

Serves 4 to 5.

Carbonnade of Beef

3 lb. chuck or round steak	salt, pepper
2 oz. (¼ cup) butter	pinch each nutmeg and sugar
2 large onions	6 to 8 pieces bread about 2 in. square (crusts removed) or use slices French bread
2 tablespoons flour	
1 clove garlic	
1 pint (2 cups) beer	
1 pint (2 cups) hot water	
bouquet garni	French mustard

Cut meat into large cubes, brown in butter. Set aside; brown sliced onions in pan. Add flour, cook slowly until brown; then add crushed garlic, beer and water. Bring to the boil, add seasonings and herbs. Put in meat, turn into ovenproof casserole. Cover, cook in very moderate oven, Mark 3, 325°F.,

until meat is tender, about 2 hours. Skim off surface fat. Spread bread squares lightly with French mustard and place on top of casserole, pushing bread down to ensure it is well soaked with gravy. Return to oven and cook, uncovered, further 10 to 15 minutes or until bread crisps on top.

Serves 6 to 8.

Boiled Beef with Dumplings

3 to 4 lb. salted silverside (bottom round)	1 onion, 2 cloves
bouquet garni	5 to 6 small onions
6 peppercorns	5 to 6 carrots
	2 small turnips

Dumplings

8 oz. (2 cups) flour	⅛ teaspoon salt
1 teaspoon baking powder	4 oz. suet
	water

Put meat into a large pan and cover with cold water. Bring slowly to boil, skimming several times. Add bouquet garni, peppercorns and onion stuck with cloves. Half cover, simmer 1¼ hours. Remove bouquet garni and onion and skim again. Add whole onions, carrots cut in quarters and turnips cut in quarters. Simmer until vegetables are just tender.

Meanwhile, prepare dumplings. Sift flour, baking powder and salt. Add suet, shredded or finely chopped and enough water to make a light dough. Divide into small pieces and roll into small balls. Drop into the boiling stock and simmer a further 15 minutes. Serve the meat on a large dish surrounded with vegetables and dumplings.

Serves 6 to 8.

Tangy Sweet Curry

2 lb. chuck steak	powder
4 sticks celery	1 teaspoon salt
1 large onion	1 tablespoon golden syrup (corn syrup)
2 large carrots	
1 cooking apple	juice ½ lemon
2 tablespoons flour	10 oz. can tomato soup
1 dessertspoon curry	½ pint (1 cup) water

Trim steak and cut into 1 in. pieces, place in a large saucepan. Dice celery, peel and chop onion, carrot and apple, add to meat. Blend flour, curry powder and salt with syrup and lemon juice. Add to meat and vegetables with tomato soup and water; mix well. Cover, simmer gently 2 hours or until meat is tender. Serve with hot rice.

Serves 6.

Easy Sukiyaki

1½ lb. braising or chuck steak	2 oz. (¼ cup) sliced beans
¼ pint (½ cup) beef stock	4 oz. mushrooms
1 teaspoon sugar	3 sticks celery
1 tablespoon soy sauce	½ bunch watercress
2 tablespoons sherry	2 tablespoons oil
½ teaspoon salt	1 onion
pepper to taste	1 teaspoon arrowroot, or cornflour

Cut steak into very thin strips. In bowl, combine stock, sugar, soy sauce, sherry, salt and pepper, add meat; marinate 1 hour. Drain well, reserving marinade.

Slice beans, mushrooms, celery and watercress. Heat oil in large deep pan, sauté meat and sliced onion 10 minutes, stirring occasionally. Add prepared vegetables, cook 5 minutes. Blend arrowroot in a little water; add reserved marinade and arrowroot to meat and vegetables, stir well, bring to boil, cook further 3 minutes.

Serves 4.

Kofta Curry

Kofta Meat Balls

1 large onion	2 teaspoons curry powder
1 clove garlic	
1 green pepper	1½ lb. lean minced beef
2 tablespoons finely shredded cabbage	salt
	1 teaspoon lemon juice
pinch ground ginger	flour seasoned with salt and pepper
pinch ground cloves	
	oil for frying

Curry

2 large tomatoes	¼ teaspoon cayenne pepper
2 oz. (¼ cup) butter	
2 onions	pinch cinnamon
1 clove garlic	1 small potato
½ teaspoon ground ginger	15½ oz. can pineapple drained and chopped
½ teaspoon turmeric	½ pint (1 cup) coconut milk (see below)
1 tablespoon curry powder	salt

Meat Balls Mince or finely chop onion, garlic and green pepper. Mix together cabbage, ginger, cloves, curry powder and meat. Season with salt and lemon juice; add minced ingredients. Roll into balls, dust with seasoned flour. Brown balls in hot oil. Drain, put aside.

Curry Skin tomatoes, slice thickly. Heat butter in pan, add sliced onions and crushed garlic,

sauté until light brown in colour. Add ginger, turmeric, curry powder, cayenne and cinnamon. Stir well, cook 3 minutes. Add tomatoes, peeled potato and diced pineapple. Cook gently 5 minutes, stirring constantly. Add coconut milk and salt to taste.

Add meat balls to sauce. Cover, simmer gently 15 to 20 minutes. Do not stir but shake pan lightly from time to time. Serve with hot fluffy rice.

Coconut Milk If fresh coconut is available, grate the flesh of half a coconut, add ½ pint (1 cup) boiling water, cover and leave to stand for 10 minutes.

If desiccated coconut is used, follow the same method, using 3 tablespoons coconut to ½ pint (1 cup) boiling water.

Serves 4 to 5.

Stuffed Vine Leaves

15 oz. can vine leaves (or use fresh cabbage leaves)	2 onions
	2 teaspoons salt
	pepper
1 lb. minced steak	15½ oz. can mushroom soup
3 oz. (½ cup) rice	
2 tablespoons chopped parsley	

Rinse and drain the vine leaves (or blanch the cabbage leaves by cooking gently in boiling water 5 minutes). Combine the meat, rice, parsley, chopped onions, salt and pepper. Place a little in the centre of each leaf and fold into a neat parcel. If the leaves are small, put 2 together.

Arrange in casserole, pour over the mushroom soup. Bake, covered, in moderately slow oven, Mark 3, 325°F., 1½ to 2 hours. Add a little water or stock to casserole, if necessary, during cooking.

Serves 4.

In place of the mushroom soup, a lightly lemon-flavoured tomato sauce can be poured over the stuffed leaves before baking. Then bake, covered, as above.

Lemon-Flavoured Tomato Sauce

1 dessertspoon oil	salt, pepper
1 large onion	2 teaspoons lemon juice
1 clove garlic	½ pint (1 cup) stock
3 tomatoes	

Heat oil, sauté chopped onion and crushed garlic. Add skinned, chopped tomatoes, salt, pepper, lemon juice, and stock; simmer gently 10 minutes.

Golden-crusted Steak and Kidney Pie—an old-fashioned favourite, just as popular today.

Chilli Con Carne

2 tablespoons oil	1 pint (2 cups) water
1 large onion	1 bayleaf
1 large clove garlic	½ teaspoon chilli
1 lb. minced (ground)	powder
steak	good pinch ground basil
1 green pepper	1½ teaspoons salt
14 oz. can whole	pepper
tomatoes	10½ oz. can kidney
	beans

Heat the oil in large saucepan, add chopped onion and crushed garlic, sauté until golden brown. Add minced steak and chopped green pepper, continue cooking until meat changes colour. Add tomatoes, water, bayleaf, chilli powder, basil, salt and pepper, bring to boil; reduce heat, and simmer gently, uncovered, until sauce thickens approximately 1½ hours). Add undrained kidney beans and reheat.

Serves 4.

NOTE: The strength of chilli powders varies greatly. With some brands, ½ teaspoon will be sufficient; with others, which may be milder, slightly more chilli powder can be used. Taste after an hour's cooking; add more chilli powder then, if necessary. Of course, a lot depends on how hot you like your Chilli.

Savoury Meatloaf

2 lb. minced (ground)	1 teaspoon oregano
steak	1 tablespoon salt
2 eggs	½ teaspoon pepper
2 medium onions	
¼ pint (½ cup) tomato	
sauce	

Brown Sauce

1 oz. (2 tablespoons)	1 chicken stock cube
butter	3 to 4 tablespoons
1 oz. (2 tablespoons)	tomato sauce
plain flour	salt, pepper
½ pint (1 cup) boiling	
water	

Combine minced steak, eggs, chopped onions, tomato sauce, oregano, salt and pepper in mixing bowl. Blend well on electric mixer (this gives very fine texture to the meatloaf) or by hand. Form meat mixture into loaf shape. Add a little stock or water if too stiff. Place in greased shallow baking dish. Bake in moderately hot oven, Mark 4, 350°F., 50 minutes, brushing occasionally with pan drippings. Serve hot, sliced, with brown sauce spooned over.

Serves 6.

Brown Sauce Melt butter in pan, stir in flour; cook until brown, stirring occasionally; do not allow flour to burn. Remove from heat, add boiling water in which stock cube has been dissolved, blend well. Return to heat, bring to boil, stirring; reduce heat, cook until smooth and thickened, stirring constantly. Stir in tomato sauce; season to taste with salt and pepper.

Indonesian Meatballs

1 lb. potatoes	1½ teaspoons salt
1 oz. (2 tablespoons)	¼ teaspoon pepper
butter	¼ teaspoon nutmeg
1 small onion	4 spring onions
2 cloves garlic	(scallions) or chives
1 lb. minced (ground)	2 eggs, separated
steak	oil for deep frying

Cook, drain, and mash potatoes. Melt butter in frying pan. Add finely chopped onion and crushed garlic. Simmer 3 to 4 minutes, then add minced steak, season with salt, pepper and nutmeg. Cook, stirring constantly. When meat is half-cooked, add finely chopped spring onions, including green tops. Remove from heat when meat is cooked.

In a bowl combine mashed potatoes with meat mixture and egg-yolks. Form mixture into small balls. Refrigerate 1 hour to firm. Beat egg-whites very lightly with fork in small bowl. Dip meat balls one at a time in egg-whites. Deep-fry in hot oil until golden brown. These can be prepared in advance and reheated for 10 minutes in moderate oven.

Makes approx. 4 dozen.

Garlic Sausage

¼ lb. lean bacon pieces	2 eggs beaten
½ lb. minced (ground)	6 oz. (2 cups) soft
steak	breadcrumbs
¾ lb. sausage meat	1 teaspoon salt
2 cloves garlic crushed	¼ teaspoon pepper

Put bacon pieces through mincer, or chop finely. Combine with remaining ingredients, mix well. Form mixture into thick sausage roll, approximately 8 in. long. Tie firmly in well-floured pudding cloth. Lower carefully into saucepan of boiling water, making sure sausage is well covered. Boil steadily, covered, 2½ hours. Remove from water, drain, and leave in cloth to cool. Refrigerate several hours or overnight. Remove cloth.

Makes approx. 2 lb. sausage.

Glazed Meatloaf

Glaze

$\frac{1}{2}$ teaspoon dry mustard
3 to 4 tablespoons tomato sauce

1 tablespoon light brown sugar

1$\frac{1}{2}$ lb. minced (ground) steak
3 oz. (1 cup) soft breadcrumbs
1 teaspoon salt
pepper
1 medium onion, chopped
1 egg, beaten

1 tablespoon Worcestershire sauce
2 tablespoons tomato sauce
6 oz. can evaporated milk
1 dessertspoon dry mustard

Combine ingredients for glaze, set aside. Mix together all remaining ingredients (mixture will be rather moist); press into greased 8 in. × 4 in. loaf tin, then turn upside down on to aluminium foil-lined oven tray, leaving tin still over loaf. Bake in moderate oven, Mark 4, 350°F., 15 minutes. Remove from oven, remove loaf tin. Brush meatloaf well with glaze. (Do not replace loaf tin). Return to oven, cook further 50 to 60 minutes.

Equally nice served hot with vegetables or cold with salads; good for sandwiches, too.

Serves 4.

Beef Olives

2 lb. skirt steak
3 oz. ($\frac{3}{8}$ cup) butter
1 small, finely chopped onion
3 oz. (1 cup) fresh breadcrumbs
2 tablespoons chopped parsley
$\frac{1}{2}$ teaspoon dried thyme
salt, pepper
little milk

3 onions diced
3 carrots diced
1 small turnip diced
1 stick of celery diced
$\frac{3}{4}$ pint (1$\frac{1}{2}$ cups) beef stock
bouquet garni
1 dessertspoon flour
1 dessertspoon butter, extra

Cut steak into thin slices about 2$\frac{1}{2}$ in. × 5 in.; mince or finely chop the trimmings. Heat 2 oz. ($\frac{1}{4}$ cup) butter in saucepan, sauté chopped onions until transparent, without allowing them to brown.

Mix together the breadcrumbs, herbs, seasonings, minced or chopped meat, and sautéed onion, bind with a little milk. Spread layer of this mixture over each slice of meat. Roll up; tie with thin string. Heat rest of butter in pan, add diced vegetables, cook until golden in colour. Pour over stock; return meat to pan with bouquet garni. Bring to boil, cover. Reduce heat.

Cook gently 1$\frac{1}{2}$ to 2 hours or until meat is tender. (Or place in casserole and cook, covered, in moderate oven, Mark 4, 350°F.) Place meat on serving dish, remove string. Mix flour with the extra butter, pour gravy from pan over this mixture, blend together. Return to pan and bring to the boil, stirring. Adjust seasoning, remove bouquet garni. Pour gravy over meat.

Serves 4.

Lamb and Mutton

English, Scotch, Welsh and New Zealand lamb is consistently tender and of good quality. Lamb, being younger, is naturally more tender than mutton and more suitable for the quick methods of cooking, i.e. frying or grilling.

Lamb is pale pink in colour, a little more so than mutton and has less fat. The main cuts of both are given below.

Cuts of Lamb and Mutton

Breast   Usually reasonably priced and can be cooked in several ways—braised, stewed, boiled or boned, stuffed and roasted.

Chops   Cut from the loin. Chump and loin chops come from the end nearest the leg. Suitable for frying or grilling.

Cutlets or neck slices   Cut from the best end of the neck, rib or rack, and may be grilled or fried.

Leg   A prime joint—can be roasted or boiled whole or divided into the fillet end and shank. The fillet end is roasted, the shank end is generally braised, stewed or used in pies. Boneless slices or 'fillets' from the top of the leg are suitable for shashlik and kebabs.

Loin   Roasted whole, boned and rolled or cut into chops.

Neck   Best end—roasted whole or divided into cutlets
Middle   —stewed, braised or boiled
Scrag   —boiled or used for soup and stock.

Saddle   A prime joint—this consists of the double loin starting from the best end of neck to the end of the loin. A choice cut, excellent roasted for dinner parties or special occasions. Can be cut as rack of lamb or crown roast.

Shoulder   A prime joint—roasted whole but large ones are often cut into two or more pieces useful for braising and pot roasting. Small pieces of shoulder meat without bone are used for grilling and for kebabs etc.

Offal

Trotters or feet—generally used in the preparation of brawn or meat moulds because they contain a large amount of gelatine.

Brains—can be simmered in milk and water or milk and added to a white sauce.

Head—used in the preparation of brawn.

Heart—can be stuffed and roasted or braised.

Kidneys—fried or grilled or used in ragouts.

Liver—fried and used in various ways, e.g. for pâté and can be braised or stewed.

Suet—not quite so hard as beef suet but can be used in puddings.

Sweetbreads—come from the pancreas, throat and heart of the animal. They are very easily digested and generally the demand exceeds the supply. Frozen sweetbreads are available.

Tongue—braised or can be boiled and pressed.

Tripe—comes from the stomach of the animal. It needs careful preparation but is very good and nutritious cooked in milk with onions.

Mint Sauce

2 tablespoons chopped fresh mint	1 tablespoon boiling water
1 tablespoon sugar	2 tablespoons vinegar

Wash and dry mint, remove stalks, chop finely. Boil sugar and water 1 minute, add vinegar, pour over mint; stand 15 minutes. Stir well before serving.

Mint sauce is the most suitable accompaniment to most custs of lamb.

Savoury Lamb—a colourful combination of vegetable and simple but subtle seasonings makes this the perfect family or party casserole.

Roast Lamb

Leg, saddle or shoulder of lamb, when roasted, gives substantial helpings for family meals. You can add subtle flavour by scoring the skin lightly in several places and inserting small slivers of garlic, sprigs of rosemary, or pieces of bayleaf. Or rub lamb well, before cooking, with a cut clove of garlic; mix 1 teaspoon of rosemary into 3 tablespoons of softened butter and rub over joint.

To give a delightfully sweet flavour to meat, baste with orange or pineapple juice while cooking—you will need about $\frac{1}{4}$ pint ($\frac{1}{2}$ cup). The Greeks use lemon and marjoram to flavour their lamb dishes.

Moderate heat is best for lamb; it ensures thorough, gentle cooking with a minimum of shrinkage. For joints, allow approximately 20 minutes per lb., and 20 minutes over. Joints which have a stuffing will take a little longer.

Some cooks like to stand lamb on a rack in baking dish to cook; some prefer to put directly into the dish, without a rack. If cooking without the rack, make sure any surplus fat is poured off during the cooking—otherwise the meat will 'stew' in the fat instead of being beautifully crisp-skinned.

When meat is cooked, remove from baking dish; pour off fat, leaving about 2 tablespoons in dish; stir in $1\frac{1}{2}$ tablespoons flour. Cook, stirring until mixture 'bubbles' and browns—do not let it burn. Gradually stir in $\frac{1}{2}$ to $\frac{3}{4}$ pint (1 to $1\frac{1}{2}$ cups) stock; cook, stirring, until gravy boils and thickens. Season to taste.

Savoury Lamb

2 lb. lean lamb	1 tablespoon lemon
4 small onions	juice
flour seasoned with	1 tablespoon
salt and pepper	Worcestershire sauce
3 tablespoons oil	1 dessertspoon dry
$15\frac{1}{2}$ oz. can tomato	mustard
soup	salt, pepper
about $\frac{3}{4}$ pint ($1\frac{1}{2}$ cups)	2 carrots
stock	1 swede or turnip
2 tablespoons sherry	4 sticks celery
1 tablespoon light	1 red pepper
brown sugar	1 green pepper

Trim lamb, cut into large pieces; peel and halve onions. Toss lamb in seasoned flour. Heat oil in large saucepan, gradually add lamb, brown well; add onions, sauté until transparent. Add remaining ingredients, except for vegetables; cover, simmer 1 hour.

Peel and slice carrots and swede, chop celery into large pieces, seed peppers, chop into 1 in. squares. Add prepared vegetables to lamb mixture, cover, simmer further $\frac{1}{2}$ to 1 hour, or until lamb and vegetables are tender.

Serves 4 to 5.

NOTE: 4 oz. (1 cup) cooked haricot beans may be added when stew is cooked, if desired.

Lamb Italienne

2 lb. lean lamb cut	1 teaspoon sugar
from leg	$\frac{1}{2}$ pint (1 cup) stock
seasoned flour	2 tablespoons tomato
2 tablespoons oil	purée
1 clove garlic	$\frac{1}{4}$ pint ($\frac{1}{2}$ cup) white
2 onions	wine
3 to 4 sticks celery	$\frac{1}{4}$ teaspoon rosemary
1 teaspoon salt	$\frac{1}{4}$ lb. mushrooms
	parsley

Cut the meat into pieces and coat with seasoned flour. Heat oil in saucepan, add meat, crushed garlic, sliced onions, chopped celery and salt and sauté until the meat is well browned. Add sugar, boiling stock, tomato purée, wine and rosemary. Bring to boiling point, cover and simmer slowly for about $1\frac{1}{4}$ hours. Add sliced mushrooms and cook a further 10 minutes.

Serve hot sprinkled with parsley.

Serves 5 to 6.

Delicious Lamb Stew

2 lb. best end neck	1 parsnip
lamb	1 stick celery
flour seasoned with	1 large cooking apple
salt and pepper	1 pint (2 cups) stock
2 tablespoons oil	1 tablespoon plum jam
2 onions	
2 carrots	

Trim meat and cut into chops. Dredge with seasoned flour and brown in heated oil. Chop onions, slice carrots, parsnip, celery and peeled apple. Add vegetables and apple to frying pan and sauté a few minutes. Stir in plum jam and stock, bring to boil, reduce heat; simmer for $1\frac{1}{4}$ hours or until tender.

If extra thickening is required, blend a little seasoned flour with water and add to stew, stirring.

Serves 4 to 5.

Crumbled Cutlets

Remove skin and excess fat from each cutlet. Dip in flour, which has been seasoned with salt and pepper; shake off excess flour.

Dip cutlets in egg beaten with a little oil (to help hold crumbs firmly), or brush over with a pastry brush. Then press firmly into breadcrumbs. Repeat process if you like a crisp coating. Refrigerate 1 hour to firm crumbs.

Shallow-fry in hot oil, turning occasionally, until crumbs are golden brown and cutlets cooked through. Make sure oil is hot before adding cutlets, otherwise crumbs will not hold firm but will drop off.

Devilled Chops

1½ lb. best end neck lamb	1 tablespoon lemon juice
10½ oz. can tomato soup	2 tablespoons sherry
1 dessertspoon prepared mustard	1 onion
1 tablespoon light brown sugar	2 to 3 sticks celery
1 tablespoon Worcestershire sauce	1 clove garlic

Trim the meat, divide into chops and put into a greased casserole. Cover, and cook in a moderate oven, Mark 4, 350°F. for 15 minutes.

Meanwhile, put tomato soup into a pan, add mustard, sugar, sauce, lemon juice and sherry. Mix well, add finely chopped onion and celery and crushed garlic and bring to boiling point. Pour off excess fat from the chops, pour the sauce over and cook a further 20 to 25 minutes.

Serves 4.

Sheep's Liver with Onions

1 oz. (2 tablespoons) butter or oil	¼ teaspoon pepper
2 oz. bacon	½ pint (1 cup) stock
1 lb. onions	1 lb. sheep's liver
2 tablespoons flour	parsley
1 teaspoon salt	mashed potato

Heat the butter in a stew pan. Cut the bacon into small pieces and fry till crisp in the butter. Remove to a plate. Add the chopped onions to the fat in the pan and fry, stirring frequently until just brown. Add the flour and seasoning, mix and cook for a minute then add the stock. Add the bacon and the liver—washed, dried and cut into slices. Cover, and simmer for about ½ hour. Serve in a border of mashed potatoes and sprinkle with parsley.

Serves 4 to 5.

Savoury Lamb Stew with Parsley Dumplings

1½ lb. scrag end neck of lamb	salt, pepper
2 pints (4 cups) water	1 bayleaf
3 carrots	¼ pint (½ cup) tomato sauce
4 potatoes	1 tablespoon finely chopped parsley
2 onions	2 tablespoons flour

Parsley Dumplings

4 oz. (1 cup) self-raising (all purpose) flour	1 tablespoon finely chopped parsley
1 teaspoon butter	milk
½ teaspoon salt	

Remove meat from bones, cut into approximately 1 in. cubes, discarding any fat. Place in saucepan with bones, cover with water, bring to boil. Reduce heat, cover and simmer 1 hour. Add peeled and diced carrots and potatoes, chopped onions, salt, pepper, bayleaf, tomato sauce and parsley. Bring to boil; reduce heat, simmer further 10 minutes. Remove bones, skim off any surplus fat.

Blend flour with little water, add to saucepan, and cook, stirring, until liquid thickens. Drop dumpling dough by heaped dessertspoonfuls on top of hot bubbling stew. Cover tightly; cook 15 to 20 minutes.

Serves 4.

Parsley Dumplings Sift together flour and salt. Rub in butter, stir in parsley. Add enough milk to make a soft, sticky dough.

Hot Curry

2 lb. boned shoulder of lamb or mutton	1 teaspoon ground black pepper
1 teaspoon ground coriander	½ teaspoon salt
1 teaspoon ground cardamom	1 finely chopped onion
1 teaspoon poppy seeds	2 in. piece green ginger
1 teaspoon ground cinnamon	2 to 3 cloves garlic
1 teaspoon ground cloves	¼ pint (½ cup) yoghurt
	2 oz. (¼ cup) butter
	1 sliced onion
	2 tablespoons slivered almonds

Cut lamb into 1 in. cubes. Combine all spices, seasonings, finely chopped onion, finely chopped ginger, crushed garlic and yoghurt. Place meat in this marinade, leave several hours.

Heat butter, fry sliced onion until golden; remove, reserve for garnish. Fry almonds, remove, reserve for garnish. Add meat and marinade to pan, stir well. Cover and simmer 45 minutes or until meat is tender. Garnish with reserved fried onion rings and almonds.

Serves 4.

Sweet Curry

2 lb. boned shoulder of lamb	2 tablespoons slivered blanched almonds
¼ pint (½ cup) sour cream	1½ oz. (¼ cup) sultanas
2 teaspoons garam masala*	2 oz. (½ cup) thinly sliced dried apricots
1 tablespoon curry powder	2 to 3 cloves garlic
4 oz. (½ cup or 1 stick) butter	2 in. piece finely chopped green ginger
	2 large onions
	salt, lemon juice

* If not available add ½ teaspoon ground cardamon and ½ teaspoon cumin seeds.

Cut meat into 1 in. cubes. Place in bowl with sour cream, garam masala, curry powder; stir well, leave to marinate several hours.

Heat butter in saucepan, fry almonds until golden, remove and drain. Fry sultanas and apricots until plumped, remove and drain. Fry sliced garlic, ginger and sliced onions until golden. Add meat and marinade, cook 5 minutes on medium heat. Add sultanas and apricots, cover and simmer 45 to 60 minutes, until meat is tender; add salt and lemon juice to taste. Garnish with the almonds.

Serves 4.

Shashlik

1 lb. lamb cut from the leg	2 medium tomatoes
2 small onions	8 mushrooms
1 green pepper	bayleaves
	marinade

Marinade

1 clove garlic crushed	salt, pepper
3 to 4 tablespoons oil	2 tablespoons finely chopped onion
2 tablespoons lemon juice	

Remove fat from meat, cut into 1½ in. cubes. Combine ingredients for marinade, add lamb, and stir until well mixed. Cover and refrigerate several hours; stir occasionally to mix.

Peel onions, cut in halves, remove centre portion. Wash pepper, slice in half, remove seeds and cut flesh in 1½ in. squares. Wash tomatoes and cut in quarters. Remove stalks from mushrooms, if desired, or leave whole.

Thread meat on to skewers, brush with marinade and, if desired, place a bayleaf at end of skewer. Thread alternate vegetables on separate skewers, brush with marinade. Cook under heated grill, turning frequently and brushing with remaining marinade or melted butter until done to taste.

Pilaf (see page 93) is a good accompaniment for Shashlik.

Serves 2.

Moussaka

3 medium eggplants or aubergines	3 oz. (⅜ cup) butter
salt	1 clove garlic, crushed
2 lb. lean lamb cut from the leg	15½ oz. can tomatoes
1 large onion	¼ pint (½ cup) white wine
8 oz. (2 cups) grated parmesan or cheddar cheese	½ teaspoon nutmeg
1½ oz. (½ cup) soft breadcrumbs	salt, pepper
	oil for frying
	melted butter, extra

Sauce

2 oz. (¼ cup) butter	salt, pepper
2 oz. (½ cup) flour	1 pint (2 cups) milk
½ teaspoon nutmeg	1 egg

Cut eggplant into ½ in. slices, sprinkle lightly with salt, stand 20 minutes. Finely chop or mince meat, finely chop onion. Combine cheese with breadcrumbs.

Heat butter, add meat, onion and garlic, sauté until meat changes colour; add drained tomatoes, wine, nutmeg, salt and pepper, cover, simmer 15 minutes, or until meat is tender.

Drain eggplant, pat dry with absorbent paper, deep fry in hot oil until golden brown; drain.

Arrange fried eggplant in base of large greased casserole dish, sprinkle with ⅓ of cheese mixture, top with meat sauce, then white sauce. Sprinkle with remaining cheese mixture, drizzle over extra melted butter. Bake in hot oven, Mark 7, 425°F., 20 minutes or until golden brown.

Serves 4 to 6.

Sauce Melt butter in saucepan, remove from heat, stir in flour, nutmeg, salt and pepper, stir until smooth, return to heat, cook 1 minute. Remove from heat, gradually add milk, return to heat, stir until sauce boils and thickens. Add beaten egg, beat until smooth.

To serve as an entrée Cut 3 small eggplants in half lengthways, scoop out centres, leaving ½ in. shell. Sprinkle inside with salt, stand until liquid appears on surface; drain. Brush egg plants inside and out with melted butter, stand on tray in ½ in. cold water. Bake in moderate oven 8 to 10 minutes.

Layer meat sauce, cheese mixture and white sauce into egg plant shells, finish with cheese mixture, drizzle with extra melted butter. Bake in hot oven Mark 7 425°F. 20 minutes, or until golden brown.

Serves 6.

Moussaka can be cooked in a casserole or cooked in the delightfully unusual way shown above, and served as an entrée.

Veal

Veal is the flesh of young calves, specially treated when killed. It should be a faint delicate pink colour and has little fat. Being an immature meat it should be well cooked.

Cuts of Veal

Breast   Can be stuffed and roasted or stewed or braised.

Chops   Cut from the loin. Chump chops are cut from the bottom end and have a round bone in the centre. Allow one per portion.

Cutlets   Cut from the best end of the neck at the top of the loin. Usually grilled, fried or braised. Allow two per portion.

Fillet   Usually the most expensive cut. Normally cut from the top of the leg and boned. It can be stuffed and roasted or cut in thin slices to make escalopes. Continental fillet is the under part of the loin. Allow 4 to 6 oz. per portion.

Neck   This is a cheaper cut and very good value. It can be stuffed and roasted and is also suitable for stewing, braising or pot roasting. It is often used to make jellied veal and veal moulds. Allow about 1 lb. per portion.

Knuckle or Shank   This is the lower part of the leg, often sold separately and is excellent for boiling, stewing and pies.

Leg   Usually roasted, frequently boned and stuffed or cut into chops for grilling or frying.

Shoulder   Can be roasted on the bone but easier to handle if boned and rolled and is then sometimes referred to as oyster. Portions of shoulder are suitable for pot roasting or braising and small pieces of boneless meat are used for pies, stews and fricassees. Allow 1 lb. per portion with bone.

Offal

Feet—used for calves foot jelly or for stock and soup.

Head—including tongue and brains—may be braised or boiled or used for brawn.

Sweetbreads—see under Lamb—page 62.

Escalopes

Allow 4 to 6 oz. per person.
To prepare   Trim escalopes carefully, then place between several thicknesses of greaseproof paper and pound with a mallet or flat blade of heavy knife. Continue pounding until escalopes are about $\frac{1}{8}$ in. thick. This breaks down the fibres of the meat, making it deliciously tender. Place escalopes on flat dish and squeeze over a little lemon juice; let stand about 1 hour, turning frequently, before cooking.

Escalopes Naturel

4 escalopes	2 oz. ($\frac{1}{4}$ cup) butter
salt, pepper	juice $\frac{1}{2}$ lemon
flour	

Sprinkle each escalope with a little salt and pepper; dip in flour, shake off excess. Sauté in heated butter, allowing 4 to 5 minutes for each side, or longer depending on thickness. Arrange drained escalopes on hot serving dish. Add lemon juice to remaining butter, pour over escalopes.
  Serves 4.

Wiener Schnitzel

4 escalopes	2 oz. ($\frac{1}{4}$ cup) melted
flour seasoned with	butter
salt and pepper	1 tablespoon oil
beaten egg	slices of hard boiled egg
fine dry breadcrumbs	rolled anchovy fillets
	lemon wedges

Toss escalopes in seasoned flour, shake off excess, and dip in beaten egg. Then roll in crumbs, pressing these on firmly; refrigerate 30 minutes to set crumbs.
  Heat oil and butter in heavy frying pan, put in escalopes and cook until golden brown on both sides. Allow 4 to 5 minutes cooking time for each side. Drain meat well, arrange on serving dish. Top each with slice of hard boiled egg and rolled anchovy fillet. Serve with lemon wedges.
  Serves 4.

Escalopes with Cream

4 escalopes	salt, pepper
flour seasoned with	chopped parsley
salt and pepper	2 oz. ($\frac{1}{4}$ cup) butter
3 to 4 tablespoons	a little oil
cream	

Dip escalopes in seasoned flour; sauté in heated butter and oil, allowing 4 to 5 minutes cooking time for each side. Transfer to serving dish; keep warm.
  Add cream to pan juices; simmer until mixture is slightly reduced and well blended. Season with

salt and pepper. Spoon over escalopes; sprinkle with chopped parsley.

Serves 4.

Veal Parmesan

3 oz. (1 cup) fresh breadcrumbs
1 teaspoon grated lemon rind
3 oz. (¾ cup) grated Parmesan cheese

4 veal escalopes
flour seasoned with salt and pepper
1 egg
2 oz. (¼ cup) butter
2 tablespoons oil

Mushroom Sauce

1 large onion
¼ lb. mushrooms
1 tablespoon oil

2 × 5 oz. cans (1½ cups) tomato purée
4 tablespoons dry sherry
salt, pepper

Combine breadcrumbs, lemon rind and Parmesan cheese. Pound escalopes, if necessary, until thin. Dip in seasoned flour, then beaten egg; press on crumb mixture. Refrigerate 1 hour.

Heat butter and oil in large frying pan, cook escalopes until golden on each side and cooked through. Remove to hot serving plates. Serve Mushroom Sauce separately.

Serves 4.

Mushroom Sauce Chop onion and mushrooms, sauté in hot oil until tender; add tomato purée, sherry, season with salt and pepper. Simmer, uncovered 5 minutes.

Veal Marengo

2 lb. veal
2 oz. (½ cup) flour seasoned with salt and pepper
1 oz. (2 tablespoons) butter
1 tablespoon oil
1 clove garlic
¼ pint (½ cup) white wine

1 pint (2 cups) boiling water
2 chicken stock cubes
1 tablespoon tomato paste
12 small white onions
2 tomatoes
½ lb. button mushrooms
chopped parsley

Trim and cut meat into serving-size pieces, toss in seasoned flour. Heat butter and oil in large frying pan, fry meat until golden; remove, place in casserole. Fry crushed garlic a few minutes, add remaining flour; cook, stirring occasionally, until lightly browned. Gradually add wine and boiling water, in which chicken stock cubes have been dissolved, bring to boil, stirring; add tomato paste. Reduce heat, simmer gently until reduced by half. Pour over meat, cover, bake in moderate oven, Mark 4, 375°F., 1 hour.

Meanwhile, parboil onions 5 minutes; remove skin from tomatoes and chop coarsely. When meat is tender, add onions, sliced mushrooms and tomatoes; cook further 15 to 20 minutes. Sprinkle with chopped parsley.

Serves 6.

Veal with Blue Cheese

1½ lb. fillet of veal
4 oz. (½ cup or 1 stick) butter
2 oz. blue cheese
flour seasoned with salt and pepper

1 egg
soft breadcrumbs
4 tablespoons oil
lemon wedges

Cut veal into 5 to 6 pieces and pound until very thin. Cream together butter and blue cheese in warmed basin. Spread some of this mixture on one side of each steak; dip steaks in seasoned flour, then beaten egg; press on breadcrumbs. Refrigerate 1 hour.

Heat oil in large frying pan, cook steaks until well browned and cooked through. Dust with chopped parsley, garnish with lemon wedges.

Serves 5 to 6.

Osso Buco

4 tablespoons oil
3 onions
2 carrots
3 sticks celery
3 or 4 veal shanks sawn into 3 in. pieces
seasoning
flour
1 bayleaf
2 cloves garlic

pinch each basil and thyme
piece lemon rind
2 tablespoons tomato paste
¼ pint (½ cup) white wine
¼ pint (½ cup) stock
2 tablespoons finely chopped celery, extra
1 tablespoon grated lemon rind

Heat oil in pan, fry sliced onions gently until soft and turning golden, place in large saucepan. Gently sauté sliced carrots and chopped celery, add to onions. Roll veal shanks in seasoned flour and brown in oil.

Arrange pieces on top of vegetables, standing upright so that marrow won't fall out during cooking. Add bayleaf, crushed garlic, thyme, basil and lemon rind. Mix tomato paste into combined white wine and stock, add seasonings and pour over. Add more stock, if necessary. Bring to boil, cover and simmer gently for approximately 4 hours or until meat is almost falling off bones. Ten minutes before serving, sprinkle with finely chopped celery and lemon rind. Serve with risotto (see page 94).

Serves 4 to 6.

Veal and Mushroom Ragout

1½ lb. veal	1 pint (2 cups) boiling
2 oz. (¼ cup) butter	water
2 onions	2 chicken stock cubes
1 tablespoon paprika	salt, pepper
15½ oz. can cream of	2 green peppers
mushroom or cream	4 oz. small mushrooms
of tomato soup	

Cut veal into 1 in. cubes. Melt butter in frying pan, sauté sliced onions and veal until onions are transparent; stir in paprika.

Combine soup and boiling water, in which chicken stock cubes have been dissolved; stir into veal, season to taste; cover, simmer gently approximately 1 hour or until veal is tender.

Add sliced peppers and whole mushrooms, cook gently until mushrooms are tender, about 7 minutes.

Serves 4.

Veal Cordon Bleu

6 veal escalopes	1 egg
6 thin slices ham	fine dry breadcrumbs
6 thin slices gruyère	2 oz. (¼ cup) butter
cheese	2 tablespoons oil
flour seasoned with	
salt and pepper	

Pound escalopes, if necessary, until very thin. Top each with slice of ham and slice of gruyère cheese. Fold in half, secure with small wooden stick. Dip in seasoned flour and beaten egg, then press on fine dry breadcrumbs. Refrigerate 1 hour.

Heat butter and oil in large frying pan. Cook escalopes turning occasionally, until cooked through. Drain well, remove small wooden sticks.

Serves 6.

Gourmet Veal

6 veal escalopes	2 tablespoons oil
½ lb. mushrooms	¼ pint (½ cup) medium
6 to 8 spring onions	cream
(scallions)	salt, pepper
2 oz. (¼ cup) butter	parsley

Pound escalopes until very thin, if necessary. Slice mushrooms, chop spring onions (scallions). Heat butter and oil in large frying pan, fry meat quickly. Remove from pan and keep warm.

Add mushrooms to pan and sauté until tender, add the chopped spring onions, cook a few minutes. Add cream and allow to heat through (do not boil). Season to taste. Pour over the cooked veal. Sprinkle with chopped parsley.

Serves 6.

Veal Chops à la Crème

12 shallots	salt, pepper
4 oz. (½ cup or 1 stick)	¼ pint (½ cup) dry white
butter	wine
6 veal cutlets	3 to 4 tablespoons
6 oz. small mushrooms	medium cream
	chopped parsley

Peel the shallots keeping them whole; cook in boiling salted water 10 minutes.

Heat butter in pan, add cutlets, and cook until golden brown on one side. Turn and cook on other side. When done, remove and keep warm on serving dish. Add the small whole mushrooms and parboiled onions to pan, season, cook until tender, and golden brown in colour. Stir in white wine, then add cream. Cook a few minutes, stirring frequently (do not allow to boil). Taste, and correct seasonings. Pour sauce over cutlets, sprinkle with parsley.

Serves 3.

Herbed Shoulder of Veal

1 boned shoulder of	salt, pepper
veal	1 oz. (2 tablespoons)
½ pint (1 cup) chicken	butter
stock	

Stuffing

1 small onion	finely grated rind 1
1 oz. (2 tablespoons)	lemon
butter	1 teaspoon mixed herbs
4 oz. (1¼ cups) fresh	pinch salt
breadcrumbs	pepper
2 tablespoons finely	
chopped parsley	

Fill shoulder with herbed breadcrumb stuffing; tie firmly into shape. Place in baking dish with stock, salt, pepper and butter. Bake in moderate oven, Mark 4, 350°F., basting frequently, allowing 30 minutes per lb.

Serves 6 to 8.

Stuffing Sauté chopped onion in melted butter; mix with breadcrumbs, parsley, grated lemon rind, herbs, salt and pepper. Beat egg, add to the mixture, and stir until it binds together.

Wiener Schnitzel—golden-crumbed veal slices, seasoned lightly with lemon, are served with traditional topping of egg and anchovy.

Pork, Ham and Bacon

For some families, there's nothing nicer than a roasted leg of pork—the crackling crisp and golden; or slices from a pink, juicy, succulent ham. In this section are the cooking methods and recipes which present pork, in its various forms, at its most appetizing best.

Cuts of Pork, Ham and Bacon

Belly This corresponds to the breast of lamb or veal. It is usually salted and then boiled (salt pork). It can also be cut into thin slices and fried or grilled like streaky bacon. Allow 4 to 6 oz. per portion.

Blade or Shoulder Butt Cut from the top part of the foreleg, suitable for roasting. Allow $\frac{1}{2}$ to $\frac{3}{4}$ lb. per portion.

Hand and Spring or Hock and Forefoot This is the foreleg, suitable for roasting, boiling or stewing. Allow $\frac{3}{4}$ lb. per portion.

Leg This is the hind leg. Can be roasted whole or boned and stuffed. Slices from the top end without bone—fillets—are used for frying and grilling.

Loin This is the best and most expensive cut. Can be roasted in the piece or cut into chops for frying or grilling. These are the chump chops and usually one is quite sufficient per portion.

Cutlets are cut from the spare rib and two per portion would be needed.

Spare Rib This is the top piece just behind the head. It is fairly lean and can be roasted, braised or stewed.

Offal

Head—used for brawn.

Liver—has a fairly strong flavour but excellent for making pâté.

Pig's Fry—is the term given to a selection of offal including kidneys and liver. It is generally fried or baked.

Trotters—can be boiled or stewed.

Apple Sauce

Peel, core and slice 3 tart apples. Cook until soft with 1 tablespoon sugar, 2 tablespoons water, pinch salt, squeeze lemon juice and 1 teaspoon of butter. Beat until smooth, serve hot.

Roast Pork

1 small leg of pork or fillet cut from leg (4 to 5 lb.)	salt ground ginger oil

Ask your butcher to score the pork rind well. Place roast in well-oiled baking dish. Rub skin with generous amount of salt and a little ground ginger. (The salt will ensure crisp crackling). Roast in hot oven, Mark 7, 425°F., 20 minutes, then reduce heat to moderate, Mark 4, 350°F.; continue cooking until meat is well browned and tender, allowing 25 to 30 minutes per lb. cooking time. Make a thin gravy from the pan drippings; serve with gravy and baked apples or apple sauce.

Sweet and Sour Pork

3 dessertspoons sugar	3 to 4 spring onions (scallions) or chives
1 tablespoon soy sauce	1 red pepper
$\frac{1}{2}$ teaspoon salt	4 oz. mushrooms
1 tablespoon dry sherry	$\frac{1}{2}$ cucumber
1 egg-yolk	cornflour (cornstarch)
2 to $2\frac{1}{2}$ lb. lean pork	3 to 4 tablespoons vinegar
$15\frac{1}{2}$ oz. can pineapple pieces	1 dessertspoon tomato sauce
2 onions	salt, pepper

Mix together sugar, soy sauce, salt, sherry and egg-yolk; stir well. Cut meat into 1 in. cubes, place in soy sauce mixture. Stir until well coated with marinade. Cover, leave 1 hour; stir occasionally.

Drain pineapple, reserve the liquid. Slice onions, cut spring onions diagonally. Remove seeds from pepper; cut into thin strips. Slice mushrooms and cucumber into chunky strips. Fry onion in a little hot oil until transparent. Add pepper and spring onions, cook further 3 to 4 minutes. Add mushrooms, cook until softened. Stir in pineapple pieces and cucumber. Remove from heat, keep hot.

Drain meat from marinade, reserve liquid. Toss meat lightly in cornflour (cornstarch). Heat oil, cook meat until golden brown and cooked through; drain well. Add meat to vegetables, keep hot.

Blend 1 dessertspoon cornflour (cornstarch) with reserved pineapple liquid. Add vinegar and tomato sauce, stir into remaining marinade. Bring to boil, stirring continually; season to taste. Pour sauce over meat and vegetables, stir to coat evenly. Serve with hot boiled rice.

Serves 6.

Ginger Pork Spareribs

4 lb. pork spareribs	juice ½ lemon
4 tablespoons soy sauce	pepper
1½ gills (¾ cup) water	½ teaspoon ground
4 tablespoons orange	ginger
marmalade	1 dessertspoon grated
1 clove garlic	green ginger

Place spareribs, meaty side down, in well-greased, shallow baking dish. Roast in hot oven, Mark 7, 425°F., 30 minutes. Turn spareribs over, lower temperature to moderate, Mark 4, 350°F., continue cooking further 30 minutes. Pour off excess fat from pan.

Combine soy sauce, water, marmalade, crushed garlic, lemon juice, pepper and gingers; blend thoroughly. Pour this sauce over spareribs, cook further ¾ hour, basting frequently with sauce.

Serves 6.

Chinese Barbecued Pork Fillets

4 slices pork fillet about 6 oz. each	2 tablespoons dry sherry
1 dessertspoon sugar	1 clove garlic, crushed
1 tablespoon honey	½ teaspoon mixed spice
3 tablespoons soy sauce	1 tablespoon Hoy Sin
1 teaspoon oil	sauce*—optional
	1 teaspoon salt

** Hoy Sin sauce is available at food halls of large department stores, or at Chinese food stores.*

Trim pork, removing surplus fat. Combine remaining ingredients in large mixing bowl, mix well. Add pork, allow to marinate a few hours or overnight, turning occasionally. Drain pork, place on wire rack. Stand rack in shallow baking tray. Bake in hot oven, Mark 7, 425°F., approximately 30 minutes, or until meat is tender, basting frequently with remaining marinade. Turn pork once during cooking. (Place a small amount of water in baking tray to prevent juices from burning).

Alternatively, meat can be grilled under hot grill until tender, turning and basting often.

Brawn

½ pig's head	5 peppercorns
1 lb. lean pork	2 cloves
1 lb. veal shoulder	1 small onion, sliced
salt	1 bayleaf
5 whole allspice	1 small carrot

Clean pig's head, soak in cold water 6 to 12 hours; change water once. Place with other meat in large saucepan, cover with boiling water. Bring to boil again, skim well; add remaining ingredients. Reduce heat; simmer covered, 1½ to 2 hours or until meat is very tender. Remove meat from bones, cut into small pieces. Measure liquid, return liquid to saucepan, continue boiling until liquid is reduced to half quantity; strain. Replace strained liquid and meat in saucepan, bring to boil, season to taste.

Pour into lightly oiled 9 × 5 in. loaf tin; cool, then refrigerate until set.

Serves 4 to 6.

Pork and Cider Casserole

2 lb. boned blade of pork	2 sticks celery
2 oz. (½ cup) flour	2 cloves garlic
salt, pepper	1 pint (2 cups) cider
1 oz. (2 tablespoons) fat	¼ pint (½ cup) yoghurt
2 onions	

Cut the meat into 1½ in. cubes and coat with seasoned flour. Heat the fat in a pan, add the meat, finely chopped onions, finely chopped celery and crushed garlic and fry altogether until lightly browned. Remove from the heat, gradually stir in cider, return to the heat and bring to the boil, stirring all the time. Add seasoning, cover and simmer slowly for 1½ hours or until meat is tender.

Blend the yoghurt with a little of the hot liquid then stir it into the stew. Correct the seasoning and serve with boiled noodles or spaghetti.

Serves 5 to 6.

Hawaiian Ham

4 gammon rashers cut ¼ to ½ in. thick or lean thickly sliced bacon	2 tablespoons light brown sugar
4 oz. (½ cup or 1 stick) butter	¼ pint (½ cup) pineapple juice

Marinate rashers in combined pineapple juice and brown sugar for 3 hours. Drain well.

Heat butter, fry gammon until golden brown on both sides; turn constantly during cooking. Canned pineapple rings, sautéed in hot butter, can be served as an accompaniment.

Serves 4.

Ham-Asparagus Rolls

canned asparagus spears	½ pint (1 cup) mornay sauce
6 slices cooked ham	(see page 105)

Drain asparagus spears well. Take 4 or 5 spears and roll these inside a slice of ham. Arrange neatly in a fireproof dish. Pour sauce over ham-asparagus rolls. Heat through in a moderate oven, Mark 4, 350°F., or under the grill.

Serves 4 to 6.

Boiled Ham

Soak ham for several hours in cold water, then drain and dry. Place in large vessel with enough tepid water to cover. Add a little parsley and thyme and 4 peppercorns. Bring slowly to boil, taking at least 1½ hours. Simmer gently (never boil) for time required, according to size.

To test whether ham is cooked, pull the small bone at the shank end that lies alongside the large one; when it is loose and slips out easily, then ham is done.

Allow to cool in liquid, then peel off skin, and glaze as desired. If boiled ham is to be eaten cold, remove skin, then return to water in which it was cooked and leave until quite cold. This helps to keep it juicy.

Cooking Time per Pound
Up to 12 lb.—20 minutes
12 lb. and over—15 minutes

To Glaze the Ham

If baking a ham that has been already cooked (by boiling), simply peel off skin; score fat into squares or diamonds with sharp knife. Place ham in large baking dish, glaze with any of the following suggested glazes; bake in moderate oven, Mark 4, 350°F., 45 minutes.

Spread orange marmalade over scored ham. Bake, baste with pan drippings.

Arrange pineapple rings and glacé cherries on ham, secure with whole cloves or cocktail sticks. Sprinkle with brown sugar; bake.

Blend together 6 oz. (1 cup) brown sugar, 1 tablespoon dry mustard; mix to a thick paste with dry sherry. Spread over scored ham; bake.

Pork Loins with Prunes

4 lb. loin pork, boned	1 large cooking apple
salt, pepper	lemon juice
4 oz. (⅔ cup) prunes	2 oz. (¼ cup) butter

Make a pocket in the loin by cutting, with a sharp knife, to within ½ in. of both ends; sprinkle with salt and pepper. Pit prunes; peel and dice apple, sprinkle with lemon juice. Stuff pocket with prunes and apple. Roll meat firmly around filling, secure with string. Rub scored crackling around loin lightly with salt.

Melt butter in baking dish; add pork. Cook in moderate oven, Mark 4, 350°F., approximately 1½ to 2 hours. Make thin gravy from pan juices. Red cabbage makes a good accompaniment.

Serves 6.

Boiled Bacon

Whilst in America it is not customary for the housewife to boil bacon, in England this is a popular dish.

The most usual cut for boiling is the gammon which comes from the hind leg of a bacon pig. It can be corner, middle, hock or slipper. The collar is also suitable and generally less expensive. The approximate weights of the joints naturally varies with the size of the pig but a corner of gammon is generally about 4 lb., middle gammon about 5 lb., hock about 4½ lb., and the slipper is a smaller joint about 1½ to 2 lb.

Perhaps 'simmering' would be a better word than boiling for this cooking process, because rapid boiling, over a period, will cause shrinkage and will affect the meat texture and the fat structure. Slow, careful cooking is necessary for best results.

Put bacon into saucepan, cover with cold water and let stand 24 hours; drain. Cover with fresh cold water, bring slowly to boil, then reduce heat until water is just simmering. Cover, cook until bacon is tender. Allow 20 to 25 minutes per lb.

When the bacon has been cooked it can be glazed and baked as a ham. Remove rind while hot, spread with some melted red currant jelly or honey, or spread with a paste of brown sugar, mustard and sherry. The fat can be cut in criss-cross squares and each square studded with a clove. Bake in moderate oven, 350°F., 20 minutes to melt glaze. Apple sauce (see page 72), spiced lightly with cinnamon, is a nice accompaniment.

Chinese Sweet and Sour Pork combines—deliciously!—tender pieces of pork with pineapple and a rich sauce.

健何
金
飛
益群
合隆
升
WING TAI JADE CHR

The Variety Meats

Simple recipes suit the variety meats best, so that their full, delicate flavour is retained. They are easily prepared and some can be cooked in minutes. Serve them often; in addition to their good taste, they are a rich source of nourishment at a low price.

Pig's Trotters (feet)

4 trotters (feet)	1 chicken stock cube
2 onions	salt, pepper
pinch ground mace	½ oz. (1 tablespoon)
strip lemon peel	flour
	parsley

Ask the butcher to split the trotters in half lengthwise. Wash them and put into a pan with the sliced onions, mace, lemon peel, stock cube, 1 pint (2 cups) water, and a little salt and pepper. Bring to boiling point, stirring occasionally, cover and simmer for about 2 hours. Remove the trotters and thicken the liquid with the flour blended smoothly with a little cold water. Boil 2 to 3 minutes. Pour over the trotters and serve hot sprinkled with chopped parsley.

Serves 2 to 4 according to the size of the trotters.

Brains

To prepare   Soak brains in cold water several hours. Then place in saucepan with 1 dessertspoon vinegar, a little salt, 1 small sliced onion, 1 small bayleaf and water to cover. Bring slowly just to boiling point. Poach gently for 10 minutes, without allowing water to boil. Drain, cover with cold water to firm; remove membranes.

Brains in Cream Sauce

4 sets brains	1 chicken stock cube
2 oz. (¼ cup) butter	2 egg-yolks
1 small onion	½ green pepper
1 tablespoon flour	1 teaspoon lemon juice
¾ pint (1½ cups) boiling	1 medium tomato
water	salt, pepper

Cut prepared brains into slices or cubes. Melt butter in saucepan, add finely chopped onion, cook 1 minute. Stir in flour, cook further 1 minute. Remove from heat, gradually stir in boiling water, in which chicken stock cube has been dissolved. Return to heat, bring to boil, stirring; reduce heat, simmer until thickened, stirring constantly.

Stir 2 tablespoons of this mixture into beaten egg-yolks, gradually add to remaining sauce, stirring constantly. Simmer 5 minutes without boiling. Add brains, chopped pepper, lemon juice, peeled and chopped tomato, salt and pepper. Place in top of double saucepan over hot water, simmer 15 minutes.

Serves 4.

Brains in Black Butter

4 sets brains	juice 1 lemon
seasoned flour	1 teaspoon capers
butter for frying	chopped parsley
4 oz. (½ cup or 1 stick)	
butter, extra	

Toss prepared brains in seasoned flour. Sauté in heated butter until golden brown, remove to hot serving dish. Add extra butter to pan, cook until it turns brown. Remove from heat, add lemon juice and capers. Pour the sizzling butter over brains, sprinkle with chopped parsley.

Serves 3 to 4.

Sweetbreads

To prepare   Wash sweetbreads well, soak in cold water 3 to 4 hours, changing water several times. Drain, place in saucepan with sufficient cold water to cover. Bring water slowly to boil, simmer 3 to 5 minutes, according to size. Drain, plunge at once into cold water. Remove as much skin and membrane as possible; dry well.

If desired, they can be spread out on a plate and weighed down by pressing another plate on top of them. In this way, they flatten as they cool. The sweetbreads are now ready to cook in a variety of ways. They can be crumbed and fried, or served in a cream sauce.

Sweetbreads à la King

1 lb. sweetbreads	¼ pint (½ cup) thin
3 oz. (⅜ cup) butter	cream
4 oz. mushrooms	1 tablespoon flour
1 green pepper	½ pint (1 cup) milk
1 red pepper	salt, pepper
3 to 4 tablespoons dry	4 slices of toast or
sherry	pastry-cases

Cut prepared sweetbreads into cubes. Melt half the butter in saucepan, add sliced mushrooms and diced peppers; cook gently 2 minutes, then add half the sherry and cream. Simmer sauce until reduced by half, then add sweetbreads.

Melt remaining butter in separate saucepan, stir in flour, cook 1 minute. Remove from heat, gradually add milk. Return to heat, bring to boil, stirring; reduce heat, simmer until thick and smooth, stirring constantly. Add sweetbread mixture, season to taste with salt and pepper. Stir in remaining sherry and cream, reheat without boiling. Spoon mixture into heated pastry cases or serve on slices of hot toast.

Serves 4.

Tripe

To prepare Tripe should be absolutely fresh; if possible, cook and serve it on the day it is bought. Although tripe, when bought, has already been parboiled in processing, a preliminary blanching before cooking is necessary.

Place tripe in large saucepan with sufficient cold water to cover; add squeeze of lemon juice. Bring slowly to the boil, simmer 5 minutes. Drain well, then prepare as desired.

Tripe in Parsley Sauce

1½ lb tripe	1 oz. (2 tablespoons)
water	flour
2 oz. (¼ cup) butter	½ pint (1 cup) milk
2 onions	2 tablespoons chopped
	parsley
	salt, pepper

Cut blanched tripe into strips. Place in saucepan with sufficient cold water to cover. Bring to boil, cover, simmer approximately 2 hours or until tender; drain, reserving ½ pint (1 cup) stock.

Melt butter in saucepan, add chopped onions, cook until transparent. Stir in flour, cook 1 minute. Remove from heat, gradually add reserved stock and milk. Return to heat, bring to boil stirring; reduce heat, simmer until thickened, stirring constantly. Add tripe and chopped parsley; heat through. Season to taste with salt and pepper.

Serves 4.

Tripe Bordelaise

1½ lb. tripe	¾ pint (1½ cups) boiling
2 onions	water
1 oz. (2 tablespoons)	1 chicken stock cube
butter	salt, pepper
1 clove garlic	bouquet garni
3 medium tomatoes	chopped parsley
1 tablespoon tomato	
paste	

Cut blanched tripe into strips. Sauté chopped onions in butter until golden. Add crushed garlic, peeled and chopped tomatoes, tomato paste, boiling water (in which chicken stock cube has been dissolved), seasoning and bouquet garni. Bring

to boil, add tripe, reduce heat; cover and simmer slowly until tripe is tender, approximately 2 to 2½ hours. Remove bouquet garni. Correct seasonings. Transfer to serving dish, sprinkle with chopped parsley.

Serves 4.

Ox Tongue

To prepare Wash the tongue. If it is highly salted, it should be soaked in water for approximately 24 hours. (If fresh, unsalted tongue is used, add some salt to water when cooking.) Place tongue in large saucepan with sufficient cold water to cover. Add a few peppercorns, 1 bayleaf, 1 sliced onion and 1 small carrot. Bring to boil, cover, reduce heat and simmer approximately 3 hours depending on size of tongue, allowing 45 to 60 minutes cooking time per lb. Remove skin from tongue while still hot.

Allow pickled tongue, which is served cold, to cool in the cooking liquid.

Glazed Ox Tongue

1 cooked ox tongue	3 cloves
½ oz. (2 tablespoons or	3 thin strips lemon rind
2 envelopes) gelatine	1 dessertspoon lemon
¾ pint (1½ cups) cold	juice
water	2 thin slices onion
¼ pint (½ cup) hot water	2 sprigs parsley
1 tablespoon white	1 teaspoon salt
vinegar	

Pack cooked tongue into tongue presser or basin. Pour in just enough aspic to cover tongue. Place saucer or plate and a weight on top. Leave to cool, then refrigerate overnight.

Aspic Jelly Soak gelatine in hot water. Place all other ingredients into saucepan, stir lightly with fork until boiling, add soaked gelatine. Cool and strain through fine strainer lined with clean cloth. Pour over tongue (you may not need all the aspic).

Kidneys

To prepare Wash kidneys, remove skin. Cut lamb's kidneys in half. Remove hard core and any fat or gristle. When frying halved kidneys, place them cut side down in pan and press lightly. This will seal the cut edge, thus retaining all juices.

Ox kidney should not be fried: it needs long, gentle simmering to soften it, as in the filling for Steak and Kidney Pie.

Kidneys Chasseur

8 lamb's kidneys
salt, pepper
4 oz. (½ cup or 1 stick) butter
1 tablespoon finely chopped shallots
1 dessertspoon plain flour
¼ pint (½ cup) madeira or port wine
¼ pint (½ cup) dry white wine
4 oz. mushrooms
triangles of fried bread
parsley

Soak kidneys in salted water for 15 minutes. Remove outer skin and fat from kidneys, cut into slices. Sprinkle with salt and pepper. Melt half the butter in frying pan, add kidneys, cook quickly until just beginning to brown; remove from pan.

Add shallots and flour to pan drippings, cook 2 minutes. Add madeira and white wine; return kidneys. Bring just to boil, simmer 5 minutes. In separate pan, sauté sliced mushrooms a few minutes in remaining butter. Spoon kidney mixture on serving dish, top with mushrooms. Serve with triangles of fried bread. Garnish with parsley.

Serves 4.

Devilled Kidneys

8 lamb's kidneys
3 oz. (⅜ cup) butter
1 clove garlic
1 small onion
salt, pepper
1 tablespoon Worcestershire sauce
1 tablespoon dry sherry
2 to 3 tablespoons finely chopped parsley

Wash kidneys, remove skin, fat and hard core; slice kidneys. Melt butter in pan, add crushed garlic, finely chopped onion, salt and pepper, cook a few minutes. Add kidneys, cook quickly on both sides. Add Worcestershire sauce, sherry and parsley to pan, blend well. Spoon on to slices of hot buttered toast—delicious as a supper dish; or serve with hot rice, into which some finely chopped parsley has been tossed.

Serves 4.

Oxtail Casserole

2 large onions
2 large carrots
4 oxtails
1 oz. (2 tablespoons) butter
1 dessertspoon dark brown sugar
4 tablespoons flour
6 tomatoes
3 cloves garlic, crushed
few sprigs parsley
1 bayleaf
½ teaspoon thyme
3 pints (6 cups) beef stock
1 pint (2 cups) red wine
salt, pepper
1 15½ oz. can cream of tomato soup
4 oz. (¼ cup) haricot beans*

Slice onions, dice carrots, cut oxtails into 2 in. sections. Heat butter, gradually add onions, carrots and oxtail pieces, sauté, stirring constantly until well browned. Drain off any surplus fat during cooking.

Place browned meat and vegetables into a large casserole dish, sprinkle with brown sugar and flour. Peel tomatoes and chop finely, add with remaining ingredients (except haricot beans) to casserole, cover, bake in slow oven, Mark 1, 275°F., 4 hours. Cool, refrigerate overnight.

Cover haricot beans well with water, stand overnight. Next day, drain, place beans in salted water, boil 1 hour, or until tender.

Remove fat from top of casserole, remove bayleaf. Reheat casserole in slow oven, Mark 2, 300°F., for approximately 1 hour; stir in beans during last 15 minutes. Adjust seasoning, serve sprinkled with parsley.

Serves 6 to 8.

* Green beans can be substituted for haricot, but do not need soaking overnight.

A wonderful meal for men—subtle blending of hearty flavours makes this Oxtail Casserole the perfect dish for cold-weather entertaining.

Poultry

Chicken, so easily available at an economical price, has become almost a standard feature on weekly menus, either for family meals or for entertaining. Turkey, too, now available in small sizes, gives lots of good eating when you have a number of people to entertain.

In this section are all the basic ways of cooking the various birds, plus a wide selection of the world's most popular ways with poultry, plus stuffings and accompaniments.

To Choose a Chicken

The skin should be white and free from wrinkles, the breast plump and the breast bone pliable. A boiling fowl may have a slightly yellow tinge to the skin.

Young birds weigh from $2\frac{1}{2}$ to 3 lb. and are suitable for roasting, grilling or frying or sautéing. Older birds weigh from $3\frac{1}{2}$ to 5 lb. and are boiled or used for fricassées, casseroles or similar dishes.

A capon is a male bird that has been specially treated and reared to make it particularly 'meaty' and may weigh up to 8 lb.

Poussins are baby chickens 4 to 8 weeks old weighing 1 to 2 lb. and may be roasted, sautéed or grilled. According to their size, they are either cooked whole or cut in half. Spring chickens are generally 8 weeks to 4 months old.

A $2\frac{1}{2}$ to 3 lb. bird is sufficient for 4 to 5 people. A larger one will serve 6 to 8 people. If the chicken is stuffed and roasted it should be weighed after stuffing in order to calculate the time for cooking. Allow 25 minutes to the lb.

Chicken joints, fresh or frozen are convenient for small families and for special occasions.

How to Joint a Chicken

Many chicken recipes call for the chicken to be jointed, or cut into sections. Here's how to do it. You'll need a good sharp knife and a pair of poultry shears or a strong pair of kitchen scissors.

A chicken will joint into 8 sections: 2 legs, 2 wings, 2 breast portions, and the backbone, which is split into 2 pieces.

To remove legs Cut through skin connecting leg to body; bend leg out, away from body, find the joint where leg hinges, cut through this (there is no need to cut any bone).

To remove wings Cut a slice of breast meat with the wing to make a better serving portion, then bend wing away from body to find where wing joins body; cut through this. Fold wing into a neat shape with breast meat tucked under.

To remove breast Separate breast and back by cutting through rib-bones along each side of body. Cut down centre of breastbone to divide breast in 2; trim away excess skin and fat. (These breast portions, when removed from the bone, are called the supremes).

The backbone Break back in 2 where ribs end. These back portions are generally not considered as individual serving portions, but can be served to accompany another portion such as a wing, or they can be used to make soup, etc.

For many recipes—particularly those to be served with a white or cream sauce—some cooks prefer to remove the skin of the chicken before cooking. However, for those recipes where the chicken pieces are browned before cooking, the skin browns more easily and gives protection to the juicy meat beneath.

Roast Chicken

For roasting, a chicken is generally stuffed (see page 89) and can be cooked in an uncovered dish, wrapped in foil or in a covered roaster. (Spring chickens and poussins are not stuffed.)

The stuffing is put in at the neck end and should not be packed too firmly.

Rub the breast and legs with butter or bacon fat and cook in a moderately hot oven, Mark 6, 400°F., for the calculated time. If the chicken is in a covered roaster or has been wrapped in foil, allow an extra 10 to 15 minutes cooking time and remove the lid or foil 15 minutes before the end of the cooking to allow the skin to brown and crisp.

Accompaniments to Roast Chicken

Bread Sauce Peel an onion and stud with 2 or 3 cloves. Put into saucepan with $\frac{1}{2}$ bayleaf, 2 or 3 peppercorns, a small blade of mace and $\frac{1}{2}$ pint (1 cup) milk. Bring slowly to boil, cover, simmer 5 minutes; strain, retaining liquid and discarding onion. Return liquid to rinsed-out saucepan, add 2 oz. (¾ cup) fresh breadcrumbs, season to taste. Simmer, stirring, 2 or 3 minutes. Stir in a little butter or cream before serving.

Giblet Gravy Melt 1 tablespoon butter in small saucepan, stir in 1½ dessertspoons flour; cook, stirring, few minutes. Gradually stir in ½ pint (1 cup) hot giblet stock (made by cooking giblets in water with a little onion and celery) season to taste. A few of the finely chopped giblets can also be added.

Or stir some flour into pan drippings, pour in the strained giblet stock; cook, stirring, until sauce boils and thickens slightly; season.

French Roast Chicken

1 chicken (2½ to 3 lb.)	giblets
prepared stuffing	½ pint (1 cup) stock or
4 oz. (½ cup or 1 stick)	water
softened butter	salt, pepper

Fill chicken with prepared stuffing, spread legs and breast with softened butter. Place in baking dish with giblets and stock or water. Roast in moderately hot oven, Mark 6, 400°F., until chicken is well browned and tender, basting and turning frequently, and adding extra water or stock if this reduces too much.

Transfer cooked bird to hot serving platter. Strain pan juices into saucepan, skim well, bring to the boil, cook 1 or 2 minutes, season to taste, strain; serve with chicken.

Serves 4.

Chicken in a Basket

This is one of the most popular chicken dishes, particularly for a small, informal party.

Allow one small chicken (about 1½ lb.) for each person; roast in usual way. Serve in small basket, lined with paper napkin. Packaged potato crisps (heat them in oven first) and fried onion rings are the correct accompaniments.

Chicken in the Basket is finger food, so serve finger bowls filled with warm water, with a slice of lemon floating in the water. As the water cools, the lemon can be used to remove any grease from fingers.

There's a correct way to eat this dish: Break off one leg first. Eat this before breaking off any further pieces. In this way the chicken retains its heat.

One hand only should be used to convey the food to the mouth. Rinse fingers often in the finger bowl. Make sure the dinner napkins are a good big size.

Chicken in Aspic

3 lb. chicken	piece of lemon rind
1 carrot	salt, pepper
1 stick celery	½ oz. (2 tablespoons or
1 medium onion	2 envelopes) gelatine
1 clove garlic	2 tablespoons chopped
1 bayleaf	parsley

Place chicken in a pan with sliced carrot, sliced celery, sliced onion, crushed garlic, bayleaf, lemon rind and a sprinkling of salt and pepper. Cover with water and bring to the boil; reduce heat and simmer until chicken is cooked.

Lift out chicken, remove meat from bone, return bones and skin to pan and allow to boil a further 10 minutes. Cut meat into small pieces, soften gelatine in a little water.

Strain bones and vegetables from stock, then strain again through muslin.

Take 1 pint (2 cups) of this stock and add the gelatine, add salt to taste. Mix together chicken, parsley and stock, pour into oiled mould. Refrigerate until set, stirring occasionally to distribute meat evenly.

Serves 4 to 5.

Coq au Vin

2 2½ lb. chickens	3 to 4 tablespoons
2 oz. (¼ cup) butter	brandy
¼ lb. lean salt pork	¾ pint (1½ cups) dry red
12 tiny onions	wine
salt, pepper	¼ pint (½ cup) stock
½ lb. mushrooms	bouquet garni
1 to 2 cloves garlic	1 oz. (2 tablespoons)
	butter, extra
	2 tablespoons flour

Joint the chickens. Heat butter in heavy saucepan, add diced pork and peeled, blanched and drained onions. Cook a few minutes, then add chicken joints; brown well, season. Add sliced mushrooms and crushed garlic, cook 5 minutes. Strain off all excess fat, add brandy. Add red wine, stock and bouquet garni.

Transfer to casserole, cover; cook in moderate oven, Mark 4, 350°F., 40 minutes or until chicken is tender. (Or cook in saucepan on top of stove.) Mix extra butter with flour and add gradually to sauce to thicken it. Stir over heat a few minutes. Check seasoning. Serve with hot garlic bread (see page 137) and a tossed green salad.

Serves 6.

Chicken Tetrazzini

3 lb. chicken	2 oz. (¼ cup) butter
½ pint (1 cup) water or chicken stock	3 tablespoons flour
½ pint (1 cup) dry white wine	¾ lb. (2 cups) spaghetti
	½ lb. mushrooms
1 onion	2 oz. (¼ cup) butter, extra
1 bayleaf	¼ pint (½ cup) heavy cream
pinch thyme	
a few bacon rinds	1 tablespoon sherry
salt, pepper	

Gently poach chicken in combined wine and water, with chopped onion, bayleaf, thyme, bacon rinds, salt and pepper. When tender, cool, drain, strain the stock and reserve.

Remove the flesh from the chicken bones and cut into thin pieces. Melt the butter, stir in the flour, and cook over gentle heat 2 minutes. Gradually add ½ to ¾ pint (1 to 1¼ cups) of the reserved stock, stirring continually until mixture boils and thickens. Cook a few minutes, then set aside.

Cook spaghetti in plenty of boiling salted water until tender; drain thoroughly, place in deep, hot serving bowl. Finely slice the mushrooms, melt extra butter in frying pan and sauté the mushrooms gently until tender. Drain the mushrooms and add to the sauce with the sliced chicken and seasoning to taste. Reheat until nearly boiling.

Stir in the cream and sherry and stir over heat until heated thoroughly. Pour over spaghetti.

Serves 4 to 6.

Chicken Chow Mein

3 lb. chicken	½ cabbage
½ lb. lean pork	3 shallots
salt, pepper	2 to 3 sticks celery
1½ teaspoons soy sauce	1 green pepper
1 teaspoon brandy or dry sherry	1 clove garlic
1 dessertspoon cornflour	1 pint or 1 packet frozen prawns (shrimp)
4 tablespoons oil	2 tablespoons water

Remove meat from uncooked chicken. Cut chicken meat and pork into fine shreds, place in bowl, sprinkle with salt. Add soy sauce, brandy, ½ teaspoon of the cornflour, and 1 teaspoon of oil; mix well.

Prepare vegetables, cut into thin strips. Heat remaining oil in pan, add crushed garlic and chicken and pork mixture. Cook quickly 3 minutes, stirring constantly, sprinkle with pepper. Add prepared vegetables, fry until vegetables are tender, but still slightly crisp. Add shelled prawns. Mix remaining cornflour with water, add to pan,

bring to boil, stirring gently. Serve on top of crisp fried noodles.

Serves 4 to 6.

Crisp Fried Noodles

Drop ½ lb. (2 cups) fine dried egg noodles into large saucepan of rapidly boiling salted water; stir with fork to separate, cook 3 to 4 minutes; drain well. Arrange on a clean teatowel over wire cake cooler, spread noodles over this to drain. Leave at least 6 hours.

When ready to serve, drop noodles, a few at a time, into shallow hot oil. (To ensure thorough cooking, it is best to fry the noodles in 3 or 4 lots). They cook in seconds; turn once during cooking.

Chicken Paprika

lard or oil for frying	2 tomatoes
2 onions	¾ pint (1½ cups) stock
4 chicken joints	salt, pepper
1 tablespoon paprika	¼ pint (½ cup) sour cream

Heat lard or oil in large frying pan, add chopped onions, sauté until tender. Add chicken pieces to pan, cook until brown. Add paprika, then peeled, chopped tomatoes, stock, salt and pepper. Cover, simmer over gentle heat 1 hour or until chicken is tender.

Remove chicken from sauce, stir in sour cream, return chicken; stir over low heat until well blended and hot.

Serves 4.

Paella

4 small joints frying chicken	1 chicken stock cube
	pinch saffron
1 onion	2 scallops
1 clove garlic	8 large prawns (shrimps)
2 tablespoons oil	
2 pints (4 cups) water	6 to 8 mussels
2 tomatoes	8 oz. (2 cups) cooked peas
4 oz. (⅔ cup) rice	
	1 red pepper

Cut up the chicken, slice onion, crush garlic and fry in the oil until golden brown. Add half the water and simmer 15 minutes. Add peeled and sliced tomatoes, rice, stock cube and remaining water. Simmer for 5 minutes then add saffron. Mix in well then add all other ingredients. Continue cooking until rice is tender and most of the liquid has been absorbed.

Chicken in a Basket—a good dish for an informal luncheon or dinner. Serve the small, golden chickens with fried onion rings, potato chips.

Chicken Casserole

1 onion
4 chicken breasts
1 teaspoon salt
4 oz. ($\frac{1}{2}$ cup or 1 stick) butter
2 teaspoons paprika
3 tablespoons flour
$\frac{1}{4}$ pint ($\frac{1}{2}$ cup) water
1 chicken stock cube
$\frac{1}{4}$ pint ($\frac{1}{2}$ cup) sour cream
$\frac{1}{2}$ pint (1 cup) white wine
14 oz. can artichoke hearts

Chop onion finely, sprinkle chicken breasts with salt. Heat butter in frying pan, add chicken breasts, fry until golden brown; drain on absorbent paper. Add onion and paprika to remaining melted butter, sauté until onion is soft. Remove pan from heat, stir in flour, return to heat, cook 1 minute. Gradually add water in which stock cube has been dissolved; stir until mixture boils and thickens. Add cream and wine, stir well, heat gently; do not boil.

Place chicken and drained artichoke hearts in ovenproof dish, top with sauce. Cover, bake in moderate oven, Mark 4, 350°F., 1 hour. If desired, before serving, garnish with crisp fried bacon and toasted slivered almonds.

Serves 4.

Burmese Chicken Curry

$\frac{1}{2}$ coconut grated*
1 pint (2 cups) chicken stock
3 lb. chicken
2 medium onions
4 tablespoons oil
3 cloves garlic
1 teaspoon ground ginger
1 dessertspoon curry powder
$\frac{1}{4}$ pint ($\frac{1}{2}$ cup) boiling water
1 teaspoon salt
2 tablespoons cornflour (cornstarch)
3 tablespoons cold water
1 lb. broad noodles, cooked
1 red chilli
2 hard-boiled eggs
3 chives

* If fresh coconut is not available use 4 oz. ($\frac{2}{3}$ cup) desiccated coconut.

Combine coconut and chicken stock in saucepan; bring to the boil stirring constantly; remove from heat, let stand 15 minutes, stirring occasionally.

Strain mixture, pressing coconut well with wooden spoon, to extract as much flavour as possible. Reserve liquid, discard coconut.

Remove meat from chicken, cut into bite-sized pieces, chop onions.

Heat oil in large saucepan, add onions, crushed garlic, and ginger, sauté 10 minutes; add curry powder, sauté further 2 minutes. Add chicken, cover, simmer 15 minutes. Stir in $\frac{1}{2}$ pint of the coconut liquid, boiling water and salt; simmer, uncovered, 30 minutes.

Blend cornflour (cornstarch) with cold water,

add to chicken mixture, stir until mixture boils and thickens, add further $\frac{1}{2}$ pint coconut liquid, bring back to boil, remove from heat. Arrange hot noodles on serving plate, sprinkle with finely chopped chilli, chopped eggs and sliced chives, top with chicken mixture.

Serves 4 to 5.

Chicken à la King

3 to 4 lb. chicken
1 small green pepper
1 oz. (2 tablespoons) butter
$\frac{1}{4}$ lb. sliced mushrooms
1 dessertspoon grated onion
1 tablespoon flour
salt
$\frac{1}{2}$ pint (1 cup) milk or light cream
$\frac{1}{2}$ pint (1 cup) chicken stock
3 egg-yolks
1 dessertspoon lemon juice
$\frac{1}{2}$ teaspoon paprika
$\frac{1}{2}$ teaspoon celery salt
2 tablespoons dry sherry

Steam chicken until tender; remove meat from bones and cut into large dice or pieces.

Remove pith and seeds from green pepper; blanch in boiling water 5 minutes. Drain and chop finely.

Heat butter in saucepan, add green pepper, mushrooms and grated onion; sauté a few minutes. Sprinkle in flour and salt, cook, stirring, 2 minutes. Gradually blend in milk or cream and stock; add chicken. Stir over gentle heat until sauce thickens, simmer 3 minutes.

Stir a little of sauce into beaten egg-yolks, return to saucepan. Add lemon juice, paprika and celery salt. Reheat very gently, stirring, but do not allow to boil. Just before serving, stir in sherry.

Serves 4 to 6.

Chicken Maryland

1 egg
1 tablespoon milk
3 lb. chicken
2 oz. ($\frac{1}{2}$ cup) seasoned flour
dry breadcrumbs
2 oz. ($\frac{1}{4}$ cup) butter
4 tablespoons oil

Beat egg and milk together. Cut chicken into joints, roll in seasoned flour, dip in the beaten egg, then coat with crumbs. Heat butter and oil in heatproof casserole, add chicken pieces, sauté until golden on all sides. Drain off excess oil, cover casserole, cook in moderate oven, Mark 4, 350°F., until tender (about 30 to 45 minutes).

Serve with fried bananas, corn fritters, bacon rolls and grilled tomato halves.

Serves 4.

Corn Fritters Sift 4 oz. (1 cup) plain flour with 1 teaspoon baking powder and $\frac{3}{4}$ teaspoon salt. Beat the yolk of 1 egg and 4 tablespoons of milk; mix with 1 11 oz. can whole kernel corn, add to dry ingredients; mix thoroughly. Beat egg-whites until stiff, fold in. Deep-fry dessertspoons of mixture in hot oil until golden. Drain well.

Fried Bananas Peel bananas, cut in halves cross-wise, dip in beaten egg, then breadcrumbs. Fry in butter until golden. Drain well.

Chicken Fricassée

3 lb. chicken	3 shallots
salt, pepper	1 oz. (2 tablespoons)
2 oz. (¼ cup) butter	butter, extra
1 clove garlic	4 oz. mushrooms
1½ gills (⅔ cup) dry	2 tablespoons flour
white wine	¼ pint (½ cup) milk
¾ pint (1½ cups) chicken	2 tablespoons light
stock	cream

Cut chicken into serving pieces, season with salt and pepper. Melt butter in large pan, add chicken joints, and cook until a light brown on all sides. Add crushed garlic, wine, chicken stock, chopped shallots, salt and pepper, cover and cook gently until chicken is tender.

Melt extra butter in separate pan and sauté sliced mushrooms for 5 minutes, drain.

When chicken is tender, remove joints from pan, blend flour with the milk, add gradually to pan, stir over gentle heat until sauce thickens. Return chicken pieces to pan, add mushrooms, reheat and adjust seasoning, if necessary. Just before serving, add cream, keep hot but do not boil.

Serves 4 to 5.

Chicken Croquettes

½ pint (1 cup) milk	2 egg-yolks
few peppercorns	½ lb. mushrooms
1 onion, sliced	salt, pepper
1 carrot, sliced	1 egg
1½ oz. (3 tablespoons)	dry breadcrumbs
butter	oil for frying
2 oz. (½ cup) plain flour	
1 lb. chopped cooked	
chicken	

Combine milk, peppercorns, onion and carrot in saucepan. Bring to boil, simmer 5 minutes; strain.

Melt butter in separate saucepan. Stir in flour, cook 1 minute. Remove from heat. Gradually stir in hot milk, blend well. Return to heat. Bring to boil, then reduce heat and simmer until thickened, stirring constantly. Remove from heat.

Add finely chopped chicken, egg-yolks, and finely chopped mushrooms which have been sautéed in a little butter. Season to taste with salt and pepper. Blend well together.

Spread mixture on greased tray, cover with greased paper. Refrigerate until cold and set. Divide mixture into 16 pieces and mould each into croquette shape approximately 2½ in. long. Dip in lightly beaten egg, then in breadcrumbs. Refrigerate 1 hour. Fry in hot oil until brown.

Makes 16 croquettes.

Chicken Chasseur

3 lb. chicken	1 oz. (2 tablespoons)
3 shallots	butter
1 lb. mushrooms	¼ pint (½ cup) dry white
2 large tomatoes	wine
flour	½ pint (1 cup) chicken
salt, pepper	stock

Joint the chicken, chop the shallots, slice the mushrooms, peel and chop the tomatoes. Dredge the chicken pieces in flour seasoned with salt and pepper. Heat butter in frying pan, sauté chicken pieces gently, browning lightly on all sides.

Remove chicken pieces from pan. Add shallots and mushrooms, cook a few minutes, then add tomatoes, wine and stock. Return chicken to the pan, bring to boil, then reduce heat, cover pan, and simmer until chicken is tender. Taste and adjust seasoning.

Serves 4 to 5.

Chicken Marengo

3 lb. chicken	salt, pepper
2 tablespoons oil	pinch mixed herbs
2 cloves garlic	½ lb. sliced mushrooms
2 tablespoons flour	1 small onion
½ pint (1 cup) dry white	3 tomatoes
wine	
½ pint (1 cup) chicken	
stock	

Cut chicken into serving pieces. Heat oil in pan, add crushed garlic and chicken pieces, brown chicken on all sides; remove from pan.

Stir flour into oil, cook a few minutes, then add wine and stock gradually, stirring, until mixture boils and thickens. Season with pepper, salt and mixed herbs, add sliced mushrooms, chopped onion and peeled, chopped tomatoes. Cook about 5 minutes, then return chicken to the pan, cover and simmer 45 minutes or until chicken is tender.

Serves 4 to 5.

Chicken Cacciatore

3 lb. chicken	1 lb. tomatoes
2 tablespoons oil	salt, pepper
2 cloves garlic	½ teaspoon oregano
2 large onions	¼ pint (½ cup) red wine
½ lb. mushrooms	

Cut the chicken into serving pieces. Heat the oil in a pan and add the crushed garlic, sliced onions, and mushrooms; brown lightly. Remove and reserve.

Add the chicken pieces and brown on all sides. Return the onions and mushrooms to the pan. Peel and chop the tomatoes and add with the salt, pepper and oregano. Pour in the red wine, bring to boil; reduce heat, cover and simmer for ½ hour. Uncover and simmer for 15 to 20 minutes longer or until sauce is reduced and chicken very tender. Sprinkle with chopped parsley, if desired.

Serve with noodles or hot fluffy rice.

Serves 4 to 5.

Assamee Chicken Curry

3 lb. chicken	¾ teaspoon ground ginger
2 oz. (¼ cup) butter	
salt	2 1 in. pieces cinnamon
1 teaspoon ground black pepper	3 to 4 cloves crushed garlic
2 to 3 bayleaves	1 in. piece green ginger
1 tablespoon turmeric	2 onions
pinch chilli powder	½ pint (1 cup) chicken stock
½ teaspoon cloves	
¾ teaspoon cardamom	2 tablespoons cornflour (cornstarch)
½ teaspoon cumin	
½ teaspoon coriander	water

Joint chicken. Heat butter in saucepan, add all ingredients except chicken, chopped onions, cornflour (cornstarch) and stock; fry 5 minutes. Add chicken joints, brown well on all sides. Add chopped onions and cook gently, stirring occasionally, 25 to 30 minutes. Gradually add stock, simmer 1 hour, or until chicken is tender.

Blend cornflour (cornstarch) with a little water, add to pan, simmer further 3 minutes. Allow to cool, refrigerate overnight. Remove any excess fat, reheat gently.

Serves 4 to 5.

Chicken Liver Risotto

4 oz. (½ cup or 1 stick) butter	½ lb. (1⅓ cups) long grain rice
2 onions	1½ pints chicken stock
3 sticks celery	2 oz. (½ cup) grated Parmesan cheese
1 lb. chicken livers	salt, pepper

Heat half the butter in large saucepan. Add finely chopped onions and sliced celery, sauté 10 minutes, stirring occasionally.

Cut cleaned chicken livers into quarters. Add to pan, cook further 5 minutes. Stir in well-rinsed rice and remaining butter, and cook further 5 minutes. Add stock, bring to the boil; reduce heat and simmer, covered, until rice is tender and liquid absorbed (about 20 to 25 minutes). Stir in cheese, adjust seasoning.

Serves 4.

Chicken Chop Suey

3 lb. chicken	oil
½ small firm cabbage	salt
3 to 4 sticks celery	chicken stock
¼ lb. carrots	16 oz. can bean sprouts
¼ lb. green beans	1 dessertspoon cornflour (cornstarch)
1 onion	

Steam chicken until tender, cool; remove meat from bones, cut into large dice.

Shred cabbage, slice celery, carrots, beans diagonally, chop onion. Heat oil in large pan, add vegetables, sauté until just tender but still crisp, season with salt. Add chicken pieces and chicken stock to cover, add drained bean sprouts. Reheat gently, then thicken with cornflour (cornstarch) which has been blended with a little water; stir until thickened.

Serves 4 to 5.

Honeyed Chicken

3 oz. (⅜ cup) butter	3 lb. chicken

Sauce

4 spring onions (scallions)	1 tablespoon honey
	1 tablespoon soy sauce
1 teaspoon finely chopped green ginger	½ teaspoon salt
	¼ pint (½ cup) sherry

Melt butter in baking dish, add chicken, brush well with butter, bake in moderately hot oven, Mark 4, 350°F., 45 minutes; baste frequently with the butter. Pour sauce over chicken, continue cooking for further 30 minutes, or until tender and golden brown. Baste chicken frequently with sauce during last 30 minutes.

Sauce Chop spring onions (scallions) finely, combine with remaining ingredients.

Serves 4 to 5.

Chicken Casserole combines tender chickens with artichoke hearts, wine, paprika; a perfect dish for a small dinner party.

DO NOT LOCK OR CLAMP THIS HANDLE BUT TURN THE LID

Roast Duck

1 duckling, 4 to 5 lb.
prepared stuffing
melted butter

1 tablespoon flour
½ pint (1 cup) chicken
    stock
salt, pepper

Fill duck with prepared stuffing (see page 89); place in baking dish, brush well with melted butter. Roast in hot oven, Mark 7, 425°F., 15 minutes, then reduce heat to moderate, Mark 5, 375°F., and cook until tender. During cooking, baste and turn bird occasionally. Allow 15 to 20 minutes per lb. Remove duck to a warm serving dish, keep hot.

Pour excess fat from baking dish, sprinkle in flour, stir over gentle heat until brown. Stir in stock, simmer, stirring, 3 or 4 minutes. Strain.

Serves 4.

NOTE: If desired, towards end of cooking time duck can be brushed with a little honey; this helps to crisp the skin. Don't use too much or skin will become too brown. For a Chinese flavour, a little crushed green ginger can be mixed into the honey.

Orange Roast Duckling

3 oranges
2 small ducklings
1 stick celery
1 carrot
1 small onion
2 oz. (¼ cup) butter
1 tablespoon sugar
1 dessertspoon vinegar
1 pint (2 cups) chicken
    stock

1 dessertspoon lemon
    juice
3 teaspoons arrowroot
¼ pint (½ cup) sweet
    sherry
salt, pepper
2 to 3 tablespoons
    Grand Marnier or
    other orange liqueur

Remove rind from 2 oranges, cut into thin strips; squeeze juice from the 3 oranges. Set aside for sauce.

Cut ducklings in half lengthwise. Place chopped celery, carrot and onion into baking dish, add butter; place ducklings on top. Roast in hot oven, Mark 7, 425°F., 15 minutes reduce heat to moderate, Mark 4, 350°F., continue cooking until ducklings are tender, allowing approximately 20 minutes per lb.; baste occasionally with pan juices. Remove from pan, keep warm.

Orange Sauce   Skim off fat from pan, strain pan juices. Add sugar and vinegar to pan, cook over gentle heat until sugar caramelises slightly. Add strained pan juices, stock, orange juice and rind and lemon juice. Cook rapidly until sauce is reduced in quantity by half. Blend arrowroot and sherry, stir gradually into sauce; cook, stirring, 6 to 8 minutes over gentle heat; season to taste.

just before serving, stir in orange liqueur.

Spoon the hot Orange Sauce over each serving of duckling, or pass sauce separately.

Serves 4.

Chinese Braised Duck

1 plump young duck
    (3½ to 4 lb.)
6 dried mushrooms
1 dessertspoon soy
    sauce
1 tablespoon dry sherry
1 teaspoon very finely
    chopped green
    ginger
water
1½ dessertspoons corn-
    flour (cornstarch)
½ teaspoon sugar

pepper
1 teaspoon soy sauce,
    extra
1 tablespoon oil
½ teaspoon salt
2 cloves garlic
1 small can bamboo
    shoots
1 small can water
    chestnuts
1 pint (2 cups) stock or
    water

Wash duck, cut into joints. Wash mushrooms, soak in hot water 20 minutes. Rinse, squeeze dry, cut in halves.

Combine dessertspoon of soy sauce, the sherry and ginger; add 1 dessertspoon water. Mix together the cornflour (cornstarch), sugar, pepper and extra soy sauce; stir in ¼ pint (½ cup) water.

Heat oil with salt and crushed garlic, add duck pieces, and fry, stirring until well browned. Add mushrooms, sliced bamboo shoots, and sliced water chestnuts; cook further 2 minutes. Stir in soy sauce mixture; cook 2 minutes, stirring. Add stock, cover, bring to boil. Reduce heat, simmer until duck is tender. Stir in cornflour (cornstarch) mixture and cook, stirring, until sauce thickens. Transfer duck to serving dish, spoon sauce over.

Serve with hot, fluffy rice.

Serves 4.

To Choose a Turkey

Turkeys should be plump with white flesh. Short spurs and smooth black legs are indications that the bird is young. Much has been done over the past years to breed small plump breasted birds. They are frequently marketed frozen and sold by dressed weight i.e. drawn with feet and legs removed and ready for the oven. They should be left in the polythene bag and allowed to thaw out slowly at room temperature which may take about 2 days.

A turkey can weigh as much as 20 lb. but for family use a medium sized bird 10 to 12 lb. is usually most popular. For roasting, the turkey is stuffed to keep it moist and add flavour. It can be roasted in the same way as chicken—see page 80—or slow roasted. The French method ensures that the flesh remains succulent and tender. See page 81.

Roast Turkey

Stuff the turkey and truss it making it as plump and even in shape as possible. Then weigh the bird and calculate the time for cooking. Allow 15 minutes per lb. and 15 minutes over for a bird up to 12 lb. Over 12 lb. allow 10 minutes per lb. and 10 minutes over.

Heat some dripping or bacon fat in the roasting tin—enough to cover the tin to a depth of 1 in. Put in the turkey, baste with the hot fat then cover with greaseproof paper and cook in a hot oven, Mark 6, 425°F., for 45 minutes then reduce the heat to moderate, Mark 4, 350°F., for the required time, basting frequently during cooking. If the turkey is cooked in foil it is not necessary to baste.

Slow roasting

Rub the turkey all over with butter or bacon fat and wrap in foil. Cook at Mark 3, 325°F., allowing 20 minutes per lb. and 30 minutes over for a bird up to 14 lb.

Unwrap about 30 minutes before the end of the cooking to allow the turkey to brown.

Accompaniments for Roast Turkey

Bread sauce or cranberry sauce, bacon rolls, chipolata sausages and watercress to garnish.

Roast Goose

1 goose (9 to 10 lb.)	flour
prepared stuffing	melted butter
1 cooking apple	

Stuff goose with prepared stuffing. Place in baking dish with quartered apple, brush with little melted butter. Put little extra melted butter in base of baking dish. Roast in hot oven, Mark 7, 425°F., 15 to 20 minutes, reduce to moderate, Mark 4, 350°F., and allow 20 to 25 minutes per lb. If bird appears to be browning too rapidly, cover with piece of well-greased paper.

When almost cooked, prick skin of bird lightly with fine-pronged fork or skewer; this will allow excess fat to run off. Do not prick flesh of bird, or juices will run out. Dredge breast lightly with flour, baste with hot fat, and continue cooking until tender.

Transfer cooked goose to serving dish, serve with well-seasoned gravy made from pan drippings.

Stuffings for Poultry

Chestnut Stuffing (for Turkey)

15 oz. can unsweetened chestnut purée	1 tablespoon chopped parsley
½ lb. (3 cups) fresh breadcrumbs	1½ oz. (3 tablespoons) melted butter
1 finely chopped onion	salt, pepper
	beaten egg to bind

Sieve chestnut purée into bowl. Blend with remaining ingredients.

Sage and Onion Stuffing (for Duck and Goose)

2 onions chopped	1 oz. (2 tablespoons) melted butter
¼ lb. (1½ cups) fresh breadcrumbs	salt, pepper
1½ teaspoons dried sage	pinch nutmeg
	½ teaspoon sugar

Place onions in saucepan. Add cold water to cover, and salt. Bring to boil; reduce heat and simmer until almost tender. Combine drained onion with remaining ingredients. Add sufficient onion water to bind, about 1 tablespoon.

Simple Herb Stuffing (for Chicken)

¼ lb. (1½ cups) fresh breadcrumbs	1 teaspoon grated lemon rind
1 oz. (2 tablespoons) softened butter	1 teaspoon mixed dried herbs
2 tablespoons chopped parsley	1 small onion chopped
	salt, pepper
	beaten egg to bind

Mix together all ingredients, except egg. Add sufficient beaten egg to bind.

Forcemeat (for Turkey)

1 small onion	pinch grated lemon rind
2 oz. ham or bacon	
1 oz. (2 tablespoons) butter	1 dessertspoon chopped parsley
½ lb. lean minced (ground) veal or sausage meat	½ teaspoon mixed herbs
	pinch nutmeg
	salt, pepper
6 oz. (1¾ cups) fresh breadcrumbs	1 egg
	milk

Chop onion and bacon finely, sauté in heated butter until onion is transparent. Add minced meat, breadcrumbs and seasonings; bind with beaten egg; add a little milk if mixture seems too dry.

Fondues

Cheese fondue is a different and delightful dish for entertaining. And the other fondues—tomato (a variation of the cheese fondue) beef, fish, and even a dessert fondue—are equally popular.

For cheese fondue, a thick earthenware pot called a 'caquelon' is used; this gives the gentle heat necessary for cheese cookery. If cooked too quickly, or overheated, cheese would become stringy. For Beef Fondue (or Fondue Bourguignonne, as it is sometimes called) a cast-iron (as shown in the picture), copper, or enamel fondue pot is used. Any small heatproof bowl or casserole can be used for the dessert fondue. For all fondues, a spirit lamp with an adjustable flame is necessary. Special fondue forks, with long handles and prongs, are available.

Cheese Fondue

crusty French bread
1 clove garlic
¾ pint (1½ cups) white burgundy
¾ lb. Gruyère cheese
¾ lb. Cheddar cheese
3 tablespoons kirsch
2 tablespoons cornflour (cornstarch)

Cut bread into cubes; each cube should have some crust on it. Push the fondue fork through the crust; this will hold the bread firmly on the fork and help prevent it dropping into the fondue.

To prepare the fondue Rub round inside of fondue dish with cut garlic clove. Add wine, heat to boiling point. Add the grated cheeses gradually, stirring continually, until cheese melts and mixes with wine. Add the kirsch, blended with cornflour (cornstarch). Continue to cook until mixture thickens (about 3 to 4 minutes) stirring all the time in the form of a figure eight.

Some like to add a light sprinkling of nutmeg or paprika, or both, to the fondue; add these with the cheese.

One after another, the guests take up a piece of bread on the prong of the fork and dip it in the thick, creamy fondue.

There's no need for hurry with fondue, but it must be stirred so it remains evenly thick. The swirling of the bread in the fondue is generally sufficient for this.

Slowly, the 'Grillon', or rich brown crust, forms at the bottom of the fondue dish. Some consider this the best part of fondue; everybody should share in this delicacy.

A crisp green salad is a good accompaniment to cheese fondue. And don't forget to have the pepper mill on the table.

If serving wine, it should be the same as used in the fondue.

NOTE: If kirsch is not available, brandy or gin can be substituted. The fondue will not have the traditional taste, but it will be very good.

There's a traditional forfeit paid by those who drop their bread in the fondue—a kiss, if it's a lady; a bottle of wine, if it's a man.

Tomato Fondue

1 clove garlic
¾ pint (1½ cups) white burgundy
1½ lb. Cheddar cheese
¼ pint (½ cup) tomato purée
2 tablespoons cornflour (cornstarch)
salt, pepper
paprika

Rub round inside of fondue dish with cut garlic clove. Add wine, heat to boiling point. Add grated cheese gradually, stirring constantly until cheese melts and mixes with wine. Add tomato purée blended with cornflour (cornstarch). Continue cooking until mixture thickens, approximately 3 to 4 minutes, stirring constantly. Season to taste with salt, pepper and paprika.

Beef Fondue (or Fondue Bourguignonne), wonderful for a party, is served with a variety of sauces and accompaniments. In smaller pictures, popular Cheese Fondue and Chocolate Dessert Fondue.

Beef Fondue

Allow about ¾ lb. steak per person. Any tender steak can be used. Remove all fat, cut steak into 1 in. cubes. Add equal quantities of oil and butter to fondue pot. The melted butter, combined with the oil, should fill fondue pot about three-quarters full. A clove of garlic can be added to the oil for flavour.

To save time, the oil and butter mixture can be heated on the stove and transferred to the fondue pot, then placed over spirit lamp.

Each guest spears a morsel of beef on a fondue fork and cooks it in the hot oil and butter, then slides it on to the plate with another fork. (The fork which has been in the fondue pot would be too hot to use for eating.) Another piece of beef can be cooking while the first is being eaten.

Have a selection of sauces and condiments. Offer at least two of the following: Bearnaise sauce, chilli sauce, mustard, bottled horseradish sauce, caper sauce, any savoury steak butter. Accompaniments can be simple—a good green salad, asparagus spears, onion rings, a baked potato or heated potato crisps, etc. Serve with hot crusty bread and a good red wine or beer.

Steaks to use   Any tender steak can be used; rump will have best flavour, but there will be less wastage with fillet because of its lack of fat.

Round steak can be used, but will need to be marinated first to make it tender.

Marinade   Combine 4 tablespoons salad oil, ¼ pint (½ cup) red wine, 1 dessertspoon chopped onion. Let meat pieces marinate in this several hours, turning occasionally. Drain well, pat dry.

Here are two variations of the classic beef fondue.

Add other meats—kidney, veal, chicken—to the beef. Put first on the fork or skewer the meat that needs least cooking; put on last the meat that needs the most cooking. If using foregoing combination, you would put the square of kidney on first, then veal, then chicken and finally the cube of beef, which will be immersed in the hot oil.

Use boiling beef bouillon in place of oil in fondue dish. Cut the steak into wafer-thin strips, wrap round the prongs of fondue forks. The steak cooks very quickly in the hot bouillon. And, when the meal is finished, don't discard the bouillon; enriched by the steak cooked in it, it makes an excellent soup for the following day.

Fish Fondue

A fish fondue can be prepared in two ways: with an oil and butter mixture (as for Beef Fondue), for shellfish, or with fish stock to cook fish fillets.

For Shellfish   Prepare oil and butter mixture as for Beef Fondue. Prawn (Shrimp) Fondue makes an excellent supper dish, but prawns (shrimps) must be uncooked; cooked prawns fried in this way would be very hard and tough.

For Chinese style Prawns (Shrimps)   Shell prawns (shrimps), cut deep slit down back of each, taking care not to cut through completely. Coat prawns (shrimps) in cornflour, shaking off excess. Dip in eggs which have been beaten lightly with soy sauce (you will need 2 eggs and 1 teaspoon soy sauce for 2 lb. or 2 pints prawns (shrimps)). Coat prawns well in breadcrumbs, pressing down with palm of hand to flatten.

Prawns (shrimps) can be prepared in this way several hours in advance, and refrigerated until guests arrive. Guests spear a prawn (shrimp) on fondue fork, lower in to the hot oil and butter for few minutes; prawns (shrimps) cook quickly. Serve with Hoi Sin Sauce (obtainable from Chinese food stores) or with Chinese Plum Sauce (see page 149) for dipping.

For Fish Fillets   Make a good fish broth. Place fish trimming and bones into saucepan (fish with firm flesh, halibut, turbot, etc. is best), add 1 chopped onion, 1 or 2 chopped sticks celery, 1 chopped carrot, a bayleaf and few parsley sprigs. Add water to cover; about 2 pints (4 cups) water should be sufficient. Bring to boil, skim well, reduce heat, simmer 20 minutes; strain. Add salt and pepper to taste.

Pour this liquid into fondue pot, add ½ pint (1 cup) dry white wine and, if desired, three slices fresh green ginger and 1 or 2 teaspoons soy sauce. Bring to boil.

Have fish cut into 1 or 1½ in. squares. Spear fish on fondue fork, dip into broth; it will cook very quickly. Serve with small dishes of soy sauce and chopped cucumber.

Fish fillets can also be cooked in the butter and oil mixture. Cut fillets into 1½ in. pieces, put piece on fondue fork, and dip into hot oil; it cooks quickly. Serve with mustard or tartare sauce (see page 148, 149).

Chocolate Dessert Fondue

2 large cans evaporated milk	8 oz. (8 squares) plain chocolate
1½ oz. (scant ¼ cup) sugar	2 teaspoons instant coffee powder
	1 dessertspoon rum

Place milk, sugar, grated chocolate and coffee powder in fondue dish. Heat to boiling point, stirring, then lower heat and simmer gently 5 minutes, stirring constantly. Stir in rum. A small fondue dish is used for this rich dessert sauce. Pineapple, pears, bananas—in fair-sized pieces—go well with the chocolate flavour. Or any other fresh or canned fruits can be used.

Rice is one of the most versatile of all grains; it can be used for sweet and savoury dishes with equal success.

In this section we give the various methods of cooking rice; all work well, it's just a matter of choosing the method which suits you best.

Hints for Cooking Rice

Add a good squeeze of lemon juice to the rice when cooking; this will whiten and flavour the grains. Some cooks also like to throw in the $\frac{1}{2}$ or $\frac{1}{4}$ of lemon from which the juice was squeezed. For additional flavour, 1 or 2 small stock cubes can be crumbled into the water.

Boiled or steamed rice can have many flavourful additions lightly forked through, such as finely chopped chives, parsley, or mint; grated carrot with finely chopped shallots; raisins, toasted halved or slivered almonds; diced, cooked vegetables; chopped hard boiled eggs. The choice is as wide as the imaginative cook cares to make it.

Rice almost triples in bulk during cooking. Allow approximately 2 oz. ($\frac{2}{3}$ cup) cooked rice for each main dish serving. In other words, 1 lb. of rice, when cooked will give 8 to 10 servings.

Fluffy and Boiled Rice

Put $3\frac{1}{2}$ pints (7 cups) water into large saucepan, bring water to rapid boil, add 1 dessertspoon salt. Then, gradually letting it dribble through your fingers so the water does not go off the boil, add 8 oz. ($1\frac{1}{3}$ cups) rice. Boil rapidly, uncovered, 12 to 15 minutes. Cooking time depends on the type of rice used and also on the way you like your rice—tender, or still with a slight firmness left in the grain. Start testing at the end of 12 minutes. Lift a few grains from the pan with a fork and bite into the grain. When cooked to your liking, drain at once in a colander.

Steamed 'Pearly' Rice

Put rice into saucepan, add water to come 1 in. above level of rice. Add salt to taste. Bring water rapidly to boil, then cover tightly, reduce heat to the lowest simmer and cook further 20 minutes. For a firmer grain, many cooks prefer to simmer the rice 15 minutes only; then remove from heat, let stand—still tightly covered—for 5 to 10 minutes.

Oven-Steamed Rice

Place $\frac{1}{2}$ lb. ($1\frac{1}{3}$ cups) rice into casserole dish, sprinkle lightly with salt. Pour over $1\frac{3}{4}$ pints ($3\frac{1}{2}$ cups) boiling water, cover tightly. Cook in moderately hot oven, Mark 4, 350°F., 20 to 25 minutes.

Reheating Rice

Rice which you have cooked in advance and stored in the refrigerator can be reheated in any of the following ways:

To reheat with steam   Place cooked rice in colander, stand over saucepan of simmering water. Cover colander with lid, steam until rice is heated through. Another method of steaming cooked rice is to pour just enough water into saucepan to cover the base of pan. When boiling, add rice, cover, steam 5 minutes or until water is absorbed and rice is hot. The size of saucepan will depend on the amount of rice to be reheated; use a large saucepan for a large amount of rice so the steam can penetrate the grains.

To reheat in oven   Spread rice in greased, shallow ovenproof dish, sprinkle with little water or milk, dot with butter. Cover dish with lid or aluminium foil. Place in moderate oven, Mark 4, 350°F., until heated through.

To reheat in frypan   Melt a little butter in frypan, add rice; stir with fork until heated through.

Pilaf

1 tablespoon butter or oil	1 tablespoon melted butter, extra
1 small onion	3 oz. ($\frac{1}{2}$ cup) raisins
12 oz. (2 cups) long grain rice	2 oz. ($\frac{1}{4}$ cup) blanched slivered toasted almonds
2 pints (4 cups) chicken stock	

Heat butter or oil in pan that can be covered tightly. Add finely chopped onion, cook gently until it is soft but not brown. Add rice, stir well over gentle heat a few minutes; add boiling chicken stock.

Cover tightly, cook in moderately hot oven, Mark 4, 350°F., 25 to 30 minutes, or until liquid is absorbed and rice is tender. Turn rice on to heated serving dish, separate grains with fork, stir in melted butter, raisins and almonds.

Serves 6 to 8.

Nasi Goreng

½ lb. (1⅓ cups) long
  grain rice
boiling salted water
½ lb. or ½ pint prawns
  (shrimps)
3 oz. (⅜ cup) butter
1 lb. fillet steak or pork
3 cabbage leaves
2 red peppers
thin omelets (see
  below)

2 medium onions
4 spring onions
  (scallions) or chives
cucumber
2 cloves garlic, crushed
salt, pepper
2 tablespoons soy sauce
1 small can bean
  sprouts

Add rice gradually to large quantity of boiling salted water, boil rapidly for approximately 15 minutes, or until tender; drain, keep hot. Shell prawns (shrimps), sauté in 1 oz. (2 tablespoons) of the butter, set aside.

Thinly slice steak or pork, cabbage, red peppers and omelets. Chop onions, cut spring onions (scallions) into 1 in. pieces. Peel and thinly slice cucumber.

Heat remaining butter in a large pan, add onion and garlic, sauté 1 minute or until onion is transparent. Add steak or pork, sauté until tender, season with salt and pepper. Add cabbage, peppers, spring onions or chives and hot rice, toss with a fork to mix well; add half the omelet strips, sautéed prawns, soy sauce and bean sprouts. Heat thoroughly, stirring continually.

Add a little more butter if mixture appears too dry; season to taste. Serve on hot platter, garnish with remaining omelet strips and sliced cucumber.
Serves 4 to 6.

Thin Omelets

5 eggs
3 tablespoons milk

salt, pepper
butter

Beat eggs lightly with milk, season to taste with salt and pepper. Grease pan with butter, when hot, pour in enough of the egg mixture to make 1 very thin omelet. When cooked, roll, slice into thin strips. Repeat with remaining egg mixture.

Risotto

1 oz. (2 tablespoons)
  butter
1 onion
12 oz. (2 cups) long
  grain rice
2½ pints (5 cups)
  chicken stock

1 dessertspoon melted
  butter, extra
1 tablespoon grated
  Parmesan cheese

Melt butter in large saucepan, sauté finely chopped onion until it starts to turn golden. Add rice, mix well. Gradually add boiling stock, about ½ pint (1 cup) at a time; wait until liquid has been absorbed before adding next quantity. Stir at each addition.

Cover pan and cook for remainder of cooking time. The rice should cook about 20 minutes from time first ½ pint (1 cup) of stock is added. The rice should be very tender, liquid all absorbed and mixture creamy at the end of this time.

Add melted butter and Parmesan cheese, mix in carefully with fork. Serve immediately, topped, if desired, with extra Parmesan cheese.

Chinese Fried Rice

Among English speaking people, this is one of the most popular of Chinese dishes. Boil or steam rice the day before you want to fry it; it then has time to dry out completely so that it will fry with every grain separate.

Rice is fried in a small quantity of hot oil, and a variety of good tasting, colourful ingredients are added.

1 tablespoon oil
¼ lb. cooked pork
½ lb. (1⅓ cups) long
  grain rice, cooked
salt
¼ to ½ pint prawns
  (shrimps)

1 egg
1 teaspoon soy sauce
1 teaspoon water
2 spring onions
  (scallions) or chives
2 oz. ham

Heat oil in frying pan, add chopped pork. Fry 1 or 2 minutes, then add rice and salt. Cook 10 minutes, stirring to prevent rice sticking. Add shelled prawns (shrimps), mix well, then clear small space in rice and drop in egg, breaking yolk. When nearly cooked, stir and mix through rice.

Add soy sauce mixed with the water, and finely chopped spring onions (scallions) or chives. Mix well, sprinkle with finely chopped ham.

Fried Rice, traditional accompaniment to many Chinese dishes, is also a colourful, good-tasting dish for a buffet party.

Pastas

Finding your way among the different macaroni foods—or pastas, as they are called—can be a little puzzling at first because of the varying names. But it is a treasure hunt that will reward you with good food for all the family.

Many nations have claimed to have invented macaroni (the generic term which is applied to all shapes and flavours of pasta), but it is in Italy that pasta-making was perfected. As a result, most of the macaronis bear Italian names. When these names are translated, they describe the shape or type of pasta.

Spaghetti, the long, tube-like strands, means 'little string', lasagne means 'broad-leafed', farfalle is 'butterfly', and so on.

Macaroni products can be divided into four basic groups—cords, tubes, ribbons and special shapes such as shells, crests, etc. There is a wide range of sizes and shapes within each of these groups.

Different shapes have evolved for different dishes. Generally, very small shapes—such as alphabet or animal noodles (these are really just for fun, and children love them!) or tubettini—are cooked in clear broths. Cut macaroni or shells are used in heartier soups or in salads. Wide ribbon shapes are for casserole use layered with sauces.

Spaghetti is available in two forms; thin spaghetti and thicker, or 'tubular' spaghetti. Cooking time is approximately the same for both.

Some of the macaronis—spaghetti, shells, elbows, noodles, crests, gnocchi, spirali, alphabets, animals, etc.—are sold in packages and are easily available. For the more unusual types you might need to shop at an Italian or Continental food store.

Green noodles—coloured with spinach juice—can also be purchased.

Oriental noodles, from China or Japan, are much finer than Italian pasta, and they are in plainer form—cords or ribbons of varying degrees of fineness. They are used in three ways: in soup, cooked noodles, drained and mixed with seasonings, or they can be fried.

How to Cook Pasta

Cook all forms of pasta in plenty of boiling water; a gallon of water to 1 lb. of pasta is not too much. Use large saucepan and bring water to a fast, rolling boil; add sprinkling of salt.

Add pasta gradually so water does not go off the boil.

When cooking spaghetti, vermicelli, or any of the 'long goods', as they are called, hold long strands at one end and place other ends into the boiling water. The pasta will begin to soften in the hot water and it is then simple to lower strands into saucepan, coiling them neatly inside pan.

Approximate Cooking Time

Spaghetti, 12 to 20 minutes; vermicelli (resembles very fine spaghetti), 6 to 10 minutes; macaroni, 12 to 20 minutes; noodles, 10 to 20 minutes, depending on width.

Cooking time of pasta varies according to individual manufacturers; freshness of the product, too, will affect cooking time. Pasta should not be overcooked; it should be tender but firm.

Start testing at the minimum cooking time given above and, when the pasta is cooked just to your liking, add a cup of cold water to the pan to stop the cooking instantly. Pour pasta into colander, drain well. If you wish, mix a knob of butter or a little oil through the pasta to prevent it sticking together.

Provided sufficient water has been used in cooking, there will be no starch adhering to the pasta, so do not rinse it under cold water; this will only cause the tender pasta to become hardened.

Spaghetti and macaroni almost double in volume during cooking; noodles remain the same in volume.

1. *Gemelli*	6. *Spirali*	11. *Large Shells*	16. *Tubettini*
2. *Spinach Noodles*	7. *Farfalle*	12. *Small Shells*	17. *Elbows*
3. *Fine Noodles*	8. *Gnocchi*	13. *Alphabets*	18. *Macaroni*
4. *Medium Noodles*	9. *Animals*	14. *Spaghetti*	19. *Lasagne*
5. *Wide Noodles*	10. *Rigatoni*	15. *Crests*	

1
2
3
4
5
6
7
8
9
10
11
12
13
14
15
16
17
18
19

Meatballs in Tomato Sauce

1 medium onion
1 lb. minced beef
1 egg
1 oz. ($\frac{1}{4}$ cup) dry
  breadcrumbs
1$\frac{1}{2}$ tablespoons grated
  Parmesan cheese

1 tablespoon chopped
  parsley
salt, pepper
oil for frying

Tomato Sauce

1 small onion
1$\frac{1}{2}$ tablespoons oil
5 oz. can tomato paste

1 pint (2 cups) water
salt, pepper

Finely chop onion, combine with remaining ingredients, mix well. Shape mixture into balls approximately the size of an egg. Fry in hot oil until evenly browned.

Remove from pan, drain well, place in prepared sauce, bring to boil; reduce heat, simmer, uncovered, for approximately 1 hour or until tender. Spoon meatballs and sauce over hot spaghetti.

Serves 4.

Tomato Sauce Finely chop onion, sauté in heated oil until soft, add remaining ingredients, stir well to combine. Bring to boil, stirring constantly.

Meatballs in Tomato Sauce have the good, rich flavour of Italian-style cooking. Spoon them over piping hot spaghetti.

Spaghetti Marinara

2 oz. ($\frac{1}{4}$ cup) butter
1 clove garlic
2 tablespoons finely
  chopped parsley
6 large tomatoes
1 8 oz. can oysters

1 lb. or 1 pint prawns
  (shrimps)
4 to 6 scallops
salt, pepper
1 lb. spaghetti

Melt butter in saucepan, add crushed garlic, parsley and peeled, chopped tomatoes. Simmer until mixture is well blended and soft; mix in oysters, shelled prawns (shrimps), and scallops cut in halves or quarters, cook gently 5 to 7 minutes. Season to taste.

Drain hot cooked spaghetti. Return to saucepan, stir the sauce through. Or, alternatively, spoon sauce over individual servings of spaghetti.
Serves 6.

Spaghetti Bolognese

1 large onion
2 tablespoons oil
1 lb. minced (ground)
  steak
1 pint (2 cups) water
8 oz. can tomato paste
2 beef stock cubes

salt, pepper
$\frac{1}{4}$ teaspoon oregano
$\frac{1}{4}$ teaspoon thyme
$\frac{3}{4}$ lb. spaghetti
grated Parmesan
  cheese

Sauté the finely chopped onion in the heated oil until golden, add minced steak; cook very well, stirring with fork all the time, until steak browns well. Pour off any surplus fat. Add water, tomato paste, crumbled stock cubes, salt and pepper to taste, and herbs.

When sauce comes to the boil, reduce heat, cook gently 1 to 1$\frac{1}{2}$ hours, uncovered, adding a little more water if sauce becomes thick too quickly. The longer this sauce is cooked the better it is.

Cook spaghetti, drain well and arrange in individual bowls, making a slight well in the centre. Spoon in the sauce. Top with grated Parmesan cheese.

Serves 4 to 6.

Spaghetti alla Carbonara

1 lb. spaghetti
boiling salted water
$\frac{3}{4}$ lb. bacon
$\frac{1}{4}$ pint ($\frac{1}{2}$ cup) white
  wine
2 eggs

2 oz. ($\frac{1}{2}$ cup) grated
  Parmesan cheese
freshly ground pepper
chopped parsley
extra grated Parmesan
  cheese

Cook spaghetti in large saucepan of salted boiling water 10 to 12 minutes or until tender but still firm. While spaghetti is cooking, remove rind from bacon, cut into $\frac{1}{2}$ in. squares. Sauté in pan until cooked through but not crisp.

Add wine, simmer gently 3 minutes. Drain spaghetti well, return to saucepan. Immediately add bacon and wine. Blend together, then add well-beaten eggs and cheese. Toss together over low heat. Add a little freshly ground pepper. Make sure spaghetti is well coated with egg-and-cheese mixture. Serve in individual dishes sprinkled with parsley and extra grated cheese.

Serves 6.

NOTE: If completed spaghetti is a little dry, add a little extra white wine to moisten.

Meatballs in Tomato Sauce have the good, rich flavour of Italian-style cooking. Spoon them over piping hot spaghetti.

Baked Rigatoni

½ lb. rigatoni noodles | grated Parmesan cheese

Filling

1 tablespoon oil
2 onions, chopped
1 clove garlic, crushed
1½ lb. minced (ground) steak

3 oz. (1 cup) fresh breadcrumbs
1 egg
1½ teaspoons salt
pepper

Sauce

oil for frying
1 onion, chopped
1 clove garlic, crushed
14 oz. can drained, peeled tomatoes

½ pint (1 cup) juice from can (made up to ½ pint (1 cup) with water if necessary)
1 bayleaf
salt, pepper

Cook rigatoni in boiling salted water until just softened (about 5 minutes); drain and, for this dish, rinse under cold water because they must be cool enough to handle immediately.

Filling   Heat oil, brown onions and garlic lightly. Combine with all remaining ingredients.

Using small teaspoon, stuff rigatoni with filling mixture. Arrange stuffed rigatoni in casserole, spoon sauce over. Top with sprinkling of grated Parmesan cheese. Bake in moderate oven, Mark 4, 350°F., 30 minutes.

Sauce   Heat a little oil in saucepan, add onion and garlic; sauté until onion is transparent. Add all remaining ingredients (crush tomatoes well), simmer uncovered until sauce has thickened.

Serves 4 to 6.

Macaroni Cheese

6 oz. macaroni
3 oz. (⅜ cup) butter
1 oz. (2 tablespoons) flour
salt, pepper
1 teaspoon dry mustard
¼ teaspoon paprika
½ pint (1 cup) milk
6 oz. (1½ cups) grated firm cheese

10 oz. can tomato soup
¼ lb. bacon
1 onion
1 small green pepper
1 teaspoon Worcestershire sauce
extra grated cheese

Cook macaroni in boiling salted water 12 to 15 minutes or until tender; drain.

Melt butter in saucepan, remove from heat, stir in flour and seasonings. Return to heat and cook 1 minute. Add milk gradually, stirring until sauce boils and thickens, remove from heat. Add grated cheese and tomato soup, mix well. Gently heat sauce, do not boil.

Fry lightly, chopped bacon, chopped onion and chopped pepper, add to sauce. Add macaroni and Worcestershire sauce, mix thoroughly. Place mixture into casserole dish, sprinkle with extra grated cheese. Bake in moderate oven, Mark 4, 350°F., 25 to 30 minutes.

Serves 4 to 6.

Lasagne

¼ lb. lasagne noodles

Meat Sauce

1½ lb. tomatoes
1 tablespoon oil
1 lb. minced (ground) steak
small can tomato juice
1 tablespoon finely chopped onion
small can or 2 oz. button mushrooms

½ clove crushed garlic
1 teaspoon oregano
¼ teaspoon basil
¼ teaspoon rosemary
1 teaspoon salt
½ teaspoon sugar

Cheese Sauce

2 oz. (¼ cup) butter
3 tablespoons flour
1 pint (2 cups) milk

4 oz. (1 cup) grated processed cheese
salt, pepper

Topping

2 oz. (½ cup) grated Parmesan cheese

3 to 4 tablespoons cream

Cook lasagne noodles in boiling, salted water until tender, 15 to 20 minutes. Drain well. Peel and chop tomatoes. Heat oil, add steak, cook, stirring, until browned. Add all other ingredients, cook until meat is tender. Place half the noodles in ovenproof dish, spread with half the meat sauce, then half the cheese sauce. Repeat layers.

Sprinkle top with grated Parmesan cheese. Cook in moderate oven, Mark 4, 350°F., 15 minutes. Five minutes before end of cooking time, pour cream over top of cheese.

Cheese Sauce   Melt butter in saucepan, stir in flour, cook gently for 2 minutes. Gradually add milk, stir over low heat until boiling. Stir in grated cheese and seasoning, stir until cheese has melted.

Serves 4 to 6.

Vegetables

Vegetables are an important part of our daily diet. We use them in salads, as colourful, good tasting accompaniments to main meals, or they can be a complete meal in themselves.

To cover or not to cover vegetables when cooking them on top of the stove is a question often debated; as with most forms of cookery, everybody has a favourite method. But experts agree on this—vegetables should be cooked as quickly as possible, so they are crisp, full of flavour, and retain as much of their vitamin contents as possible.

Artichoke

There are two types of artichoke— the Jerusalem and the globe. Many people consider the globe artichoke to be the most delicately flavoured and refined of all vegetables.

Globe Artichokes Wash artichokes, then cut off stem at base. Remove any old outside leaves, shorten the tips with scissors. Plunge into large saucepan of boiling salted water; add juice of ½ lemon, cover and cook 30 to 40 minutes, according to size. Artichokes are cooked when leaves come away easily when pulled gently. Drain well, place on individual serving dishes. Serve with bowl of melted butter, with juice of lemon and salt and pepper added.

Each diner pulls off the leaves, dips them in melted butter and eats fleshy end. Remove central hairy 'choke', when reached, and eat base.

Artichokes cooked in this way can also be served cold, with a vinaigrette sauce.

Jerusalem Artichokes Not really an artichoke but a member of sunflower family. Does not look or taste like the globe artichoke, but resembles a knotty potato. Has a sweet nutty flavour.

The tubers are small and irregular in size and shape. Scrub them well, soak in slightly salted cold water 30 minutes, then drain and rinse well. Cover with cold salted water, cook 20 to 30 minutes until tender, depending on size.

Some cooks prefer to peel the artichokes before cooking; small, sharp-pointed knife should be used for this.

However, it is much easier to peel the skins off after cooking. They are now ready to be used in a variety of ways, or they can be served topped with butter.

Asparagus

Cut off tough ends of asparagus, scrape spears a few inches up from end, tie in a bunch. Stand in deep, tall saucepan (top of double boiler is also suitable), and add boiling salted water to come half way up spears. Cover tightly, bring to boil, reduce heat and simmer until asparagus is tender (about 20 minutes, although very young, tender asparagus will take only 10 to 15 minutes). Drain asparagus well. Serve with melted butter.

Aubergine

See Eggplant.

Beans

Broad Beans Seasonal: April to July. Very young broad beans (fresh from the garden) can be cooked whole. But usually they should be shelled, as for peas, and the pods discarded. Cook beans in boiling salted water until tender (15 to 20 minutes). Top with butter and sprinkling of finely chopped parsley.

French or Runner Beans, (Green or Shap Beans) Wash beans, then top and tail, remove strings. Young beans can be left whole for cooking, but older beans should be sliced. Cook in small amount of boiling salted water until tender (10 to 15 minutes). Drain well, season with salt and pepper, top with pat of butter. Serve at once.

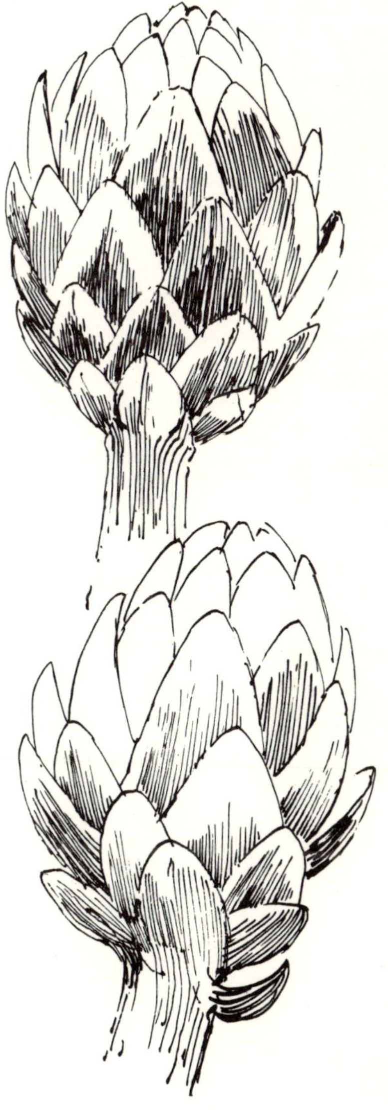

Artichoke

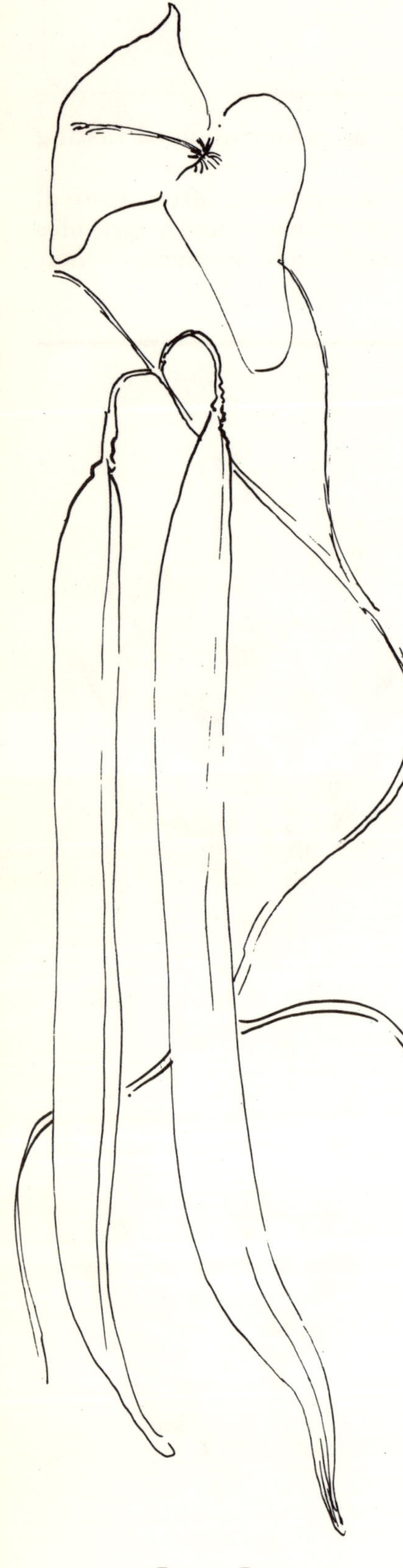

Runner Beans

Spanish Beans

1 large onion	1 dessertspoon
1 tomato	flour
1 chilli	1 to 1½ pints (2 to
1 red or green	3 cups) stock
pepper	1 lb. runner
1 oz. (2 table-	(green) beans
spoons) butter	1 teaspoon salt

Slice the vegetables thinly. Cook the onion, tomato, chilli and pepper in the butter until soft and golden brown. Add the flour, stir until brown then add the boiling stock. Bring again to boiling point, add the sliced beans and salt and cook about ½ hour. Serve as an accompaniment to meat or as a savoury.

Serves 3 to 4.

Runner (Green) Beans with Carrots

½ lb. young	salt, pepper
carrots	2 tablespoons oil
1 lb. runner	
(green) beans	

Scrape the carrots and cut into very thin rounds. String and slice the beans thinly. Put 1 in. water into a strong saucepan, add the carrots, salt and pepper, cover and cook for 10 minutes. Add the beans and oil and continue cooking further 20 minutes or until tender. Correct the seasoning as necessary.

Serves 4.

French Beans Almondine

1 lb. French	1 oz. (3 to 4 table-
(green) beans	spoons)
2 oz. (¼ cup)	slivered
butter	almonds
pinch salt	1 dessertspoon
	lemon rind

Top and tail beans. Cook whole, or sliced, in little boiling salted water until tender; drain. Melt butter over low heat, add almonds, sauté a few minutes. Stir in salt and lemon juice. Pour over hot beans.

Serves 4.

Beetroot

Wash well. Leave on 1 in. or more of stems and root end. If cut too near stem the bright colour will leak into water, leaving cooked beetroot a pale pink instead of its bright natural colour. Cook, covered, in boiling salted water to cover until tender when tested with fork. Small young beetroot will take 30 to 40 minutes, older beetroot up to 1½ hours. When tender, drain and slip off skins, root and stems.

Broccoli

Wash broccoli, trim off ends of stalks and coarse leaves. Cut deep cross in base of extra thick stalks to facilitate cooking. Place in saucepan with small amount of boiling salted water; boil until tender (10 to 15 minutes). Drain, add salt, pepper, pat of butter and squeeze of lemon juice. Serve at once.

For additional flavour, add ½ clove garlic to cooking water. Remove garlic before serving.

Broccoli with Lemon-Cream Sauce

1½ oz. (3 table-	1 lb. cooked
spoons butter	broccoli spears
1 dessertspoon	(or use quick-
flour	frozen broccoli)
salt, pepper	1 oz. (3 to 4
large can	tablespoons
evaporated	blanched,
milk or cream	slivered
2 egg-yolks	almonds
1½ tablespoons	
lemon juice	

Melt ½ oz. (1 tablespoon) butter in a saucepan, add flour and seasonings, stir until smooth. Cook 1 minute. Gradually add the evaporated milk. Bring to the boil, stirring constantly. Remove from heat. Beat egg-yolks, slowly beat a little hot sauce into the eggs, return to sauce in the pan, stir in remaining butter and lemon juice carefully.

Place the cooked broccoli spears in a shallow dish, pour over the hot sauce and garnish with almonds.

Serves 4.

Brussels Sprouts

Remove any wilted outer leaves from sprouts, remove hard end of stem; cut a cross in base of stems to ensure even cooking. Wash thoroughly. Cook in little boiling salted water until tender (10 to 15 minutes depending on size). Drain well, dot with butter, sprinkle with salt and pepper. Serve at once.

At top, from left, Zucchini, Eggplant. Below, Beans.

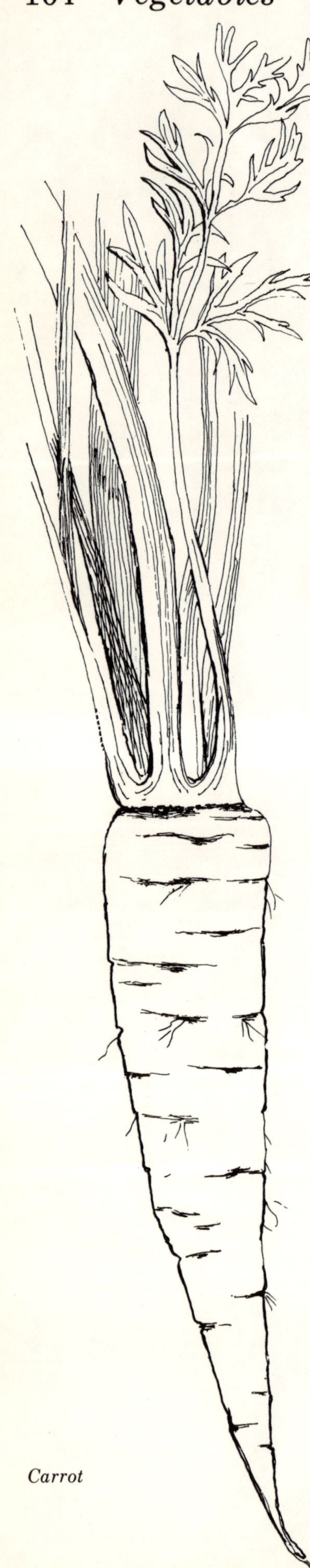

Carrot

Cabbage

Remove coarse outer leaves from cabbage, cut out hard core. Wash thoroughly, cut into fine shreds. Place in saucepan, add little salt, lump of butter and squeeze of lemon juice. Add minimum amount of boiling water, let water come again to boil, then stir cabbage well. Boil rapidly, covered, until tender.

Alternatively, put cabbage into saucepan with salt, add boiling water to cover: bring water rapidly again to boil, boil 3 minutes, then drain. Season with freshly ground pepper, top with knob of butter. This gives a very crisp vegetable, in the Chinese style.

Half a cup of chopped celery added to cabbage when cooking gives a new and delightfully fresh flavour.

Cabbage American

1 medium sized cabbage	$\frac{1}{2}$ teaspoon curry powder
3 oz. ($\frac{3}{8}$ cup) butter	grated rind and juice of 1 lemon
1 teaspoon chutney	

Shred the cabbage and cook for 4 minutes in 1 quart (4 cups) boiling salted water. Drain well. Brown the butter in a small pan, add curry, chutney, orange rind and juice. Pour over the cabbage and leave in a warm place for 10 minutes before serving.

Serves 4.

Dolmas

12 cabbage leaves	$\frac{1}{4}$ teaspoon Tabasco
1 lb. lean pork	$\frac{1}{2}$ teaspoon marjoram
1 onion	
$\frac{1}{4}$ teaspoon garlic salt	$\frac{1}{2}$ pint (1 cup) cider
$\frac{1}{4}$ teaspoon black pepper	sliced cooked carrots for garnish

Wash the cabbage leaves and cook for 5 minutes in boiling salted water until just soft and pliable, drain well.

Mince or grind the pork and onion, add seasoning, Tabasco and marjoram. Spread over the cabbage leaves, roll firmly and put into a casserole. Add the cider, cover and cook in a very moderate oven, Mark 3, 325°F. for 1 hour. Arrange in a hot dish and garnish with carrots.

Makes 12 dolmas.

If liked the remaining cider can be thickened with a little cornflour and served with the dolmas. When thickened add seasoning and a little tomato purée.

Red Cabbage

This, unlike green cabbage, is never boiled in water. It should be finely shredded or grated and then cooked slowly, covered, with butter or lard and vinegar; water may then be added. This initial cooking with butter and vinegar ensures a rich purple colour to the cabbage; if cooked with water, the cabbage will 'bleed' and become pale pink.

$\frac{1}{2}$ red cabbage	1 apple
1 oz. (2 tablespoons) lard	$\frac{1}{4}$ pint ($\frac{1}{2}$ cup) water
2 oz. bacon	6 peppercorns
1 medium onion	1 bayleaf
3 tablespoons sugar	4 whole cloves
$\frac{1}{4}$ pint ($\frac{1}{2}$ cup) white vinegar	1 teaspoon salt

Finely shred cabbage, discarding any coarse leaves. Melt lard in large saucepan, add chopped bacon and onion, sauté until onion is golden. Add sugar, cook over medium heat 1 minute. Add shredded cabbage, vinegar, peeled and chopped apple; cover, simmer gently 10 minutes, turning occasionally. Stir in water and seasonings, cover; simmer gently further $1\frac{1}{2}$ hours. Serve as accompaniment to any meats.

Serves 4.

Capsicums

See Peppers

Carrots

One of the most popular root vegetables. Their bright colour adds appetite appeal to many dishes, especially when served raw in salads; their sweet fresh taste teams well with many foods. Carrots are rich in vitamins.

Carrots Vichy

1 lb. young carrots	2 oz. ($\frac{1}{4}$ cup) butter
1 teaspoon sugar	water
salt, pepper	chopped parsley

Scrape carrots and cut into slices about $\frac{1}{2}$ in. thick. Put in pan with the sugar, seasoning and butter, barely cover with water. Cook quickly, turning occasionally, until all the water has evaporated and the carrots are tender, and lightly coated in butter. Sprinkle with parsley.

Serves 4.

Cauliflower

Trim cauliflower, removing outer green leaves and part of core. Make several deep cuts in core to facilitate cooking. Place in saucepan, add boiling water almost to cover cauliflower. Add salt to flavour, and a teaspoon of lemon juice or little milk; this will help keep cauliflower white. Cook gently 20 to 30 minutes or until tender (do not overcook); drain.

Alternatively, the cauliflower can be broken into flowerets and cooked for a shorter time.

Cauliflower au Gratin

1 cauliflower	fresh bread-
Mornay sauce	crumbs
(see below)	melted butter
grated Parmesan	
or Cheddar	
cheese	

Cook cauliflower until tender, drain well. Spread about $\frac{1}{4}$ pint ($\frac{1}{2}$ cup) Mornay Sauce in ovenproof dish, place drained cauliflower on top of this. Spoon over $\frac{1}{2}$ pint (1 cup) of Mornay Sauce, or more, if necessary, to cover. Sprinkle with grated cheese and fine, fresh breadcrumbs. Spoon over little melted butter. Cook in hot oven, Mark 7, 425°F., or place under hot grill until top is lightly brown.

Mornay Sauce

2 egg-yolks	1 dessertspoon
1 tablespoon	butter
cream	2 tablespoons
1 pint (2 cups)	finely grated
hot white	Parmesan or
sauce (see	Cheddar
page 146)	cheese

Mix egg yolks and cream into hot white sauce. Cook, stirring constantly, until mixture just reaches boiling point; remove from heat. Stir in butter and grated cheese.

Celery

Trim heads thoroughly—for best results for cooked celery, only the tender inner stalks should be used. Scrub these, plunge into boiling water; cook 10 minutes. Then drain, dry and tie tops of heads together; cook as desired.

The simplest way to cook celery is to blanch it as above, then continue cooking in boiling salted water until tender (about 20 minutes). Drain, serve with a well-seasoned white sauce.

Don't throw away the discarded leaves and outer stalks—these are a wonderful addition to the stock or soup pot, and young, fresh celery is delicious, of course, to eat fresh or use as a salad ingredient.

Celery Victor

1 head celery	tomato wedges
stock	few strips
well-seasoned	anchovy
French	shredded lettuce
dressing	ripe olives
freshly ground	
black pepper	

Clean celery, cut head in halves lengthwise. Trim off top and if head is large, cut in half again crosswise. Place in saucepan with hot stock to cover, cook until tender. Drain well, place in shallow dish to cool. Pour over sufficient French dressing to moisten well. Refrigerate, turning pieces occasionally. At serving time, arrange on platter on bed of shredded lettuce. Sprinkle with pepper, lay few strips of anchovy over each piece. Decorate with tomato wedges, black olives.

Serves 4 to 6.

Braised Celery

2 small heads	1 small onion
celery	1 tablespoon
$\frac{1}{2}$ pint (1 cup)	flour
chicken stock	paprika
1 tablespoon	salt, pepper
butter	

Trim and blanch celery as directed, drain and tie up. Place in saucepan with chicken stock, cover, bring to boil; simmer until tender. Drain, remove string, keep warm; reserve cooking liquid. Heat butter in saucepan, add finely chopped onion, sauté until golden. Blend in flour, gradually add cooking liquid. Cook, stirring, until mixture boils and thickens, adding little extra stock if sauce seems too thick. Season to taste. Spoon sauce over celery, sprinkle with paprika.

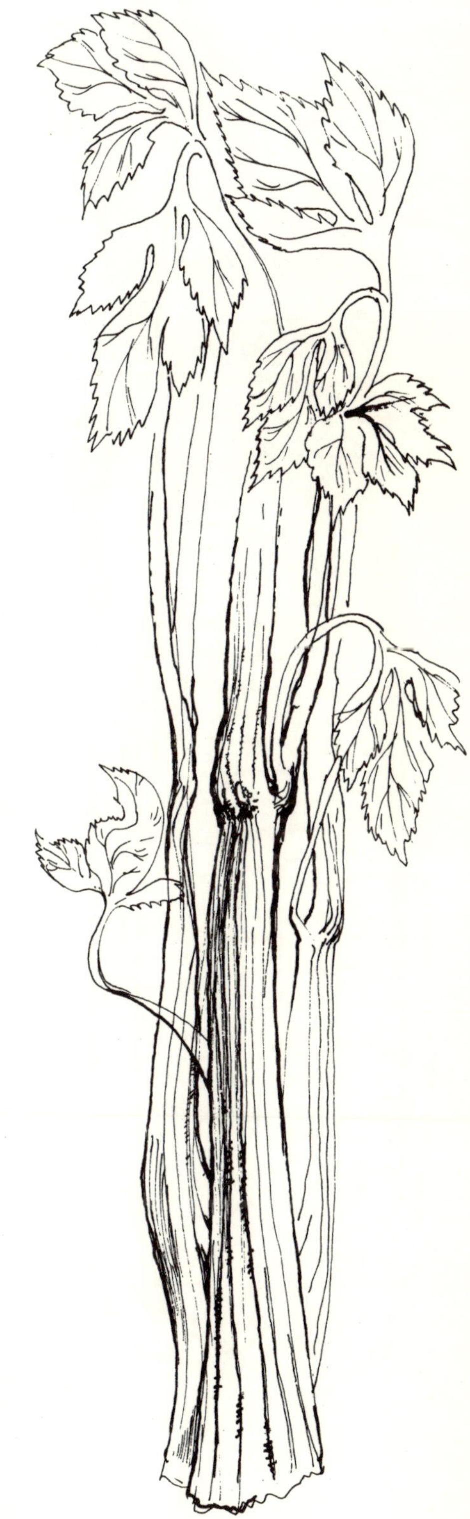

Celery

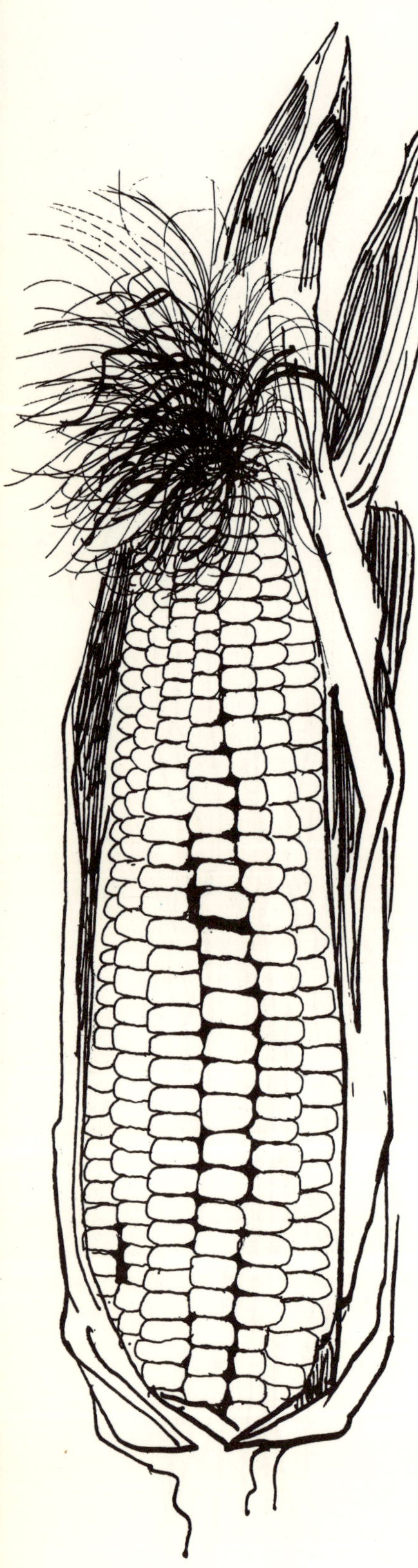

Corn

Celery au Gratin

1 head celery	2 oz. (½ cup)
1 oz. (2 table-	grated
spoons) butter	Parmesan or
1 oz. (2 table-	Cheddar
spoons) flour	cheese
¼ pint (½ cup)	salt, cayenne
celery water	pepper
¼ pint (½ cup)	browned bread-
milk	crumbs

Prepare the celery and cut into dice. Cook in a little boiling salted water until tender, drain well. Make a white sauce with the butter, flour, celery stock and milk. Add half the cheese and season carefully. Fill a greased fireproof dish with alternate layers of sauce and celery. Sprinkle the rest of the cheese and a few breadcrumbs on top. Reheat in the oven or under the grill.

Serves 3 to 4.

Celery and Fruit Jelly

1 pkt. lemon jelly	1 teaspoon salt
1 pkt. lime jelly	1 pint (2 cups)
1 pint (2 cups)	cold water
hot water	3 oz. (½ cup)
4 tablespoons	diced celery
lemon juice	1 apple
2 small bananas	

Dissolve lemon and lime jellies in the hot water. Add lemon juice, salt and cold water. Chill in the refrigerator until slightly thickened. Fold in celery, diced bananas and diced unpeeled apple. Pour into 1 large or 8 individual moulds and refrigerate until set. Serve on lettuce with mayonnaise (see page 121).

Serves 8.

Chicory (Endive)

Generally imported. In France this vegetable is called Endive Belge. It is generally eaten raw in salads or can be braised.

Chicory (Endive) Soufflé

6 to 8 heads of	3 eggs
chicory	salt, pepper
(endive)	nutmeg
½ pint (1 cup)	grated firm
bechamel	cheese
sauce (see	
page 146)	

Wash the chicory (endive), removing the outside leaves and cook in boiling salted water for 20 minutes. Drain and chop finely. Add to the sauce with beaten egg-yolks, salt, pepper and nutmeg to taste.

Fold in the stiffly beaten egg whites, turn into a buttered soufflé dish and bake in a moderately hot oven, Mark 5, 375°F., for 20 minutes. Serve with a sprinkling of grated cheese.

Serves 4.

Chilli

See Peppers

Corn

Corn deteriorates more rapidly after picking than any other vegetable. The sugar in the corn rapidly converts to starch. Freshly picked young corn is sweet to taste; corn which has been picked for some time develops a floury taste. Ideally, corn should be cooked as soon as possible after picking. Look for corn with dark green, fresh husks, with plump, well-filled kernels. Fresh corn looks moist and juicy; if you scratched a grain with your fingertips it would be soft. Old corn looks hard and dull. Do not buy corn that has had the husks removed.

Do not remove husks until ready to cook the corn. Have ready a deep saucepan filled with boiling water; water should be deep enough to cover cobs when they are in saucepan. Salt can be added to the water, but some cooks believe this tends to toughen the kernels; instead, they add a little sugar. Remove green leaves and the silky 'hair' from cobs, drop cobs into the boiling water, let water return to the boil, then cook for 20 minutes. Overcooking will toughen the kernels; the corn becomes harder, not softer, through longer boiling.

Lift cobs from water with tongs. Serve with butter and pepper.

Corn is also good for a barbecue. Remove husk and silk from corn. Spread cobs generously with softened butter, season well with salt and pepper. Wrap each cob in a double thickness of aluminium foil, twisting or folding ends to make a seal. Place on grill of barbecue over hot coals. Cook, turning often, 15 to 20 minutes, depending on heat of fire.

Or cobs can be boiled for 10

Mild, sweet peppers (or capiscums) come in a variety of colours. Yellow-green Banana Chillies (mild as peppers) and small, hot red chilli are also shown.

minutes, removed from the water, and brushed generously with melted butter; then barbecued on grill over hot coals for 10 minutes, and brushed occasionally with melted butter.

Cucumbers

Although generally used as a salad vegetable, cucumbers are excellent when cooked and served hot.

Buttered Cucumbers

2 to 3 cucumbers	salt, pepper
boiling salted water	lemon juice
2 tablespoons melted butter	2 tablespoons chopped parsley

Peel cucumbers, score them with fork. Cut into quarters, lengthwise, or into $\frac{1}{2}$ in. slices. Drop into boiling salted water, simmer 2 minutes, drain.

Melt butter in frying pan, add well-drained cucumber, sprinkle with salt and pepper. Cook, turning once, until cucumbers are lightly golden; do not overcook. Add a good squeeze of lemon juice, stir this lightly through cucumbers. Sprinkle with parsley.

This is a delicious accompaniment to fish.

Serves 4.

Cucumbers in Sour Cream

2 medium cucumbers	2 tablespoons chopped chives
1 tablespoon salt	salt, pepper to taste
1 tablespoon vinegar	pinch cayenne
$\frac{1}{4}$ pint ($\frac{1}{2}$ cup) sour cream	

Peel cucumbers and slice thinly. Sprinkle slices with salt and vinegar, let stand 30 minutes. Drain off liquid, and mix cucumber with sour cream, chives and seasonings to taste. Serve well chilled. Excellent as a curry accompaniment.

Serves 4 to 6.

Eggplant or Aubergine

To prepare for cooking, simply wipe with damp cloth and remove stem and calyx. Can be peeled or left unpeeled. Eggplant is a watery vegetable; if cut into thick slices, salted and covered with plate with weight on top, some of the excess moisture will drain away.

When frying eggplant, do not cover pan—the slices should be crisp.

Cut unpeeled eggplant crosswise in thin slices. Coat lightly with seasoned flour, fry in hot butter until pale golden brown. Serve piping hot as vegetable accompaniment with meat, fish, etc.

Aubergines à la Boston

4 aubergines	2 oz. ($\frac{1}{2}$ cup) grated Parmesan cheese
salt, pepper	
flour	
oil for frying	
2 onions	$\frac{1}{4}$ pint ($\frac{1}{2}$ cup) thin white sauce (see page 146)
$\frac{1}{2}$ oz. (1 tablespoon) butter	
1 egg	

Cut unpeeled aubergines in half lengthways. Run the point of a knife round the inside of the skin to a depth of 1 in. and make several cuts across the fleshy part.

Sprinkle with salt and leave to stand for $\frac{1}{2}$ hour. Drain, dry with a cloth and sprinkle with flour. Fry for about 8 to 10 minutes on the cut side only. Remove from the pan and leave to cool. Then, with a metal spoon, scoop out the flesh and chop up. Soften the peeled and chopped onions in the butter, add to the aubergine flesh with beaten egg, cheese and seasoning. Fill the aubergine cases with this mixture, place in a fire-proof dish and cook for 10 minutes in a hot oven, Mark 7, 425°F. Pour over the sauce and serve in the same dish.

Mild, sweet peppers (or capsicums) come in a variety of plain and variegated colours—red, green, yellow; shown, also, is the rarer creamy-white pepper. Yellow-green Banana Chillies (mild as peppers) and the small, hot red chilli are also shown.

Kale

This is a vegetable of the cabbage family. The leaves are closely curled, prettily variegated in colours of green, white and mauve.

Cut leaves from heavy stems, wash well. Cook as for spinach over gentle heat, but allow slightly longer cooking time. Drain, season with a little grated nutmeg, top with butter.

Kale can also be substituted in any recipe that calls for spinach.

Leek

Kohlrabi

Looks like a turnip and has similar taste, but more delicate grain. Actually, is a member of the cabbage family. Select leaves that are pale green and crisp, roots about the size of medium-sized onion. Trim off leaves, peel roots, slice. Cook in boiling salted water to cover until tender, about 25 minutes. Drain, season with salt, pepper, melted butter, or serve with a medium white sauce.

Leeks

Cut off roots, trim green tops, leaving about 3 in. of green part. Peel off outside layer, then make 2 cuts, about 2 in. long, first one way and then the other, on top of green parts of leek. This makes it easy to ruffle back the tops when washing. (This is essential because all particles of grit lying between leaves must be removed.) Then place leeks in saucepan with little boiling salted water. Cover, bring to boil, simmer until tender (about 30 minutes). Drain well, season with salt and pepper, pour over little melted butter.

Leeks Vinaigrette Cook leeks as directed, drain and cool. Serve with vinaigrette sauce (three parts oil mixed with one part vinegar, with salt and pepper to taste), sprinkle with chopped parsley or chives.

Braised Leeks

8 small leeks	½ pint (1 cup)
1 tablespoon	chicken stock
butter	salt, pepper
1 small onion	slices of buttered
	toast

Wash leeks thoroughly and trim. Melt butter in wide shallow saucepan, add chopped onion, sauté until soft and golden. Add leeks, pour in stock; add salt and pepper. Cover, simmer until leeks are just tender. Serve on slices of buttered toast.
    Serves 4.

Lettuce

Widely used as a salad vegetable, lettuce can also be cooked to serve as a green vegetable. Remove wilted leaves, wash lettuce under running water. Cut heads into quarters. Put into saucepan with a little chicken stock (about 2 tablespoons for each medium-size lettuce). Cover, cook until tender, about 5 to 10 minutes. Drain, season with salt and pepper, pour over a little melted butter.

Marrow (Squash)

When small known as Courgettes or Zucchini (see picture on page 102 and page 115). Seasonal April to August, sometimes imported.

    Peel marrow, cut into neat pieces, cook in boiling salted water until just tender, or steam over boiling water. Serve topped with butter or parsley sauce. Marrows can also be filled with a savoury stuffing and baked in the oven.

Stuffed Vegetable Marrow (Acorn or Hubbard Squash)

1 medium vegetable marrow (squash)	salt, pepper
	1 dessertspoon chopped parsley
½ lb. (1½ cups) cold cooked meat	2 oz. (½ cup) grated Cheddar cheese
3 oz. (1 cup) diced cooked vegetables	1 oz. (scant ½ cup) soft breadcrumbs
1 tomato	1 dessertspoon butter
about ¼ pint (½ cup) white sauce (see page 146)	

Cut marrow in half lengthwise, do not peel, remove seeds. Mince or dice meat finely, skin and chop tomato. Combine meat, vegetables, tomato, white sauce, salt, pepper and parsley; fill into each half of marrow. Sprinkle tops with combined cheese and breadcrumbs, dot with butter. Place marrow (squash) in baking dish with small quantity of water in bottom of dish, bake in moderate over, Mark 4, 350°F., for approximately 45 minutes or until tender.
    Serves 4.

Mushrooms

Classified as a fungus rather than a vegetable, but used as a vegetable they are delicious! Two kinds of mushrooms are generally available —the cultivated mushrooms, pink-brown underneath with creamy-white top; and the darker, generally larger and more open-capped field mushroom, which grows wild.

    Mushrooms should be used when they are fresh. From the time they

Mushrooms

are picked, they gradually lose weight by dehydration; they contain 75 per cent of water.

To help cut down evaporation, if they are to be kept, store in plastic bag, or well wrapped in plastic food wrap or waxed paper, in refrigerator. Don't try to keep them too long—a week is maximum, if they are to have any flavour.

Before cooking, wash mushrooms lightly. Don't let them soak in water, because this dilutes their flavour. For cultivated mushrooms, a wiping with clean, damp cloth is generally sufficient.

To prepare, slice off dry end of stem. It is not necessary to peel the cultivated mushrooms, but you might like to remove darker skin of field mushrooms before cooking. They can be sliced, if large, or left whole.

Here is a simple way of cooking mushrooms.

Prepare as directed above. Sauté in heated butter until barely tender (about 5 minutes). Add squeeze of lemon juice to pan, with a small clove of crushed garlic, some chopped parsley, salt and pepper. Cook a further moment or two. Nice with grills.

Stuffed Mushrooms

½ lb. small mushrooms	1 dessertspoon chopped parsley
2 oz. (¼ cup) butter	1 small shallot
1 small clove garlic	2 tablespoons soft bread- crumbs, approx.
salt, pepper	oil

Wash and stem mushrooms; chop stems finely. Melt butter in frying pan, add stems and crushed garlic, sauté 2 minutes. Add salt and pepper to taste, parsley and very finely chopped shallot, cook gently 1 minute. Remove from heat and add enough breadcrumbs to mix to a light stuffing.

Fill mushroom caps with this mixture, spreading evenly. Place in shallow, well-greased ovenproof dish, pour 1 teaspoon oil over each mushroom. Bake in moderate oven, Mark 4, 350°F., 10 to 15 minutes. The mushrooms should not be over-cooked.

Serve as a first course or as an accompaniment to meat.

Sautéed Mushrooms

3 tablespoons butter	⅛ teaspoon ground nut- meg and clove mixed
1 teaspoon flour	salt
1½ lb. mushrooms	4 tablespoons sherry

Melt butter in a shallow pan over low heat. Add flour, then gradually add mushrooms turning each over to absorb some of the butter. Just cover with water, add salt, cover and cook slowly for 10 minutes. Uncover, increase heat a little and cook until liquid has been well reduced. Add sherry and spice, bring to the boil and serve at once.

Serves 4.

Onions

A versatile vegetable, they adapt themselves well to almost all ways of cooking. Can be sliced and fried to top a succulent grill; baked whole with the joint; boiled and served with parsley sauce; or can be chopped, boiled, and added to a savoury white sauce to top corned beef.

Fried Onion Rings

4 onions	¼ teaspoon salt
½ pint (1 cup) milk	4 oz. (1 cup) plain flour
1 egg	oil for frying

Skin onions, slice thinly, separate into rings. Put into bowl, add the milk, let stand 1 hour. Drain, reserve milk. Beat egg well, beat in reserved milk, salt and sifted flour. Dip each onion ring into batter, drop into hot oil a few rings at a time so heat of oil does not decrease. Fry until golden brown. Drain well, sprinkle with salt.

Stuffed Onions

4 large onions	2 tablespoons grated Parmesan cheese
1 clove garlic	
1 stick celery	
1½ teaspoons oil	
1 teaspoon thyme	salt, pepper
2 oz. (½ cup) dried bread- crumbs	2 tablespoons melted butter

Peel onions, cut off top ¾ of the way up onion. Cut out enough of the inside to leave a shell about ¾ in.

Onion

thick. Salt the cavities well and let the onions stand while making the stuffing. Chop onion pulp finely with crushed garlic and celery. Fry slowly in oil for 5 minutes, then add thyme, breadcrumbs, cheese, salt and pepper to taste. Mix thoroughly, fill the onions; stand them flat in an oven-proof dish in which there is the melted butter and a little salt and pepper. Cover and bake in a moderately hot oven, Mark 5, 375°F., for 1 hour, or until onions are tender.

Spoon over the juices in base of the casserole.

Parsnips

Wash, trim and peel. Slice, if desired, or leave whole. Cook in small amount of boiling water until tender (about 25 to 30 minutes for whole parsnips—sliced parsnips will not take as long). Drain, season with salt and pepper, pour over little melted butter.

Parsnips are also delicious if baked around a roast. Peel parsnips and cut in halves, lengthwise. Place in baking dish with meat, spooning little of hot fat from pan over each. Bake about 45 minutes or until tender and browned.

Parsnip Croquettes

2 rashers bacon	1 small egg
1 lb. parsnips	2 tablespoons
1½ gills (⅔ cup)	plain flour
milk	salt, pepper
1 oz. (2 table-	seasoned flour
spoons) butter	egg glazing
2 to 3 table-	dried bread-
spoons finely	crumbs
chopped chives	oil for frying

Remove rind from bacon, cut bacon into small pieces. Fry until crisp, drain, set aside. Peel parsnips, cut into small pieces; put into saucepan with milk. Simmer, covered, until parsnips are tender and liquid is almost absorbed; mash. Add butter, chopped chives, egg, plain flour, and bacon. Season with salt and pepper, mix well. Drop tablespoons of mixture into seasoned flour, shape into croquettes; roll in flour, dip in beaten egg, toss in dry breadcrumbs. Press crumbs firmly on to croquettes. Refrigerate 1 hour. Deep fry in hot oil until golden brown.

Makes approx. 1½ dozen small croquettes.

Peas

Shell peas just before cooking, place in saucepan with small amount of boiling salted water. Add salt, little sugar and sprig of mint; cook until peas are tender. Cooking time will depend on age of peas, but is usually from 10 to 15 minutes. Drain, season with salt and pepper; add nut of butter; serve at once.

Peas Bonne Femme

1 heart of lettuce	1 dessertspoon
1½ to 2 lb. peas	flour
1½ oz. (3 table-	½ pint (1 cup)
spoons) butter	chicken or
6 chives or	vegetable
spring onions	stock
(scallions)	bouquet garni
2 rashers bacon	salt, pepper

Shred lettuce finely, shell peas. Melt butter in saucepan, add sliced chives and chopped bacon, shake over heat for a few minutes. Stir in flour, cook 2 to 3 minutes, then add lettuce. Pour on stock, bring mixture to boil, add peas, bouquet garni, salt and pepper. Cover, cook gently 20 to 30 minutes, stirring frequently. Remove bouquet garni.

Serves 6 to 8.

Peppers

Size of pepper usually indicates how to use it in cooking. Small pointed varieties (chillies) are very hot. Like garlic, a small amount goes a long way in seasoning casseroles, pickles, relishes, etc. Banana chillies are long, pale greenish-yellow in colour, are mild in flavour, like the big red and green peppers (or capsicums). Peppers can be used in many dishes; they add flavour to casseroles, and are a popular, colourful addition to salads.

To prepare peppers for cooking, remove slice from stalk end, scoop out seeds and membranes. Young, tender peppers can be used fresh, but older peppers should be blanched in hot water for 2 to 3 minutes to soften.

Perhaps the most popular way of using peppers is to stuff them with a savoury mixture and bake them; they make an easy, economical dish.

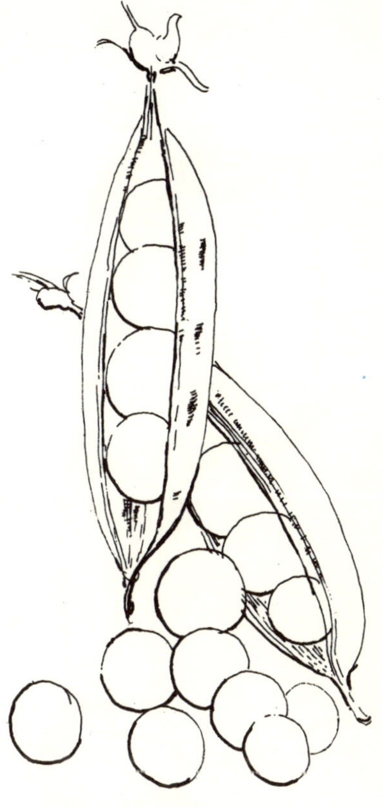

Peas

Peppers

Stuffed Peppers

4 green peppers	2 to 3 sticks
1 tablespoon oil	chopped celery
salt, pepper	½ lb. minced (1
2 oz. (¼ cup)	cup ground)
butter	raw meat
1 small onion	2 oz. (⅔ cup)
	cooked rice

Cut tops from peppers, or cut peppers in half lengthwise; remove seeds and membranes. Place peppers in boiling water with oil, boil 5 minutes; drain well. Season inside of peppers with salt and pepper. Heat butter, add finely chopped onion and celery, sauté until tender; add meat and rice, season with salt and pepper. Cook, stirring constantly, until meat changes colour.

Place meat mixture into pepper halves, place in shallow baking dish, cover. Bake in moderate oven, Mark 4, 350°F., 30 to 40 minutes, serve at once.

Serves 4.

Stuffed Peppers with Frankfurters

4 peppers	2 oz. butter

Filling

1 onion	3 dessert apples
1 can frank-	1½ oz. (3 table-
furters	spoons) butter
(medium size)	seasoning

Sauce

½ oz. (1 table-	1 cooked cabbage
spoon) butter	2 tablespoons
½ oz. (1 table-	water
spoon) flour	2 tablespoons
¼ pint (½ cup)	tomato purée
liquid from	seasoning
frankfurters	

Cut the tops off the peppers, remove core and seeds. Cook in hot butter for about 7 minutes, drain and keep hot. Peel and chop onion, chop frankfurters, chop unpeeled apple. Add remaining butter to that left in the pan, add onion, frankfurters and apple and fry until tender. Season. Fill the peppers and keep hot.

For the sauce—melt the butter, stir in the flour and cook for a few minutes. Add the liquid from the can of frankfurters gradually, stir until boiling. Add the tomato purée and cook until thickened. Season well. Arrange the cooked cabbage round the peppers and pour the sauce over.

Potatoes

They are eaten boiled, baked, roasted and fried—there are a hundred different methods of cooking them.

New Potatoes Scrub well before cooking. Cook in boiling salted water to which a sprig of mint or chopped parsley has been added until tender, 15 minutes or a little longer, depending on size. (Don't add too much mint, this darkens the potatoes). Drain, peel potatoes, return to pan, toss in butter, sprinkle with a little finely chopped mint. Or, as the skins on new potatoes are very thin, some cooks prefer to serve them unpeeled; just cut them in half for serving, top with a little butter and mint.

Baked Potatoes Choose potatoes of uniform size so they will finish cooking at the same time; scrub skins well, prick several times with a fine-tined fork. Rub over well with oil (this will ensure a crisp skin), sprinkle with salt. Bake in moderately hot oven, Mark 5, 375°F., 1¼ to 1½ hours, depending on size of potatoes; the skins should be crisply brown.

Remove from oven, make 2 cuts in top of each potato, forming a cross. Press sides of each potato so it opens out. Top each with knob of butter and sprinkling of salt and freshly ground pepper.

If desired, add sprinkling of chopped chives, parsley or crumbled bacon, spoonful of thick sour cream or sprinkling of grated Parmesan cheese.

Alternatively (and this is a delicious course at a dinner party) scoop out inside of cooked potato carefully, mash well, mix with some cooked cod's roe and enough sour cream to give a firm but rather creamy consistency. Spoon back into potato jacket.

Pommes Dauphinoise

2 lb. potatoes	1 cut clove garlic
salt, pepper	1 egg
nutmeg	4 tablespoons
½ pint (1 cup)	grated Gruyère
milk	cheese
few onion slices	butter

Peel potatoes, slice thinly. Arrange in ovenproof casserole, sprinkle with salt, pepper, grated nutmeg. Heat milk with onion slices and garlic, strain, combine with beaten egg; pour over potatoes. Sprinkle with cheese, dot with butter. Bake in moderate oven, Mark 4, 350°F., 45 to 50 minutes, or until potatoes are soft when tested with skewer.

Serves 4 to 6.

Paprika Potatoes

2 lb. potatoes
3 oz. ($\frac{3}{8}$ cup) lard or butter
3 chives
salt, pepper
$\frac{1}{4}$ pint ($\frac{1}{2}$ cup) sour cream
2 tablespoons milk
$1\frac{1}{2}$ teaspoons paprika

Peel and wash potatoes, cut into 1 in. cubes. Heat lard in large frying pan, add potatoes; cover and cook over low heat, stirring occasionally, until potatoes are tender and lightly golden brown. Add chopped chives, cook few minutes longer; season with salt and pepper. Mix together sour cream, milk and paprika, add to potatoes. Heat slowly over low heat (do not boil). Serve immediately.

Serves 4.

Potato Scallops

1 lb. potatoes
boiling water
$\frac{1}{2}$ lb. (2 cups) plain flour
$\frac{1}{2}$ teaspoon salt
1 egg
1 tablespoon oil
about $\frac{1}{2}$ pint (1 cup) hot water

Peel potatoes, wash well. Cut into slices $\frac{1}{4}$ in. thick. Place in heatproof basin, cover with boiling water, let stand 1 hour.

Meanwhile, prepare batter. Sift flour and salt into basin. Make a well in centre, add beaten egg and oil; beat in enough hot water to make a fairly thick coating batter. Beat until smooth.

Drain potatoes, pat dry. Coat each slice well with batter, deep-fry in hot oil, a few at a time, until batter is golden brown and crisp. Drain on kitchen paper, sprinkle with salt.

Potatoes Anna

2 lb. potatoes
water
approx. 4 oz. ($\frac{1}{2}$ cup or 1 stick) butter
salt, pepper
parsley

Peel potatoes, slice as thinly as possible. Drop them into iced water, let them stand 30 minutes. Drain, dry well. Take round mould or small baking dish, butter generously. Place layer of potatoes in base, spread over some softened butter. Repeat layers of potatoes and butter, ending with butter; sprinkle each layer with salt and pepper. Bake in hot oven, Mark 7, 425°F., 45 to 55 minutes, or until potatoes are soft when tested with thin skewer. To serve, invert on to serving dish. Garnish with parsley.

Serves 4.

Duchesse Potatoes

3 lb. potatoes
salt, pepper, nutmeg
4 egg-yolks
2 oz. ($\frac{1}{4}$ cup) butter
melted butter

Peel potatoes, boil in salted water until tender, then drain well, mash or push through strainer. Place in bowl, season with salt, pepper and nutmeg; add yolks and softened butter, work to smooth paste. Place in piping bag with star tube, pipe small pyramids on greased baking sheets. Brush with little melted butter. Bake in hot oven, Mark 7, 425°F., until tipped with brown.

Pumpkin and Squash

Of the same family and sometimes classed as fruit. Both are popular in America and Australia and are becoming popular in Britain. Pumpkin is good made into soup and for the American favourite—pumpkin pie. As a vegetable, it can be cooked and mashed like turnips. See Marrow (page 109).

Spinach

Should be thoroughly washed before cooking and every speck of dirt removed. Can be cooked in either of the following ways:

Wash spinach thoroughly. One popular variety of spinach has rather coarse white stems; these should be cut out before cooking. Place spinach in saucepan with only the water clinging to leaves. Cover tightly, cook until tender. Drain, pressing out all moisture, return to pan with salt, pepper and squeeze of lemon juice. Shake over heat 2 or 3 minutes before serving.

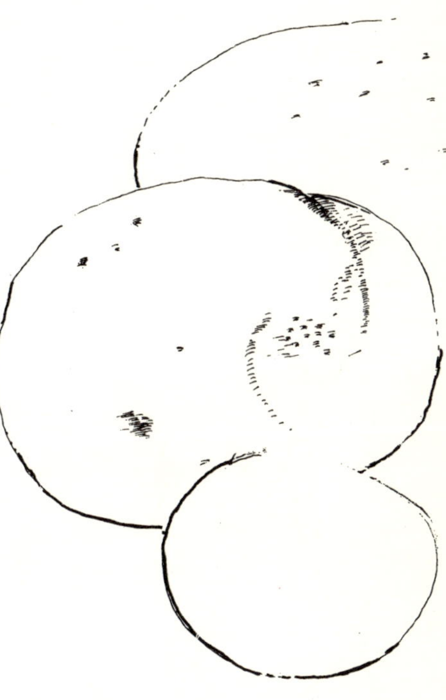

Potatoes

Spinach and Mushroom Cream

2 lb. spinach	nutmeg
¼ lb. mushrooms	salt, pepper
1 oz. (2 table- spoons) butter	1 hard boiled egg

¼ pint (½ cup)
  white sauce
  (see page 146)	

Prepare and cook spinach as usual. Drain well, chop finely and keep hot.

Sauté the chopped mushrooms in butter, add them to the white sauce together with grated nutmeg and seasoning.

Reserve the yolk of the hard boiled egg for garnish, chop the white and add to the sauce. Arrange the spinach in a border on a hot dish. Reheat the sauce and pour in the centre. Garnish with sieved egg yolk.

Serves 4.

Spinach à la Creme

2½ lb. spinach	lemon juice
2 oz. butter	freshly ground

2 tablespoons
  flour
	pepper
	  fried croutons

1½ gills milk	(see page 14)
salt, pepper	1 to 2 table-
sugar, nutmeg	spoons hot medium cream

Cook the spinach and drain well. Put into a pan over gentle heat to dry off, add half the butter and stir in the flour. Cook for a few minutes then add the milk, salt, pepper and a pinch of sugar. Bring to boiling point, cover and simmer over low heat for about 15 minutes. Add a pinch of nutmeg and adjust the seasoning. Just before serving add the remaining butter in small pieces, a squeeze of lemon juice and a dash of pepper. Serve with croutons and if liked, add 1 to 2 spoonfuls of hot cream.

Serves 4.

Sweet Potato

This is an edible tuber resembling an ordinary potato in appearance but with a sweetish flavour. Sweet potatoes are also known as yams. They can be boiled or baked, and are delicious if simply scrubbed and baked in their jackets; this will take 1 to 1½ hours, depending on size. When cooked, serve them split open and topped with a pat of butter.

They can also be peeled, quartered, or halved and cooked with roast meat in the same way as ordinary potatoes.

Peel them just before cooking; if left to stand after peeling, their colour rapidly darkens.

Tomatoes

Should be washed thoroughly before use. Some recipes require peeled tomatoes. This is quite simple; place tomatoes in bowl, pour over sufficient boiling water to cover. Leave a moment, then drain and plunge into cold water. Skins will slip off easily.

Other recipes require juices and seeds to be discarded and only firm flesh of tomato used. To remove juices and seeds, halve tomatoes, squeeze out seeds and juice into basin. Strain juice, if desired, and use in place of some of liquid in recipe.

Baked Tomatoes

6 large tomatoes	2 to 3 table-
salt, pepper	spoons
1 teaspoon sugar	chopped
1 onion	parsley
	soft white breadcrumbs
	1 oz. (2 table- spoons) butter

Peel tomatoes, cut into firm slices. Arrange layer of tomatoes in greased ovenproof dish. Sprinkle with salt, pepper, sugar, finely chopped or grated onion and parsley. Top with another layer of tomatoes, sprinkle over any remaining onion, parsley, etc. Top with layer of breadcrumbs, dot with butter. Bake in moderately hot oven, Mark 5, 375°F., about 20 minutes. Delicious with roast meats.

Serves 4 to 6.

Tomato Concassé

1 lb. tomatoes	butter

2 shallots or 1
  small onion
	1 clove garlic
	  crushed

	salt, pepper

Plunge tomatoes into boiling water, then into cold water. Skin, seed and chop. Chop shallots or onion finely. Sauté shallots in little hot butter until softened, but not browned. Add tomatoes, garlic, salt and pepper to taste. Simmer gently, pressing mixture with fork occasionally.

Serve over chops, steaks or sausages; delicious as filling for omelets.

Turnips

Young, small turnips can be washed, peeled and cooked whole in boiling salted water to cover until soft (about 30 minutes). Bigger turnips can be cut into large dice or halved. Drain them well, toss in a little butter and serve sprinkled with chopped parsley.

Swede Turnips Peel, dice or cut into quarters and cook as above. They are best served mashed with salt, pepper and a little butter.

Stuffed Turnips

4 medium sized turnips	salt, pepper
1 tablespoon chopped parsley	$\frac{1}{2}$ lb. (2 cups) cooked peas
	2 oz. ($\frac{1}{4}$ cup) butter

Peel the turnips and cook whole in boiling water until tender. Drain and scoop out the centres, leaving the cases about $\frac{1}{2}$ in. thick. Heat the parsley, seasoning, peas and butter and fill the turnip cases.

Serves 4.

Zucchini or Courgettes

Small Italian marrows; French name is courgettes. Delicately and delightfully flavoured. To prepare, trim stems. Young, small zucchini can be cooked whole and unpeeled in boiling salted water until just tender. Serve with butter. Or, when cooked, slice and mix with some finely chopped mushrooms which have been sautéed until tender in a little butter.

Zucchini with Mushrooms

1 lb. zucchini	2 oz. ($\frac{1}{4}$ cup) butter
1 clove garlic	salt, pepper
4 oz. mushrooms	2 tablespoons chopped parsley
1 large onion	

Cut zucchini diagonally into 1 in. slices, crush garlic, slice mushrooms, chop onion. Melt butter in large frying pan, add vegetables, sauté until golden brown and tender. Season with salt and pepper. Sprinkle with chopped parsley and serve.

Herbs and Flavourings for Vegetables

Aubergine	Basil, dill, garlic, marjoram, oregano, rosemary.
Beetroot	Celery or caraway seeds, dill, mustard, tarragon, thyme.
Broccoli	Basil, garlic, lemon, mustard, nutmeg, onion, oregano.
Brussels Sprouts	Basil, celery seed, curry powder, lemon, mustard, oregano.
Cabbage	Dill, onion, nutmeg, chives, parsley, tarragon.
Carrots	Bayleaf, basil, curry powder, garlic, ginger, mint, nutmeg, onion, parsley, rosemary, thyme.
Cauliflower	Basil, caraway seed, chives, mace, lemon, oregano, parsley, rosemary.
Celery	Basil, onion, parsley, tarragon.
Green Beans	Basil, chilli powder, garlic, nutmeg, onion, tarragon, thyme.
Mushrooms	Basil, chives, garlic, parsley.
Peas	Chives, mint, garlic, onion.
Peppers	Basil, garlic, onion, oregano.
Spinach	Basil, garlic, lemon, nutmeg, onion, rosemary.
Tomatoes	Celery salt, chives, garlic, onion, oregano, parsley, tarragon, basil.

Salads

Salads can be a light, colourful accompaniment to a main meal, or substantial enough to be a main meal in themselves. All types of salad recipes are given here—old favourites, such as coleslaw, rice, potato— as well as wonderful new salads. And we've given a selection of good-tasting salad dressings.

Classic Green Salad

1 lettuce
salt, pepper

French dressing (see page 121)

Wash lettuce, dry thoroughly; place in plastic bag in refrigerator to crisp. At serving time, tear into small pieces; place in salad bowl. Sprinkle with salt and pepper; pour over sufficient dressing to moisten, then toss lightly.

There should be just enough dressing to lightly coat each leaf.

The classic green salad uses lettuce only; however, other greens—endive, young spinach, etc.— can be added for contrasting colours of green.

Prawn and Rice Salad

2 medium onions
3 oz. ($\frac{3}{8}$ cup) butter
4 oz. mushrooms
$\frac{1}{2}$ lb. ($2\frac{2}{3}$ cups) cooked long grain rice
3 oz. ($\frac{3}{4}$ cup) cooked peas
1 green pepper

2 tablespoons chopped parsley
4 oz. ham
1 lb. or 1 pint prawns (shrimps)
French dressing (see page 121)
shredded lettuce
sliced tomatoes and cucumber

Sauté finely chopped onions in 1 oz. (2 tablespoons) heated butter until lightly browned; remove from pan. Add remaining butter to pan. Fry sliced mushrooms in this until tender (about 3 minutes). Spoon onion and mushroom mixture into rice, adding pan juices as well. Mix in peas, chopped green pepper, parsley, chopped ham and shelled prawns (shrimps) (reserving about 1 dozen with tails still on for garnishing).

Mix together lightly, pour over enough French dressing to moisten; mix lightly. Arrange rice in ring on large platter. Surround with shredded lettuce and alternate slices of tomato and cucumber. Fill centre of ring with shredded lettuce, arrange reserved prawns in crown shape on top of rice ring.

Serves 4 to 6.

Creamy Potato Salad

2 lb. potatoes
$\frac{1}{4}$ pint ($\frac{1}{2}$ cup) French dressing (see page 121)
3 to 4 sticks sliced celery
few chopped spring onions

$\frac{1}{4}$ pint ($\frac{1}{2}$ cup) mayonnaise (see page 121)
4 tablespoons sour cream
$1\frac{1}{2}$ teaspoons prepared mustard
salt
$\frac{1}{4}$ small cucumber, diced

If using old potatoes, peel and cook until tender but still firm; if new potatoes, cook in their jackets and peel when cooked. Slice potatoes or cut into large dice while still warm. Put into bowl, pour over the French dressing, toss gently to coat potato pieces. Let stand 1 hour. Add celery and spring onions. Combine mayonnaise, sour cream and mustard, blend well; mix into potato, together with salt to taste; refrigerate. Just before serving mix in the cucumber.

Serves 4 to 6.

Indian Curry Salad

$\frac{1}{4}$ pint ($\frac{1}{2}$ cup) French dressing (see page 121)
$\frac{1}{2}$ teaspoon Worcestershire sauce
salt, pepper
$1\frac{1}{2}$ teaspoons curry powder

$\frac{1}{2}$ small cauliflower
$\frac{1}{4}$ lb. ($\frac{2}{3}$ cup) long grain rice, cooked
2 lb. or 2 pints prawns (shrimps)
1 green pepper
$\frac{1}{2}$ head celery, sliced
2 small onions, finely sliced

In basin combine French dressing, Worcestershire sauce, salt, pepper and curry powder. Cut cauliflower into small flowerets, mix with cooked, drained rice; pour the combined dressing over and marinate $1\frac{1}{2}$ hours, stirring occasionally. Shell prawns, cut into $\frac{1}{2}$ in. pieces. Cut green pepper into thin 2 in. strips. Stir remaining vegetables and prawns into rice. Refrigerate until required.

Serves 6 to 8.

Delicious Garden Salad

½ small cauliflower
1 large onion
1 small cucumber
1 large green pepper
1 large red pepper
½ lb. young spinach

1 teaspoon paprika
2 teaspoons sugar
1 teaspoon thyme
¼ pint (½ cup) French
  dressing (see
  page 121)
salt, pepper

Soak cauliflower in salted water 30 minutes, wash and drain, trim off leaves and stems leaving small flowerets. Dice onion and unpeeled cucumber; cut green and red peppers into thin strips. Wash and dry spinach, remove stalks, roughly chop leaves. Combine prepared vegetables with remaining ingredients, toss lightly with fork. Refrigerate well before serving.

Serves 6 to 8.

Haricot Bean Salad

1 lb. haricot beans
boiling salted water
2 oz. (⅓ cup) green
  olives
1 clove garlic,
  crushed

¼ pint (½ cup) French
  dressing (see
  page 121)
1 oz. (½ cup) chopped
  parsley
salt, pepper
2 oz. (⅓ cup) black
  olives

Cover beans well with water, allow to stand overnight. Drain, add to boiling salted water, boil 1 to 1½ hours or until tender, drain well; allow to become cold. Pit and slice green olives, add to beans with garlic, dressing and parsley. Season with salt and pepper, toss lightly to combine. Garnish with black olives. Refrigerate before serving.

Serves 6.

Chicken Salad with Lychees

4 lb. cooked chicken
4 to 5 sticks chopped
  celery
1 small green pepper,
  chopped

¼ pint (½ cup) French
  dressing (see
  page 121)
salt, pepper
large can lychee nuts
salad greens

Mayonnaise Dressing

6 tablespoons mayonnaise (see page 121)
2 tablespoons sour
  cream
2 teaspoons curry
  powder

2 tablespoons grated
  onion
2 tablespoons chopped
  parsley

Remove meat from chicken, chop into cubes. Add celery and green pepper, season with salt and pepper. Add French dressing, toss until all ingredients are lightly coated. Refrigerate ½ hour, tossing occasionally.

Heap chicken salad on to serving platter. Drain lychees, arrange on top of salad. If desired, some canned mandarin segments can be used for garnish; slip one segment into each lychee nut. Serve with salad greens. Serve the mayonnaise dressing separately to spoon over individual servings.
Mayonnaise Dressing Blend together all ingredients. Refrigerate until well chilled.

Serves 6.

Home-Style Potato Salad

2 lb. potatoes
2 medium carrots
1 dessertspoon finely
  chopped onion
1 teaspoon finely
  chopped mint

pinch cayenne pepper
4 tablespoons mayonnaise (see page 121)
2 oz. (½ cup) cooked
  peas

Peel and dice potatoes and carrots. Cook in boiling salted water until tender; drain and allow to cool. In a basin combine onion, mint, cayenne and mayonnaise, mix well; fold in potatoes, carrots and cooked peas. Refrigerate before serving. Spoon servings into crisp lettuce leaves.

Serves 6.

Party Chicken Salad

¼ lb. mushrooms
¼ pint (½ cup) French
  dressing (see
  page 121)
2 small lettuce
1 cooked chicken
  (3½ lb.)

1 small can artichoke
  hearts
1 small red pepper
½ lb. (2 cups) sliced
  cooked green beans
salt, pepper
2 oz. (¼ cup) slivered
  almonds

Slice mushrooms thinly, place in shallow dish. Pour French dressing over, stand 1 hour, stirring occasionally. Wash and drain whole lettuce, discarding outer leaves. Cut each lettuce crossways into 6 wedges, arrange in base of large deep salad bowl. Discard bones and skin of chicken, chop meat roughly. Drain and lightly wash artichoke hearts, slice pepper into thin strips.

In separate basin, combine chicken meat, artichoke hearts, cooked beans, strips of pepper, mushrooms and dressing. Toss lightly, adding salt and pepper to taste. Refrigerate until ready to serve. Toast almond slivers under grill until lightly brown, remove from heat. To serve, spoon chicken mixture over lettuce in large salad bowl, toss lightly. Sprinkle over toasted almonds.

Serves 6.

Waldorf Salad

3 red skinned eating apples
juice of 2 lemons
6 sticks celery
2 oz. (½ cup) chopped walnuts
lettuce leaves
mayonnaise (see page 121)

Core and dice unpeeled apples, sprinkle with lemon juice. Add sliced celery and walnuts. Toss together with enough mayonnaise to moisten thoroughly. Pile into salad bowl lined with lettuce leaves.
Serves 4 to 6.

Caesar Salad

2 small lettuce (Romaine)
2 slices bread
1 clove garlic, crushed
1 oz. (2 tablespoons) butter
2 rashers bacon
chopped parsley
grated Parmesan cheese

Dressing

¼ pint (½ cup) French dressing (see page 121)
1 teaspoon salt
1 coddled egg
1 teaspoon prepared mustard

Wash lettuce well, discard tough outer leaves. Tear leaves into pieces, mix with dressing. Cut bread into ½ in. cubes. Brown cubes with garlic in hot butter. Cook chopped bacon separately until crisp. Drain on absorbent paper.

Scatter bread croutons over salad with bacon pieces, chopped parsley and grated cheese.
Dressing   To coddle egg, gently lower egg into boiling water, boil 1 minute. Remove egg from shell; combine with remaining ingredients. Blend well.
Serves 4 to 6.

Oregano-Tomato Salad

1 lb. firm tomatoes
2 small white onions
1 teaspoon ground oregano
1 teaspoon sugar
1 teaspoon salt
freshly ground pepper
2 tablespoons dry white wine
2 tablespoons oil
chopped parsley

Wash, dry and slice tomatoes; peel and thinly slice onions. Layer tomatoes and onions in bowl. In another bowl mix together seasonings, add oil and wine; stir until well mixed. Pour over tomatoes and onions, refrigerate several hours. Serve sprinkled with chopped parsley. Garnish, if desired, with black olives.
Serves 6.

Prawn (Shrimp) and Green Bean Salad

1 lb. green beans
salted water
2 tablespoons French dressing (see page 121)
½ lb. or ½ pint shelled prawns (shrimps)
little extra French dressing
2 hard-boiled eggs

Top, tail and string beans, cook in boiling salted water until tender. Drain, pour the 2 tablespoons French dressing over. Toss lightly, arrange on platter.

Top with shelled prawns and sprinkle these with a little additional French dressing. Garnish with the eggs cut into quarters.
Serves 6.

Ratatouille

3 to 4 tablespoons oil
2 large onions
2 cloves garlic
2 small eggplants (aubergines)
4 zucchini (courgettes)
2 green peppers
1 small head celery
1 lb. ripe tomatoes
1 teaspoon dried basil
1½ teaspoons salt
pepper

Heat oil in shallow pan, add sliced onions and crushed garlic; cook slowly until soft. Add the eggplant, cut into cubes, sliced zucchini, peppers cut into strips and sliced celery. Mix well, cook quickly 5 minutes. Add peeled, chopped tomatoes and seasonings, cover and simmer about 1 hour, stirring occasionally. Then remove cover and allow mixture to cook down until most of liquid has evaporated and mixture is thick. Serve cold.
Serves 4 to 6.

Asparagus Rice Salad

½ lb. (1⅓ cups) long grain rice
boiling salted water
1 large onion
1 oz. (2 tablespoons) butter
7 oz. can asparagus tips
2 tablespoons chopped parsley
2 tablespoons French dressing (see page 121)
salt, pepper

Add rice gradually to large quantity of boiling salted water, boil rapidly 10 minutes or until tender. Drain, allow to cool. Dice onion, sauté in butter 2 to 3 minutes until tender (do not brown). Drain asparagus well, discard liquid.

Add onion mixture, asparagus, parsley and French dressing to rice, season with salt and pepper, toss lightly.
Serves 6.

Chicken Salad with Lychees—perfect for a summer luncheon, as shown with Oregano Tomato Salad and classic Green Salad. Flamed Caramel Pineapple—delightfully informal dessert; guests cook their own. It's a perfect dessert for a summer barbecue.

Almond Coleslaw

½ medium cabbage	¼ pint (½ cup) mayonnaise (see page 121)
2 sticks celery	
½ cucumber	1 tablespoon vinegar
½ green pepper	salt, pepper
1 large onion	1 oz. (¼ cup) toasted flaked almonds

Wash cabbage; discard outer leaves and hard central stalk. Shred finely. Chop celery, slice cucumber; thinly slice pepper, finely chop onion. Combine prepared vegetables in bowl.

Mix together mayonnaise and vinegar; season to taste with salt and pepper. Add mayonnaise mixture to vegetables, and mix with two forks until evenly coated. Top salad with almonds.

Serves 4 to 6

Coleslaw

½ medium cabbage	4 sticks celery
2 carrots	1 red skinned apple
3 to 4 spring onions	

Dressing

1 tablespoon lemon juice	good pinch cayenne
¼ pint (½ cup) mayonnaise (see page 121)	½ tablespoon salt
	freshly ground black pepper
½ teaspoon dry mustard	3 tablespoons cream

Remove stalk and shred cabbage very finely; grate carrots. Cut celery and spring onions, including green parts, into diagonal pieces. Wash, but do not peel apple, core and cut into dice. Mix together all prepared vegetables and apple and add enough dressing to give even coating. Mix well.
Dressing Place all dressing ingredients in small basin, mix well.

Serves 4 to 6.

Rice Coleslaw

½ medium cabbage shredded finely	1 medium sized onion
6 oz. (1 cup) long grain rice	10 oz. can whole kernel corn
½ small red and ½ small green pepper, chopped	¼ pint (½ cup) French dressing (see page 121)
6 to 8 sliced radishes	½ teaspoon dry mustard
1 teaspoon salt	pinch pepper
	1 dessertspoon sugar
	1 clove garlic, crushed

Cook rice in usual way, drain well. Place cabbage into large bowl. Add rice, red and green peppers, radishes, grated onion and drained corn. Place remaining ingredients into screwtop jar, shake well. Pour over rice and vegetables, toss thoroughly.

Serves 6.

Smoked Oyster Salad

½ lb. (1⅓ cups) long grain rice	1 teaspoon curry powder
¼ pint (½ cup) French dressing (see page 121)	6 chives or spring onions (scallions)
	1 red or green pepper
	2 cans smoked oysters

Cook rice in usual way, drain well. Combine French dressing and curry powder in small jar, shake well.

Arrange rice in serving dish, pour dressing over; fork dressing lightly through rice. Cool.

Chop celery, chives and pepper. Add to rice with the drained smoked oysters, toss lightly.

Serves 4 to 6.

Mushroom Salad

1 lb. very fresh mushrooms	chopped parsley
salt	juice of ½ lemon
garlic	freshly ground pepper
oil	lettuce leaves

Wipe mushrooms, slice finely. Place little salt in bowl, rub bowl with garlic. Add mushrooms, pour over sufficient oil to moisten. Mix lightly, set aside until mushrooms have absorbed most of oil (about 5 minutes).

Sprinkle with lots of chopped parsley, add lemon juice and pepper. Taste mixture, add a little more salt, pepper, lemon juice if needed. Serve on lettuce.

Serves 4.

Egg and Bacon Salad

¼ lb. bacon	1 clove garlic, crushed
1 lettuce	3 to 4 tablespoons French dressing (see page 121)
2 to 3 chives or spring onions (scallions), chopped	
3 to 4 sticks celery, diced	2 tomatoes
	4 quartered hard boiled eggs

Cook bacon until crisp, crumble into pieces. Tear lettuce into bite-sized pieces, place in salad bowl. Add half the crumbled bacon, with chives and celery. Add garlic to French dressing, shake well, pour over salad. Toss. Garnish with tomatoes and eggs cut into wedges. Top with remaining bacon.

Serves 4.

Salad Dressings

A simple salad can become something really special when you add a well-flavoured dressing.

Mayonnaise

2 egg-yolks	1½ teaspoons vinegar
½ teaspoon salt	½ pint (1 cup) olive or
½ teaspoon dry mustard	salad oil
	½ teaspoon lemon juice

Rinse bowl with hot water; dry well. Put in egg-yolks, salt, mustard and 1 teaspoon vinegar. Beat vigorously with beater or at low speed with electric mixer; add oil, drop by drop, until a little more than a quarter of the oil has been added. Add ½ teaspoon vinegar, still beating, then very slowly pour in remainder of oil in thin stream, beating continually. When all oil has been added, add lemon juice.

Cooked mayonnaise

2 tablespoons vinegar	½ teaspoon salt
2 tablespoons water	½ to 1 teaspoon dry
2 tablespoons sugar	mustard
½ oz. (1 tablespoon)	1 beaten egg
butter	

Combine all ingredients in saucepan, stir over low heat until butter melts and mixture thickens slightly. Remove from heat, cool.

French Dressing

3 parts olive or salad	½ teaspoon salt
oil	½ teaspoon freshly
1 part white vinegar	ground pepper

Place all ingredients in screw-top jar, shake thoroughly before pouring over salad.
NOTE: Crushed garlic, dry or prepared mustard or chopped herbs can be added, if desired. The garlic, salt, pepper and mustard are first mixed with the oil, then the vinegar is added. Herbs are added last.

The above are the classic proportions for French dressing. However, equal parts of oil and vinegar can be used, if you like a less oily dressing.

Russian Dressing (1)

½ pint (1 cup) mayon-	1 to 2 teaspoons
naise	chopped chives
1½ tablespoons chilli	
sauce	

Blend chilli sauce and chives into mayonnaise; a little chopped red pepper or canned pimento can also be added. Use with egg or vegetable salads or with fish.
NOTE: Strength of chilli sauce varies greatly. With a mild, American chilli sauce, the above quantity is correct. If using a hot chilli sauce, add only ½ teaspoon at first; then taste, and add a little more if desired.

Russian Dressing (2)

½ pint (1 cup) mayon-	1 to 2 teaspoons bottled
naise	horseradish sauce
3 to 4 tablespoons	
finely chopped	
cooked beetroot	

Combine mayonnaise and beetroot, blend in bottled horseradish sauce or relish.

Thousand Island Dressing

½ pint (1 cup) mayon-	1 tablespoon finely
naise	chopped green olives
1 tablespoon chilli	1 dessertspoon finely
sauce	chopped chives

Combine all ingredients, mix well. Good with meat or fish salads. See Russian Dressing for note on chilli sauce.

Aioli

2 egg-yolks	3 teaspoons lemon juice
2 cloves garlic	salt, pepper
½ pint (1 cup) oil	

Beat egg-yolks in bowl with crushed garlic. Add oil, drop by drop. When half the oil has been used, add half the lemon juice, then beat in remaining oil, drop by drop. Season with salt and pepper and add remaining lemon juice.

Green Goddess Dressing

1 clove garlic	2 tablespoons cream
1 oz. (½ cup) parsley	3 dessertspoons tar-
2 tablespoons chopped	ragon vinegar
chives	1 dessertspoon anchovy
½ pint (1 cup) mayon-	paste
naise	

Crush garlic; finely chop parsley. Combine all ingredients and stir until dressing is smooth. Serve with seafood salads.

International cookery

Every year more and more people spend their holidays travelling abroad and eating unfamiliar dishes. Once back home, they like to re-capture some of the enjoyment and try out for themselves some of the interesting food of other countries.

Many people too, enjoy dining in Chinese and Indian restaurants, and in this chapter—apart from popular Continental dishes we give you some very good recipes for dishes from the South Pacific, China and India.

Unusual ingredients are explained or alternatives given. Green ginger is used in some dishes and this is quite often available, but if ground ginger is substituted, use only $\frac{1}{4}$ of the amount specified.

The food of each country can be presented as a complete menu. Quantities given will serve 4 to 6. The Hawaiian menu is suggested as an outdoor party, a wider choice of dishes is given and quantities will serve 8.

Germany

German cooking varies from district to district and, as with Switzerland, the cooking in the various sections is influenced by the other countries on the borders. Recipes given here are representative of Bavaria, Southern Germany.

German food is hearty, and not highly spiced. Black and rye breads are popular; potato and cabbage are part of everyday meals. Beer, wine and Schnapps are the popular drinks. Kirsch and Kummel are famous German liqueurs.

Sauerkraut

2 15 oz. cans sauerkraut
2 tablespoons oil
6 oz. fat pork in one piece
1 medium onion
$\frac{1}{2}$ teaspoon whole peppercorns
1 dessertspoon flour
1 pint (2 cups) water
1 large potato

Drain sauerkraut, wash lightly under cold running water. Heat oil in large saucepan, add pork, cook few minutes on both sides. Add chopped onion; cook, covered, over low heat until soft but not brown. Lightly mix in sauerkraut, peppercorns and flour; add 1 pint (2 cups) water. Bring to boil; cover, cook for 30 minutes, stirring occasionally. Peel potato, grate finely, stir into mixture. Continue cooking, stirring occasionally, further 30 minutes, adding little more water if necessary. Remove pork; discard.

Serve sauerkraut hot or cold.

NOTE: To keep sauerkraut a good colour, place a sheet of plain white paper on top of mixture, under lid, during boiling.

Roast Pork

1 leg or loin of pork
salt, pepper
1 large onion
1 large carrot
approx. 1 pint (2 cups) boiling water

Wipe meat with clean cloth, score skin into small squares with sharp knife (or have butcher do this for you). Sprinkle over plenty of salt and pepper. Place meat skin-side down in large, greased baking dish. Add peeled and sliced onion and carrot, carefully pour over boiling water. Bake in hot oven until meat is tender (allow approximately 30 to 35 minutes per lb.). You may need to add more boiling water during cooking. Halfway through cooking time turn meat so that skin is uppermost.

Serve with potato balls and sauerkraut.

Flamed Caramel Pineapple—delightfully informal dessert; guests cook their own. It's a perfect dessert for a summer barbecue.

Potato Balls

1 lb. potatoes	1 teaspoon salt
½ lb. (2 cups) plain flour	1 large or two small eggs

Steam potatoes in their jackets over boiling water until cooked. Cool, refrigerate overnight. Next day, peel and mash well.

Sift together flour and salt, add alternately to potato with lightly beaten egg. Knead well. Mixture should not be sticky. Roll mixture into small balls, and drop gently into large saucepan of boiling water. Boil steadily, uncovered, 15 minutes. Drain, serve immediately.

Apple Strudel

Pastry

½ lb. (2 cups) plain flour	approx. ¼ pint (½ cup) warm water
½ teaspoon salt	
2 oz. (¼ cup) butter	

Sift flour and salt into bowl, rub in softened butter. Add a little warm water gradually, kneading to soft dough. Turn out on lightly floured surface, continue kneading and adding water until mixture is smooth and shiny. This should take about 15 minutes. Hit dough a few times with heavy wooden spoon during kneading. Form dough into a ball, place in warmed bowl or saucepan. Cover and stand in warm place 1 hour.

Filling

4 or 5 cooking apples	extra sugar
4 tablespoons sugar	extra cinnamon
finely grated rind 1 small lemon	½ pint (1 cup) sour cream
2 teaspoons cinnamon	melted butter
2 oz. (⅓ cup) sultanas	icing sugar

Filling Peel, core and slice apples very thinly, stir in sugar, lemon rind and cinnamon, mix well. Place sultanas in small bowl, add enough hot water to cover, set aside.

Divide pastry into thirds; roll each piece out very thinly on floured surface. Spread ⅓ apple mixture in centre of dough, sprinkle over a little extra sugar and cinnamon. Drain sultanas, pat dry; sprinkle a few over apples. Lightly spread ⅓ of sour cream over mixture. Roll up pastry into a long shape and seal edges.

Prepare remaining two rolls in the same way. Grease a deep 8 in. round tin. Place rolls side by side in tin, curving them carefully to fit. Bake in moderately slow oven, Mark 3 or 325°F., approximately 1¾ hours. Brush a little melted butter over strudel several times during cooking.

When golden brown and crisp, remove from oven, glaze again with melted butter. Leave in tin 15 minutes before turning out on to serving plate. Sift over a little icing sugar. Serve with whipped cream.

Hawaii

Hawaiian food is very similar to that of other islands in the South Pacific. All types of fish are easily available; pork is popular—particularly for a luau, or feast, when it is cooked in a pit, under the ground. Bananas, baked, are eaten as a vegetable, in addition to sweet potatoes or yams.

Tropical Dip

¼ pint (½ cup) mayonnaise (see page 121)	1 teaspoon dry mustard
⅛ pint (2 tablespoons) whipping cream	lemon juice
1 tablespoon bottled horseradish relish	salt, pepper

Combine whipped cream, mayonnaise, horseradish relish and dry mustard; blend well. Season to taste with lemon juice, salt and pepper. Refrigerate. Place into serving bowl. Place all kinds of interesting titbits in sauce, such as shelled prawns, oysters, ripe olives, water chestnuts, raw vegetables, etc. Each guest arms himself with a cocktail stick and 'fishes' in the sauce.

Makes approx. ⅜ pint.

Avocado Chicken Salad

3 avocados	1 teaspoon paprika
3 to 4 lb. steamed chicken	½ teaspoon nutmeg
1 cucumber	1 teaspoon salt
4 sticks celery	½ teaspoon pepper
½ green pepper	¼ pint (½ cup) cream
2 oz. (¼ cup) blanched slivered almonds	2 tablespoons mayonnaise (see page 121)

Peel, stone and slice avocados. Remove chicken meat from bones. Cut meat into 1 in. cubes. Slice cucumber, celery and green pepper and layer in dish or bowl with toasted almonds, chicken and half the avocado slices.

Blend paprika, nutmeg, salt and pepper with

cream, mayonnaise and lemon juice; pour over chicken and vegetables. Decorate with remaining avocado slices, sprinkle with extra paprika.

NOTE: If preparing this dish in advance, dip avocado slices in lemon juice so they will keep their fresh colour.

Baked Honeyed Pork

1 leg pork	2 teaspoons ground
2 tablespoons grated	ginger
green ginger	2 teaspoons salt
2 tablespoons oil	3 to 4 tablespoons
	honey

Get the butcher to score the pork thoroughly. Run knife between the skin and meat to form a pocket. Using long-bladed knife, spread grated green ginger into pocket. In basin mix oil, ground ginger and salt. Place pork in baking dish, brush leg with oil and ginger mixture. Bake in moderate oven, Mark 4, 350°F., allowing 30 minutes per lb.; brush occasionally with remaining oil and ginger mixture. Fifteen minutes before the end of cooking time, brush leg completely with honey. Serve hot or cold.

Hawaiian Chicken

4 tablespoons soy sauce	4 oz. ($\frac{1}{2}$ cup or 1 stick)
$\frac{1}{4}$ pint ($\frac{1}{2}$ cup) white	butter
wine	2 onions
juice 1 lemon	flour seasoned with
1 clove garlic	salt and pepper
$\frac{1}{2}$ teaspoon curry	$\frac{3}{4}$ lb. (2 cups) rice
powder	2 large cans pineapple
$\frac{1}{2}$ teaspoon ground	slices
ginger	1 oz. (2 tablespoons)
$\frac{1}{4}$ teaspoon pepper	butter, extra
4 lb. chicken pieces	2 oz. ($\frac{1}{4}$ cup) toasted
	slivered almonds
	1 red pepper

Mix together soy sauce, half the white wine, lemon juice, crushed garlic, curry powder, ginger and pepper. Pour over chicken, marinate several hours, turning occasionally. Melt butter in frying pan, add sliced onions, cook until golden brown, remove onions. Dry chicken, coat with seasoned flour. Cook in frying pan until brown. Add onions and marinade, cover and simmer gently 45 minutes or until tender, uncovering pan for the last 15 minutes.

Meanwhile, cook and drain rice and keep hot. Cut pineapple slices in half and brown in extra butter, also fry chopped pepper until tender.

To serve, mix rice, toasted almonds and pepper. Heap on large serving platter, arrange chicken pieces and pineapple slices round edge. Add remaining white wine to pan drippings, heat well and pour over.

Flamed Caramel Pineapple

Take a ripe pineapple, cut into 4 pieces, cutting carefully through the green top. With sharp knife, slice off the hard core. Cut pineapple down into wedges, then run a knife along base of wedges, releasing them from the shell.

(If the pineapples are not too large, allow 1 pineapple for 4 persons).

Take another pineapple, cut off top about quarter-way down. Hollow out inside of pineapple to take a small metal bowl. (The hollowed-out pineapple pieces can be reserved and used to replenish the pineapple quarters as they empty.)

Place metal bowl in position. Place hollowed-out pineapple in centre of heat-proof dish (a large wooden plate is good), arrange pineapple quarters decoratively around.

Arrange small bowls of rum or brandy, brown sugar and whipped cream round dish. Have a small fork and plate for each guest.

When ready to serve the dessert, three-quarters fill metal bowl with methylated spirit and set aflame.

Guests use fork to spear a juicy piece of pineapple, dip it in the rum, roll it in brown sugar, then hold it over the flame until the sugar caramelizes —it will take about a second. Then dip in the whipped cream—and eat!

Strawberries are delicious served this way, too, but have more flavour if allowed to stand in rum 10 to 15 minutes. Serve small bowls of rum-soaked strawberries round the pineapple.

NOTE: When lit, methylated spirit will burn for some time. If necessary to use more spirit, put it in another perfectly clean bowl; do not add more spirit to that already burning; do not pour fresh spirit into a hot bowl.

Bananas with Rum

8 bananas	2 oz. ($\frac{1}{3}$ cup) dark
1 oz. (2 tablespoons)	brown sugar
butter	3 tablespoons rum
juice of 1 lemon	cream

Peel and halve the bananas and arrange in a well buttered dish. Mix the lemon juice with 2 tablespoons water and pour over the fruit. Sprinkle with the sugar.

Bake in a moderately hot oven, Mark 5, 375°F. for 20 minutes. Add the rum and cook another 2 minutes.

Serve hot with cream.

Scandinavia

The smorgasbord—or 'cold table'—is part of the hospitality of all Scandinavian countries. Norway, Denmark, Sweden, all have their own individual versions—but, basically, the cold table of each country offers a selection of hot and cold dishes, as set out below.

Scandinavian cooking is simple. Fish of all types is widely used; potatoes, beetroot, cucumber are favourite vegetables; dill is used often for seasoning.

Smorgasbord

The Smorgasbord is said to have originated long ago at Swedish country parties, to which each housewife brought the speciality of her own kitchen. All these dishes were arranged on a long table round which the guests walked, filling their plates several times.

A Smorgasbord can be as comprehensive and varied as desired, with rich and inviting delicacies; or it can be a simple, well-chosen and well-prepared selection, comprising only a few dishes.

There is a definite rule in the procedure of dishes. Fish dishes begin the meal; favourites are pickled herrings, anchovies, herring salad—with them might be served potatoes flavoured with dill. A hot, baked fish dish might also be offered.

Then come the meats; meatballs—very important to a Smorgasbord—smoked sausages, ham, roasted pork with apple sauce and prunes. And so it goes on . . . ending with cheese.

A typical Smorgasbord might comprise a wide variety of fish dishes such as herrings, sardines, anchovies; small meatballs, sliced ham, pâté and other meats; lobster or potato salad, cucumber, radishes, pickled beetroot, mushrooms; egg dishes, tiny omelets with assorted fillings; plain boiled potatoes, cheese and assorted breads with butter.

A simple Smorgasbord can be prepared by choosing a selection from any of these dishes. A whole ham, sliced, or a sliced canned ham; herrings (from the delicatessen) with pickled onion and chopped gherkin; potato salad; smoked oysters; canned salmon with white onion rings, chopped shallots and a light vinegar dressing; smoked tuna; slices of cold roast beef, pork, lamb or seasoned veal; sliced pickled beetroot; salami or other Continental sausage; canned sardines; condiments, such as chutney, etc.; smoked salmon with scrambled eggs; cheese board.

Lamb in Cabbage

3 lb. leg of lamb	2 teaspoons
½ large cabbage	peppercorns
1 oz. (2 tablespoons)	2 medium carrots
butter	1½ pints (3 cups) water
2 oz. (½ cup) flour	or stock
salt	1 tablespoon finely
	chopped parsley

Trim meat, cut into large cubes; do not remove bones, these add extra flavour to the stock. Remove coarse outer leaves from cabbage. Cut cabbage into thick segments, removing centre core. Melt butter in large saucepan. Place alternate layers of meat and cabbage in pan, starting with meat and finishing with cabbage. Sprinkle flour, salt and peppercorns between each layer. Place peeled, sliced carrots on top. Pour water or stock down side of saucepan. Bring to boil, cover, reduce heat and simmer 1½ to 2 hours or until meat is tender. Shake pan occasionally; do not stir during cooking to avoid disturbing the arranged layers. Season to taste; sprinkle with chopped parsley. Serve with boiled potatoes.

NOTE: Peppercorns can be tied in muslin bag for easy removal after cooking.

Strawberry Mousse

1 lb. strawberries	3 oz. (⅜ cup) castor
1 dessertspoon water	(superfine) sugar
½ oz. (2 tablespoons or	½ pint (1 cup) whipping
2 packets) gelatine	cream
2 egg-whites	1 tablespoon lemon
	juice

Wash and hull strawberries, mash well. There should be about ½ pint purée. Add gelatine to water, stand 5 minutes, dissolve over hot water. Beat egg-whites until soft peaks form, gradually add sugar, beating until dissolved. Whip cream until soft peaks form; fold into egg-white mixture. Add strawberries, lemon juice and gelatine, fold in lightly. Pour into wetted mould, or into individual serving dishes. Refrigerate until set.

Cheeseboard has pride of place on a Smorgasbord. Offer a variety of cheeses. Shown here are, from back, Cheddar, Danish Tilsit, Edam, Blue Cheese.

China

The Oriental, it is said, 'eats with his tongue'—flavour is all-important. And Chinese food, with its subtle, well-balanced blending of flavours, has become very popular.

There are five main schools of Chinese cooking, named after the areas in which they originated. They are:

Canton Has succulent pork, chicken and duck dishes, delicious soups. Quick-frying is the favourite method of cooking; fried rice and crisp noodles are popular. Cantonese dishes, served with a variety of sauces, are delicately flavoured, not highly seasoned. Because the majority of Chinese restaurants outside China are owned or operated by Southern Chinese, Cantonese food has become better known throughout the world than the other styles of Chinese cooking.

Fukien Sucking pig is a favourite dish; soups of many varieties are served between courses. Popular Spring Roll is from this school.

Szechuen Also famous for soups. Foods, generally, are hot and highly spiced.

Shanghai Concentrates on steamed, rather than fried foods. More highly spiced than Cantonese, but less than Szechuenese.

Peking Peking-Duck is a world-renowned dish; so is Bird's-Nest Soup. Food is well spiced, of great variety.

Crab and Sweet Corn Soup

1 dessertspoon oil	$1\frac{1}{4}$ pints ($2\frac{1}{2}$ cups)
$\frac{1}{4}$ clove garlic	chicken stock
1 thin slice green	1 egg-white
ginger	1 tablespoon cornflour
$6\frac{1}{2}$ oz. can crab meat	(cornstarch)
1 dessertspoon dry	salt, pepper
sherry	
1 small can cream-style	
sweet corn	

Heat oil in large heavy saucepan, add crushed garlic, finely chopped ginger and crab meat which has been drained and shredded. Fry quickly 1 minute, stirring constantly. Add sherry, corn and stock. Bring to boil, reduce heat and simmer 5 minutes. Whisk egg-white lightly, stir into soup with fork. Mix cornflour (cornstarch) with a little cold water; add to soup, stirring constantly until mixture thickens. Add salt and pepper to taste. Mix well, serve immediately.

Prawn (Shrimp) Omelet

2 oz. mushrooms	1 lb. or 1 pint prawns
oil	(shrimps)
3 to 4 chives	8 eggs
2 sticks celery	10 oz. can bean sprouts
	salt, pepper

Sauce

1 dessertspoon corn-flour (cornstarch)	$\frac{1}{2}$ pint (1 cup) chicken stock
2 tablespoons cold water	1 teaspoon sugar
	1 tablespoon soy sauce
	salt

Chop mushrooms, cook in a little hot oil until tender; drain, set aside. Chop chives and celery finely; chop shelled prawns, if large. Beat eggs lightly, as for omelet. Add prawns, chives, celery, mushrooms and drained bean sprouts. Add seasonings and mix lightly. Heat a little oil in fry-pan, pour in enough omelet mixture to make small omelets about 5 in. in diameter. (Several can cook at the same time.) When firm on one side, turn, cook other side. Stack on warm plate while cooking remainder of omelets; keep warm. To serve, stack 3 omelets on top of each other; for each serving spoon sauce over.
Sauce Blend cornflour (cornstarch) with cold water. Place remaining ingredients in small saucepan, bring to boil. Stir in blended cornflour. Cook, stirring, until sauce boils and thickens.

Chicken and Almonds

4 chicken breasts	$\frac{1}{2}$ red pepper
$1\frac{1}{2}$ teaspoons salt	4 oz. mushrooms
1 tablespoon cornflour (cornstarch)	$\frac{1}{2}$ 10 oz. can water chestnuts
1 egg-white	2 tablespoons chopped
$1\frac{1}{2}$ tablespoons sherry	chives
oil	1 oz. (2 to 3 table-spoons) toasted
4 oz. green beans	almonds
2 sticks celery	

Sauce

$\frac{1}{2}$ pint (1 cup) water	1 tablespoon soy sauce
1 chicken stock cube	1 tablespoon cornflour

Bone chicken breasts, cut meat into $\frac{1}{2}$ in. cubes. Combine chicken pieces, salt, cornflour, egg-white and sherry in bowl. Heat oil in fry-pan. Deep-fry chicken until just changing colour;

drain. String beans (or use quick-frozen beans). Cut beans, celery and pepper into 1 in. strips; parboil 5 minutes. Slice mushrooms. Drain water chestnuts, cut in half. Pour off excess liquid from pan and leave enough to sauté all vegetables together. Add prepared vegetables and return chicken to pan. Season to taste, heat through thoroughly. Pour sauce over chicken mixture. Arrange on warm serving dish, sprinkle with toasted almonds.

Serves 4 to 6.

Sauce Combine water, crumbled chicken stock cube, soy sauce and cornflour (cornstarch) in saucepan; blend well. Stir over low heat until sauce boils and thickens, simmer 2 minutes.

Almond Junket

1½ dessertspoons gelatine
¼ pint (½ cup) cold water
¾ pint (1½ cups) evaporated milk
3 oz. (⅜ cup) sugar
¼ pint (½ cup) boiling water
few drops almond essence

Soften gelatine in cold water, add sugar. Pour boiling water over and stir until sugar and gelatine have dissolved. Add milk and almond essence, stir well. Pour mixture into four individual serving dishes, set aside until cool, then refrigerate until firm. Top with sliced preserved ginger, with a little of the ginger syrup poured over.

Italy

Like most European countries, Italy draws heavily on the natural products of her provinces—the luscious fruits and olives, the wonderful seafood which abounds in the waters bordering her shores.

Antipasto—the equivalent of the French hors d'oeuvre—is a pleasant start to any meal and, with a bowl of soup to follow, can be a complete meal in itself. Pasta is used in many forms.

Italian wines are very cheap in their own country, and very pleasant; the Chianti is world-famous. Wine is drunk with all main meals, and the meals are usually preceded by a glass of sweet or dry vermouth or Campari, the latter, a deep red and tangy bitters, and one of the most famous Italian aperitifs.

Antipasto

8 oz. can tuna
mayonnaise (see page 121)
1 tablespoon capers
thinly sliced celery
sliced peeled tomatoes
sliced salami
thinly sliced ham
black and green olives
anchovy fillets
quarters of hard boiled eggs
canned artichoke hearts

Arrange drained tuna (in one piece) in centre of large, round platter. Coat with mayonnaise, sprinkle with capers. Arrange remaining ingredients in decorative pattern round tuna.

Bechamel Sauce

1 bayleaf
parsley stalks
1 slice onion
4 peppercorns
sprig of thyme or parsley
½ pint (1 cup) milk
½ oz. (1 tablespoon) butter
1 tablespoon flour
salt, pepper

Tomato Sauce

1 dessertspoon oil
1 onion
1 clove garlic
2 large ripe tomatoes
2 tablespoons tomato paste
salt, pepper
bayleaf

Cannelloni

Batter

4 oz. (1 cup) plain flour
pinch salt
1 egg
½ pint (1 cup) milk

Filling

oil for frying
1 onion
1 clove garlic
1 lb. minced (ground) steak
1 tablespoon flour
¼ pint (½ cup) red wine
pinch mixed herbs
salt, pepper
1 dessertspoon tomato paste
1 teaspoon paprika

Batter Sift flour and salt into bowl. Make well in centre, add egg. Mix with wooden spoon, blending in a little of the flour from the side. When mixture begins to thicken, gradually begin to add the milk, blending thoroughly. Heat a little oil in small frying pan. Pour in enough batter to cover base. Tilt pan until batter spreads. Keep pancake as thin as possible. When cooked on one side, turn and cook the other side. Remove from pan, cook the next pancake, stacking them as you cook.

Filling Put a little oil in saucepan; when hot gently sauté chopped onion and crushed garlic. When tender add the meat, cook until brown, stirring occasionally with fork. Add the flour blended with the wine, stir well. Add remaining ingredients, simmer gently ½ to ¾ hour until liquid is absorbed.

Divide mixture between pancakes, roll up. Arrange in casserole.

Bechamel Sauce   Place bayleaf, parsley stalks, onion slice, peppercorns and thyme in saucepan, add milk. Bring slowly to boiling point, remove from heat, stand 5 minutes. Melt butter in saucepan, remove from heat, add flour, stir until smooth, gradually add strained milk, stirring constantly. Return to heat, stir until sauce boils and thickens. Season to taste with salt and pepper. Pour over pancakes.

Tomato Sauce   Heat oil, fry chopped onion and crushed garlic until tender but not brown. Add skinned, chopped tomatoes, tomato paste, salt, pepper and bayleaf. Simmer gently 20 minutes.

Spoon carefully over the white sauce.

If desired, sprinkle with a little grated cheese. Bake pancakes in hot oven, Mark 7, 425°F., 10 to 15 minutes.

Zabaglione

5 egg-yolks
1½ oz. (3 tablespoons) sugar
¼ pint (½ cup) marsala

Beat egg-yolks and sugar in top of double boiler. Add the marsala, and cook, beating constantly, until thick and foamy, approximately 10 minutes. Serve warm. Sponge fingers are a good accompaniment.

India

Through the centuries, Arabia, Persia, Central Asia and Mongolia have all contributed towards the unique cuisine of India. The success of Indian cookery rests on the subtle use of a variety of spices. The art of curry-making lies not in hot spicing but in the delicacy of flavour blending.

In such a vast country, with varying climatic and agricultural conditions, it is natural to expect a great variation in curries, also. In the north, curries are mild—like those of Pakistan. The farther south you travel, the hotter the curries become. In Madras, chillies grow abundantly and are used generously; Madras curries, therefore, are much hotter than those of the north.

Rice is the traditional accompaniment to curry. A choice of side dishes or sambals can also be served; choose from coconut, plumped raisins, crumbled bacon, chopped hard-boiled eggs, cucumber in yoghurt, wedges of lemon, bananas dipped in lemon juice, chopped dried apricots, peanuts.

Beef Vindaloo

2 large onions
3 cloves garlic
2 red chillies or
¼ teaspoon cayenne pepper
1 teaspoon ground ginger
2 tablespoons curry powder
1 tablespoon vinegar
salt
2 lb. topside or round of beef
1 dessertspoon butter
1 teaspoon turmeric
¼ teaspoon dry mustard
3 cardamom seeds (crushed)
1 teaspoon chopped mint

Place 1 chopped onion, 1 crushed clove garlic, 1 finely chopped chilli, ginger, 1 tablespoon curry powder, vinegar and salt into a bowl. Mix well together. Cut beef into 1 in. cubes, add to mixture in bowl. Mix thoroughly and allow to stand at least 3 hours.

Melt butter in frying pan and fry the remaining chopped onion, crushed garlic and chopped chilli until light brown. Add turmeric, remaining curry powder, mustard, cardamom and meat mixture. Cook 5 minutes, reduce heat to simmer, add sufficient hot water just to cover the meat; add salt to taste. Cook gently, covered, until meat is tender,

approximately 1 hour 20 minutes; add a little extra water, if necessary, during cooking time. Lastly add mint. Serve with hot rice.

Chicken Tandoori

1 chicken
2 oz. (¼ cup) butter

Marinade

1 clove garlic
½ pint (1 cup) yoghurt
1 teaspoon ground ginger
1 teaspoon garam masala (see page 145)
1 teaspoon salt

Crush garlic and mix into the yoghurt with spices and salt. Joint chicken and marinate in yoghurt mixture for 6 hours or overnight. Melt butter in baking dish, add chicken pieces. Bake uncovered in moderate oven, Mark 4, 350°F., 45 minutes to 1 hour, basting frequently.

Serve with chopped onion and lemon wedges.

Canneloni—pancakes filled with a savoury mixture, topped with sauces, baked until piping hot.

Fruit Taj

2 large oranges
2 large bananas
lemon juice
¼ pint (½ cup) softened
  vanilla ice-cream

1 egg-yolk
¼ pint (½ cup) whipped
  cream
½ to 1 tablespoon rum
1 tablespoon slivered
  dates

Peel and section oranges; arrange sections in serving bowls or glasses. Peel and slice bananas and place over oranges, sprinkle with lemon juice. Stir together softened ice-cream, beaten egg-yolk, whipped cream and rum; spoon over fruit, garnish with dates.

Indonesia

Spices are an integral part of Indonesian cookery, for these are the Spice Islands of history. Many countries have had an effect on the history of Indonesia—India, China, Arabia, Portugal, Holland; the influence of these countries is reflected in Indonesian recipes.

Sambel Oelek, mentioned in some of the recipes on this page, is obtainable in jars from most large food stores; it is made up of finely minced red chillies, seasoned with salt. If unobtainable, use same amount of finely crushed chillies; season well with salt.

See page 94 for Nasi Goreng—Indonesia's famous version of Fried Rice.

Saté Kambing

Cut 1½ lb. lean lamb into ¾ in. cubes, thread on to thin bamboo skewers. Place 4 or 6 cubes on each skewer. There should be enough meat cubes for about 15 skewers. Grill until meat is done, turning several times. Serve hot with either of these Saté sauces.

Soy Sauce

4 tablespoons soy
  sauce
3 chives or spring
  onions (scallions)

1 teaspoon sambal
  oelek
2 tablespoons lemon
  juice

Slice chives thinly crosswise; combine with remaining ingredients in oblong dish. This shape makes it easy to dip the saté sticks.

Peanut Sauce

1 small onion
2 cloves garlic
1 tablespoon butter
1 teaspoon sambal
  oelek
½ pint (1 cup) water

2 oz. (¼ cup) peanut
1½ tablespoons soy
  sauce
½ teaspoon sugar
1 tablespoon lemon
  juice

Thinly slice onion. Sauté onion and garlic in butter until transparent, add sambal oelek. Reduce heat, stir well. Add water, then peanut butter, bring slowly to boil. Continue stirring until mixture becomes smooth. Season with soy sauce, sugar and lemon. Taste; add a little salt if necessary.

Serundeng

½ lb. (1⅛ cups) raw
  peanuts
½ pint (1 cup) oil
1 beef stock cube
4 tablespoons hot
  water
½ lb. (1⅓ cups) desic-
  cated coconut

1 teaspoon sugar
1 medium onion
2 cloves garlic
2 teaspoons coriander
1 bayleaf
salt, pepper

Wash and dry peanuts, deep-fry in hot oil until crisp. Dissolve beef stock cube in hot water, pour over coconut, season with sugar. Add grated onion, grated garlic, coriander and bayleaf, all of which have been sautéed in little hot butter. Add salt and pepper to taste. Mix thoroughly by hand so all spices blend with the coconut.

Put into small baking dish or ovenproof dish. Pour over the oil. Cook in moderately slow oven, Mark 3, 325°F., 30 minutes, stirring occasionally to keep from burning. Reduce heat to low, cook until coconut is golden brown. Remove from oven, stir in peanuts. Put in colander to drain and cool.

NOTE: Serundeng will keep in airtight jar about 2 weeks. It is very tasty if sprinkled on individual helpings of vegetables.

Gado-Gado

3 medium potatoes
½ lb. green beans
2 to 3 carrots
¼ cabbage
1 lettuce
2 medium tomatoes

3 to 4 hard boiled eggs
1 tablespoon crisp fried
  onion flakes
peanut sauce (see
  page 132)

Boil potatoes in their jackets; skin and dice. Cut beans into thin, diagonal slices; boil and drain. Scrape carrots, cut into matchstick-sized strips; boil and drain. Shred cabbage very finely. Put into boiling water, bring to boil again (don't over-cook); drain. Arrange vegetables on a platter as follows:

First, the washed, well-crisped lettuce, then potatoes, cabbage, beans, carrots, sliced or quartered tomatoes, sliced or quartered eggs. This gives a nice contrast of colours.

Pour over the Peanut Sauce just before serving; sprinkle with onion flakes, see Goreng Bawang.

This goes very well with a grill, or serve it as a barbecue salad. For a quick, tasty salad, pour the sauce over hard boiled eggs, lettuce and tomatoes.

The peanut sauce is nice to serve hot in winter and at room temperature in summer.

Sambal Goreng Udang

1 to 2 tablespoons
  butter
1 onion, chopped
2 cloves garlic, crushed
2 pints prawns
  (shrimps)
2 teaspoons sambal
  oelek (or 4 or 5
  chillies)

3 or 4 pieces green
  ginger, about 1 in.
  thick
1 lb. green beans
1 pint (2 cups)
  coconut milk (see
  page 58)
1 firm tomato
3 to 4 spring onions
  (scallions)

Heat butter, fry onion and garlic until they change colour. Add shelled, deveined prawns (shrimps), sambal oelek, ginger and beans, which have been sliced diagonally, thinly and evenly. Cook about 3 minutes; add coconut milk. Stir continually to avoid curdling; bring to boil. Add peeled, chopped tomato, spring onions (scallions) cut into 2 in. length, including green tops. Stir constantly. When beans are tender, remove from heat.

This dish goes very well with Serundeng.

Goreng Bawang

These fried onion flakes are widely used as a garnish for Indonesian dishes. They also give an interesting flavour when sprinkled over European-style soups just before serving; nice with chicken, beef or vegetable soups.

Skin, wash and slice onions; cut them into very thin and even slices. Heat a little oil in fry-pan fry the onions, stirring evenly. When partly cooked, reduce heat to very low; turn onions frequently so they become evenly browned without burning. If it seems they might burn, remove from heat before they are fully browned and keep stirring. The heat of the oil should be sufficient to complete the cooking.

When cooked pour onions and oil quickly into strainer over basin. This is to avoid some of the flakes becoming over-brown and ensures the onion flakes will be left crisp and dry.

Telur Balado

1 medium onion
4 to 5 tablespoons oil
2 tablespoons sambal
  oelek

2 tomatoes
1 chicken stock cube
salt to taste
6 hard boiled eggs

Fry thinly sliced onion in hot oil. When onion changes colour, reduce heat to low. Add sambal oelek, peeled, chopped tomatoes, crumbled chicken cube, salt to taste; simmer 5 minutes, stirring continuously. Add shelled eggs, simmer another 5 minutes. Turn eggs occasionally. Remove pan from heat.

Cut the eggs neatly in halves with sharp knife, arrange on platter, pour over the chilli sauce.

Barbecues

It is pleasant to be able to take advantage of a good fine day and cook and eat out of doors. The recipes below are simple and do not require lengthy preparation.

Barbecued Sausage

2 lb. pork sausages
butter
3 to 4 sticks chopped
  celery
2 large onions
3 to 4 tablespoons
  vinegar
$1\frac{1}{2}$ gills ($\frac{2}{3}$ cup) tomato
  sauce
3 to 4 tablespoons
  water

1 dessertspoon light
  brown sugar
1 dessertspoon
  prepared mustard
1 teaspoon
  Worcestershire sauce

Cook sausages until well browned, pricking several times. (This can be done in pan over barbecue.) Melt a little butter in saucepan, add celery and chopped onions, sauté until tender. Add remaining ingredients, stir well; add sausages. Simmer 10 to 15 minutes.

Serves 4 to 6.

NOTE: To hasten cooking time, put sausages into saucepan of cold water, bring slowly to boil, simmer 5 minutes; drain. This can be done some hours beforehand. Then brown or barbecue, and add to sauce, as above.

Barbecued Corn

Remove husk and silk from corn. Spread cobs generously with softened butter, season well with salt and pepper. Wrap each cob in double thickness of aluminium foil, twisting or folding ends to make a seal. Place on grill of barbecue over hot coals. Cook, turning often, 15 to 20 minutes, depending on heat of fire. Or cobs can be boiled for 10 minutes, removed from water, and brushed generously with melted butter, then barbecued on grill over hot coals for 10 minutes, brushing occasionally with melted butter.

NOTE: Quick-frozen corn can be used in either of the above ways, too; because it has gone through preliminary processing, cooking time is much shorter. Specific cooking times are given on packet.

Barbecued Chicken

1 small chicken
oil

salt, pepper

NOTE: This quantity makes 2 servings.
Split chicken in half lengthwise. Break drumstick, wing joints and thigh so chicken stays flat during cooking. Brush joints with oil and season well with salt and pepper. Place on grill with bone side nearest fire. When one side is well browned, turn and brown skin side, brushing with oil.

Salad Kebabs

8 oz. processed cheese
4 oz. grapes or pitted
  black olives
1 bunch radishes
2 slices pineapple

lettuce
1 small cucumber
French dressing (see
  page 121)

Cut cheese into 1 in. cubes. Wash grapes and radishes, and cut pineapple into pieces. Wash lettuce and place in plastic container in refrigerator until crisp: tear into neat pieces. Cut thick slices of cucumber in half. Thread pieces of cheese alternately with the other ingredients on to individual skewers with lettuce between. Dip each skewer into dressing before serving or serve dressing separately.

Makes 4 to 6.

Foil Baked Potatoes

potatoes
oil

salt

Scrub potatoes well, dry. Brush generously with oil, sprinkle with salt; wrap in foil. Roast in the coals about 1 hour. Or place on barbecue grill; allow about $1\frac{1}{4}$ hours for cooking, turning frequently. Split open, top with butter or sour cream.

Well-chilled melon slices make a wonderful dessert at the barbecue.

Seekh Kabab

2 lb. lean minced (ground) lamb or beef	½ teaspoon salt
1 small onion	½ teaspoon cardamom
2 tablespoons finely chopped spinach	½ teaspoon cinnamon
pinch chilli powder	½ teaspoon ground cloves

Pound the meat well in a basin and mix it thoroughly with grated onion, spinach, chilli powder and spices. Let stand for 10 minutes. Then lightly grease skewers and form meat firmly around skewers in 3½ in. long kebabs. Cook over the barbecue until brown, turning occasionally.

Serves 4 to 6.

Hamburgers

3 lb. minced (ground) steak	1 teaspoon allspice
1 oz. (½ cup) chopped parsley	1 small onion, finely chopped
1 tablespoon Worcestershire sauce	salt, pepper

Blend all ingredients together as lightly as possible. Form into flat cakes. The less handling the uncooked mixture receives, the more tender the hamburgers will be. Grill slowly, allowing 5 to 10 minutes for each side.

Makes approx. 1 dozen large hamburgers.

Red Cabbage Salad

½ pint (1 cup) white vinegar	1 tablespoon salt
3 oz. (⅜ cup) sugar	12 peppercorns
1 clove garlic	1 small red cabbage
2 bayleaves	2 red apples

Place vinegar, sugar, crushed garlic, bayleaves, salt and peppercorns into saucepan, slowly bring to boil, simmer 5 minutes. In bowl, mix together finely shredded cabbage and unpeeled, grated apples, strain over hot liquid; stir, refrigerate. Can be bottled in sterilised jars and kept 1 to 2 weeks in refrigerator.

Parsley Salad

1 very big bunch parsley	1 cucumber
4 spring onions (scallions)	½ lb. bourghol (cracked wheat)
1 lb. tomatoes	juice 6 large lemons
leaves from 5 or 6 mint sprigs	1½ gills (⅔ cup) oil
	pinch chilli powder
	salt

Wash parsley, spring onions, tomatoes and mint; dry. Chop parsley, spring onions (including green tops) and mint very finely. Peel and chop tomatoes and cucumber very finely. Combine prepared vegetables, bourghol, lemon juice, oil, chilli powder and salt in bowl; mix well.

Serve garnished with slices of lemon, cucumber and tomato. A bowl of crisp lettuce leaves is the correct accompaniment to this salad. Some of the salad is spooned into the centre of lettuce leaf, which is rolled round filling and eaten in this way. The crispness of the lettuce makes a good contrast with the flavour of this wonderful salad.

NOTE: Cracked wheat is available at some health-food shops, or at Continental food stores or delicatessens.

Barbecued Fish

1 small whole fish per person (mullet, trout, herring)	salt, pepper
	butter
	lemon juice

Mullet, barbecued this way, is delicious. Clean and scale fish; if using mullet, make sure all black lining of fish is removed. Sprinkle inside of fish with salt and pepper and squeeze of lemon juice. Arrange each fish on square of well-greased aluminium foil, sprinkle top of fish with salt and pepper, add small knob of butter. Wrap fish neatly and securely in foil. Place on barbecue; cook, turning occasionally, approximately 20 minutes.

Serve in the foil. Serve with chopped parsley and lemon wedges.

Barbecue Sauce

1 tablespoon oil	1 teaspoon salt
1 onion	1 teaspoon paprika
¼ pint (½ cup) tomato purée	¼ teaspoon black pepper
1½ gills (⅔ cup) water	1 teaspoon curry powder
2 tablespoons vinegar	1 tablespoon brown sugar
1 tablespoon Worcestershire sauce	

Heat oil in saucepan, add finely chopped onion and cook until brown. Add remaining ingredients and simmer, stirring for 5 minutes. Strain through fine strainer. Serve with chops, steaks or sausages.

Makes approx. $\frac{3}{4}$ pint.

Garlic Bread

1 long loaf crusty French bread	salt, pepper 2 cloves garlic
4 oz. ($\frac{1}{2}$ cup or 1 stick) butter	

Slice loaf, cutting just to bottom crust but not right through. Melt butter and add salt, pepper and crushed garlic. Fan slices of bread apart, and pour a little garlic butter between each slice. Brush top with any remaining butter. Wrap in aluminium foil, heat on barbecue.

Or salt, pepper and garlic can be blended into softened butter and spread on the cut slices. Spread any remaining butter over top of loaf before wrapping in foil.

NOTE: If desired, some chopped parsley and chopped chives, can be added to softened butter and crushed garlic, then spread on both sides of each slice.

Cabbage Relish

1 small cabbage	1½ dessertspoons mustard seeds
3 carrots	
1 lb. white onions	pinch cayenne pepper
4 green peppers	2 pints (4 cups) white vinegar
1 to 2 tablespoons salt	
1 lb. (2 cups) sugar	1½ dessertspoons celery seeds
	bayleaves

Wash cabbage and shred finely; slice carrots thinly; chop onion and peppers into small dice. Place all vegetables into large earthenware bowl, sprinkle salt over, mix well. Cover, stand overnight.

Next day, drain vegetables well, discard liquid. Pack vegetables firmly into hot, sterilised jars, placing a bayleaf in each jar. Combine all remaining ingredients in saucepan, stir over heat until sugar dissolves. Bring to boil, reduce heat, simmer 5 minutes. Cover vegetables with hot vinegar. Seal when cold.

Makes approx. 6 pints.

Delicious with any hot or cold meats served at the barbecue.

Barbecued Mushrooms and Bacon

chicken livers	bacon rashers
mushrooms	

Wash, trim and dry chicken livers; cut in half. Cut mushrooms in half or leave button mushrooms whole. Cut bacon rashers into three if large, or two pieces if small. Roll half a mushroom and half a chicken liver into each piece of bacon. Thread bacon rolls on to skewers. Place on barbecue until bacon is crisp, turning occasionally.

Grilled Pineapple

1 large ripe pineapple   melted butter

Cut unpeeled pineapple into 6 or 8 wedges. Remove core from each wedge. Brush generously with melted butter, grill on barbecue until lightly browned. Serve as is, warm, with cream. The skin will come away easily as the slices are eaten.

Melons

On a hot day, there's nothing nicer to serve for a barbecue dessert than a slice of well-chilled melon. Or, for a more formal type of dessert, melons can be cut into balls or dice and refrigerated. At serving time, spoon into individual glasses or serving dishes, spoon over a little well-chilled sweet white wine.

A ripe melon can be made into a basket to hold fresh fruit salad. Choose a large melon, cut 2 sections from the upper half to leave an arched piece resembling handle of a basket. Carefully cut away melon flesh from under handle and from inside of basket; cut into cubes, drain, removing seeds, then refrigerate. Pile the melon back into the shell, together with any other fresh fruit, cut to similar size. Sprinkle with sugar, a little lemon juice and, if desired, some sweet white wine. Decorate basket with grape or other leaves.

Barbecued Bananas

Choose firm, ripe bananas. Place on barbecue, cook until skins turn black, turning occasionally. Remove from heat with tongs, peel back top layer of skin. If serving as an accompaniment to savoury dishes, season with salt and pepper; if serving as a dessert, sprinkle with equal amounts of cinnamon and sugar, serve with whipped cream.

Herbs and Spices

The correct use of herbs, spices and aromatic seeds gives flavour and appetizing fragrance to even the most simple foods. The herbs and spices listed here are those most commonly used in cookery; many are easy to grow in the home garden.

Herbs

Fresh herbs from the home garden or dried herbs bought at a food store add new flavour interest to familiar dishes; if substituting dried herbs for fresh in a recipe, use less of the dried variety.

Herbs should enhance, not dominate, the food's natural flavour.

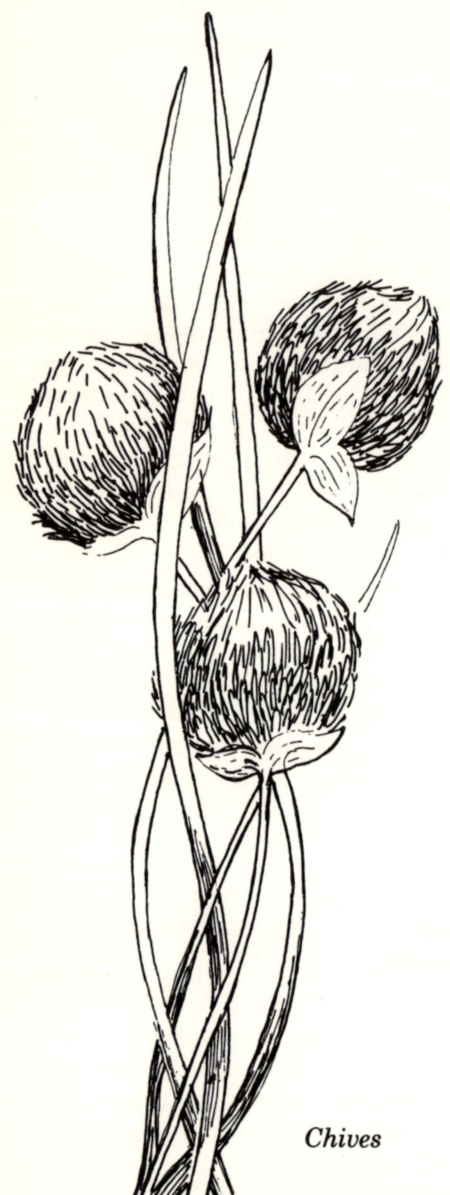

Chives

Balm

Balm, or lemon balm as it is frequently called, is not widely used in the kitchen, although it can be added to salads, mushroom dishes and sweet jellies. The crushed leaves give off a pleasant lemon scent, and a few, added to a teapot with tealeaves, will produce a refreshing drink. Balm is an important ingredient in potpourri, where its tang helps to offset the sweetness of the flower scents.

Variegated balm is another variety of the plant, but is grown more for ornamental than practical purposes.

Basil

There are more than 40 varieties of this sharp, piquant herb, but the best known are the sweet, bush and purple basils. Purple basil has deep purple-greenish leaves; its flavour is inferior to the bush and sweet types. Sweet basil is particularly suitable for drying and therefore the easiest to obtain in dried form.

Basil is traditionally teamed with tomatoes, but its flavour also adds interest to pasta dishes, and combines well with rice, liver, kidneys and fish. Try a little in omelets and with scrambled eggs; if available, use the chopped fresh leaves sprinkled on a green salad. Generally, $\frac{1}{4}$ teaspoon of dried basil with eggs, and $\frac{1}{2}$ teaspoon in a meat recipe is quite sufficient.

Bayleaves

The bay tree is a member of the laurel family. Planted in a pot and clipped to a pleasing shape, this tree can be both attractive and useful. Bayleaves are always an ingredient of bouquet garni; they can also be used by themselves to enhance the flavour of soups, stews, stock, fish, meat and poultry. Whether used fresh or dried, bayleaves are strong, and $\frac{1}{2}$ to 1 leaf is ample in most recipes.

Bouquet Garni

A bouquet garni, or faggot as it is sometimes called, generally consists of a bayleaf, a sprig of fresh thyme, and several parsley sprigs. These are tied together at the stems with cotton or thin string to make removal easier at the end of cooking time. When dried herbs are used it is best to tie them in a piece of muslin.

Use a bouquet garni to flavour stock, soups, stews and fish dishes.

Chervil

Chervil has a serrated and fernlike leaf, with a flavour reminiscent of aniseed. It is sometimes difficult to obtain fresh, but fortunately chervil dries most successfully, retaining both its colour and aroma.

Use dried chervil with discretion in soups, stews, sauces, gravies and with fish and meat. Fresh, the leaves can be chopped and sprinkled fairly liberally on salads and cooked vegetables.

Parsley, sage
rosemary
& thyme
NUTMEG
CLOVES
PEPPER
GINGER
bouquets

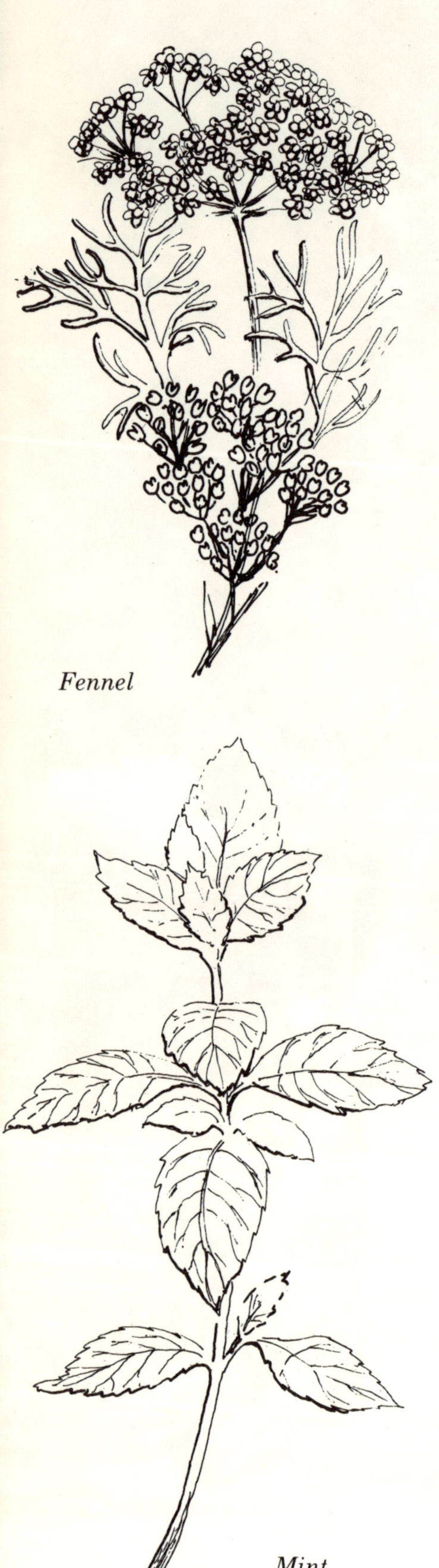

Fennel

Mint

Chives

Chives are easy to grow. Stemming from a small bulb, this member of the lily family seems to thrive in the garden or in a pot; however, if it is impossible to grow your own, bunches can usually be bought. The onion-like leaves, believed to stimulate the appetite, have a mild onion flavour.

Chopped chives add interest to cream cheese, scrambled egg and mashed potato. Try them as a garnish for some soups or sprinkled over a green salad.

Dill

Dill—a favourite herb in Scandinavian and Russian cooking—has a flavour reminiscent of fennel, but milder. Either chopped, fresh leaves or seeds can be used.

In dill pickles the herb helps to make the cucumber more digestible. Flavours of fish and dill combine well—add a few dill seeds to the poaching liquid. Try the chopped, fresh leaves in salads, dressings, sauces or with coleslaw. If fresh dill is difficult to obtain, the dried and powdered variety can be used in recipes where the herb is cooked with other ingredients.

Fennel

Perennial fennel and annual Florence fennel are the two best-known varieties. Seeds of both can be used in cooking, but leaves and stems of Florence fennel have a more pleasant flavour than those of the perennial; leaves, stems, roots and seeds all have an aniseed taste.

Try the raw stems stuffed with cream cheese and cut into 1 in. slices or use to make a delicious salad. Cook the seeds with fish or add to bread and pastries; for a change, use them as a flavouring with apple. Chop the fresh leaves and add to soups and sauces.

Fenugreek

Fenugreek is grown extensively in India, where the leaves are used for fodder. The seeds, which form in long, thin pods, are sold in ground form and are a component of curry powder. Fenugreek can be used in some pickles and with dried beans; also in soups and casseroles.

Fines Herbes

The 'fines herbes' are a combination of parsley, chervil, chives and tarragon. Finely chopped, their most frequent use is in Omelet Fines Herbes, but this combination is also called for in some French recipes for meat, chicken and fish.

Garlic

Garlic is the bulb of a plant belonging to the lily family. In appearance it resembles an irregular-shaped white onion. This is composed of several 'cloves' or segments, each one encased in flaky, white skin. Generally a recipe incorporating garlic will specify one clove to be used, but the strength will depend on the age of the root (young garlic is less pungent than an older bulb) and also the method of cooking.

Garlic is used extensively in Spanish, Italian, and French cooking. It can be added to very many savoury dishes, including soups, stews, roasts, poultry, steaks, stuffings, salad dressings and salads, pickles chutneys.

Before being added to a dish, the garlic clove is peeled, then chopped or crushed. To peel and crush, bring down the flat side of a knife blade sharply on to the clove—the skin can be lifted off quite easily. Add a little salt to the garlic and mash, again using the flat of a knife. Alternatively, peel garlic and crush in a garlic crusher.

Marjoram

There are many varieties of marjoram. In addition to oregano (wild marjoram), knotted (or sweet) is the type most widely used in cooking. The plant grows to about 2 ft. in height and its grey green leaves have a spicy, mint flavour. This herb is sometimes included in a bouquet garni.

Use marjoram mixed with other herbs in stuffings, but try it by itself with eggs, beef, pork, lamb, mutton and in soups, sauces, cheese and fish dishes. Available in powdered form.

Mint

Fresh mint can usually be bought, but it is easy to grow in the home garden; it prefers a sunny position. The most common variety, also best for drying, is spearmint, but there are many others.

Cook several sprigs of fresh mint, or a teaspoon of dried mint, with vegetables, especially peas and new potatoes. Serve some in iced tea and summer fruit drinks. Mint sauce or mint jelly is, of course, the traditional accompaniment to roast mutton or lamb.

Oregano

Oregano, the wild marjoram of Italy and Spain, is prominent in the cooking of these two countries. Available in powdered form, oregano has a strong, pungent flavour and is one of the ingredients in chilli powder.

This herb gives a piquant flavour to such dishes as pizza and chilli con carne, and combines well with tomatoes. Try a little in scrambled eggs and omelets or with pork, veal, beef and fish dishes; add a pinch to French dressing.

Parsley

One of the most widely used and versatile of all herbs, parsley is rich in vitamin C and also contains iron, calcium and vitamin A.

Unlike other herbs, which should be used with discretion, a liberal amount of chopped parsley can be added to many kinds of dishes. Use fresh or fried sprigs as a garnish; add chopped or dried parsley to soups, stews, mashed potatoes, egg dishes, dumplings, sauces.

Peppermint

A herb of the mint family, used for flavouring candies and in liqueurs. The variety known as Black peppermint may be dried for winter use or the fresh leaves may be infused. It has excellent digestive properties.

Rosemary

The variety of rosemary generally cultivated today grows to about 3 ft. in height and is a straight-branched bush with grey-green spiny leaves. It is the leaves that are used in cooking—either fresh or dried and crumbled.

Rosemary has a slight pine flavour that is particularly good with lamb, but it can also be combined with chicken, veal and pork, in soups, sauces, stuffings or chopped and scattered on salads. Try a little in minestrone or pea soup. Rosemary can often be substituted for thyme in a recipe.

Sage

There are many varieties of this particularly pungent herb, but the grey-leafed type with purple flowers is the most popular and is available whole, crushed or ground.

Use as a seasoning for rissoles, meat loaves, cheese and egg dishes or with fish—and, of course, in sage and onion stuffing. Try rubbing a joint with sage before roasting—but remember its strength, so use sparingly.

Savory

The two best known types of savory are the annual summer and perennial winter varieties—they are similar in flavour and resemble a mild form of sage. Winter savory makes an attractive hedge to a herb garden.

Traditionally associated with beans, savory can be used also with lamb, pork and veal, or combined with other herbs in stuffings, omelets and salads. It is available in dried, powdered form.

Tarragon

There are two varieties of tarragon —French and Russian—but the French, with its superior flavour, is used most in cooking.

Tarragon is an essential ingredient in bearnaise sauce. Its sharp taste blends well with fish and shellfish; for an interesting result, try a little in a chicken stuffing. Mayonnaise, hollandaise sauce and French dressing benefit from a pinch of tarragon and, fresh and chopped, it is delicious sprinkled over salads.

Thyme

Of the many varieties of thyme, lemon-scented and garden thyme are the best known and most often used in the kitchen—both are available in dried-leaf form.

A sprig of thyme is one of the bouquet garni ingredients. Use it also to season meats, soups, stuffings and forcemeat, and vegetables—especially aubergines (eggplants), mushrooms, onions, beetroot, zucchini and marrows.

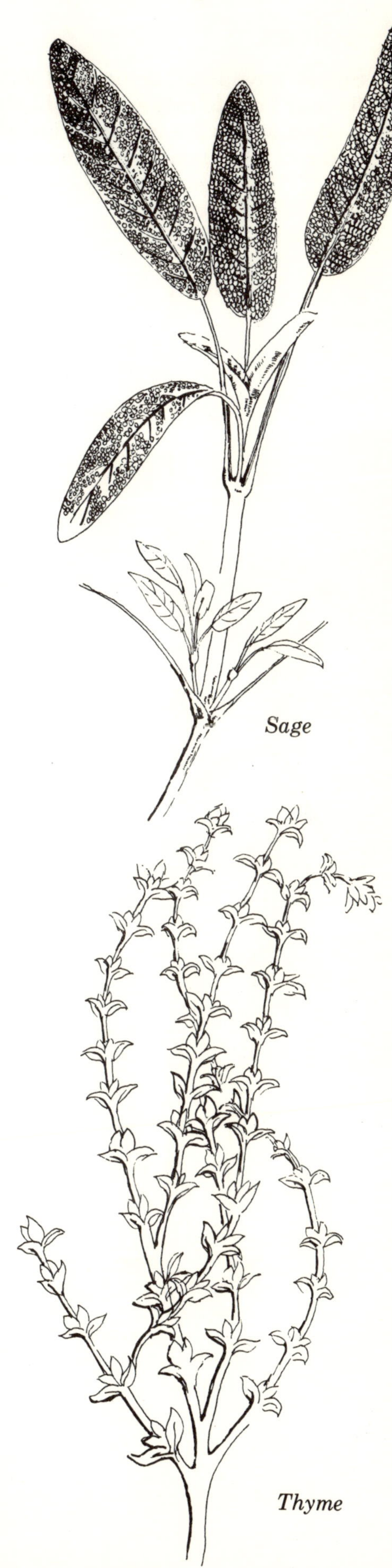

Sage

Thyme

Spices

Spices have little or no food value, but the volatile oils which give them their aroma and distinctive flavour help to make simple foods appetising and interesting.

Most spices are imported and therefore are relatively expensive. For home use buy in small quantities and retain maximum freshness and flavour by storing in airtight containers in a dark, dry, cool place.

Ginger

Allspice

Allspice (also known as Jamaican Pepper) is the dried fruit of the pimento tree—and no relation to the pepper of that name. It is so named because of its resemblance to the combined flavours of nutmeg, cloves and cinnamon.

Available whole or ground, allspice is used for pickling, fruit preserving, soups, gravies, cakes, puddings, boiled meats.

Cayenne

Cayenne pepper is made from the ground, brilliant red, whole pods of the chilli or capsicum. The plant is ornamental, and is grown in many parts of the world, but chiefly in the East Indies and Africa. Depending on its country of origin, cayenne varies in pungency, but all types are very hot and should be used with discretion. It is an important ingredient in curry powder.

Add a little cayenne to meat, fish and egg dishes, to savory batters, sauces and salad dressings, in cheese dishes and with shellfish.

Cinnamon

The cinnamon tree is an evergreen laurel. The thin bark is peeled from the tree and rolled into sticks as it dries, forming stick cinnamon. True cinnamon grows in Ceylon and India; cassia, a member of the same family, comes from South-East Asia, and is almost identical in flavour. The Saigon variety is recognised as being the best-quality ground cinnamon.

Cinnamon has a mellow, slightly sweet flavour that blends with both sweet and savoury foods. When a recipe calls for stick cinnamon, it will usually give the amount to be used in inches, for example, 'a 2 in. stick cinnamon'.

Use ground cinnamon in cakes, milk and fruit puddings or with grilled or stewed meats. Add a cinnamon stick to hot drinks such as mulled wine, use in pickles and with boiled meats and when stewing fruits.

Cloves

Cloves are the buds of an evergreen tree. Used extensively in cookery, they are available whole or ground. Their penetrating, aromatic flavour makes careful use essential—2 or 3 cloves are generally sufficient for most dishes.

Use cloves in some soups, with eggs, fish, meat, stuffings, sauces and gravies, pickles and chutneys. Try a clove-studded orange added to boiling ham or bacon, and an onion stuck with cloves, cooked with boiled chicken. A traditional use is in apple pie; ground cloves are added to cakes and biscuits.

Ginger

Ginger, the root of the plant, can be obtained in four different forms— green (fresh root); ground (dried and powdered root); preserved (cooked in syrup and bottled); crystallized cooked, drained and rolled in sugar).

Green ginger is used with savoury foods (if substituting ground ginger, use only $\frac{1}{4}$ amount specified for green ginger in recipe). Ground ginger is used in savoury and sweet recipes. Preserved and crystallized gingers are interchangeable in recipes, but if no sugar is used in the recipe, rinse sugar coating off the crystallized ginger.

Mace

Mace, the fleshy covering of nutmeg, with a similar but stronger flavour, is available in 'blade' and powdered form, although blade mace is more difficult to obtain. Use it in preserving, flavouring fish, fish sauces and stuffings. Try a pinch of mace on grilled lamb or veal chops. A little added to whipped cream makes an interesting variation—so does a pinch in pie pastry.

Mixed Spice

Mixed spice, as the name implies, is a blend of certain spices in finely ground form. Generally these will be caraway, allspice, coriander, cumin, nutmeg and ginger, but other spices, such as cinnamon, may be included.

Mixed spice is used in cakes, puddings and with fruit.

Nutmeg

From the same tree as mace, nutmeg is the kernel of the fruit; available in whole nut and ground form, the nuts should be grated before use. One nutmeg will generally produce 3 teaspoonfuls when grated, but, for full flavour, prepare only as much as needed at the time, then store remainder of nut until required again.

Although generally included in sweet recipes, nutmeg is also used with meats and poultry, such as chicken, and in sauces.

Paprika

Best quality paprika is made from the dried, ground pods of a variety of sweet red pepper or capsicum imported from Hungary. Has a mild, slightly sweet flavour.

Paprika brightens otherwise insipid-looking dishes when used as a garnish. It can be mixed with breadcrumbs to use as topping for dishes such as macaroni au gratin, or used with breadcrumbs for coating chicken joints for frying.

Pepper

Black and white pepper both come from the berry of a perennial vine. Black pepper is the whole peppercorn, white the inner seed with black outer covering removed. Whole peppercorns keep their flavour better than ground pepper; grind in a peppermill as needed.

Pepper is almost indispensable in savoury cooking. Usually, black is preferable, although it is better to use white in pale coloured foods or cream sauces.

Saffron

Saffron is obtained from the dried stigmas of a type of crocus grown in Europe, mostly in Spain. Since it takes 225,000 stigmas to make 1 lb. of saffron, and each one is hand picked, it is not surprising that this is the world's most expensive spice.

Saffron is used widely in Spanish cooking to impart yellow colour and subtle flavour; available in stigma or powdered form, it should be used very sparingly.

Steep saffron in a little warm water before use. Meat and poultry dishes generally incorporating rice, fish soups such as bouillabaisse, and some traditional breads and cakes include this spice.

Turmeric

Turmeric is the root of a plant of the ginger family. It originated in China and Indonesia, is now produced in India, Haiti and Jamaica.

Deep yellow in colour, it is often a curry ingredient and is used commercially in mustard, curry powder and some pickles. At home, use it in sauces and dressings, marinades for chicken and shellfish and in some pickles and chutneys.

Saffron

Aromatic seeds

The seeds listed below can be used in sweet or savoury dishes; most can be obtained in whole seed or ground form.

Anise

Anise is an annual plant growing to 18 in. in height and producing flat-topped bunches of white flowers. The seeds and fresh leaves are used in cooking, and its sharp, distinctive aroma is unmistakable in the liqueur Anisette.

If you have anise in the garden, chop the fresh leaves and sprinkle them over salads. Use the seeds as a flavouring with shellfish, meat and stuffings. In scones, rolls, bread and biscuits the seeds can be included in the dough or sprinkled on top.

Caraway

Caraway is the aromatic seed of a biennial member of the parsley family.

Most widely used in seed cake and bread, caraway can be cooked with meat, some vegetables and cheese. Add a pinch to stews and marinades, sprinkle a little on pork before roasting; use as a flavouring in cheese dishes or crushed with cottage cheese.

Cardamom

Cardamom is an Indian native plant extensively in Indian cookery. Cardamom pods or the whole or ground seeds can be bought. The off-white pods are about $\frac{1}{2}$ in. in length and contain about 12 to 16 seeds. The seeds are very hard, so they should be crushed before use to release their pungent flavour.

Whole cardamom seeds are used in fruit punches, pickles and marinades. In their ground form they are included in bread and cakes, meatballs and roast pork. The flavour of cardamom combines very well with coffee and, in its ground form, is a component of curry powder.

Celery Seed

Celery seeds do not come from the well-known vegetable, but from a plant related to the parsley family. They are available whole or ground. Sprinkle whole seeds on herb breads or include in the dough; scatter on canapés; add to marinades for beef or sprinkle on roast veal; include in pickles.

Use ground celery seeds with eggs, cheese, in salads and salad dressings and with vegetables such as potatoes, aubergines, tomatoes, peppers.

Coriander

Coriander is available in whole seed or ground form. It is a comparatively mild spice, has a flavour similar to nutmeg. The longer the seeds are kept (they should be stored in a dry place) the more pronounced the flavour becomes. Seeds can be left whole in cooking but it is usual to crush them first.

Use with dried pea and bean soups, spicy sauces, roast or stewed meat, some fish dishes, omelets, baked eggs and some cakes and pies such as coffee cake, Danish pastries and apple pie. When using coriander to flavour custards or milk puddings, include a small piece of lemon or orange rind; the two flavours blend well.

Cumin Seed

Cumin, a low-growing annual from the Mediterranean, is used in Near and Middle Eastern cookery, and is a basic ingredient of curries. The dried ripe fruit of the plant forms the spice. With its pungent aroma, cumin is used by the Dutch and Swiss to flavour cheese, by the Germans in sauerkraut and by the Hebrews in unleavened bread. It is available ground or in whole seed form.

Use cumin in rye bread, pickles, chutney, rice cabbage and bean dishes with pork and lamb.

Mustard

The hardy annual mustard plant will grow in almost any temperate area of the world. There are two main varieties, both native to Europe and producing seeds that vary in strength and flavour. Ready-mixed mustards are becoming more and more popular.

Use mustard seed in casseroles, pickles, salads, dressings and vegetable dishes. Prepared mustards, traditional accompaniment of beef, steak and ham, can be added to cheese dishes, sauces and dressings.

Poppy Seeds

Grown mainly in Holland, poppy seeds are the non-narcotic seeds of the poppy. They can be used whole or ground. For best flavour bake in moderate oven, Mark 4, 350°F., approximately 10 minutes, or toast in dry frying pan over low heat. Sprinkle whole on breads, pastries, salads, pasta, baked or grilled fish, buttered new potatoes and cauliflower. Use ground in cakes or strudel fillings. Purists, however, believe in using poppy seeds only in sweet foods.

Sesame Seeds

Sesame seeds are small, flat and round—and light brown, high in mineral and protein content. In many parts of the world, oil extracted from the seeds is used for cooking. The faintly nutty flavour of the seeds is brought out by baking 20 minutes in moderate oven, Mark 4, 350°F.

Sesame seeds are sprinkled on breads, buns, cakes and pastries. They can also be added to cheese mixtures and fish dishes, sprinkled on canapés, added to salad dressings.

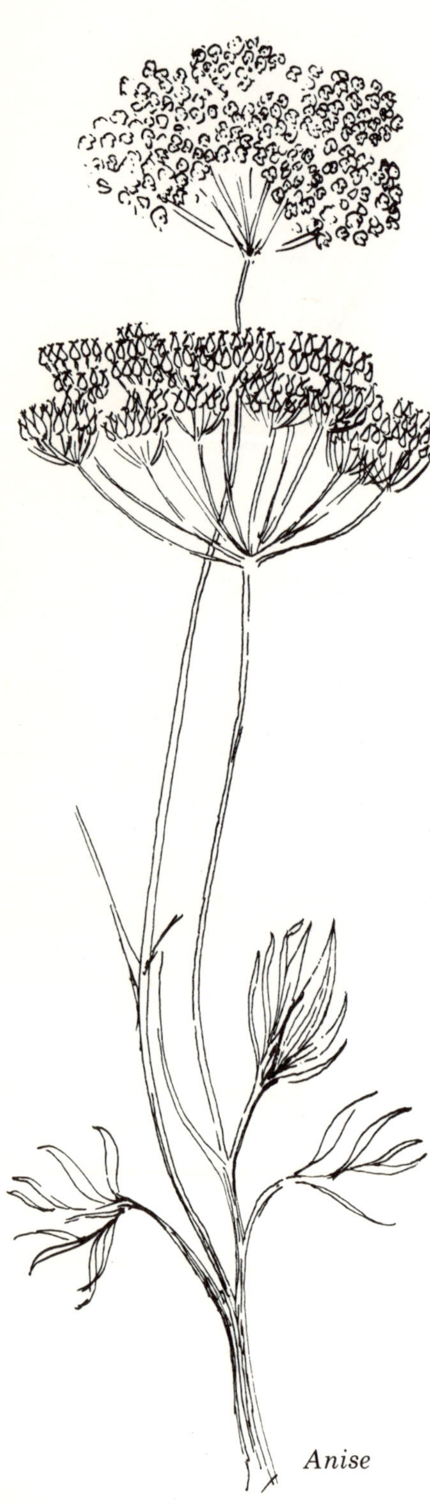

Anise

Miscellaneous

Below we list a variety of ingredients which add zest to your cooking.

Capers

The floral bud of the caper bush, that grows along the Mediterranean shores of southern Europe. Once picked, the buds are dried and pickled in vinegar.

Capers add a sharp and piquant flavour to sauces accompanying boiled meat and fish, particularly caper sauce served with boiled mutton. Try them also in salads, or as a garnish.

Curry Powder

Curry powder is a blend of at least 6 spices which may include cumin, coriander, fenugreek, turmeric, ginger, pepper, mace, cardomom and cloves.

In addition to curries, use curry powder with eggs, in marinades, sprinkled on grilled fish, or to flavour sauces and butters. Amount used will vary according to the brand of curry powder and strength desired. Curry powder should be fried at start of making a curry—this releases its full flavour and also cooks the spices.

Garam Masala

Garam Masala is the mixed spice of India; it is a combination of ground coriander seeds, cumin seeds, cloves, cinnamon, peppercorns, nutmeg and cardamom seeds. Unlike curry powder, it should be added to a dish at the end of cooking time so its delicate flavour is retained. The spices included in the mixture and quantities used are variable. Garam Masala is used extensively in Indian cooking.

Horseradish

Horseradish is the root of a perennial plant, a member of the mustard family. It can be bought in jars, blended in a creamy sauce.

Horseradish, the traditional accompaniment to roast beef, can be combined with mayonnaise to give a sharp and piquant dressing. The young and tender leaves of the plant can be chopped and used in salads.

Monosodium Glutamate

Monosodium Glutamate or MSG, as it is commonly known, is widely used in Chinese cookery. It is the sodium salt of glutamic acid present in nearly all animal and vegetable protein, and is used in cookery to give accent to flavour.

It is used in some savoury foods only and should not be added to sweet foods, fruits or dairy products.

Salt

Salt, or sodium chloride as it is scientifically known, is a mineral mined in many parts of the world; it is also contained naturally in most foods. Salt added to food during cooking will help to bring out the flavour, and will also stimulate the appetite. A certain amount of salt in the diet is essential for health, while too much can be harmful. Salt also acts as a preservative.

Vanilla

The vanilla bean is the seed pod of a yellow-flowered orchid native to Central America; the pods are odourless and flavourless. Over a period of 6 months, they are subjected to alternate heat and darkness to induce fermentation. When almost black in colour, the vanilla bean, as we know it, emerges.

Vanilla extract is produced by steeping the cured pods in a mixture of alcohol and water.

Keep a vanilla bean in a jar containing sugar—the flavour is imparted to the sugar to be used in cakes and custards. Heat the whole pod, or a small piece, in milk for any sweet dish requiring these two ingredients. The bean can be washed and dried afterwards to be stored and used again. An alternative method is to split the bean and remove the seeds. Store the bean in a sugar jar and use the seeds—the part with the strongest flavour—for heating with milk.

Vanilla flavour is popular for many sweet recipes, including custards, ice-cream, cakes, puddings, confectionery.

Nutmeg

Sauces

Basically, there are two types of savoury sauces—brown and white; nearly all sauces are variations of these. In addition, there are the butter sauces—Hollandaise and Bearnaise, and the compound sauces, Mayonnaise (see page 121) and its variations. All the favourite savoury sauce recipes are given here. See Desserts section, page 222, for a selection of delicious dessert sauces.

Basic White Sauce

1 oz. (2 tablespoons) butter	1 pint (2 cups) hot milk
2 tablespoons flour	salt, pepper

Melt butter over low heat, remove from heat, stir in flour, working until smooth. Return to heat, cook few minutes, remove from heat. Gradually stir in heated milk, return to heat; cook, stirring constantly until boiling point is reached. Reduce heat, simmer further 3 minutes, season to taste.

The amount of flour and butter used in sauces depends on the consistency desired.

Thin Sauce Use 1 oz. (2 tablespoons) butter and 2 tablespoons (approximately 1 oz.) flour to 1 pint (2 cups) liquid.

Medium Sauce Use 1½ oz. (3 tablespoons) butter and 3 tablespoons (approximately 1½ oz.) to 1 pint (2 cups) liquid.

Thick Sauce Use 2 oz. (¼ cup) butter and 4 tablespoons (approximately 2 oz.) flour to 1 pint (2 cups) liquid.

Parsley Sauce Stir 2 to 3 tablespoons finely chopped parsley and a squeeze of lemon juice into 1 pint (2 cups) medium-thickness white sauce.

Onion Sauce Chop 2 onions finely, cook in boiling salted water until tender, drain. Add onions, a squeeze of lemon juice and 1 teaspoon finely chopped parsley to 1 pint (2 cups) medium-thickness white sauce. (Cooking liquid from onions can be used as part of liquid in making the white sauce).

Mornay Sauce Make up thick white sauce, remove from heat, stir in 4 oz. (1 cup) grated cheese; add a sprinkling of nutmeg. Stir, off heat, until cheese melts completely.

Mushroom Cream Sauce

½ lb. mushrooms	1 gill (½ cup) medium
1 oz. (2 tablespoons) butter	white sauce
1½ gills (⅔ cup) medium cream	salt, pepper

Chop mushrooms very finely, sauté in hot butter until lightly browned. Add cream, cook over low heat 5 minutes. Stir in white sauce, season to taste; heat through gently.

Béchamel Sauce

bayleaf	½ pint (1 cup) milk
parsley stalks	½ oz. (1 tablespoon) butter
slice of onion	
4 peppercorns	1 tablespoon flour
sprig thyme	salt, pepper

Place bayleaf, parsley stalks, onion slice, peppercorns and thyme into milk in small saucepan over low heat. Gradually bring to boiling point, remove from heat, let stand 5 minutes. Melt butter in saucepan, add flour, stir until smooth; remove pan from heat, gradually add the strained milk, stirring constantly. When thoroughly blended, return to heat and stir until sauce boils and thickens. Season to taste with salt and pepper.

Brown Sauce

1 carrot	1 pint (2 cups) boiling water
1 medium onion	
1 stick celery	1 tablespoon tomato purée
1 clove garlic	
3 tablespoons oil	bayleaf
2 tablespoons flour	parsley stalks
2 beef stock cubes	sprig of thyme

Coarsley chop carrot, onion and celery; crush garlic. Heat oil in saucepan. Sauté carrot, onion, celery and garlic until lightly browned. Stir in flour and cook until well browned; do not allow to burn. Dissolve stock cubes in boiling water. Add to pan with tomato purée and herbs. Simmer, uncovered, 30 minutes. Strain, adjust seasoning.

A well-flavoured sauce can transform simple grilled or roasted meats into gourmet dishes.

Quick Sauce Bordelaise

2 small onions
6 mushrooms
butter
1½ gills (⅔ cup) dry
  white wine
1½ gills (⅔ cup) stock
1 tablespoon tomato
  purée or paste
salt, pepper

Chop onions very finely, slice mushrooms. Sauté in a little butter until lightly browned. Add wine and stock and simmer until reduced to ½ pint (1 cup) of liquid. Stir in tomato purée or paste; season to taste.

Oyster Sauce

½ pint (1 cup) milk
¼ pint (½ cup) water
½ carrot
1 slice of onion
few peppercorns
parsley sprig
1 small bayleaf
1 oz. (2 tablespoons)
  butter
2 tablespoons flour
1 dessertspoon lemon
  juice
salt, pepper
1 bottle or can of
  oysters (10 to 12
  oysters)
3 to 4 tablespoons
  heavy cream

Place milk, water, diced carrot, onion slice, peppercorns, parsley and bayleaf in saucepan. Bring to boil; reduce heat, simmer very slowly, uncovered, 5 minutes. Strain, reserve stock. Melt butter in saucepan, stir in flour, cook 1 minute, remove from heat. Gradually add strained stock. Return to heat, simmer until smooth and thickened, stirring constantly.

Add lemon juice, season to taste. Add drained, chopped oysters, simmer very slowly further 5 minutes. Stir in cream. Reheat gently, do not boil. Serve over grilled (broiled) steaks or steamed or poached fish.

Sauce Bercy

1 tablespoon finely
  chopped shallots
½ oz. (1 tablespoon)
  butter
1 wineglass white wine
2 wineglasses white
  stock
salt, pepper
juice of ½ lemon
1 dessertspoon chopped
  parsley
½ oz. (1 tablespoon)
  butter
½ oz. (1 tablespoon)
  flour

Sauté the shallots in butter. Add wine and reduce by half. Add stock, seasoning, lemon juice and parsley, bring to the boil.

Mix flour and butter smoothly, add to the pan in small pieces, stirring well. Boil for 1 minute, adjust seasoning.

Mustard Sauce

1 oz. (2 tablespoons)
  butter
1½ tablespoons flour
½ pint (1 cup) stock
salt, pepper
1 teaspoon dry mustard
½ teaspoon vinegar
1 tablespoon heavy
  cream
1 egg-yolk

Melt butter in saucepan. Stir in flour, cook until lightly brown; remove from heat. Gradually add stock, blend well. Return to heat, bring to boil; reduce heat, simmer until smooth and thickened, stirring constantly. Season to taste with salt and pepper.

Blend mustard and vinegar with a little of the sauce until smooth. Add to sauce, blend well. Remove from heat, stir in cream and beaten egg-yolk.

Stroganoff Sauce

1 oz. (2 tablespoons)
  butter
1 large onion
½ lb. mushrooms
½ teaspoon dry mustard
salt, pepper
½ pint (1 cup) sour
  cream

Melt butter in pan, add finely chopped onion, sauté gently until onion is tender. Add sliced mushrooms, cook until mushrooms are well softened. Add mustard, salt, pepper to taste, then stir in sour cream; heat together gently, simmer 5 minutes.

This sauce is equally good spooned over grilled (broiled) or pan-fried steaks, or over thick slices of roasted beef fillet.

Madeira Sauce

½ oz. (1 tablespoon)
  butter
1 rasher bacon
2 shallots
1 dessertspoon flour
1 teaspoon tomato
  paste
4 mushrooms
¾ pint (1½ cups) boiling
  water
2 beef stock cubes
salt, pepper
pinch mixed herbs
¼ pint (½ cup) madeira

Heat butter in pan, add finely chopped bacon and shallots, cook over low heat until lightly browned. Stir in flour, add paste, finely chopped mushrooms. Gradually stir in boiling water, in which stock cubes have been dissolved. Season, bring to boil. Reduce heat, simmer 20 minutes. Add herbs, bring to boil again further 5 minutes; strain.

Let sauce simmer over low heat until reduced to half quantity. Add madeira, reboil gently until sauce thickens.

Mushroom Sauce

½ oz. (1 tablespoon) butter
1 small onion
2 oz. mushrooms
4 tablespoons white wine
1 tablespoon cornflour (cornstarch)
½ pint (1 cup) milk
salt, pepper
1 to 2 tablespoons cream

Melt butter, fry the chopped onion and sliced mushrooms, but do not brown. Add wine, cook gently for 1 minute. Blend the cornflour (cornstarch) with the milk, add to pan. Bring to boil, stirring continually, and cook 1 minute. Remove from heat, season to taste, stir in the cream.

Chinese Plum Sauce

3 oz. ($\frac{3}{8}$ cup) butter
1 onion
½ lb. (1 cup) plum jam
2 tablespoons soy sauce
1 tablespoon wine vinegar
½ teaspoon ginger
¼ teaspoon dry mustard

Melt butter in saucepan and sauté chopped onion until tender. Remove pan from heat, add remaining ingredients; heat gently, stirring, until well combined.

Serve with pork or veal.

Bearnaise Sauce

4 tablespoons tarragon
6 peppercorns, crushed
1 shallot
1 bayleaf
3 egg-yolks
4 oz. (½ cup or 1 stick) butter
salt, pepper

Boil vinegar, peppercorns, chopped shallot and bayleaf together until liquid is reduced to 2 tablespoons, strain. Beat egg-yolks lightly in top of double boiler and stir in strained liquid. Gradually beat in cooled melted butter and stir continuously over simmering water until thickened. Season with salt and pepper.

Tartare Sauce

1½ gills ($\frac{2}{3}$ cup) mayonnaise (see page 121)
2 tablespoons capers
2 tablespoons chopped gherkins
½ teaspoon chopped chives
1 tablespoon chopped parsley

In bowl combine mayonnaise, finely chopped capers, gherkins, chives and parsley. Serve with fish.

Hollandaise Sauce

3 tablespoons wine vinegar
6 peppercorns
½ bayleaf
4 oz. (½ cup or 1 stick) butter
2 egg-yolks
salt, pepper
few drops lemon juice

Simmer vinegar, peppercorns and bayleaf gently together until liquid is reduced to half the quantity, strain. Work butter until slightly soft. Cream egg-yolks with a little of the butter and a pinch of salt in the top of a double saucepan; stir in strained liquid. Stir over gentle heat until just beginning to thicken. Add remaining butter in small pieces, stirring continually. When all the butter has been added, add lemon juice to taste.

Sauce Remoulade

½ pint (1 cup) mayonnaise (see page 121)
2 tablespoons finely chopped dill pickle or gherkin
1 dessertspoon finely chopped capers
1 teaspoon prepared mustard
1 dessertspoon finely chopped parsley
dash of Worcestershire or anchovy sauce
2 tablespoons whipped cream

Combine all ingredients except cream, mix well. Stir in cream. Serve with any seafood.

Caper Sauce

¼ pint (½ cup) mayonnaise (see page 121)
1 tablespoon chopped, drained capers
1 teaspoon vinegar from capers
1 tablespoon finely chopped parsley

Combine all ingredients, mix well to blend.

Cucumber-Mayonnaise Sauce

1 large cucumber
4 stuffed olives
¼ pint (½ cup) mayonnaise (see page 121)
4 tablespoons sour cream
1½ tablespoons milk
1½ tablespoons chopped parsley
1 tablespoon lemon juice
salt

Peel, seed, grate and drain cucumber, chop olives. Heat mayonnaise and cucumber in small saucepan over low heat. Combine remaining ingredients in bowl, stir into cucumber mixture. Keep over low heat a few seconds, stirring constantly. Serve with fish.

Tea cakes, coffee cakes, small cakes, butter cakes, fruit cakes, slices, a superb torte and gateau—there's an irresistible selection of cakes to choose from, for every occasion.

Butterscotch Teacake

4 oz. ($\frac{1}{2}$ cup or 1 stick) butter
6 oz. (1 cup) brown sugar
1 large egg

8 oz. (2 cups) plain flour
3 teaspoons baking powder
$\frac{1}{4}$ pint ($\frac{1}{2}$ cup) milk

Butterscotch Icing

$4\frac{1}{2}$ ($\frac{2}{3}$ cup) dark brown sugar
4 dessertspoons milk
pinch salt

1 oz. (2 tablespoons) butter
3 to 4 oz. (about $\frac{3}{4}$ cup) icing (confectioners') sugar
chopped almonds

Cream butter and sugar until light and fluffy. Add egg, beat well. Fold in sifted flour and baking powder alternately with the milk. Turn mixture into greased 8 in. sandwich tin. Bake in moderate oven, Mark 4, 350°F., 40 to 45 minutes, or until cake is cooked. Turn cake on to a wire tray. When cold, top with Butterscotch Icing.

Icing Place all ingredients except icing sugar and almonds in a saucepan and cook, stirring constantly, until mixture begins to boil. Boil steadily, without stirring, 4 to 5 minutes. Allow to cool until warm, beat in sifted icing sugar, adding more icing sugar, if necessary, to give a spreading consistency. Spread over cake, sprinkle with chopped almonds.

Apple Teacake

1 to 2 apples
2 oz. ($\frac{1}{4}$ cup) butter
4 oz. ($\frac{1}{2}$ cup) castor (superfine) sugar
1 egg

6 oz. ($1\frac{1}{2}$ cups) self raising (all purpose) flour
pinch salt
8 tablespoons milk
2 teaspoons cinnamon
extra sugar

Peel and core apples, cut into thin slices, cut each slice in half.

Cream butter, add sugar and beat until light and fluffy; beat in egg. Fold in sifted flour and salt alternately with milk, mix well. Spread mixture into well-greased 8 in. sandwich tin, arrange a whirl of apple slices on top, sprinkle with combined cinnamon and extra sugar. Bake in moderate oven, Mark 4, 350°F., approximately 45 minutes.

Streusel Coffee Cake

6 oz. ($\frac{3}{4}$ cup) butter
8 oz. (1 cup) sugar
1 teaspoon vanilla
3 eggs

5 oz. ($1\frac{1}{4}$ cups) self raising (all purpose) flour
3 oz. ($\frac{3}{4}$ cup) plain flour
3 tablespoons milk

Topping

4 oz. (1 cup) plain flour
1 tablespoon cinnamon

3 oz. ($\frac{1}{2}$ cup) dark brown sugar
3 oz. ($\frac{3}{8}$ cup) butter

Cream together butter and sugar until light and fluffy, add vanilla. Add eggs one at a time, beating well after each addition. Sift flours, add alternately with milk, mix thoroughly. Spread into greased 9 in. square cake tin. Sprinkle topping over cake. Bake in moderately hot oven, Mark 5, 375°F., 35 to 40 minutes, or until cooked when tested with a skewer.

Topping Sift together dry ingredients. Rub in butter thoroughly, roll into a ball. Refrigerate until firm.

Butterscotch Teacake, Chelsea Butter Bun and Almond Meringue Cake—full-of-flavour cakes that go equally well with tea or coffee.

Orange Loaf Cake

4 oz. ($\frac{1}{2}$ cup) castor (superfine) sugar
8 tablespoons milk
4 oz. ($\frac{1}{2}$ cup or 1 stick) butter

1 dessertspoon grated orange rind
2 eggs
8 oz. (2 cups) self raising (all purpose) flour

Dissolve sugar in 4 tablespoons of milk in a small mixing bowl. Add butter and orange rind and cream well. Add beaten eggs a little at a time. Sift flour, fold in alternately with remaining milk. Spoon mixture into greased and lined 9 in. × 5 in. loaf tin. Bake in moderate oven, Mark 4, 350°F., 40 minutes.

Patty Cakes

4 oz. ($\frac{1}{2}$ cup or 1 stick) butter
4 oz. ($\frac{1}{2}$ cup) castor (superfine) sugar
2 eggs

little milk
$\frac{1}{2}$ teaspoon vanilla
8 oz. (2 cups) self raising (all purpose) flour

Cream butter and sugar together until light and fluffy. Add vanilla, then gradually beat in the lightly beaten eggs. Fold in the sifted flour, adding a little milk if necessary, mix well. Drop dessertspoonfuls of mixture into well greased, deep patty tins. Bake in moderately hot oven, Mark 5, 375°F., 10 to 15 minutes.

Makes 2 dozen.

Butterfly Cakes Cut a slice from top of cooled patty cake, then cut this slice in half to form two wings. Pipe or spoon whipped cream across top of cake, set the wings in position. Dust with sifted icing (confectioners') sugar; top, if desired, with a halved strawberry.

Ginger Cake

1 lb. (4 cups) plain flour
$\frac{1}{2}$ teaspoon salt
2 dessertspoons baking powder
3 dessertspoons ground ginger
1 teaspoon bicarbonate of soda

12 oz. (1 cup) treacle
6 oz. ($\frac{3}{4}$ cup) butter
12 oz. (2 cups) light brown sugar
1 egg
$\frac{1}{2}$ pint (1 cup) milk

Lemon Icing

12 oz. (2 cups approx.) icing (confectioners') sugar
$\frac{1}{2}$ oz. (1 tablespoon) butter
lemon juice

Sift flour, salt, baking powder, ginger and bicarbonate of soda into a basin. Place treacle, butter and brown sugar into a saucepan, stir over a low heat until sugar dissolves. Cool. Add to dry ingredients; mix in egg and warmed milk. Pour into greased and paper-lined 10 in. square or large oblong cake tin.

Bake in moderately hot oven, Mark 5, 375°F., 1 hour. Cool slightly before turning out on to a wire tray. When cold, top with lemon icing.

Lemon Icing Sift icing sugar. Soften butter with a wooden spoon, then gradually add icing sugar, working well in, until the mixture is crumbly. Add sufficient lemon juice, a little at a time, to make a smooth spreading consistency.

Basic Butter Cake

4 oz. ($\frac{1}{2}$ cup or 1 stick) butter
6 oz. ($\frac{3}{4}$ cup) castor (superfine) sugar
1 teaspoon vanilla
2 eggs

8 oz. (2 cups) self raising (all purpose) flour
pinch salt
3 to 4 tablespoons milk

Cream butter, sugar and vanilla together until light and fluffy. Add eggs one at a time, beat well. Fold in sifted dry ingredients alternately with the milk. Spoon into a greased and lined 7 in. or 8 in. cake tin. Bake in a moderate oven, Mark 4, 350°F., 50 to 60 minutes.

Variations

Light Fruit Cake
Add 6 oz. (1 cup) mixed fruit and $\frac{1}{2}$ teaspoons mixed spice, nutmeg and grated lemon or orange rind.

Marble Cake
Divide mixture into three portions. Colour one portion pink; to second portion add 3 dessertspoons cocoa blended smoothly with 3 dessertspoons warm milk; leave third portion plain. Spoon mixtures into tin in alternate spoonfuls. Cut through two or three times with knife blade or skewer, to give pattern.

Lamingtons
Pour cake mixture into a well-greased 7 in. × 11 in. tin. Bake in moderate oven, Mark 4, 350°F., 30 to 40 minutes. Allow to stand in the tin for a few minutes before turning out on to wire tray.

It is best to make the cake the day before you want to cut and ice the lamingtons, as fresh cake will usually crumble.

Cut cake into squares. Dip in chocolate icing, then toss in coconut.

Chocolate Icing for Lamingtons Sift 1 lb. (3 cups) icing (confectioners') sugar and 4 dessertspoons cocoa into a basin. Add 1 dessertspoon melted butter to 6 to 8 tablespoons warmed milk. Add sufficient milk mixture to icing sugar mixture to make a smooth coating consistency; beat well.

One-Egg Butter Cake

8 oz. (2 cups) plain
  flour
pinch salt
2½ teaspoons baking
  powder
3 oz. (⅜ cup) butter

8 oz. (1 cup) castor
  (superfine) sugar
1 egg
1 teaspoon vanilla
4 to 5 tablespoons milk

Sift together flour, salt and baking powder. Cream butter until soft, gradually add sugar and beaten egg, beat well until light and fluffy; add vanilla. Add dry ingredients alternately with the milk. Spoon into a well-greased 7 in. cake tin. Bake in moderate oven, Mark 4, 350°F., approximately 55 minutes.

Two-Egg Butter Cake

4 oz. (½ cup or 1 stick)
  butter
8 oz. (1 cup) castor
  (superfine) sugar
2 large eggs, or 3
  smaller eggs
12 oz. (3 cups) plain
  flour

4 teaspoons baking
  powder
pinch salt
about ¼ pint (½ cup)
  milk
1 teaspoon vanilla

Cream butter, add sugar and 1 egg; beat until light and fluffy. Add remaining egg, beat well. Sift together dry ingredients; add alternately with milk to creamed mixture; add vanilla. Pour into well-greased 8 in. cake tin.

Bake in moderately slow oven, Mark 3, 325°F., approximately 1¼ to 1½ hours. Let cake cool in tin 5 to 10 minutes before turning out.

Cherry Cake

4 oz. (½ cup) glacé
  cherries
6 oz. (¾ cup) butter
6 oz. (¾ cup) castor
  (superfine) sugar
3 eggs

3 oz. (¾ cup) plain flour
3 oz. (¾ cup) self
  raising (all purpose)
  flour
3 dessertspoons milk

Snow Glaze

10 oz. (2 cups) icing
  (confectioners')
  sugar
1 teaspoon softened
  butter

¼ teaspoon vanilla
1 to 2 dessertspoons
  milk

Cut cherries into thirds. Cream butter and sugar until light and fluffy. Gradually add well-beaten eggs. Fold in sifted flours alternately with milk; lastly fold in cut cherries. Place mixture into a large, well-greased baba mould, or greased 8 in. round cake tin.

Bake in moderate oven, Mark 4, 350°F., approximately 1 hour, or until golden brown and cooked when tested with skewer. Allow to stand 10 minutes before turning out; cool.

When cold, ice with Snow Glaze and decorate with glacé cherry halves, if desired.

Snow Glaze   Combine sifted icing (confectioners') sugar, butter and vanilla in small basin. Gradually beat in milk until mixture is smooth and of a coating consistency; a little more milk may be necessary. Spread over cake; or warm over low heat and allow to trickle over top of cake and down the sides.

Madeira Cake

6 oz. (¾ cup) butter
5 oz. (⅝ cup) castor
  (superfine) sugar
grated rind medium
  size lemon

3 large eggs
8 oz. (2 cups) plain flour
2 teaspoons baking
  powder
candied peel

Cream butter until light and fluffy, gradually beat in sugar. Add grated lemon rind, mix well. Beat eggs lightly, add gradually to mixture, beat well. Sift flour with baking powder; lightly fold into beaten mixture. No extra liquid should be added. Turn mixture into greased, lined 7 in. cake tin. Bake in moderate oven, Mark 4, 350°F., approximately 1 hour. Place small pieces of candied peel on top, decoratively, after ¾ hour of cooking time.

Apple Shortcake

4 oz. (½ cup or 1 stick)
  butter
4 oz. (½ cup) castor
  (superfine) sugar
1 egg
4 oz. (1 cup) self
  raising (all purpose)
  flour
4 oz. (1 cup) plain flour

¼ teaspoon salt
1 tablespoon
  marmalade
3 peeled, coarsely
  grated apples
grated rind and juice
  ½ lemon
extra sugar

Cream butter and sugar lightly, add egg, beat well; mix in sifted flours and salt. Divide mixture into two, roll each piece into a round; place one round in base of 8 in. greased sandwich tin, cover with grated apple and marmalade. Sprinkle with grated lemon rind and juice, then with 1 tablespoon extra sugar. Cover with second round of dough, pressing well at sides. Brush with water, sprinkle evenly with extra castor sugar. Bake in moderate oven, Mark 4, 350°F., 35 to 40 minutes.

Chelsea Butter Bun

12 oz. (3 cups) self raising (all purpose) flour
½ teaspoon salt

1½ oz. (3 tablespoons) butter
¼ to ½ pint (½ to 1 cup) milk

Filling

2 oz. (¼ cup) butter
2 oz. (⅓ cup) light brown sugar
2 oz. (⅓ cup) sultanas
2 oz. (⅓ cup) currants

2 oz. (¼ cup) chopped glacé cherries
2 oz. (⅓ cup) mixed peel
1 teaspoon cinnamon

Glaze

2 dessertspoons water
2 dessertspoons sugar

1 teaspoon gelatine

Sift flour and salt into a basin, rub in butter lightly. Mix to a firm dough with milk. Roll dough into oblong shape, ¼ in. in thickness.
Filling Cream butter and brown sugar together. Spread over dough; sprinkle with fruit and cinnamon. Roll up lengthwise; cut roll into 14 thick slices. Pack into a greased 8 in. sandwich tin, cut side down. Bake in a moderate oven, Mark 4, 350°F., 25 to 30 minutes.

Brush bun with glaze, while still hot.
Glaze Place ingredients into a small bowl, stir over hot water until gelatine and sugar dissolve.

Christmas Cake

10 oz. (1¼ cups) butter
10 oz. (1⅓ cups) dark brown sugar
1 tablespoon black treacle
grated rind of 1 lemon
grated rind of 1 orange
5 large eggs
2 tablespoons brandy
12 oz. (3 cups) plain flour
½ teaspoon cinnamon

½ teaspoon nutmeg
½ teaspoon mixed spice
1¼ lb. (3⅔ cups) currants
12 oz. (2 cups) sultanas
8 oz. (1½ cups) raisins
4 oz. (¾ cup) prunes
4 oz. (¾ cup) dates
4 oz. (1 cup) almonds
4 oz. (¾ cup) candied peel
4 oz. (½ cup) glacé cherries

Prepare a 9 in. round tin at least 3 in. deep. Line the sides and bottom with a double layer of greased grease-proof paper and tie a deep band of brown paper round the outside of the tin, standing 1 to 2 in. above the top of the tin.

Beat the butter, sugar, treacle, lemon and orange rind together until very soft and creamy. Gradually add the beaten eggs and brandy, adding a little sifted flour if the mixture shows signs of curdling. Sieve flour and spices together. Mix all the fruit—the last six ingredients should be chopped. Stir the flour and fruit into the creamed mixture, mix well but do not over beat. Put into the prepared tin and bake in the centre of a very moderate oven, Mark 3, 325°F., for 1½ hours, then reduce heat to Mark 2, 300°F., for a further 3 hours. Allow to cool in the tin, and when quite cold, wrap securely in foil and store till required.

Chocolate Fruit Cake

1 lb. (2⅔ cups) sultanas
8 oz. (1½ cups) raisins
4 oz. (⅔ cup) currants
4 oz. (1½ cups) glacé cherries
3 oz. (½ cup) mixed peel
2 oz. (⅓ cup) glacé pineapple
2 oz. (⅓ cup) glacé apricots
2 oz. (⅜ cup) prunes or dates
1 oz. (⅜ cup) dried apricots
6 tablespoons brandy
8 oz. (1 cup) butter
9 oz. (1½ cups) dark brown sugar

1 teaspoon grated orange rind
1 teaspoon grated lemon rind
1 teaspoon vanilla
¼ teaspoon almond essence
2 tablespoons marmalade
4 oz. (4 squares) plain chocolate
4 eggs
10 oz. (2½ cups) plain flour
1 teaspoon mixed spice
¼ teaspoon nutmeg
1 teaspoon cinnamon
pinch salt

Chop fruit and place in a basin, pour over brandy, mix well, cover and stand overnight. Cream butter with sugar, add grated fruit rinds, essences, marmalade and melted chocolate; mix thoroughly. Drop in the eggs one at a time, beating well after each addition. Fold in sifted dry ingredients alternately with the prepared fruits; mix well. Place mixture into deep 9 in. cake tin, which has been lined with 1 thickness white paper and 2 thicknesses brown paper. Bake in slow oven, Mark 1, 275°F., approximately 4 hours, or until cooked, when a skewer, inserted, comes out clean. Allow to cool completely in tin. Then remove from tin, peel off brown paper layers. Wrap in clean towel or aluminium foil, store in a reasonably cool place until required.

At top, from left. Madeira Cake, Chocolate Fruit Cake, topped with Marzipan Fruits, Cherry Cake; below, Ginger Cake, Patty Cakes, Easy Dundee Cake.

Easy Dundee Cake

2 oz. (⅓ cup) mixed peel
8 oz. (1½ cups) raisins
10 oz. (2½ cups) plain
  flour
1 teaspoon baking
  powder
½ teaspoon mixed spice
6 oz. (¾ cup) castor
  (superfine) sugar
6 oz. (¾ cup) softened
  butter
8 oz. (1⅓ cups) currants
8 oz. (1⅓ cups) sultanas
2 oz. (¼ cup) cherries
5 eggs
little milk if required
1 oz. (¼ cup) blanched
  almonds

Chop peel and raisins, sift dry ingredients. Place softened butter in a large bowl, add all remaining ingredients with the exception of the almonds; beat together until smooth and thoroughly mixed (this is best done in an electric mixer). Place in an 8 in. round deep cake tin that has been lined with 2 layers of greaseproof paper. Decorate top with almonds and, if desired, glacé cherries.

Bake in a moderately slow oven, Mark 3, 325°F., 2 to 2½ hours.

When cake is cooked, cover with a clean tea-towel and leave to cool in tin.

Strawberry Hazelnut Gateau

4 egg whites
pinch salt
10 oz. (1¼ cups) castor
  (superfine) sugar
4½ oz. (1 cup) ground
  hazelnuts
1 teaspoon vinegar
½ teaspoon vanilla
4 dessertspoons black
  coffee

Filling

1 lb. strawberries
1 pint (2 cups) whipped
  cream
6 oz. (6 squares) plain
  chocolate
water

Beat egg-whites with salt until stiff; gradually add sugar; beat until mixture is of meringue consistency. Fold in remaining ingredients. Spread in 2 greased and floured 8 in. springform pans. Bake in moderate oven, Mark 4, 350°F., approximately 35 minutes; release sides of pans. Cool on base of pan.

Remove from base, place a layer of meringue on serving plate. Spread with thin layer of chocolate, which has been melted with the water. Spread ¾ in. layer of cream over chocolate. Top with layer of sliced strawberries; reserve remainder for decoration.

Spread second layer of meringue with remaining chocolate mixture, place on strawberry layer, chocolate-side up. Cover and top with remaining cream.

Refrigerate several hours, or preferably overnight. Serve decorated with reserved strawberries.

Sultana Cake

1½ lb. (3⅔ cups) sultanas
8 oz. (1 cup) butter
8 oz. (1 cup) castor
  (superfine) sugar
5 eggs
10 oz. (2½ cups) plain
  flour
1 oz. (¼ cup) self
  raising (all purpose)
  flour
pinch salt
4 oz. (1 cup) blanched
  almonds
2 to 3 tablespoons
  brandy
½ teaspoon vanilla

Cover sultanas with warm water, soak for 2 hours. Drain, let dry at least 24 hours.

Cream butter and sugar together until light and fluffy. Add eggs one at a time, beating well after each addition. If necessary, add a little flour towards the end of the egg additions, to prevent curdling. Add sifted flours and salt alternately with the sultanas, then add chopped almonds, reserving a few to decorate the top of cake. Fold in brandy and vanilla. Place mixture into a greased and paper lined 8 in. or 9 in. square cake tin. Bake in moderately slow oven, Mark 3, 325°F., approximately 1¾ hours.

Devil's Food Cake

2 oz. (¼ cup) butter
8 oz. (1 cup) sugar
2 eggs
6 oz. (1¼ cups) self
  raising (all purpose)
  flour
4 tablespoons sour milk
6 tablespoons black
  coffee
2 oz. (2 squares) plain
  chocolate
1 teaspoon bicarbonate
  of soda
1 teaspoon vanilla
  essence

Frosting

1 egg white
3 dessertspoons cold
  water
7 oz. (⅞ cup) sugar
¼ teaspoon cream of
  tartar
½ teaspoon vanilla
little melted chocolate

Grease two 9 in. sandwich tins.

Cream butter and sugar until light and fluffy. Beat in eggs gradually. Add flour and sour milk alternately. Pour boiling coffee on to melted choclate and add bicarbonate. Cool a little, add to mixture with vanilla. Bake in a moderate oven, Mark 5, 375°F., for 25 minutes. When cold, fill and spread with frosting.

To make frosting Whisk all ingredients except vanilla in a basin over hot water for about 7 minutes until mixture stands in peaks then add vanilla.

Dribble a little melted chocolate over the top.

Dark Chocolate Cake

1½ gills (⅔ cup) hot
  coffee
2 oz. (½ cup) cocoa
10 oz. (1¼ cups) sugar
4 oz. (½ cup or 1 stick)
  butter
3 eggs, separated
1 teaspoon salt
1 teaspoon vanilla

1 teaspoon bicarbonate
  of soda
¼ pint (½ cup) sour
  cream
8 oz. (2 cups) plain
  flour
4 oz. (½ cup) sugar,
  extra
whipped cream

Sour Cream Frosting

4 oz. (4 squares) plain
  chocolate
¼ pint (½ cup) sour
  cream

pinch salt
4 dessertspoons icing
  (confectioners')
  sugar

Stir hot coffee gradually into cocoa. Combine sugar with butter, egg-yolks, salt, vanilla and half the cocoa mixture. Beat until light and creamy. Mix bicarbonate of soda and sour cream together. To butter and sugar mixture add sour cream and cocoa-coffee alternately with sifted flour. Beat egg-whites until stiff, gradually add the extra 4 oz. (½ cup) sugar, beat until meringue stands in stiff peaks. Fold into chocolate mixture. Pour into 9 in. or 10 in. greased and paper lined deep cake tin. Bake in moderate oven, Mark 4, 350°F., 1 to 1¼ hours.

Cool completely on wire tray, then cut into 2 layers and join with whipped cream. Spread frosting in a thin layer over top and sides of cake, decorate with walnut halves and cherries if desired.

Refrigerate until Sour Cream Frosting is firm. *Sour Cream Frosting* Melt chopped chocolate over hot water. Remove from heat, allow to cool slightly, then stir in sour cream and salt. Add sifted icing sugar and beat until a spreading consistency.

Date and Walnut Loaf

4 oz. (1 cup) self raising
  (all purpose) flour
4 oz. (½ cup) sugar
½ teaspoon bicarbonate
  of soda
2 teaspoons cinnamon

2 oz. (⅜ cup) chopped
  dates
2 oz. (½ cup) chopped
  walnuts
1 oz. (2 tablespoons)
  butter
¼ pint (½ cup) water

Sift flour, sugar, bicarbonate of soda and cinnamon into a basin. Add the chopped dates and walnuts, mix well. Heat butter and water in a saucepan until water just comes to the boil. Make a well in the centre of the dry ingredients, add hot liquid and mix thoroughly. Spoon into greased 10 in. × 3 in. tin. Bake in a moderate oven, Mark 4, 350°F., approximately 40 minutes. Serve with butter.

Mocha Torte

6 eggs, separated
4 oz. (½ cup) castor
  (superfine) sugar
4 oz. (4 squares) plain
  chocolate

1 teaspoon instant
  coffee powder
4 dessertspoons water
2 dessertspoons plain
  flour

Coffee Cream

1 dessertspoon instant
  coffee powder
½ pint (1 cup) cream

2 oz. (¼ cup) castor
  (superfine) sugar

Beat egg-yolks and sugar until pale and creamy. Melt chopped chocolate over hot water, allow to cool slightly; add to egg-yolk mixture, mixing well. Stir coffee into water, add to chocolate mixture. Gently fold in sifted flour and lightly beaten egg-whites. It is important not to overmix.

Pour mixture into 3 greased and lined 8 in. sandwich tins, bake in moderately slow oven, Mark 3, 325°F., 30 to 35 minutes; cool on wire rack.

When cold, join together with Coffee Cream. Cover top and sides of cake with remaining Coffee Cream, decorate with toasted almonds; drizzle a little melted chocolate over, if desired. Refrigerate. *Coffee Cream* Combine all ingredients in mixing bowl, refrigerate at least 1 hour. When ready to use beat until thick.

Orange Date Cake

¼ pint (½ cup) orange
  juice
1 lb. (2½ cups) dates
1 lb. 2 oz. (4½ cups) self
  raising (all purpose)
  flour
pinch salt
8 oz. (½ cup) butter

1 lb. (2 cups) castor
  (superfine) sugar
3 oz. (½ cup) mixed
  peel
3 eggs
½ to ¾ pint (1 to 1½ cups)
  warm milk
½ teaspoon vanilla

Pour orange juice over chopped dates, cover, leave overnight.

Next day sift flour and salt into bowl. Rub in butter until mixture resembles fine breadcrumbs; mix in castor sugar. Add mixed peel, dates and orange juice, rub through lightly, separating the pieces. Make well in centre of dry ingredients. Add beaten eggs alternately with milk to which vanilla has been added, stirring until all dry ingredients are well mixed. Place mixture into greased and paper lined 10 in. square cake tin. Bake in moderate oven, Mark 4, 350°F. 30 minutes, reduce heat to moderately slow, Mark 2, 300°F., and continue cooking further 1½ hours. Leave in tin to cool.

Chocolate Orange Cake

6 oz. ($\frac{3}{4}$ cup) butter
6 oz. ($\frac{3}{4}$ cup) castor (superfine) sugar
3 eggs

6 oz. ($1\frac{1}{2}$ cups) self raising (all purpose) flour
2 tablespoons milk
grated rind 2 oranges

Chocolate Icing

6 oz. (1 cup) icing (confectioners') sugar

1 tablespoon cocoa
$\frac{1}{2}$ teaspoon butter
water to mix

Cream butter and sugar until light and fluffy, beat in eggs one at a time, beating well after each addition. Sift flour, fold in alternately with milk; add grated orange rind. Place mixture in greased and paper lined 9 in. × 5 in. loaf tin. Bake in moderate oven, Mark 4, 350°F., approximately 1 hour or until skewer inserted in centre comes out clean. Leave in tin a few minutes before turning out on to wire tray. When cold, top with chocolate icing.
Chocolate Icing   Sift icing sugar and cocoa into bowl, add butter, then mix to a stiff consistency with a little cold water. Place over hot water and stir until a pouring consistency; this will take only a minute or two. Pour on top of cake and spread with spatula, swirling icing with tip of spatula.

Almond Meringue Cake

4 oz. ($\frac{1}{2}$ cup or 1 stick) butter
4 oz. ($\frac{1}{2}$ cup) castor (superfine) sugar
4 egg-yolks

1 teaspoon vanilla
4 oz. (1 cup) self raising (all purpose) flour
pinch salt
4 to 5 tablespoons milk

Topping

4 egg-whites
6 oz. ($\frac{3}{4}$ cup) castor (superfine) sugar
2 dessertspoons sugar, extra

$\frac{1}{2}$ teaspoon cinnamon
1 oz. ($\frac{1}{8}$ cup) blanched, slivered almonds

Cream butter and sugar until light and fluffy. Beat in yolks and vanilla. Sift flour and salt; add alternately with milk. Spread mixture into a greased 8 in. springform pan.
Topping   Beat egg-whites until stiff, gradually add sugar, beating well. Spread this meringue over mixture in pan. Mix together the extra sugar and cinnamon, sprinkle over meringue. Sprinkle with almonds. Bake in moderate oven, Mark 4, 350°F., 60 to 65 minutes, or until cake is cooked when tested with a skewer. Leave in pan 10 minutes before turning out.

Pineapple Fruit Cake

8 oz. (1 cup) sugar
15 oz. can crushed pineapple
1 lb. ($2\frac{3}{4}$ cups) mixed fruit
1 teaspoon bicarbonate of soda

1 teaspoon mixed spice
4 oz. ($\frac{1}{2}$ cup or 1 stick) butter
4 oz. (1 cup) plain flour
4 oz. (1 cup) self raising (all purpose) flour
2 eggs

Place sugar, contents of can of pineapple, chopped mixed fruit, bicarbonate of soda, spice and butter into a saucepan. Bring to boil, boil 3 minutes; remove from heat, cool completely.
Sift flours together, mix into cold fruit mixture with well-beaten eggs. Place mixture into greased and lined 8 in. cake tin.
Bake in moderate oven, Mark 4, 350°F., approximately $1\frac{1}{2}$ hours, reduce heat to moderately slow, Mark 2, 300°F., bake further 20 to 30 minutes or until a skewer, inserted, comes out clean.

Pineapple Teacake

15 oz. can crushed pineapple
4 oz. ($\frac{1}{2}$ cup or 1 stick) butter
6 oz. ($1\frac{1}{2}$ cups) self raising (all purpose) flour
pinch salt

4 oz. ($\frac{1}{2}$ cup) sugar
1 egg
scant $\frac{1}{4}$ pint (7 tablespoons) milk
4 oz. ($\frac{1}{3}$ cup) honey
1 oz. ($\frac{1}{4}$ cup) coconut

Drain pineapple (the juice is not needed for this recipe). Melt 2 oz. ($\frac{1}{4}$ cup) butter and allow it to cool slightly.
Sift flour and salt, add sugar. Combine beaten egg, milk and melted butter, add to dry ingredients; mix well. Pour into a greased deep 8 in. round cake tin, spread pineapple over the batter. Cream remaining butter and honey well, spoon over pineapple; sprinkle with coconut. Bake in moderately hot oven, Mark 4, 350°F., 35 to 40 minutes.
When cool, sprinkle top with sifted icing sugar.

Strawberry Hazelnut Gateau—thin wafers of hazelnut cake are sandwiched together with whipped cream and chocolate and red, ripe strawberries in this delicious dessert cake.

Rock Cakes

8 oz. (2 cups) self raising (all purpose) flour	3 oz. ($\frac{3}{8}$ cup) butter
2½ oz. (good ¼ cup) sugar	3 oz ($\frac{1}{2}$ cup) sultanas or currants
pinch salt	1 oz. (¼ cup) mixed peel
¼ teaspoon cinnamon	1 egg
	4 to 5 tablespoons milk
	extra sugar

Sift dry ingredients into a bowl. Add butter, and, using fingertips rub in until mixture resembles fine breadcrumbs. Add fruit and peel, mix well. Beat egg and add to mixture, then add sufficient milk to make a moist but still stiff consistency. If mixture is too soft, cakes will spread widely during cooking instead of retaining shape. Use teaspoons or dessertspoons, depending on size of cake required, to spoon mixture out in rough heaps on to greased trays. Leave space between each to allow for slight spreading. Sprinkle cakes with extra sugar. Bake in a moderately hot oven, Mark 5, 375°F., 10 to 20 minutes, depending on size of cake. Loosen on trays while hot; allow to cool on trays.

Fruit Slices

6 oz. (1½ cups) self raising (all purpose) flour	4 oz. (½ cup or 1 stick) butter
1½ oz. (⅓ cup) ground rice	2 oz. (¼ cup) castor (superfine) sugar
2½ tablespoons corn-flour (cornstarch)	1 egg

Filling

½ lb. (1¼ cups) dates	1 dessertspoon sugar
grated rind and juice 1 lemon	1 oz. (2 tablespoons) butter
4 oz. (⅔ cup) sultanas	1 teaspoon mixed spice
4 oz. (⅔ cup) raisins	1½ gills (⅔ cup) water
1 oz. (2 tablespoons) mixed peel	1 tablespoon arrowroot
2 oz. (¼ cup) glacé cherries	1 tablespoon rum or orange juice

Sift flour, ground rice, cornflour (cornstarch) into basin, rub in butter until mixture resembles fine breadcrumbs. Stir in sugar and beaten egg. Knead lightly on floured board, roll out half the pastry, fit into greased and lined 11 in. × 7 in. tin.

Cover with prepared filling. Roll out remaining pastry; cover filling.

Glaze with little cold water, sprinkle with extra castor (superfine) sugar. Bake in hot oven, Mark 7, 425°F., 25 to 30 minutes. Cool; cut into slices.

Filling   Place in saucepan chopped fruit and all ingredients except arrowroot and rum; place over low heat, stirring continually, until thick. Blend arrowroot with rum or orange juice, stir into fruit mixture; return to heat, stirring, 3 minutes. Remove, cool completely.

Apple Slice

4 oz. (½ cup or 1 stick) butter	4 oz. (1 cup) plain flour
4 oz. (½ cup) castor (superfine) sugar	1 teaspoon cinnamon
1 egg	1 teaspoon mixed spice
	½ pint (1 cup) stewed apple, well drained

Cream butter and sugar together until light and fluffy, add egg and beat well. Sift flour with spices fold lightly into creamed mixture. Spread half mixture on base of a greased 8 in. square cake tin, cover with well drained apples, spread remaining cake mixture on top. Bake in moderate oven, Mark 4, 350°F., approximately 45 minutes, or until golden brown. Serve hot or cold, cut into squares, sprinkled with sifted icing sugar.

Peanut Slice

8 oz. shortcrust pastry (see page 200)	2 oz. (½ cup) cake crumbs
raspberry jam	1 dessertspoon cocoa
1 egg-white	½ teaspoon vanilla
6 oz. (¾ cup) castor (superfine) sugar	½ lb. (1¼ cups) roasted peanuts
	vanilla

Roll out pastry, line greased 7 in. × 11 in. tin, bake in moderately hot oven Mark 5, 375°F., 15 minutes; cool. Spread with jam.

Beat egg-whites until stiff, gradually beat in sugar. Lightly fold in cake crumbs, cocoa, peanuts; flavour with vanilla. Spread over raspberry jam, brush with water. Bake in moderate oven, Mark 4, 350°F., approximately 25 minutes. Cut into slices.

Vanilla Custard Slice

10 oz. puff pastry (see page 201-2)	4 tablespoons custard powder
1¾ pints (3½ cups) milk	¼ pint (½ cup) milk, extra
6 oz. (¾ cup) sugar	
2 oz. (¼ cup) butter	1 dessertspoon vanilla
2 oz. (½ cup) cornflour (cornstarch)	1 egg

Roll out pastry thinly, cut into two 10 in. squares; place on ungreased oven tray, bake in very hot oven, Mark 8, 450°F., approximately 15 minutes.

Cool, trim to make two 8 in. squares. Place one layer on base of ungreased 8 in. square cake tin.

Place milk, sugar, butter in large saucepan. Blend cornflour (cornstarch) and custard powder with extra milk; add to saucepan, bring to boil, stirring until smooth and thick. Remove from heat, beat in vanilla and egg. While still hot, pour over layer of pastry in tin; top with second square of pastry, pressing down firmly. Cool, top with lemon icing. (See page 152). Refrigerate until firm; cut into slices.

Chocolate Rough Slice

4 oz. (1 cup) self raising (all purpose) flour	2½ oz. (⅓ cup) castor (superfine) sugar
1 dessertspoon cocoa	1 oz. (¼ cup) coconut
pinch salt	4 oz. (½ cup or 1 stick) butter

Topping

3 tablespoons condensed milk	1 oz. (2 tablespoons) butter
1 tablespoon cocoa	4 oz. (1 cup) coconut
6 oz. (1 cup) sifted icing (confectioners') sugar	1 teaspoon vanilla

Sift dry ingredients into basin, add sugar and coconut; stir in melted butter, mixing well. Press into greased and lined 11 in. × 7 in. tin. Bake in moderate oven, Mark 4, 350°F., 25 minutes.

Cool slightly; cover with Chocolate Rough Topping while still warm. Cut into slices when cold.

Chocolate Rough Topping Combine all ingredients in basin, mix well.

Raspberry Coconut Slice

4 oz. (1 cup) self raising (all purpose) flour	4 oz. (1 cup) coconut
8 oz. (1 cup) sugar	few drops almond essence
1 tablespoon butter	extra coconut
2 eggs	
raspberry jam	

Sift flour and 4 oz. (½ cup) sugar into basin, rub in butter until mixture resembles fine breadcrumbs. Mix to stiff dough with 1 beaten egg. Knead lightly, roll out to 8 in. square. Place on base of greased and lined shallow 8 in. square tin. Spread with little raspberry jam.

Beat remaining egg and sugar together until pale and thick, carefully fold in coconut and almond essence; spread over jam. Sprinkle with little extra coconut. Bake in moderate oven, Mark 4, 350°F., 30 to 35 minutes or until golden. Cut into slices while still warm.

Spicy Apple Slice

Pastry

3 oz. (⅜ cup) butter	6 oz. (1½ cups) plain flour
2 oz. (¼ cup) castor (superfine) sugar	½ teaspoon baking powder
1 egg-yolk	
1 teaspoon water	

Filling

4 large apples	2 tablespoons water
4 oz. (½ cup) sugar	little lemon rind

Spicy Topping

3 oz. (¾ cup) plain flour	2½ tablespoons sugar
3 teaspoons cinnamon	2 oz. (¼ cup) butter

Cream butter and sugar until light and fluffy, beat in egg-yolk and water. Knead in sifted dry ingredients until mixture comes together in a ball. Roll out on floured board, line greased 7 in. × 11 in. tin.

Filling Peel, core, and slice apples thinly. Place in saucepan with sugar, water and lemon rind, cook gently until apples are tender, cool. Place cold apple mixture in uncooked pastry shell.

Spicy Topping Sift dry ingredients into bowl, rub in butter using fingertips, shape into a ball, chill until firm. Press ball of topping through colander or grate on to apples.

Bake in moderately hot oven, Mark 5, 375°F., 35 to 40 minutes. Cool and cut into slices.

Pineapple Upside Down Cake

Topping

1 oz. (2 tablespoons) butter	1 small can pineapple rings
1 oz. (2 tablespoons) light brown sugar	glacé cherries

Cake

6 oz. (1½ cups) flour	4 oz. (½ cup) castor (superfine) sugar
1½ teaspoons baking powder	3 eggs
2 oz. (⅓ cup) semolina	½ teaspoon vanilla essence
4 oz. (½ cup or 1 stick) butter	

Melt the butter and brown sugar and pour into a 7 in. cake tin. Arrange the pineapple in the tin and place a glacé cherry in the centre of each ring. Sift the flour, semolina and baking powder. Cream the butter and sugar until light and fluffy. Beat in half the eggs, then fold in half the flour mixture. Add rest of eggs and vanilla and a little milk. Fold in rest of flour mixture. Spread evenly over fruit.

Bake in a moderately hot oven, Mark 5, 375°F., for about 20 minutes.

Turn out and serve hot or cold.

Sponge cakes

Everybody loves the light, airy melt-in-the-mouth goodness of a sponge cake. Filled with cream and fruit, they make a delicious dessert; and they're ideal for a child's birthday cake. They're not difficult to make—here we give you all the hints you need to turn out perfect sponge cakes.

The lightness of a sponge depends upon the amount of air incorporated during the mixing.

Sift dry indredients well so mixture is aerated.

Beat eggs with sugar until sugar is dissolved; this could take 10 to 15 minutes. Castor (superfine) sugar is the best to use for sponge cakes; it is finer than granulated sugar, dissolves more easily, gives a more even texture to finished cake. Some recipes require the eggs to be separated. If so, the whites are whipped until stiff, sugar being added gradually. This is important; if the sugar was added all at once it would deflate the mixture.

Once yolks are added, beat only until mixture is thick and of creamy consistency. Do not over-beat or mixture will become thin; the air beaten into egg-whites would be broken down.

Sift dry ingredients evenly over surface of batter and fold in. A large metal spoon is good for this. Dip spoon right to bottom of basin, turn spoon over gently to bring it out, so flour is 'folded' inside egg mixture. Do this lightly, smoothly, until all traces of flour have disappeared.

Dissolve the butter in hot water and fold in all at once, carefully and quickly. Hot water is absorbed into mixture more quickly than cold; therefore, less folding-in, which disturbs the air, is necessary.

Grease tins lightly; sprinkle lightly with flour or, for a sugary crust, castor (superfine) sugar. Shake to cover inside surface, tap out any surplus.

Do not line tins with paper. Sponge cakes do not contain fat in any quantity and, if bottom of tin was protected with paper, the cakes would have a moist, crustless appearance when paper was removed—instead of the delightful, golden colour.

The exception to this is the Swiss Roll, which has the tin lined with greased paper.

To test if cake is cooked, press top lightly with fingertip; if no impression is left and cake springs back lightly it is ready to take from oven. It will also shrink away a little from sides of tin.

Turn out on to wire cooling tray covered with teatowel; this will prevent wire marking top of cake. Quickly place another wire tray on top of cake; carefully invert so top of cake is uppermost. (Be careful not to apply pressure or cake will be squeezed between trays.) Remove top tray and tea-towel. Let cake stand until quite cool.

Sponge Cakes

4 eggs
6 oz. ($\frac{3}{4}$ cup) castor (superfine) sugar
5 oz. ($1\frac{1}{4}$ cups) self raising (all purpose) flour
1 teaspoon butter
3 tablespoons hot water

Beat whole eggs until light. Gradually beat in sugar; continue beating until mixture is thick and sugar is completely dissolved (approximately 10 to 15 minutes). Sift flour several times; melt butter in hot water. Sift dry ingredients over egg mixture, fold in; then, working quickly, fold in the hot water and butter. Pour into greased deep 8 in. cake tin, or until cake is elastic to touch and shrinking slightly from sides of tin. Turn out at once on to wire tray. When cold fill and decorate as liked.

Sponge Sandwich

3 large eggs
4 oz. ($\frac{1}{2}$ cup) castor (superfine) sugar
4 oz. (1 cup) self raising (all purpose) flour
3 tablespoons hot water
1 teaspoon butter

Separate eggs; beat whites stiffly, gradually beat in sugar, beating well after each addition to dissolve sugar thoroughly. Add yolks all at once, beat only until colour is evenly mixed through. Sift flour several times, then sift over egg mixture; fold in carefully. Combine hot water and butter, stir until butter melts (or heat together a few minutes to dissolve butter); pour all at once into mixture, fold through quickly, thoroughly.

Pour into 2 deep 7 in. greased and lightly floured sandwich tins, bake in moderate oven, Mark 4, 350°F., approximately 20 minutes or until lightly browned and elastic to the touch. Turn immediately on to wire tray. When cold, join with whipped cream.

Deliciously light, delicate in texture, Sponge Cake is everybody's favourite. Filling can be whipped cream, jam, lemon butter.

Honey Sponge

3 eggs
4 oz. (½ cup) castor (superfine) sugar
½ teaspoon vanilla
3 oz. (¾ cup) self raising (all purpose) flour
3 dessertspoons arrowroot
pinch salt
1 dessertspoon honey
1 dessertspoon butter
3 dessertspoons hot milk

Separate eggs, beat whites stiffly, gradually add sugar, beating well after each addition. Add vanilla, beat well; add yolks all at once, beat again. Sift dry ingredients several times, fold gently into egg mixture. Add honey and the butter, which has been melted in the milk. Pour into 2 greased and lightly floured 7 in. sandwich tins, bake in moderate oven, Mark 4, 350°F., approximately 20 to 25 minutes. When cooked, turn immediately on to wire tray. When cold, join cakes together with whipped sweetened cream.

Swiss Roll

For Swiss Roll, make up the Sponge Sandwich recipe on page 162 and mix as directed. Pour mixture into greased, greaseproof paper lined swiss roll tin, approximately 10 in. × 14 in.; spread mixture out lightly. Bake in moderate oven, Mark 4, 350°F., approximately 12 to 15 minutes, or until lightly coloured and elastic to touch. Be careful not to over-cook or sponge will become dry and crack when rolled.

While sponge is cooking, prepare for the rolling. Place sheet of greaseproof paper on slightly dampened teatowel; dust paper with castor sugar.

When sponge is cooked, turn immediately from tin on to greaseproof paper; peel off lining paper; with sharp knife trim off crisp edge from long sides of cake. Gently roll up sponge, rolling the greaseproof inside as you go. Cover sponge with clean teatowel, let stand for 1 minute. Unroll, remove paper, re-roll, let stand until quite cold before filling. When cold, gently unroll, spread with jam or whipped cream (or both), roll up again. Dust top with extra castor sugar, if desired.

Chocolate Sponge

4 eggs
8 oz. (1 cup) castor (superfine) sugar
1½ tablespoons butter
2½ tablespoons cocoa
4 tablespoons boiling water
5 oz. (1¼ cups) self raising (all purpose) flour

Beat eggs together in basin, gradually add sugar; beat 15 minutes. Combine butter, cocoa, and boiling water, fold into egg mixture. Sift flour several times, sift over egg mixture, fold in, making sure no streaks of colour remain. Fill into 2 greased 7 in. sandwich tins; bake in moderate oven, Mark 4, 350°F., 20 to 25 minutes, or until elastic to touch and shrinking slightly from sides of tin. Remove from tins, cool. When cool, join together with whipped cream; top, if desired, with chocolate icing.

Ginger Fluff Sponge

4 eggs
4 oz. (½ cup) castor (superfine) sugar
2 oz. (¼ cup) arrowroot
2 tablespoons plain flour
2 teaspoons ginger
2 teaspoons cinnamon
2 teaspoons cocoa
2 teaspoons cream of tartar
1 teaspoon bicarbonate of soda
1 dessertspoon golden or corn syrup

Separate eggs; beat whites stiffly, gradually add sugar, beating well after each addition to dissolve sugar thoroughly. Add yolks all at once, beat only until colour is evenly mixed through. Sift dry ingredients at least four times to combine thoroughly. Sift on to egg mixture, fold through gently until colour is even and dry ingredients are mixed in. Pour in warmed syrup, fold through gently. Pour into 2 greased deep 7 in. sandwich tins, bake in moderate oven, Mark 4, 350°F., approximately 15 to 20 minutes or until elastic to touch and shrinking slightly from sides of tin. Turn on to wire tray. When cold, join with whipped cream.

Honey Roll

3 eggs
2 oz. (¼ cup) castor (superfine) sugar
2 tablespoons honey
½ teaspoon bicarbonate of soda
1 dessertspoon hot water
4 oz. (1 cup) plain flour
1 teaspoon cinnamon
whipped cream
extra sugar

Beat eggs 3 minutes, or until light in colour. Gradually add sugar, beat until dissolved. Add honey, beat until mixture resembles thick cream. Add bicarbonate of soda dissolved in hot water. Lightly fold in sifted flour and cinnamon. Pour mixture into greased paper-lined 10 in. × 14 in. swiss roll tin. Bake in moderately hot oven, Mark 5, 375°F., 12 to 15 minutes.

Follow method for Swiss Roll; spread with whipped cream.

Cheesecakes

Cheesecake is among the most popular of all desserts. It's so rich, so luscious, you need to serve it only in small slices. One cheesecake will go a long way; in an 8 or 9 in. size, it will give up to 12 servings. They're best made the day before they're to be served, so can be made ahead for a party.

Cheesecakes can be baked in the oven, or unbaked (set in the refrigerator); there's a wide variety of both types of recipes here and everyone delicious!

To Make Cheesecakes

When making baked cheesecakes, cooking times should be followed carefully. Don't overcook them. At the end of the specified cooking time, the cheesecake might still appear soft in the centre; but it becomes firmer as it stands.

An overbaked cheesecake develops grainy texture; it is inclined to shrink, crack, become dry as it cools. If you cool the cheesecake by the following method you'll find there is very little shrinking, and the cheesecake does not fall in the centre.

When baking time is over, turn off the oven heat, leave the oven door ajar, and let the cheesecakes stand undisturbed in the oven until it is quite cool. This helps to set the soft centre and prevent it falling. It will not cause overbaking. When the cheesecake is cool, refrigerate until set firmly.

Large cheesecakes are best if made the day before they are to be served, then refrigerate overnight; filling sets firmly and they're easier to cut.

For a crumb crust that will hold its shape without crumbling, and cut well, the ideal proportions are half the amount of butter to the weight of biscuit crumbs. For example, a crumb crust which used 8 oz. (2 cups) biscuit crumbs will hold together well with 4 oz. ($\frac{1}{2}$ cup) melted butter.

The exception to this is when a biscuit which has a good proportion of butter added to it during the manufacturing process (such as shortbread biscuits) is used for the crumb crust. This type of crust needs slightly less melted butter added. Specific quantities are given in recipes in this book.

The recipes which use a crumb crust specify them in a particular size to hold the quantity of filling: for example, '8 in. crumb crust,' '9 in. crumb crust.'

As a general guide, we give below the various proportions of biscuit crumbs and butter needed for each size. To this can be added a little cinnamon, nutmeg, etc.

For 7 in. sandwich tin with removable base: use 6 oz. ($1\frac{1}{2}$ cups) plain sweet biscuit crumbs and 3 oz. ($\frac{3}{8}$ cup) butter.

For 8 in. springform pan: use 8 oz. (2 cups) plain sweet biscuit crumbs and 4 oz. ($\frac{1}{2}$ cup) butter.

For 9 in. springform pan: use 12 oz. (3 cups) plain sweet biscuit crumbs and 6 oz. ($\frac{3}{4}$ cup) butter.

For 10 in. to 11 in. springform pan: use 1 lb. (4 cups) plain sweet biscuit crumbs and 8 oz. (1 cup) butter.

For 8 in. to 9 in. pie plate: use 6 oz. ($1\frac{1}{2}$ cups) plain sweet biscuit crumbs and 3 oz. ($\frac{3}{8}$ cup) butter.

Wonderful Basic Cheesecake

$1\frac{1}{2}$ lb. cream cheese	grated rind 1 lemon
1 teaspoon vanilla	1 dessertspoon lemon
4 eggs	juice
8 oz. (1 cup) sugar	8 in. crumb crust

Press cream cheese through strainer, blend with vanilla. Beat eggs until thick, beat in sugar gradually. Continue beating while adding cheese mixture in small proportions, mixing each time until smooth. Mix in lemon rind and juice. Spread into crumb crust, bake in moderate oven, Mark 4, 350°F., 25 to 30 minutes. Cool, then refrigerate. Just before serving, top with whipped cream, sprinkle with cinnamon or nutmeg.

Superb Sour Cream Cheesecake

8 oz. packaged cream cheese	8 oz. (1 cup) sugar
	$\frac{1}{4}$ pint ($\frac{1}{2}$ cup) milk
8 oz. (1 cup) cottage cheese	$\frac{1}{2}$ pint (1 cup) sour cream
3 eggs	grated rind 2 lemons
4 dessertspoons cornflour (cornstarch)	1 teaspoon lemon juice
	8 in. crumb crust

Beat cheeses together until smooth. Add eggs, one at a time, beating well after each addition. Add cornflour (cornstarch) and sugar, mix well. Blend in milk, sour cream, lemon rind and juice. Pour mixture into crumb crust. Stand pan on oven tray. Bake in moderately slow oven, Mark 3, 325°F., 50 to 60 minutes; cool in oven. Refrigerate several hours before serving.

Minted Cheesecake

Crumb Crust

5 oz. shortbread biscuits	2 oz. ($\frac{1}{4}$ cup) butter

Topping

1 dessertspoon gelatine	$\frac{1}{2}$ teaspoon vanilla
2 tablespoons cold water	1 teaspoon peppermint essence
2 tablespoons boiling water	2 dessertspoons lemon juice
8 oz. packaged cream cheese	1 small can evaporated milk, chilled
4 oz. ($\frac{1}{2}$ cup) sugar	

Crumb Crust Crush biscuits. Combine crumbs and melted butter in a mixing bowl; reserve 1 to 2 tablespoons crumbs for topping. Press remaining mixture on to base of greased 7 in. springform pan. Refrigerate until firm.

Topping Soak gelatine in cold water 5 minutes, then dissolve in boiling water; cool. Cream together cheese and sugar until smooth and fluffy. Add vanilla, peppermint essence and lemon juice; beat well. Blend in cooled gelatine and chilled evaporated milk; beat well again. Pour cheese mixture on to prepared crumb crust, sprinkle with remaining crumbs. Refrigerate several hours or overnight.

Strawberry-Glazed Cheesecake

Crumb Crust

6 oz. plain sweet biscuits	3 oz. ($\frac{3}{8}$ cup) butter

Filling

1$\frac{1}{2}$ lb. cream cheese	2 eggs
1 oz. ($\frac{1}{4}$ cup) self raising (all purpose) flour	6 oz. ($\frac{3}{4}$ cup) sugar
rind $\frac{1}{2}$ large lemon	1$\frac{1}{2}$ gills ($\frac{2}{3}$ cup) milk
$\frac{1}{4}$ pint ($\frac{1}{2}$ cup) sour cream	

Strawberry Glaze

1 lb. strawberries	3 dessertspoons cornflour (cornstarch)
water	2 oz. ($\frac{1}{4}$ cup) sugar

Crumb Crust Crush biscuits finely, add melted butter and combine well. Press over base only of 8 in. springform pan.

Filling Beat together sieved cream cheese, sifted flour, grated rind, and sour cream. Beat eggs and sugar together until light and fluffy, add milk. Gradually beat into cheese mixture. Pour mixture on to crumb crust. Bake in a moderately slow oven, Mark 3, 325°F., 1$\frac{1}{2}$ hours.

Strawberry Glaze Crush half of the strawberries, add the water and cook 2 minutes; strain. Mix cornflour (cornstarch) with sugar, stir into strained strawberry liquid. Cook gently, stirring constantly until liquid is clear, approximately 3 minutes. (A few drops of red colouring can be added.) Cool slightly. Cut remaining strawberries in half and arrange on top of cooled cheesecake; spoon glaze over. Refrigerate.

Luscious Gourmet Cheesecake

1 lb. cream cheese	4 eggs, separated
8 oz. (1 cup) castor (superfine) sugar	$\frac{1}{2}$ pint (1 cup) sour cream
2 dessertspoons plain flour	juice of 1 lemon
pinch salt	2 dessertspoons sugar, extra
1 whole egg	10 in. crumb crust

Beat cream cheese until softened, combine with sugar, flour and salt, beat well. Beat in the whole egg plus the 4 egg-yolks, sour cream and lemon juice. Beat egg-whites until stiff but not dry, beat in extra sugar, fold into cream cheese mixture. Pour into prepared crumb crust. Bake in a moderately slow oven, Mark 3, 325°F., 1$\frac{1}{4}$ to 1$\frac{1}{2}$ hours. Allow to cool in oven. Refrigerate until firm.

Chocolate-Cream Cheesecake

3 oz. (3 squares) plain chocolate	1 teaspoon vanilla
3 eggs	1$\frac{1}{2}$ oz. (3 tablespoons) plain flour
6 oz. ($\frac{3}{4}$ cups) sugar	pinch salt
8 oz. cream cheese	pinch bicarbonate of soda
1$\frac{1}{2}$ gills ($\frac{2}{3}$ cups) whipping cream	extra whipped cream
2 dessertspoons rum	extra melted chocolate
	8 in. crumb crust

Chop chocolate, melt over hot water, set aside. Beat eggs until thick and fluffy. Add sugar gradually, beating well until thick and lemon-coloured. Beat together cream cheese and cream until smooth and thickened. Add melted chocolate, stir until well blended. Fold egg mixture into chocolate cream mixture with rum and vanilla. Sift together flour, salt, and bicarbonate of soda; add to creamed mixture. Pour into crumb crust. Bake in slow oven, Mark 2, 300°F., 55 to 60 minutes. Allow to cool, then refrigerate until well firmed.

Top with whipped sweetened cream, drizzle melted chocolate over.

Strawberry-Glazed Cheesecake—light, lovely texture and flavour, with a beautiful glaze of crushed fresh strawberries.

Step 1

Put biscuits into a plastic bag, crush finely with rolling-pin, then put through fine sieve to separate any large lumps. Larger lumps can be rubbed through sieve with fingers. Or, if using an electric blender, break up biscuits roughly, drop into blender a few at a time.

Step 2

Add to crumbs the melted butter, sugar, any flavourings; mix to combine well. Mixture should cling together when pressed between fingers. Grease inside of pan lightly, scatter mixture across base, then press on firmly with dessertspoon.

Step by Step to Perfect Crumb Crust

Continental Cream Cheese Slice

Pastry

6 oz. (1½ cups) plain flour

2 oz. (½ cup) custard powder

4 dessertspoons icing (confectioners') sugar

½ teaspoon baking powder

4 oz. (½ cup or 1 stick) butter

milk

Filling

2 oz. (¼ cup) butter

10 oz. cream cheese

2 eggs

2 oz. (¼ cup) sugar

2 oz. (⅓ cup) sultanas

grated rind of 1 lemon

2 dessertspoons lemon juice

Pastry Sift into basin the flour, custard powder, icing sugar and baking powder. Rub in butter, add sufficient milk to make into a stiff dough (approximately 4 to 6 dessertspoons of milk). Roll out ⅔ of the pastry and line 7 in. × 11 in. greased tin, bringing pastry ½ inch up the sides. Prick base and bake in moderate oven, Mark 4, 350°F., 10 minutes; cool. *Filling* Cream butter with cream cheese until soft and creamy. Beat eggs and sugar until light and fluffy. Gradually add to cream cheese mixture, beat until smooth. Fold in sultanas, lemon rind, and juice. Smooth filling over cooked pastry shell.

Cut remaining pastry into long strips and place diagonally over filling in lattice form. Brush pastry with milk. Bake in moderate oven, Mark 4, 350°F., 35 to 45 minutes; while still warm, cut into slices; leave in tin until cool, then refrigerate.

Coffee-Cream Cheesecake

4 oz. (1 cup) cottage cheese

12 oz. cream cheese

2 dessertspoons gelatine

4 dessertspoons cold water

4 dessertspoons boiling water

2 dessertspoons grated lemon rind

2 dessertspoons lemon juice

½ pint (1 cup) cream

4 dessertspoons coffee essence

1 egg-white

6 oz. (¾ cup) sugar

8 in. crumb crust

Sieve cheeses into a bowl, beat well. Soften gelatine in cold water, add boiling water, stir until dissolved. Add to cheese mixture with lemon rind and juice, continue beating until smooth. Whip cream until stiff, fold in coffee essence. Beat egg-white, gradually add sugar, continue beating until of meringue consistency. Fold whipped cream, then egg-white, carefully into cheese mixture. Pour into prepared crumb crust. Refrigerate several hours or until set. If desired, decorate top, just before serving, with grated chocolate.

Step 3
Now turn pan on its side and put large spoonfuls of crumbs in place on side; press on with back of spoon. Continue until all sides of pan are coated with a firm, even layer of crumbs. You can relax while doing this. Sit down with the pan on your lap.

Step 4
Stand pan firmly on table, take smooth-sided glass or jar, work it smoothly over base and sides of pan until crust is even. Hold thumb on top of crust as you press to keep top even. Refrigerate 1 hour or bake 10 minutes to set crumbs.

Step 5
Do not remove filled crumb crust from pan until well refrigerated, preferably overnight. Then release catch at side of pan, loosen gently round top with knife. Stand on top of glass or jar, slide side of pan down; make sure cake doesn't slip off jar.

Step 6
When the cheesecake has been removed from the pan, neaten the edge of crumb crust by pressing a sharp knife across, as shown above; work carefully to avoid cracking the crust. Use a pastry brush to brush off gently any crumbs on the top.

Chocolate Cheesecake

Crumb Crust

4 oz. plain chocolate biscuits

1½ oz. (3 tablespoons) melted butter

Filling

8 oz. packaged cream cheese

4 oz. (½ cup) sugar

1 teaspoon vanilla

2 eggs, separated

4 oz. (4 squares) plain chocolate

pinch salt

½ pint (1 cup) whipping cream

2 dessertspoons finely chopped walnuts

Crumb Crust Combine crushed biscuit crumbs and melted butter, mix well. Press mixture on to base of 8 in. springform pan. Bake in moderately slow oven 8 minutes; cool.

Filling Beat cheese until smooth, add half the sugar and the vanilla, beat well. Add lightly beaten egg-yolks and chocolate, which has been melted over hot water. Beat egg-whites and salt until peaks form, gradually beat in remaining sugar; fold into chocolate mixture. Finally, fold through whipped cream and the walnuts. Pour into prepared crumb crust. Refrigerate until set.

To serve, decorate with extra whipped cream and grated chocolate.

Strawberry Cheesecake

Filling

8 oz. packaged cream cheese

4 oz. (½ cup) castor (superfine) sugar

3 egg-yolks

3 dessertspoons plain flour

1 teaspoon vanilla

pinch salt

½ pint (1 cup) scalded medium cream

2 egg-whites

Topping

fresh strawberries

4 oz. (1 cup) red currant jelly

3 dessertspoons sweet sherry

Crumb Crust Crush 4 oz. coconut biscuits and combine with 2 oz. (¼ cup) melted butter. Press mixture on to base only of greased 8 in. springform pan. Refrigerate until firm.

Filling Beat together cheese and sugar until smooth and fluffy, approximately 8 minutes. Add egg-yolks, beat well. Add sifted flour, vanilla and salt, beating continually. Gradually pour in hot scalded cream, beating all the time. Lasty fold in stiffly beaten egg-whites. Pour cheese mixture on to crumb crust. Stand pan on oven tray, bake in slow oven, Mark 2, 300°F., 1½ hours. Cool, then refrigerate.

Topping Place jelly and sherry in a saucepan. Dissolve over low heat, stirring with a wooden spoon. Refrigerate until commencing to set. Decorate when cold with strawberries cut into quarters. Spoon jelly mixture over, refrigerate until set.

Cheesecake Squares

4 oz. (1 cup) plain flour

4 oz. (1 cup) self raising (all purpose) flour

2 oz. (½ cup) cornflour (cornstarch)

2 oz. (½ cup) custard powder

1½ oz. (¼ cup) icing (confectioners') sugar

6 oz. (¾ cup) butter

2 to 3 tablespoons water

1 teaspoon lemon juice

4 oz. (½ cup) apricot jam

egg glazing

icing (confectioners') sugar

Filling

2 eggs

3 oz. (⅜ cup) butter

2 oz. (¼ cup) sugar

2 oz. (⅓ cup) raisins

½ teaspoon grated lemon rind

10 oz. (1¼ cup) cottage cheese

⅛ pint (¼ cup) sour cream

Sift dry ingredients into basin, rub in butter until mixture resembles fine breadcrumbs. Mix to dry dough with water and lemon juice. Turn out on to floured board and knead lightly. Divide in half, roll out one half to fit base of greased lamington tin, spread with apricot jam, then spread cheese filling over evenly.

Filling Separate eggs. Cream butter, add egg-yolks, sugar, raisins, lemon rind, cottage cheese and sour cream; mix well. Fold in stiffly beaten egg-whites, spread over pastry. Roll out remaining pastry, place on top of cream mixture. Trim edges, brush with beaten egg. Bake in moderate oven, Mark 4, 350°F., 30 to 40 minutes; cool. Cut into squares to serve. Sprinkle with sifted icing sugar.

Lemon Jelly Cheesecake

¼ pint (½ cup) boiling water

1 pkt. lemon jelly

scant ¼ pint (½ cup) lemon juice

1 teaspoon lemon rind

1 large can condensed milk

8 oz. cream cheese

1 teaspoon vanilla

8 in. crumb crust

Pour boiling water over jelly and stir until dissolved. Add lemon juice and rind; cool. Whip chilled condensed milk until thick. Beat cream cheese until soft, add milk, vanilla and jelly, mix well. Pour into crumb crust, refrigerate until set.

Cheesecake Squares—one of the most popular of all cheesecakes. A delicious pastry holds a filling of cream cheese, sour cream, raisins, apricot jam.

Meringues

Here are recipes for meringues using 1, 2, 3 or 4 egg-whites; ingredients and method for each are slightly different. It's just a matter of choosing which type you like the best.

The ingredients

There are several different types of meringues; recipes can vary in ingredients and in method. Below are the ingredients used and the reasons for their use.

Egg-whites Eggs a few days old are best for making meringues; when very fresh, straight from the nest, the egg-white is thin and does not beat up to a great volume. Egg-whites should be firm, jelly-like in consistency; they should be at room temperature before beating.

Frozen egg-whites, brought back to room temperature, can be used.

In methods where whites are beaten first and sugar added gradually, beat whites until firm before adding sugar.

Once meringue is made, quickly add other ingredients; if left to stand, beaten egg-whites will lose their volume as the tiny air-bubbles collapse; once collapsed, they will not beat up again.

For the same reason, when the complete meringue mixture is made, it should be handled quickly and baked as soon as possible.

Cream of tartar and salt Used to strengthen and stabilise egg-whites, helping them hold their aerated volume.

Sugar In some recipes castor (superfine) sugar is used for quick dissolving; for others, granulated sugar gives a firmer result.

It is important, when beating sugar into egg-whites, to make sure all sugar is dissolved—otherwise, the undissolved sugar will melt during cooking, and give a 'weepy', sticky meringue.

Where sugar is added gradually, make sure each addition of sugar is dissolved before any more sugar is added; otherwise, the weight of undissolved sugar will break down egg-white aeration and mixture will collapse.

To test if sugar is dissolved, rub a little of the mixture between two fingers; any undissolved sugar crystals can be quickly detected.

If using electric mixer, make sure the bowl is continually rotating and evenly dissolving sugar; it may be necessary to assist the bowl gently round

with your fingers—mixing may slow down as egg-whites whip up firmly and mixture becomes thick.

Like all rules, there are exceptions to it; the exception to the firm beating of sugar to dissolve all crystals completely, is the Classic Meringue (see recipe overleaf).

In this recipe, the last quantity of sugar is mixed with cornflour (cornstarch) and just lightly folded in at the last minute. The cornflour (cornstarch) prevents sugar 'weeping'. This method gives a very characteristic meringue—crisp and crunchy on outside, with soft, marshmallowy centre.

Cornflour (cornstarch) Helps to dry out meringue; the more cornflour (cornstarch) used, the drier will be the meringue.

Vinegar and lemon juice This combination helps to form the marshmallowy centre; also whitens the meringue.

The equipment

Bowls A bowl with small rounded base and deep, gently sloping sides is considered best. The small bowl of electric mixer can be used in mixtures with up to 3 egg-whites.

It is most important that all equipment—bowls, beaters, etc.—be clean, dry, free from any dust, moisture, or fat (this includes egg-yolk). These could prevent egg-whites whipping up to good volume.

Preparation of trays

There are several different methods of preparing trays; each is effective, the meringue does not stick. They are:

Cornfloured Cover that part of baking tray on

which you are going to spoon meringue mixture with a thick, even layer of sifted cornflour (cornstarch). Suitable for large or small meringues.
Greased and Cornfloured   Brush tray lightly with melted butter, dust with sifted cornflour (cornstarch); shake off excess cornflour (cornstarch). Best suited to small individual meringues.
Lined, Greased and Cornfloured   Place sheet of greaseproof paper, trimmed to size of tray, on greased baking tray; brush paper lightly with melted butter, dust with sifted cornflour (cornstarch). Shake off excess cornflour (cornstarch). Suitable for all types of meringue.
Aluminium Foil   Cover tray with layer of aluminium foil—there is no need to grease. Place meringue mixture directly on foil. When meringue has cooked and cooled, it is easy to peel off foil gently. Suitable for all types of meringues—particularly good for large ones.

Removing from trays

Allow meringue to cool completely on its tray, then loosen with spatula or broad, flat-bladed knife. Make sure spatula or knife blade is kept flat on tray—do not try to lever meringue up, or it will break.

If syrup from undissolved sugar has 'weeped' out during cooking, thus making meringue difficult to remove, place tray over low heat for a second to melt greasing, then loosen again carefully, as above.

How to bake

Baking times and temperatures vary, according to the varying recipes.

Place baking tray with meringue in low position in oven, leave for stipulated cooking time, then turn off heat, and, if possible, allow meringue to remain in oven, with door ajar, until it has completely cooled. This dries it out and makes it crisp.

This method has been used for all recipes in this section.

If you are making meringue in a hurry, and cannot wait for it to cool in oven, allow a little longer cooking time than given in individual recipe. Remove from oven, cool on tray. Meringues should be light, dry, pale in colour.

How to store

Provided meringues have been cooked to correct dryness, we recommend the following keeping times for recipes in this section. Keep meringues in air-tight tin.
One-Egg Meringue: 1 to 2 weeks
Easy Two-Egg Meringue: 10 days
Classic Meringue: 10 days
Stored Heat Meringue: 1 week
Marshmallow Meringue: 2 days
Marshmallow Meringue is best stored in air-tight tin in refrigerator; the others can be stored in dark cupboard.

The Easy Two-Egg Meringue, because it is a dry mixture, can be wrapped and frozen; keeps 2 months frozen.

One-Egg Meringue

1 egg-white	good pinch cream of
2 tablespoons boiling	tartar
water	7 oz. ($\frac{7}{8}$ cup) granulated
pinch salt	sugar

Place all ingredients in small, deep, heat-proof basin. Stand basin over saucepan of boiling water; reduce heat, beat with electric mixer or rotary beater until mixture is stiff and glossy, approximately 7 minutes. (Do not allow water to boil; there should be just enough heat to keep water hot.) Remove immediately from hot water and spread quickly on prepared trays. This mixture makes one 8 in. meringue or 4 small individual meringue shells.
Baking   Large meringue; bake in very slow oven, Mark 1, 275°F., 1$\frac{1}{2}$ to 2 hours, cool in oven. Individual meringues; bake in very slow oven, Mark 1, 275°F., 30 to 45 minutes, cool in oven.

Easy Two-Egg Meringue

2 egg-whites	1 teaspoon cornflour
12 oz. (1$\frac{1}{2}$ cups) castor	(cornstarch)
(superfine) sugar	4 tablespoons boiling
$\frac{1}{2}$ teaspoon vanilla	water
1 teaspoon vinegar	

Place all ingredients into small bowl of electric mixer, beat on high speed until mixture is very stiff (approximately 15 minutes). Spread on to prepared trays. This mixture makes one 11 in. meringue or 15 small shells.
Baking   Large meringue; bake in very moderate oven, Mark 3, 325°F., 10 minutes, reduce heat to slow, Mark 2, 300°F., bake further 45 minutes, cool in oven. Small individual meringues; bake in very moderate oven, Mark 3, 325°F., 10 minutes reduce heat to slow, Mark 2, 300°F., bake further 30 minutes, cool in oven.

Pavlova Classic Meringue

3 egg-whites
pinch salt
6 oz. (¾ cup) castor (superfine) sugar

1 oz. (¼ cup) granulated sugar
1 tablespoon cornflour (cornstarch)
1 teaspoon lemon juice

Beat egg-whites and salt until stiff and dry; add castor (superfine) sugar gradually, beating well between each addition. Make sure sugar is completely dissolved. Mix together granulated sugar and cornflour (cornstarch), lightly fold into meringue with lemon juice. This mixture will make one round, 6 to 7 in. It can also be used for 2 smaller ones, 4 to 5 in., and they can be arranged in tiers, as shown in colour picture. To do this, mark prepared tray with 5 in. circle and another prepared tray with 7 in. circle. Spread approximately ¼ in. layer of mixture to fit each circle. With remainder of mixture, pipe or spoon swirls round edges to form shell. Bake in slow oven, Mark 2, 300°F., 30 to 45 minutes, cool in oven.

To assemble the 2-tiered pavlova (as shown in picture), when completely cooled, place larger shell on serving dish. Spread over generous layer of whipped cream, then any fresh fruit or well-drained canned fruit. Place smaller shell on top, fill centre with fresh or canned fruit. See next page for other fillings.

Stored heat Meringue

(Cooks in oven overnight).

4 egg-whites
½ teaspoon cream of tartar
¼ teaspoon salt

10 oz. (1¼ cups) granulated sugar
1 teaspoon lemon juice
1 teaspoon vanilla

Beat egg-whites until foamy, add cream of tartar and salt; beat until stiff. Gradually add sugar, a tablespoon at a time, beating well until all sugar is dissolved. Continue beating until all sugar is added and mixture is thick and glossy. Stir in lemon juice and vanilla. Spread or pipe mixture on to prepared trays, making two 8 in. rounds, or 15 small individual shells.
Baking Large round; place in very hot oven, Mark 8, 450°F., close door, turn off heat, leave in oven overnight. Small meringue shells; preheat oven to hot, Mark 7, 425°F., put in meringues. Turn off heat, leave in oven overnight.
NOTE: It is important not to open door until it is time to take baked meringues from oven—otherwise stored heat will be lost and meringue will not crisp correctly.

Marshmallow Meringue

4 egg-whites
8 oz. (1 cup) castor (superfine) sugar

1 dessertspoon cornflour (cornstarch)
1 teaspoon vinegar

Beat egg-whites, until stiff, add 4 oz. (½ cup) castor (superfine) sugar, beat thoroughly until sugar is dissolved (approx. 5 minutes). Add remaining sugar, a tablespoon at a time, beating well after each addition. Lightly fold in sifted cornflour (cornstarch), then vinegar. Take 30 in. length of aluminium foil, fold in half lengthwise. Make a circle of foil and secure. Place on thickly cornfloured tray, fill meringue mixture into foil; level off top (do not make into a shell). This mixture will make one deep 9 in. meringue case. Do not use this mixture to make small individual meringues.
Baking Preheat oven to moderate, Mark 4, 350°F., reduce heat to slow, Mark 2, 300°F., bake 1¼ hours, cool in oven.

Be very careful when peeling off collar, so as not to break crisp coating.
NOTE: This is a favourite type of meringue with its deep, soft, marshmallowy centre and crisp, slightly chewy coating. It has, when cooked, a rather 'untidy' appearance, compared with other mixtures—but the taste, texture and flavour are delightful. In the preliminary cooking, this mixture rises very high; toward end of cooking time, the centre falls, leaving a high, crisp shell around. (It will fall a little more as meringue cools.) The filling or topping is put inside the high, crisp shell.

Fresh fruit salad or strawberries make a colourful topping, spread whipped cream over. Or fill with whipped cream and spread fruit over top. Do this as near to serving time as possible.

Classic Pavlova has the traditional crisp shell with the soft, marshmallow centre. Fill with whipped cream and any fresh or canned fruit; we've used strawberries and colourful Chinese gooseberries.

Fillings for Meringues

Whipped cream, or ice-cream, with fresh or canned fruit are favourite fillings for meringues. But they can be made even more special with any of the luscious fillings given here.

Frozen Fruit Cream

15 oz. can crushed pineapple
grated rind 2 oranges
1 tablespoon marsala

large family size block vanilla ice-cream
orange segments

Drain pineapple. Mix drained pineapple with grated orange rind and marsala. Fold in vanilla ice-cream, pour into freezer trays, allow to set slightly. Just before serving, arrange layer of orange segments on base of meringue. Spoon over partially frozen pineapple cream. Decorate with extra orange segments. Serve at once.

Lemon Chiffon

1 dessertspoon gelatine
3 to 4 tablespoons cold water
2 eggs, separated
2 oz. ($\frac{1}{4}$ cup) castor (superfine) sugar

juice and rind 2 lemons
$\frac{1}{4}$ pint ($\frac{1}{2}$ cup) whipping cream

Soak gelatine in cold water. Beat egg-yolks, sugar and lemon rind over boiling water until thick, creamy, and pale in colour. Dissolve gelatine over boiling water, add lemon juice. Add gelatine mixture to cooled egg mixture, off heat, and continue beating until mixture begins to thicken. Beat egg-whites until stiff, and whip cream; gently fold into meringue case, refrigerate until firm. Decorate with extra whipped cream.

Mocha-Chiffon

1 tablespoon gelatine
3 to 4 tablespoons water
2 tablespoons cornflour (cornstarch)
2 eggs, separated
4 oz. ($\frac{1}{2}$ cup) sugar
$\frac{3}{4}$ pint ($1\frac{1}{2}$ cups) milk

vanilla
2 oz. (2 squares) grated chocolate
1 dessertspoon instant coffee powder
$\frac{1}{4}$ teaspoon cream of tartar
2 tablespoons sugar, extra

Soak gelatine in cold water. In saucepan, blend cornflour (cornstarch), egg-yolks and sugar with a little of the milk, add remaining milk, stir over low heat until custard boils and thickens. Flavour with vanilla. Measure out half of this custard mixture, reserve. To remaining custard add chocolate and instant coffee; stir until melted and well blended. Cool, spread over base of meringue. Dissolve soaked gelatine over boiling water, stir into reserved custard; cool. Beat egg-whites and cream of tartar until stiff, gradually beat in extra sugar. Lightly whisk in cooled custard. When starting to set, spoon over mocha layer. Refrigerate until firm. Serve topped with whipped cream and chocolate shavings.

Chestnut Cream

9 oz. can cream of chestnuts (in vanilla flavoured syrup)

1 tablespoon brandy
$\frac{1}{2}$ pint (1 cup) whipping cream

Beat chestnut cream until soft, add brandy, stir in whipped cream. Fill into 8 in. meringue shell and refrigerate.

NOTE: There are two types of canned chestnuts; one is pure chestnuts puréed, with no sweetening added. The second has sugar, glucose, and vanilla added; this is the best for above filling. Check ingredients on can.

Brandy Bavarian Cream

$1\frac{1}{2}$ teaspoons gelatine
1 tablespoon water
2 egg-yolks
2 oz. ($\frac{1}{4}$ cup) sugar

$\frac{1}{2}$ pint (1 cup) hot milk
$\frac{1}{4}$ pint ($\frac{1}{2}$ cup) whipping cream
1 tablespoon brandy

Soften gelatine in cold water. Beat egg-yolks and sugar until thick and light in colour, stir in hot milk gradually. Stir over boiling water until mixture coats back of spoon. Add softened gelatine, stirring until dissolved; cool, stirring occasionally to prevent skin forming. Whip cream and brandy together, fold into cooled custard. Pour into meringue case, refrigerate until set. Delicious topped with brandied stawberries.

Rich Chocolate Custard

2 egg-yolks
3 tablespoons cocoa
2 tablespoons cornflour (cornstarch)

4 oz. ($\frac{1}{2}$ cup) sugar
$\frac{3}{4}$ pint ($1\frac{1}{2}$ cups) milk
$\frac{1}{4}$ pint ($\frac{1}{2}$ cup) whipping cream

Place egg-yolks, cocoa, cornflour (cornstarch), and sugar into saucepan; gradually add milk, stirring until well blended. Stir over medium heat until mixture boils and thickens; cool. Whip cream and fold into cooled chocolate custard. Pour into meringue case, refrigerate. Serve decorated with whipped cream and almond slivers.

Wedding cakes

A good, rich fruit cake is the basis for the traditional wedding cake. Fruit cake recipes given on these pages also make excellent Christmas cakes; they have rich flavour, keep well, cut well.

The cakes are named according to the amount of butter and sugar used in each. For example, Quarter-pound Cakes uses ¼ lb. of butter; Half-pound Cake used ½ lb., and so on.

Method for Fruit Cakes

This method of preparing the four cakes is the same:

NOTE: See the four fruit cake recipes that follow for the quantities of ingredients required.

Prepare fruits by washing, drying, and removing stems. Chop and place in basin, pour over spirits, and mix well. Cover, stand overnight. Cream butter with brown sugar, grated fruit rinds, and essences, add marmalade and caramel. Drop in eggs one at a time, beating well after each addition. Fold in prepared fruit alternately with sifted dry ingredients, mix well.

Fill into lined tin (see page 178), smooth top. Bake as directed in individual recipes. When cooked, cake should feel firm, and a thin-bladed knife, when inserted into centre of cake, should come out clean.

Immediately cake is removed from oven, wrap in clean towel, or aluminium foil, to ensure soft surface on top of cake. Store in a cool place.

Quarter-Pound Cake

¾ lb. (2 cups) sultanas
¼ lb. (⅔ cup) raisins
2 oz. (⅓ cup) currants
2 oz. (¼ cup) crystallized or glacé cherries
2 oz. (⅓ cup) shredded mixed peel
3 to 4 tablespoons rum, brandy or sherry
4 oz. (½ cup or 1 stick) butter
4 oz. (⅔ cup) light brown sugar
½ teaspoon grated orange rind
½ teaspoon grated lemon rind
few drops almond essence
½ teaspoon vanilla
1 tablespoon marmalade
½ teaspoon caramel
2 eggs
5 oz. (1¼ cups) plain flour
pinch salt
½ teaspoon mixed spice
⅛ teaspoon cinnamon
⅛ teaspoon nutmeg

Prepare and mix ingredients as directed in Method for Fruit Cakes on this page. Fill into 6 in. round or square cake tine lined with 1 thickness of white paper and 1 thickness of brown paper.

Bake in slow oven, Mark 2, 300°F., approx. 2½ hours.

Half-Pound Cake

1½ lb. (4 cups) sultanas
½ lb. (1⅓ cups) raisins
4 oz. (⅔ cups) currants
4 oz. (½ cup) glacé cherries
4 oz. (⅔ cup) shredded mixed peel
8 tablespoons rum, brandy or sherry
8 oz. (1 cup) butter
8 oz. (1¼ cups) light brown sugar
1 teaspoon grated orange rind
1 teaspoon grated lemon rind
few drops almond essence
1 teaspoon vanilla
2 tablespoons marmalade
1 teaspoon caramel
4 eggs
10 oz. (2½ cups) plain flour
pinch salt
1 teaspoon mixed spice
¼ teaspoon cinnamon
¼ teaspoon nutmeg

Prepare and mix ingredients as in Method for Fruit Cake (page 177). Fill into 8 in. round or square cake tin lined with 1 thickness white paper and 2 thicknesses brown.

Bake in slow oven, Mark 2, 300°F., approx. 3 hours.

One-Pound Cake

3 lb. (8 cups) sultanas
1 lb. (2⅔ cups) raisins
½ lb. (1⅓ cups) currants
½ lb. (1 cup) crystallized or glacé cherries
½ lb. (1⅓ cups) shredded mixed peel
1½ gills (⅔ cup) rum, brandy or sherry
1 lb. (2 cups) butter
1 lb. (2½ cups) light brown sugar
2 teaspoons grated lemon rind
½ teaspoon almond essence
2 teaspoons grated orange rind
2 teaspoons vanilla
4 tablespoons marmalade
1 dessertspoon caramel
8 eggs
1¼ lb. (5 cups) plain flour
pinch salt
2 teaspoons spice
½ teaspoon cinnamon
½ teaspoon nutmeg

Prepare and mix ingredients as in Method for Fruit Cakes. Fill into 10 in. cake tin lined with 1' thickness white paper and 2 thicknesses brown.

Bake in slow oven, Mark 2, 300°F., approx. 4½ hours.

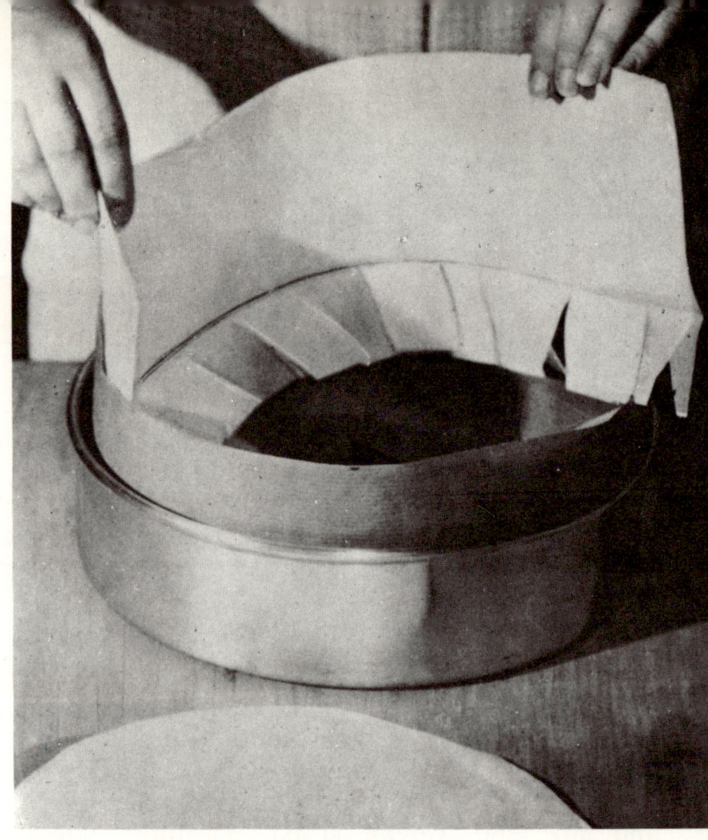

Tins in which rich fruit cakes are to be baked need linings to protect the mixture during the long cooking time. Line tin with two layers of brown paper, then one of greaseproof paper; this is the inside layer next to cake.

For square tin: Cut 3 pieces of lining paper the width of tin, and to come 1½ in. higher than the sides. Fit them into tin, overlapping them in opposite directions. Corners must be even.

For round tin: Stand tin on paper, trace circle around with pencil, then cut out the circle. Cut out strip 3 in. higher than depth of tin, fold over 1½ in. of strip and cut diagonally into the fold at 1 in. intervals.

Preparing the Cake Tin

One-and-a-half Pound Cake

4½ lb. (12 cups) sultanas
1½ lb. (4 cups) raisins
¾ lb. (2 cups) currants
¾ lb. (1½ cups) crystallized or glacé cherries
¾ lb. (2 cups) shredded mixed peel
2½ gills (1½ cups) rum, brandy or sherry
1½ lb. (3 cups) butter
1½ lb. (3¾ cups) light brown sugar
3 teaspoons grated lemon rind
3 teaspoons grated orange rind
1 teaspoon almond essence
3 teaspoons vanilla
6 tablespoons marmalade
1 tablespoon caramel
12 eggs
1 lb. 14 oz. (7½ cups) plain flour
½ teaspoon salt
3 teaspoons spice
¾ teaspoon cinnamon
¾ teaspoon nutmeg

Prepare and mix ingredients according to Method for Fruit Cakes on previous page. Fill mixture into round or square 12 in. cake tin lined with one thickness white paper and two thicknesses brown paper.

Bake in slow oven, Mark 1, 275°F., about 6 to 6½ hours.

NOTE: Mixed fruit can be used in place of the sultanas, raisins, currants, cherries, and peel listed in the ingredients in the four cake recipes named according to butter content, which appear above and on previous page.

These substitutions are as follows:
Quarter-Pound Cake: Use 1 lb. 6 oz. (3⅔ cups) mixed fruit.
Half-Pound Cake: Use 2¾ lb. (7⅓ cups) mixed fruit.
One-Pound Cake: Use 5½ lb. (14⅔ cups) mixed fruit.
One-and-a-Half-Pound Cake: Use 8¼ lb. (22 cups) mixed fruit.

Covering the Cakes

Brush cake with lightly beaten egg-white or sieved apricot jam, apply almond paste.

After applying almond paste, let cake stand for at least 24 hours. Then take a little lightly beaten egg-white and brush evenly over cake. Now apply the fondant.

Almond Paste

2 lb. (5½ cups) icing (confectioners') sugar
8 oz. (1⅓ cups) ground almonds
4 egg-yolks
good squeeze lemon or orange juice
almond essence
4 tablespoons sherry

Sift icing sugar into basin, add ground almonds,

Fit strips of paper *round sides of tin, pressing the cut edges flat at the base of tin. Then take the paper circle previously cut out and fit it into base of tin to cover cut-out side sections; press paper out evenly.*

Settle mixture into tin *by lifting up about 12 in. and letting it drop sharply on a firm, hard surface. This ensures that the mixture settles into tin, resulting in a good shape for cake; this also breaks up any air bubbles that may form in mixture.*
For smooth top to cake, *wet your hand and smooth the surface of the raw mixture before putting cake in oven to cook. This will ensure a flat even top and give a nice gloss to finished cake.*

---

mix well. Beat egg-yolks with sherry and fruit juice, mix into dry ingredients. Turn on to board lightly dusted with extra icing sugar; knead well. Flavour with a little almond essence.

If too dry, add more fruit juice.

Fondant

2 lb. (5½ cups) icing (confectioners') sugar
2 egg-whites

4 tablespoons liquid glucose
1 tablespoon glycerine

Sift icing sugar into bowl. Remove about ½ lb. (1½ cups) icing sugar, put aside. Make well in centre of icing sugar in basin, add egg-whites, cover lightly with icing sugar from sides. Add glycerine and warmed glucose, mix well. Sprinkle reserved icing sugar on to board; turn fondant on to this, knead well, working in reserved icing sugar, until mixture is of correct consistency. Extra icing sugar may be needed.

Flavour and colour as desired.

Wedding Cakes

When assembling wedding cakes, it is very important to have good balance in the height of cakes that will form the tiers.

If cake for top tier is deeper than bottom tier, the complete cake will look top-heavy.

Average height for a wedding cake tier is 3 in. to 3½ in. deep.

Tier heights can be graduated; for example, base cake, 4 in. deep; the middle cake, 3½ in. deep; top tier, 3 in. deep.

Wedding-Cake Sizes

Large Wedding Cakes Three-tier, bake base in 12 in. tin; middle cake in 9 in. tin; top cake, 6 in. tin.

Two-tier: Base cake, 12 in. tin; top cake, 6 in. tin.
Small to Average Cakes Three-tier, base cake, 10 in. tin; middle cake, 8 in. tin; top cake, 6 in. tin.

Two-tier: Base cake, 10 in. tin; top cake, 6 in. tin.
Single-tiers Bake in 10 in. or 12 in. tin.

Batters

Pancakes, drop scones or Scotch pancakes, waffles, sweet or savoury fritters—these are just some of the good things which can be made with a versatile batter, which can be mixed in minutes.
The basic recipes for many types of batters are given here, together with delightful variations.

Drop Scones or Scotch Pancakes

4 oz. (1 cup) self raising (all purpose) flour
pinch salt
¼ teaspoon bicarbonate of soda
¼ pint (½ cup) sour milk
3 tablespoons sugar
1 egg
1 dessertspoon melted butter

NOTE: Fresh milk soured with 1 teaspoon vinegar or lemon juice can be used in place of the ¼ pint (½ cup) of sour milk listed above.

Sift dry ingredients, add sugar. Mix to a smooth batter with beaten egg and milk, add melted butter. Heat and grease pan, drop batter by dessertspoonfuls on to pan, cook until bubbly on top, light brown underneath. Turn, cook other side.

For variety add 2 tablespoons sultanas to batter. When cooked, wrap scones in a clean cloth to keep moist.

Makes 12 to 18.

Drop Scones with Orange

½ pint (1 cup) milk
juice ½ lemon
2 eggs
3 tablespoons sugar
pinch salt
6 oz. (1½ cups) self raising (all purpose) flour
grated rind and juice 1 orange
butter

Combine milk and lemon juice, stand aside in warm place to turn sour. Separate eggs. Place egg-yolks in basin, add 1 tablespoon of the sugar and beat well. Beat egg-whites in separate basin until stiff, and fold in sifted flour and salt, sour milk, juice and rind of orange. Mix to smooth batter. Heat frypan, grease lightly with butter. Drop dessertspoonfuls of batter on to pan, cook until bubbles appear on top of scones. Turn and cook other side.

For variety substitute grated rind and juice of 1 lemon for orange juice and rind in above recipe.

Makes about 24.

Rich Drop Scones

4 oz. (1 cup) self raising (all purpose) flour
2½ teaspoons baking powder
½ teaspoon salt
1 tablespoon sugar
1 egg
1 oz (2 tablespoons) melted butter
¼ pint (½ cup) milk
2 tablespoons light cream

Sift together flour, baking powder, and salt; stir in sugar. Beat egg lightly, add butter, milk and cream. Beat liquid into flour mixture until smooth. Heat frying pan or griddle; spoon 1 tablespoon mixture on to greased heated griddle. Cook until bubbly and browned at edges, turn and cook on other side. Serve warm, buttered with honey or lemon juice.

Makes 12 to 18.

Fritter Batter 1

8 oz. (2 cups) plain flour
1 teaspoon salt
1 egg
1 tablespoon oil
about ½ pint (1 cup) hot water

Sift flour and salt into basin. Make a well in centre, add beaten egg and oil. Add enough water to make a coating batter. Beat until smooth. Use to coat fish, meat, etc.

Fritter Batter 2

1 egg
2 oz. (½ cup) plain flour
pinch salt
4 to 5 tablespoons tepid water
1 tablespoon oil

Separate eggs. Mix sifted flour and salt gradually with water. Beat in egg-yolk and oil until batter is smooth. Leave to stand at room temperature 2 hours. Then whisk egg-white and fold into batter. Use to coat fruit, such as apple slices, pineapple, bananas, etc.

Fritter Binding Batter

7 oz. (1¾ cups) self raising (all purpose) flour
½ teaspoon salt

2 eggs
½ pint (1 cup) milk
1 dessertspoon melted butter

Sift flour and salt. Combine lightly beaten eggs, milk, and melted butter, stir into dry ingredients and beat until smooth. Use to bind ½ to ¾ lb. (1½ to 2 cups) of filling. Drop by spoonfuls into hot oil, cook until brown all over. Drain well on absorbent paper.

NOTE: Finely chopped, cooked meat, chicken etc., can be used with this batter; it's an excellent way to use up small quantities of left-over meat or fish.

Brandied Prune Fritters

12 large prunes
½ pint (1 cup) white wine
12 blanched almonds
1½ oz. (3 tablespoons) self raising (all purpose) flour
pinch salt

1 tablespoon brandy
water
oil for frying
2 oz. (2 squares) grated chocolate
3 tablespoons dark brown sugar

Place prunes with wine in saucepan, simmer slowly 10 minutes. Drain, cool, stone and replace each prune stone with an almond. Sift flour, add salt and brandy and a little water to make a smooth batter. Dip prunes in batter, fry until golden in hot oil. Drain and roll in mixed chocolate and brown sugar.

Yorkshire Pudding

4 oz. (1 cup) plain flour
pinch salt
1 egg

½ pint (1 cup) milk
1 to 2 tablespoons dripping from roast

Sift flour and salt into basin. Make a well in the centre, add egg. Beat into flour, then gradually add ½ milk, beating constantly and incorporating flour from sides of bowl. When a thick batter consistency has formed, beat well about 5 minutes. Stir in remaining milk, cover, refrigerate 30 minutes. Place the dripping from the roasting meat in small baking dish and heat. When very hot, add the batter and bake in hot oven, Mark 7, 425°F., until well browned (20 to 25 minutes). Serve with roast beef.

Serves 4.

Basic Waffles

2 eggs
1 dessertspoon sugar
1½ gills (⅔ cup) milk
¼ pint (½ cup) water
1 teaspoon vanilla
pinch salt

½ lb. (2 cups) self raising (all purpose) flour
2 tablespoons cornflour (cornstarch)
4 oz. (½ cup or 1 stick) butter

Separate eggs. Beat egg-yolks and sugar together, add milk, water and vanilla; beat again. Add sifted dry ingredients. Pour in melted butter; beat well. Finally fold in stiffly beaten egg-whites. Allow batter to stand 10 minutes. Spoon into hot, greased waffle iron, cook approximately 5 minutes or until golden brown and crisp.

Makes about 6, according to size of waffle iron.

Crisp Golden Waffles

4 oz. (1 cup) self raising (all purpose) flour
1 dessertspoon sugar
½ teaspoon salt

2 eggs
½ pint (1 cup) light cream
1 tablespoon melted butter

Sift flour, sugar and salt. Separate eggs, beat egg-yolks until thick. Add cream and mix lightly. Stir in sifted dry ingredients all at once, and stir only until smooth. Stir in melted butter. Beat egg-whites until stiff and fold into mixture. Cook in hot, greased waffle iron until golden brown.

Makes about 4.

Chinese Fried Prawns (Shrimps)

1 lb. or 1 pint prawns (shrimps), shelled and cleaned
1 tablespoon brandy or lemon juice
½ teaspoon soy or Worcestershire sauce

oil for deep frying
mayonnaise (see page 121) seasoned with horseradish or capers

Frying Batter

2 oz. (½ cup) plain flour
pinch salt
1 dessertspoon melted butter

1 egg, beaten
¼ pint (½ cup) beer
1 egg-white, extra

Marinate prawns (shrimps) in brandy and sauce. Meanwhile, make the frying batter; sift flour and salt into bowl, stir in butter and egg. Add beer gradually, stirring only until mixture is smooth. Let batter stand in warm place for 1 hour, then fold in stiffly beaten egg-white. Drain prawns (shrimps) then dip into the batter and fry, a few at a time, in deep, hot oil until golden brown. Drain and serve with mayonnaise.

Pancakes

4 oz. (1 cup) plain flour   1 egg
pinch salt   ½ pint (1 cup) milk

Sift flour and salt into bowl, make well in centre. Add whole egg, work flour in from sides, add milk a little at a time. Beat well until bubbles rise to surface; stand 1 hour. Heat pan, grease lightly. From small jug pour 2 to 3 tablespoons batter into pan, cook slowly, loosening edges with knife until set and lightly browned underneath. Toss or turn, brown on other side. Lift on to kitchen paper, sprinkle with lemon juice and sugar. Roll up and serve.

Makes 8 to 12.

German Potato Pancakes

1 oz. (2 tablespoons)   1 tablespoon chopped
   plain flour   onion
1½ teaspoons salt   1 tablespoon chopped
¼ teaspoon baking   parsley
   powder   2 lb. potatoes
pinch pepper   2 oz. (¼ cup) butter
2 eggs

Sift dry ingredients into bowl. Beat eggs well, add to dry ingredients with chopped onion and parsley; blend well. Wash, peel, and grate potatoes. Place in cloth and squeeze out excess liquid, add potatoes to egg mixture. Beat thoroughly with wooden spoon. Heat butter in frying pan. Spoon about 2 tablespoons batter into pan, flatten slightly with spoon. Cook over medium heat until golden brown and crisp on one side. Turn carefully, brown other side. Drain on absorbent paper. Add more butter to pan for remainder of pancakes, if necessary.

Makes 6 to 8.

French Crêpes

1½ oz. (3 tablespoons)   1 tablespoon oil
   plain flour   pinch salt
1 egg   ½ pint (1 cup) milk
1 egg-yolk, extra

Sift flour into bowl, add egg, egg-yolk, oil, salt and 2 tablespoons milk. Beat until smooth with small whisk. Mix in remainder of milk; refrigerate ½ hour. Heat heavy pan, grease with butter. Pour thin layer of pancake batter into pan, brown on one side. Turn, brown other side. Turn out on to plate. Repeat until all batter is used; keep warm. These can be filled with any savoury or sweet filling; seafood or chicken in a well-flavoured white sauce is good—and, for a sweet filling, try spreading pancakes with warmed apricot jam mixed with a little brandy, roll up, spoon lightly whipped cream over.

Makes 8 to 10.

Crêpes Suzette

2 oranges   4 to 5 tablespoons
1 lemon   Grand Marnier
2 oz. (¼ cup) butter   French Crêpes, see
2 tablespoons sugar   above

Squeeze oranges and lemon. Melt butter in pan, add sugar. Continue cooking over low heat until sugar melts and begins to caramelise. Pour in fruit juices. Cook rapidly over high heat until liquid reduces slightly and the caramelized sugar dissolves. Reduce heat, add the pancakes, one at a time, swirling them around in the sauce. Then, using fork and spoon, fold them in half, then in quarters. Allow pancakes to cook for a few minutes to soak up sauce, turning them once. Pour over the grand marnier; when warm, set aflame. Arrange pancakes on warmed plates (allow 2 to a serving). Spoon the hot sauce over.

Cream Cheese Blintzes

1 egg   8 oz. (2 cups) plain flour
1 tablespoon sugar   oil for deep frying
½ teaspoon salt   sour cream
1¼ to 1½ (2½ to 3 cups)
   pints milk

Cream Cheese Filling

½ lb. cream cheese   1 tablespoon melted
½ lb. (1 cup) cottage   butter
   cheese   3 oz. (½ cup) raisins,
yolk of 1 egg   plumped in warm
4 oz. (½ cup) sugar   water
pinch salt   little chopped
little grated lemon   preserved ginger
   rind

Break egg in bowl, add 1 tablespoon of sugar, the salt, ½ pint (1 cup) of milk, and mix. Then gradually stir in the sifted flour and remainder of milk. Heat the pan, grease with butter, pour in just enough batter to cover bottom of pan. As soon as one side is done take the pancake out and continue to cook remainder. Cook on one side only. (The pancakes must be very thin; add more milk to the batter if necessary). Put a tablespoon of filling on to cooked side of each pancake, fold into envelope shape, brushing the last fold with some of the batter to hold it. Just before serving, drop pancakes, one or two at a time, into deep, hot oil. Cook a few minutes until crisp and golden; drain well. Serve topped with sour cream.

Filling Sieve the cheeses, add egg-yolk, sugar, salt, lemon rind, butter, and mix thoroughly. Stir in the raisins and ginger.

Makes about 12.

Drop Scones are mixed and cooked in minutes. Serve them hot, well-buttered—they're good, light eating at any time.

Made without baking

There's no need to light the oven in hot weather to make pies, biscuits and cakes. There are recipes for all types—all delicious!—including some special-occasion biscuits to serve with after-dinner coffee.

Coffee Cream Roll

½ lb. plain sweet
  biscuits
4 oz. (¾ cup) icing
  (confectioners')
  sugar

3 oz. (½ cup) ground
  almonds
¼ pint (½ cup) hot black
  coffee
½ teaspoon vanilla
extra sugar

Butter-Cream Filling

6 oz. (¾ cup) sugar
4 to 5 tablespoons
  water

4 oz. (½ cup or 1 stick)
  butter
1 to 2 teaspoons rum

Cream Filling

½ pint (1 cup) whipping
  cream
1½ oz. (¼ cup) icing

(confectioners')
  sugar
1 to 2 teaspoons rum

Crush biscuits very finely; place in mixing bowl with sifted icing sugar and ground almonds. Mix well, make a well in centre, stir in coffee and vanilla. Mix together well to form a soft dough. Sift a little extra icing sugar on to a large sheet of greaseproof paper. Roll out mixture on grease-proof paper to rectangular shape approximately 9 in. × 12 in. Spread filling over evenly. Holding paper with both hands, gently roll into swiss roll shape. Roll in greaseproof paper, refrigerate until firm.

We've given a choice of two fillings for the roll—cream or butter-cream. If you want to make the Coffee Cream Roll several days in advance, use the butter-cream filling; the whipped cream filling will soften the biscuit crumbs if kept for more than 1 day. However, if making the roll to use the same day the whipped cream filling is delicious.

Butter-Cream Filling Place sugar and water in saucepan, place over low heat, stirring, until sugar dissolves. Bring to the boil, boil 5 minutes. Remove from heat, cool. Beat butter until creamy, gradually add cold syrup, beating well after each addition. Add rum to taste, beat well.

Cream Filling Beat cream until stiff, gradually adding sifted icing sugar and rum.

Chocolate Caramel Crisps

8 oz. (8 squares) plain
  chocolate
4 oz. (½ cup or 1 stick)
  butter
4 oz. (½ cup) sugar

about 4 oz. (¾ cup)
  chopped dates
about ½ lb. Rice
  Crispies

Melt half chopped chocolate over hot water, spread over base of well-greased tin, approximately 11 in. × 7 in.; refrigerate.

Put butter, sugar and dates in saucepan; cook, stirring, until dates are soft. Stir in sufficient Rice Crispies to make a firm but spreadable mixture, and spread over chilled chocolate.

Melt remaining chocolate, spread over as a topping; refrigerate until firm. Cut into small squares.

Makes approx. 2 dozen.

Continental Chocolate Slice

4 oz. (½ cup or 1 stick)
  butter
4 oz. (½ cup) sugar
3 dessertspoons cocoa
1 egg
1 teaspoon vanilla

½ lb. crushed wheat-
  meal biscuits
3 oz. (¾ cup) coconut
3 oz. (½ cup) chopped
  walnuts

Topping

2 oz. (¼ cup) butter
10 oz. (2 cups) icing
  (confectioners')
  sugar
2 dessertspoons custard
  powder

4 dessertspoons hot
  water
4 oz. (4 squares) plain
  chocolate

Combine butter, sugar, and cocoa in saucepan. Stir over low heat, until well blended. Stir in beaten egg and vanilla. Cook, stirring, 1 minute. Remove from heat, stir in biscuit crumbs, coconut and walnuts, mix well. Press mixture into greased tin, approximately 11 in. × 7 in., refrigerate until set.

Topping   Cream butter well. Sift together icing (confectioners') sugar and custard powder, add to butter alternately with hot water. Beat until light and fluffy. Spread over biscuit base, refrigerate.

Melt chopped chocolate over hot water, spread evenly over topping, refrigerate. Cut into small squares to serve.

Makes approx. 2 dozen.

Chocolate Fruit Squares

4 oz. (¼ cup) drinking chocolate	1½ oz. (¼ cup) chopped walnuts
4 oz. (1 cup) coconut	1 teaspoon sherry or fruit juice
2 oz. (⅓ cup) sultanas	
2 oz. (½ cup) crushed cornflakes	2 tablespoons crushed sweet biscuit crumbs
3 oz. (3 squares) plain chocolate	4 tablespoons condensed milk

Place all ingredients except chocolate into mixing bowl; mix well together. Press mixture into lightly greased 7 in. square tin, smooth the surface. Melt chocolate over hot water, spread evenly over surface of mixture; mark with fork. Refrigerate; when set and firm, cut into small bars or squares.

Makes approx. 1½ dozen.

Mocha Rum Torte

2 lb. stale sponge cake	4 dessertspoons instant coffee powder
10 oz. (1¼ cups) sugar	
8 oz. (1 cup) butter	1 dessertspoon gelatine
1 pint (2 cups) milk	4 dessertspoons water
	3 to 4 tablespoons rum

Icing

4 oz. (4 squares) chocolate	1 teaspoon rum
½ oz. (1 tablespoon) solid white vegetable shortening	

Rum Balls

extra cake crumbs	chocolate vermicelli
egg-white	

Crumble cake into crumbs. Place sugar, butter, and milk in saucepan. Stir over low heat until sugar dissolves and butter melts. Bring to boiling point, stir in instant coffee. Pour on to cake crumbs.

Soak gelatine in water, then place over hot water to dissolve. Stir into cake mixture with rum. Take out 4 tablespoons of mixture and reserve for rum balls.

Turn remaining mixture into a well-greased, 8 in. springform pan. Refrigerate overnight.

Rum Balls   To reserved mixture add enough extra cake crumbs to make firm dough. Roll mixture to make the size of golf balls. Refrigerate. Cut firmed balls into halves, brush with lightly beaten egg-white or warmed jam. Toss in chocolate vermicelli.

Icing   Mix together chopped chocolate, vegetable shortening and rum. Place over hot water until chocolate melts. Stir well until smooth.

Pour icing over cake while still in tin. Refrigerate at least 2 hours until firm. Before removing cake from tin, slip point of very sharp knife round chocolate to release from tin. (To make icing easier to cut, mark it lightly into wedges with a knife before chocolate is quite set).

To assemble   Place cake on serving dish. Using a little egg-white, press rum balls in position, circling top of cake.

Hazelnut Truffles

5½ oz. (1 cup) icing (confectioners') sugar	3 to 4 tablespoons whipping cream
4 oz. (⅔ cup) ground hazelnuts	12 oz. (12 squares) plain chocolate
1 egg-white	1 teaspoon rum
	chocolate vermicelli

Sift icing sugar into bowl, mix with hazelnuts. Stir in just enough egg-white to make a firm paste; add cream. Chop chocolate, place in top of double saucepan, stir over hot water until melted. Blend into hazelnut mixture, stirring with wooden spoon; add rum. Turn mixture into shallow tin lined with greased greaseproof paper; refrigerate until set. When firm, cut into small squares, then roll into balls between palms of hands; roll in chocolate vermicelli. Refrigerate.

Makes approx. 2½ dozen.

Rum Balls

9 oz. (3 cups) cake crumbs	1 tablespoon rum
3 tablespoons cocoa	2 tablespoons water
3 tablespoons apricot jam	2 tablespoons apricot jam, extra
	chocolate vermicelli

Mix together cake crumbs, cocoa, 2 tablespoons of sieved apricot jam, and rum until a stiff paste is formed. Make into approximately 24 balls. Warm 2 tablespoons of sieved jam with water; dip the balls in this jam mixture, then coat with chocolate vermicelli. Place in paper patty cases.

Makes approx. 2 dozen.

Chocolate Peppermint Squares

Base

4 oz. (½ cup or 1 stick) butter
3 dessertspoons cocoa
4 oz. (½ cup) castor (superfine) sugar
1 egg

few drops vanilla
4 oz. (1 cup) coconut
3 oz. (½ cup) walnuts
about ½ lb. wheatmeal biscuit crumbs

Filling

5½ oz. (1 cup) icing (confectioners') sugar
1 oz. (2 tablespoons) solid white vegetable shortening

3 dessertspoons milk
½ teaspoon peppermint essence

Topping

6 oz. (6 squares) plain chocolate

1 oz. (2 tablespoons) butter

Combine butter, cocoa and sugar in saucepan, stir over low heat until well blended. Remove from heat, add beaten egg and vanilla. Stir in coconut, chopped walnuts, and enough biscuit crumbs to make a fairly stiff mixture; mix well. Press into greased 13 in. × 10 in. slab tin. Refrigerate until set. Spread with peppermint filling and return to refrigerator to firm. Smooth chocolate topping over, refrigerate. When set, cut into squares.

Filling Sift icing sugar, add melted shortening, milk and essence; mix well.

Topping Coarsely chop chocolate, place in basin with butter. Stand basin in saucepan of boiling water until chocolate and butter are melted, stirring occasionally.

Makes approx. 3 dozen.

Summer Pies

A simple crumb crust is used in place of pastry base for these pies, and there's a delightful selection of fillings; all can be made without lighting the oven.

Crumb Crust

8 oz. plain sweet biscuits
½ teaspoon nutmeg

4 oz. (½ cup or 1 stick) butter

Crush biscuits into fine crumbs, place in bowl with nutmeg. Melt butter, add enough to crumbs so a tablespoon of mixture squeezed in the hand forms firm ball. Press this mixture firmly round sides and base of well-greased 7 in. sandwich tin with removable base or 9 in. pie plate. Refrigerate while preparing filling.

Serves 5 to 6.

Lemon Cream Pie

1 teaspoon gelatine
4 dessertspoons hot water
6 oz. (¾ cup) lemon curd

½ pint (1 cup) whipping cream
crumb crust

Dissolve gelatine in hot water. Add lemon curd, stir until smooth. Fold whipped cream into lemon mixture. Pour into prepared pie case. Refrigerate several hours or, preferably, overnight.

Chocolate Rum Pie

1 dessertspoon gelatine
1 pint (2 cups) milk
4 oz. (½ cup) sugar
3 dessertspoons cornflour (cornstarch)
4 eggs

4 oz. (4 squares) plain chocolate
3 dessertspoons rum
¼ pint (½ cup) whipping cream
little grated chocolate
crumb crust

Soften gelatine in 4 tablespoons of the milk; scald remaining milk. Blend sugar with cornflour (cornstarch), stir in hot milk. Separate eggs. Beat yolks, add cornflour (cornstarch) mixture. Cook in top of double saucepan over simmering water, stirring until mixture thickens. Add softened gelatine and chopped chocolate, stir until gelatine dissolves and chocolate melts; add rum. Allow to cool slightly. Beat egg-whites until soft peaks form; fold into chocolate mixture. Pour into prepared crumb crust. Refrigerate until set. Whip cream. Sweeten, if desired, with little sugar and vanilla. Spread evenly over chocolate filling. Decorate with grated chocolate.

Coffee Cream Roll and, at back, Continental Chocolate Slice— two of the delicious cakes and biscuits which can be made without lighting the oven. See page 184-5.

Biscuits

There are biscuits here to suit every taste, and every occasion—from wholesome biscuits for the children, to pack into their lunches, or for when they come home from school—or just for any time good eating, to luxurious little mouthfuls for special afternoon-teas, or to serve with coffee.

Butter Oat Biscuits

4 oz. ($\frac{1}{2}$ cup or 1 stick) butter

4 oz. ($\frac{1}{2}$ cup) castor (superfine) sugar

1 dessertspoon treacle or golden syrup (cornsyrup)

4 oz. (1 cup) self raising (all purpose) flour

9 oz. (2 cups) rolled oats

1 teaspoon bicarbonate of soda

4 tablespoons boiling water

Cream butter and sugar, add treacle, and cream well. Blend in sifted flour and oats. Dissolve soda in boiling water and add to mixture while still hot. Mix to a stiff dough. Roll teaspoons of mixture into balls; place on greased baking tray allowing room for spreading; press flat. Bake in moderate oven, Mark 4, 350°F., approximately 15 minutes. Cool on trays.

Makes approx. 4 dozen.

NOTE: 3 oz. flaked almonds can be added with the oats.

Chocolate Peppermint Slices

Biscuit Layer

6 oz. (1$\frac{1}{2}$ cups) self raising (all purpose) flour

3 oz. ($\frac{1}{2}$ cup) brown sugar

6 oz. (1$\frac{1}{2}$ cups) desiccated coconut

6 oz. ($\frac{3}{4}$ cup) butter

Peppermint Icing

1 oz. (2 tablespoons) vegetable shortening

6 oz. (1 cup) icing (confectioners') sugar

3 dessertspoons milk

$\frac{1}{2}$ teaspoon peppermint essence

Chocolate Icing

3 oz. ($\frac{3}{8}$ cup) vegetable shortening

2 oz. ($\frac{1}{2}$ cup) drinking chocolate

Biscuit Layer Sift flour, mix dry ingredients together, melt butter and pour over dry ingredients; mix well. Press into greased and lined 12 × 8 in. swiss roll tin, bake in moderate oven, Mark 4, 350°F., 20 minutes. While still warm, top with Peppermint Icing.

Peppermint Icing Melt shortening over gentle heat. Sift icing sugar into basin, add melted shortening, milk, and essence. Mix well, spread over biscuit layer. When cold top with Chocolate Icing.

Chocolate Icing Pour melted shortening over drinking chocolate and mix well. Cool slightly, then pour evenly on top of Peppermint Icing. Leave to set, then cut into slices to serve.

Makes approx. 3 dozen.

Almond Fingers

Pastry

5 oz. ($\frac{5}{8}$ cup) butter

3 oz. ($\frac{3}{8}$ cup) sugar

6 oz. (1$\frac{1}{2}$ cups) plain flour

Filling

$\frac{1}{4}$ pint ($\frac{1}{2}$ cup) whipping cream

2$\frac{1}{2}$ oz ($\frac{1}{2}$ cup) ground almonds

brown sugar

1 teaspoon cinnamon

1 egg-yolk

Icing

3 oz. ($\frac{1}{2}$ cup) icing (confectioners') sugar

lemon juice

Pastry Cream together butter and sugar in bowl until light and fluffy. Stir in sifted flour. Press dough, with lightly floured hand, into greased 11 in. × 7 in. tin. Bake in moderately slow oven, Mark 3, 325°F., 20 minutes. Remove from oven cool slightly.

Filling Whip the cream and add almonds, sugar and cinnamon. Mix in lightly beaten egg-yolk. Spread cream mixture over cooled pastry. Bake in moderately slow oven, Mark 3, 325°F., further 40 minutes. Remove from oven, cool, then refrigerate several hours. Spread icing over top. Refrigerate until icing is firm. Cut into fingers.

Icing Sift icing sugar into bowl. Add enough lemon juice to make spreading consistency. Blend until smooth; spread evenly over filling.

Makes approx. 2 dozen.

Hazelnut Chocolate Biscuits

6 oz. ($\frac{3}{4}$ cup) butter
8 oz. (1 cup) castor (superfine) sugar
1 egg
$\frac{1}{2}$ teaspoon vanilla
8 oz. (2 cups) self raising (all purpose) flour
2 oz. ($\frac{1}{3}$ cup) ground or chopped hazelnuts
2 oz. (2 squares) plain chocolate or chocolate pieces
3 oz. ($\frac{3}{4}$ cup) desiccated coconut
melted chocolate

Cream together butter and sugar until light and fluffy. Beat in egg and vanilla, beat well. Beat in sifted flour, blending thoroughly. Stir in hazelnuts, chopped chocolate and coconut, mix well. Roll into small balls about the size of a walnut; place on greased baking tray, allowing room to spread. Bake in moderate oven, Mark 4, 350°F., 15 minutes or until golden. Leave plain or dip half the biscuit in melted chocolate or drizzle chocolate over top.

Makes approx. $4\frac{1}{2}$ dozen.

Lunch-Box Cookies

3 oz. ($\frac{3}{8}$ cup) butter
$2\frac{1}{2}$ oz. ($\frac{1}{2}$ cup) dark brown sugar
4 oz. ($\frac{1}{2}$ cup) castor (superfine) sugar
1 teaspoon vanilla
1 egg
6 oz. ($1\frac{1}{2}$ cups) plain flour
$\frac{1}{2}$ teaspoon baking powder
$\frac{1}{2}$ teaspoon bicarbonate of soda
$\frac{1}{2}$ teaspoon salt
$\frac{1}{2}$ teaspoon ginger
$\frac{1}{2}$ teaspoon cinnamon
6 oz. ($1\frac{1}{4}$ cups) rolled oats
2 oz. ($\frac{1}{4}$ cup) marmalade
4 oz. ($\frac{3}{4}$ cup) chopped raisins

Cream butter and sugars, beat in egg and vanilla. Sift dry ingredients together, add to creamed mixture, then fold in oats, marmalade and raisins. Drop by teaspoons on to greased oven trays. Bake in moderately hot oven, Mark 5, 375°F., approximately 15 minutes or until evenly browned.

Makes approx. $3\frac{1}{2}$ dozen.

Anzac Biscuits

$4\frac{1}{2}$ oz. (1 cup) rolled oats
4 oz. (1 cup) plain flour
8 oz. (1 cup) sugar
$4\frac{1}{2}$ oz. (1 cup) desiccated coconut
4 oz. ($\frac{1}{2}$ cup or 1 stick) butter
1 tablespoon golden syrup (cornsyrup)
$1\frac{1}{2}$ teaspoons bicarbonate of soda
2 tablespoons boiling water

Combine rolled oats, sifted flour, sugar, and coconut. Combine butter and golden syrup (cornsyrup), stir over gentle heat until melted. Mix soda with boiling water, add to melted butter mixture, stir into dry ingredients. Spoon dessertspoonfuls of mixture on to greased oven trays; allow room for spreading. Bake in slow oven. Mark 2, 300°F.

Makes approx. 3 dozen.

Easy Florentines

3 oz. ($\frac{1}{2}$ cup) sultanas
4 to 6 oz. (about 2 cups) crushed cornflakes
3 oz. ($\frac{1}{2}$ cup) raw peanuts
2 oz. ($\frac{1}{2}$ cup) chopped cherries
6 oz. (small can) condensed milk
3 oz. (3 squares) plain chocolate

Combine all ingredients except chocolate in mixing bowl; mix well. Grease flat baking trays, line with greaseproof paper; grease paper, then dust lightly with cornflour. Shake trays to remove any excess cornflour. Place dessertspoonfuls of mixture in small heaps on trays. Bake in moderate oven, Mark 4, 350°F., 15 to 20 minutes. Leave on trays to cool before lifting off carefully with spatula. Melt chopped chocolate over hot water, remove from heat, and stir until thickened slightly. Spread chocolate over flat side of biscuit, mark with fork. Allow chocolate to set before storing in airtight tins.

Makes approx. $2\frac{1}{2}$ dozen.

Viennese Biscuits

8 oz. (1 cup) butter
2 oz. ($\frac{1}{4}$ cup) castor (superfine) sugar
$\frac{1}{2}$ teaspoon vanilla
8 oz. (2 cups) plain flour
pinch salt
melted chocolate

Cream together butter and sugar until light and fluffy. Add vanilla and carefully fold in sifted flour and salt. Fill into piping bag fitted with large star pipe. Pipe into finger lengths on lightly greased oven tray. Bake in moderately hot oven, Mark 5, 375°F., 15 to 20 minutes. Cool on tray. Leave plain, or dip one end in melted chocolate for pretty effect.

Makes approx. 3 dozen.

Australian Honey Raisin Bars

3 oz. ($\frac{3}{8}$ cup) butter
6 oz. ($\frac{1}{2}$ cup) honey
3 eggs
6 oz. ($1\frac{1}{2}$ cups) plain flour
1 teaspoon baking powder
6 oz. (1 cup) raisins
4 oz. ($\frac{3}{4}$ cup) chopped nuts

Cream butter and honey until soft and light, beat in the eggs one at a time. Add flour and baking powder sifted together, raisins and nuts. Spread in a greased tin, about 9 × 12 in. and bake in the centre of a moderate oven, Mark 4, 350°F., for about 30 minutes. Cool in the tin, cut into bars and lift out carefully.

These keep well and should be 'chewy' and moist.

Makes 16 to 20.

Brandy Snaps

2 tablespoons golden
   syrup (cornsyrup)
2 oz. ($\frac{1}{4}$ cup) butter
2 oz. ($\frac{1}{3}$ cup) dark
   brown sugar
2 oz. ($\frac{1}{2}$ cup) plain flour
2 teaspoons ground
   ginger
pinch salt

Place syrup, butter and brown sugar into saucepan, heat slowly until butter has melted, stirring occasionally. Sift flour, ginger, and salt into a bowl, stir in syrup and butter mixture; mix well. Drop dessertspoons of mixture on to greased trays, allowing room for spreading. Bake in moderate oven, Mark 4, 350°F., 5 to 7 minutes, or until golden brown. Remove from oven, cool 1 minute. With knife, lift brandy snap from tray. Roll immediately around the handle of a wooden spoon. Allow to firm and cool on spoon handle. Just before serving, fill with whipped cream.

Makes 6 to 8 brandy snaps.

NOTE: Two brandy snaps will fit comfortably on to a baking tray. It is a good idea to bake only two at a time. If they firm up before you have time to mould them into shape, return to the oven for a few minutes to soften again.

Ginger Nuts

8 oz. (2 cups) plain
   flour
8 oz. (1 cup) castor
   (superfine) sugar
$\frac{1}{2}$ teaspoon bicarbonate
   of soda
1 teaspoon cinnamon
pinch salt
2 teaspoons ground
   ginger
4 oz. ($\frac{1}{2}$ cup) butter
1 very small egg
1 teaspoon golden
   syrup (cornsyrup)

Sift into basin the flour, sugar, soda, cinnamon, salt and ginger. Rub in butter until mixture is of very fine crumb consistency. Beat egg with syrup, add to dry ingredients. Work into a firm dough with hands. Roll into small balls about size of half a walnut, place on greased baking trays, about 2 in. apart. Bake in moderately slow oven, Mark 3, 325°F., approximately 15 minutes. Loosen, cool on oven slide.

Makes approx. $3\frac{1}{2}$ dozen.

Macaroons

2 egg-whites
6 oz. ($\frac{3}{4}$ cup) castor
   (superfine) sugar
$3\frac{1}{2}$ oz. ($\frac{3}{4}$ cup) ground
   almonds
grated rind 1 lemon

Beat egg-whites until peaks form. Gradually beat in sugar, beat until sugar is dissolved; mixture should be of meringue consistency. Fold in ground almonds and grated lemon rind. Using 2 teaspoons, spoon mixture on to greased and cornfloured oven trays, allowing room for spreading. Bake in moderate oven, Mark 4, 325°F., approximately 15 to 20 minutes until firm.

Makes approx. 3 dozen.

Chocolate Cherry Bars

8 oz. (8 squares) plain
   chocolate
2 small eggs
4 oz. ($\frac{1}{2}$ cup) castor
   (superfine) sugar
6 oz. ($1\frac{1}{2}$ cups) coconut
2 to 3 oz. (about $\frac{1}{4}$ cup)
   glacé cherries
icing (confectioners')
   sugar

Chop chocolate roughly. Place in top of double saucepan over hot water; heat gently, stirring, until melted and smooth. Spread chocolate over base of well greased 11 in. × 7 in. tin. Refrigerate until firm. Beat together eggs and sugar until light and frothy; gently fold in coconut and chopped cherries. Spread over firm chocolate. Bake in moderate oven, Mark 4, 350°F., 10 to 15 minutes until topping is lightly golden and firm to the touch. Cool, then refrigerate. Before serving, sprinkle with sifted icing sugar, cut into small fingers.

Makes approx. 2 dozen.

Butter Coconut Crisps

4 oz. ($\frac{1}{2}$ cup) butter
6 oz. ($1\frac{1}{2}$ cups) self
   raising (all purpose)
   flour
8 oz. (1 cup) sugar
1 egg
desiccated coconut

Melt butter. Sift flour and sugar into bowl, add beaten egg and melted butter, mix thoroughly. Form into small balls the size of a walnut, roll in coconut, and place on greased trays, allowing room to spread. Bake in moderate oven, Mark 4, 325°F., 10 to 15 minutes. Loosen and leave until cold on tray.

Makes approx. $2\frac{1}{2}$ dozen.

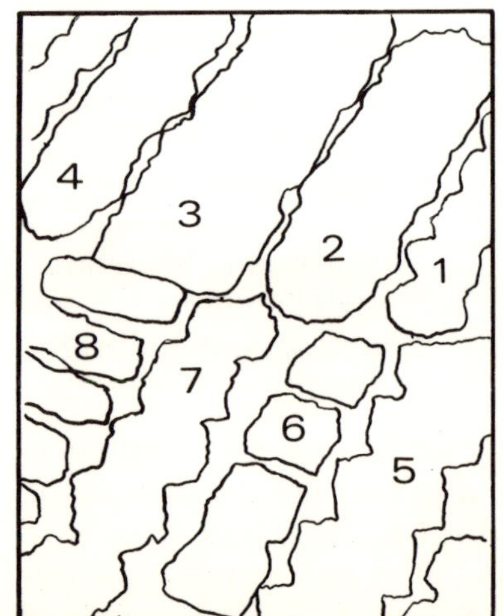

1. *Macaroons*
2. *Butter Coconut Crisps*
3. *Almond Bread*
4. *Butter Oat Biscuits*
5. *Chocolate Cherry Bars*
6. *Chocolate Mint Slices*
7. *Easy Florentines*
8. *Viennese Biscuits*

Clover Leaf Cookies

2 oz. (¼ cup) butter
2 oz. (¼ cup) sugar
1 small egg
4 oz. (1 cup) plain flour

few caraway seeds
½ teaspoon ground ginger
1 teaspoon grated lemon rind

Cream butter and sugar, add beaten egg and flour alternately to make a smooth dough. It may not be necessary to use all the egg. Knead well then divide the dough into three portions and work a different flavouring into each. Roll into small balls and group one ball of each flavour together. Put on to a greased tray and press flat to form a clover leaf shape. Bake in a moderately hot oven, Mark 5, 375°F, for 10 to 15 minutes. Cool on a wire tray.

Makes about 15.

Ginger Crunch Biscuits

4 oz. (½ cup) butter
2 oz. (¼ cup) sugar
4 oz. (1 cup) plain flour

1 teaspoon baking powder
1 teaspoon ground ginger

Topping

2 oz. (⅓ cup) icing (confectioners') sugar
2 oz. (¼ cup) butter

1 teaspoon ground ginger
3 teaspoons golden syrup (cornsyrup)

Cream butter and sugar together. Add sifted dry ingredients, mix well until thoroughly absorbed. Spread into greased 11 in. × 7 in. tin and bake in moderate oven, Mark 4, 350°F., until lightly browned, approximately 15 to 20 minutes.
Topping Place all ingredients in saucepan, stir over gentle heat until butter is melted and ingredients well mixed. Pour over biscuit layer while both are still warm. Cut into squares or fingers when cold.

Makes approx. 1½ dozen.

Easy Ratafias

2 egg-whites
pinch salt
8 oz. (1 cup) sugar
6 oz. (½ cup) instant mashed potato flakes (dry)

6 oz. (1½ cups) desiccated coconut
few drops almond essence
almond flakes to decorate

Beat egg-whites with salt until very stiff. Gradually add sugar, beat until thick and sugar is dissolved. Fold in potato flakes, coconut, and essence. Place teaspoons of mixture on greased baking tray, top with almond flakes. Bake in moderate oven, Mark 4, 350°F., 15 to 20 minutes.

Makes approx. 3 dozen.

Crisp Coconut Biscuits

4 oz. (½ cup) butter
8 oz. (1 cup) castor (superfine) sugar
1 egg
8 oz. (2 cups) self raising (all purpose) flour

pinch salt
6 oz. (1½ cups) desiccated coconut
extra sugar

Cream butter and sugar, beat in egg, add sifted flour, salt and coconut. Roll into balls and press flat between hands. Dip the top side into extra sugar. Place on greased baking trays, allow for spreading. Bake in moderately hot oven, Mark 5, 375°F., 10 to 15 minutes.

Makes approx. 2 dozen.

Shortbread

8 oz. (2 cups) plain flour
1½ oz. (¼ cup) icing (confectioners') sugar

1 tablespoon ground rice
6 oz. (¾ cup) butter

Sift flour, sugar and ground rice into bowl. Rub in butter and knead until mixture is smooth. Roll mixture out to ¼ in. thickness on lightly-floured board; cut into 2 in. rounds with cutter. Place on ungreased trays, bake in moderate oven, Mark 4, 350°F., 15 to 20 minutes or until pale golden.

Makes approx. 2½ dozen.

Mixture can also be pressed into ungreased 7 in. × 11 in. tin. Cut with knife into finger shapes, bake as above.

Makes approx. 2 dozen.

Butterscotch Bars

Base

4 oz. (1 cup) plain flour
3 oz. (⅜ cup) butter
pinch salt

2½ oz. (½ cup) dark brown sugar

Topping

6 oz. butterscotch toffees
1 tablespoon golden syrup (cornsyrup)
1 tablespoon water

1 oz. (2 tablespoons) butter
pinch salt
4 oz. (⅔ cup) walnuts

Base Combine ingredients in small bowl of electric mixer; blend at low speed until well combined and particles are small (or rub butter into sifted dry ingredients until mixture resembles fine breadcrumbs).

Press mixture into paper-lined 8 in. square shallow tin. Bake in moderately hot oven, Mark 5, 375°F., 10 to 12 minutes. Remove from oven, spread topping over. Return to oven for 8 to 10 minutes.

Cool on wire rack; when cold cut into small squares.

Topping   Combine all ingredients except walnuts in small saucepan, stir over low heat until butterscotch has dissolved. Stir in chopped walnuts. Spread evenly over hot partially baked base.

Makes approx. 16.

Caramel Shortbread Squares

4 oz. (1 cup) plain flour
pinch salt
3 oz. (½ cup) icing sugar
4 oz. (½ cup) butter

Caramel

4 oz. (½ cup) butter
2½ oz. (¼ cup) golden syrup (cornsyrup)
2½ oz. (½ cup) dark brown sugar
1 teaspoon gelatine
8 oz. (⅔ cup) condensed milk

Sift flour, salt and icing sugar into bowl. Rub in butter. Press into greased 8 in. square shallow tin. Bake in moderate oven, Mark 4, 350°F., 20 to 25 minutes. Leave to cool in tin, then pour caramel over. Refrigerate several hours or overnight until topping is quite firm.

Carefully turn biscuit over on to plastic food wrap and, with biscuit base uppermost, cut into small squares. (It is easier to cut biscuit this way.)

Makes approx. 25.

Caramel   Melt butter and syrup in saucepan over low heat; add sugar, gelatine and condensed milk; beat thoroughly. Continue stirring over low heat until sugar dissolves, then bring to boil and boil 4 minutes, stirring constantly. Remove from heat, beat well with wooden spoon. Pour over biscuit.

Almond Bread

3 egg-whites
4 oz. (½ cup) castor (superfine) sugar
4 oz. (1 cup) plain flour
4 oz. (⅔ cup) whole unblanched almonds

Beat egg-whites until stiff, gradually beat in castor sugar until mixture is of good meringue consistency, forming thick peaks. Fold in sifted flour and whole almonds. Fill into very lightly greased 8 in. × 4 in. loaf tin. Bake in moderate oven, Mark 4, 350°F., 30 to 40 minutes. Leave in tin until completely cold. Wrap in aluminium foil, put aside for one or two days. Using very sharp knife, cut into wafer thin slices. Place slices on oven tray, put into slow oven, Mark 2, 300°F., 45 minutes to dry out completely.

Serve just one slice with after dinner coffee. Or serve as a delightfully crisp biscuit with ice-cream.

Flaky Cheese Biscuits

2 oz. (¼ cup) butter
2 oz. (½ cup grated) Cheddar cheese
½ egg-yolk
salt
good pinch paprika
2 oz. (½ cup) plain flour

Beat butter until creamy, gradually add finely grated cheese, egg-yolk, salt and paprika. Work in sifted flour. When well blended, refrigerate 1 hour. Knead lightly, roll out on floured board to ¼ in. thickness. Cut out in 1 in. rounds; place on lightly greased oven trays, bake in hot oven, Mark 7, 425°F., 10 minutes.

Makes approx. 2½ dozen.

Cheese and Sesame Wafers

4 oz. (1 cup) plain flour
½ teaspoon salt
pinch cayenne pepper
½ teaspoon dry mustard
½ teaspoon ground ginger
½ teaspoon sugar
2 oz. (½ cup) grated Cheddar cheese
2 to 3 tablespoons toasted sesame seeds
1 egg-yolk
2 oz. (¼ cup) butter
1 tablespoon water

Sift together dry ingredients into bowl. Stir in cheese and toasted sesame seeds. Combine lightly beaten egg-yolk, melted butter and water. Stir into dry ingredients; form into a ball. Wrap in greaseproof paper; refrigerate 30 minutes. Roll out to ⅛ in. thickness on lightly floured board. Cut into 1 in. × 2 in. strips or 2 in. squares. Place on ungreased oven tray, bake in moderate oven, Mark 4, 350°F., 15 minutes. Cool on tray.

Makes approx. 4½ dozen.

To toast sesame seeds   Place seeds on baking tray, bake in moderate oven, Mark 4, 350°F., 15 minutes, shaking tray occasionally.

Paprika Biscuits

3 oz. (⅜ cup) butter
3 oz. (¾ cup) Cheddar cheese
4 oz. (1 cup) plain flour
1 teaspoon paprika
½ teaspoon salt
½ teaspoon dry mustard
1 dessertspoon poppy seeds or 1 teaspoon caraway seeds

Beat together butter and grated cheese until soft and creamy. Sift together dry ingredients, add to cheese mixture, beat until well blended. Take dessertspoons of mixture and roll into small balls, using floured hands. Place on greased oven tray, flatten slightly, sprinkle poppy seeds lightly over each biscuit. Bake in moderate oven Mark 4, 350°F., 15 to 20 minutes or until lightly golden brown. Loosen and cool on tray.

Makes approx. 1½ dozen.

Scones

It's easy to whip up a batch of feather-light scones and, in this section, we give a wide variety of recipes for plain and sweet scones.

To make sure they turn out perfect every time, it is important they be mixed and baked correctly—and we show how to do this in step-by-step pictures.

Here is a list of the basic ingredients used in scone making, and the reasons for their use.

Basic Ingredients

Self-raising flour Should be as fresh as possible, to guarantee maximum rising power. Stale flour will give poor results.

Salt Used to accent flavour.

Sugar Small amount used adds flavour, but does not sweeten. For a sweet scone, perhaps with sultanas, use 1 tablespoon sugar.

Butter Scones are best eaten the day they're made. Small amount of butter used does not give keeping quality, but adds flavour and colour.

Milk and water Combination of equal quantities of milk and water will produce a lighter scone than all milk.

Scones

8 oz. (2 cups) self raising (all purpose) flour	1 oz. (2 tablespoons) butter
½ teaspoon salt	approx. 8 tablespoons milk and water
1 teaspoon sugar	

Sift flour and salt into basin, stir in sugar. Rub in butter until mixture resembles fine breadcrumbs. Pour nearly all the liquid in at once and mix to a soft dough. (Flours vary in the way they absorb liquid; if mixture is not soft enough, add remaining liquid.) Place on floured surface and knead lightly. Pat dough out to approximately ¾ in. thickness, and, using a 2 in. cutter, cut into rounds. Place on to a greased baking tray, glaze with a little milk. Bake in a very hot oven, Mark 8, 450°F., for 10 minutes or until golden brown.

Makes approx. 1 dozen.

Cream Scones

1 egg	4 tablespoons milk
2 dessertspoons sugar	8 oz. (2 cups) self
4 tablespoons light cream	raising (all purpose) flour

Beat egg and sugar together until light and creamy. Add cream and milk, mix thoroughly. Add sifted flour and mix to soft dough. Turn on to floured surface and knead lightly. Pat dough to ¾ in. in thickness, cut into rounds with 2 in. cutter. Place on a greased baking tray; glaze with a little milk. Bake in very hot oven, Mark 8, 450°F., 10 to 12 minutes.

Makes 1 dozen.

Cheese-Topped Scones

12 oz. (3 cups) self raising (all purpose) flour	1½ oz. (3 tablespoons) butter
½ teaspoon salt	about ½ pint (1 cup) milk

Cheese Topping

3 oz. (⅜ cup) butter	pinch pepper
3 oz. (¾ cup) tasty cheese	pinch salt
	½ teaspoon dry mustard

Sift flour and salt into basin. Rub in butter until mixture resembles fine breadcrumbs. Pour nearly all the milk in at once and mix to a soft dough; add remainder of milk, if necessary. Place dough on a floured surface and knead lightly. Pat out to approximately ¾ in. in thickness, and, using a 2 in. cutter, cut into rounds. Place on greased baking tins, place a teaspoon of cheese topping on to each scone. Bake in a very hot oven, Mark 8, 450°F., 10 to 15 minutes, or until golden brown.

Cheese Topping Melt butter in a small saucepan, allow to cool slightly. Add grated cheese, pepper, salt and mustard; mix thoroughly.

Makes approx. 15.

So easily and quickly made, scones are everybody's favourite. Serve them hot with strawberry jam or honey.

Step 1

Rub in butter correctly: *Sift dry ingredients, then rub in butter. Use tips of fingers only for rubbing in; these are the coolest part of the hand, and butter will not be softened or melted during rubbing in process. To rub in, rub thumbs over fingertips in circular motion, lifting hands above bowl so flour falls through fingers to bowl beneath; this aerates and lightens the mixture.*

Some prize-winning cooks heat a little of the milk and melt the butter in it before adding it, with the rest of the milk, to the flour mixture. This gives even distribution throughout the scone and prevents any uneven butter-patches.

Step 2

Mix lightly: *Add the liquid to rubbed in mixture almost all at once (this is important to avoid over mixing), then lightly stir and cut liquid through mixture, adding remainder of liquid, if required. Dough should be soft, sticking to sides of bowl. Use a knife for mixing; it is light, functional, makes it easier to avoid over-mixing dough.*

Step by Step Perfect Scones

Sultana Scones

12 oz. (3 cups) self raising (all purpose) flour	2 oz. ($\frac{1}{4}$ cup) sugar
	4 oz. ($\frac{2}{3}$ cup) sultanas
$\frac{1}{2}$ teaspoon salt	1 egg
2 oz. ($\frac{1}{4}$ cup) butter	approx. $\frac{1}{2}$ pint (1 cup) milk

Sift flour and salt, rub in butter until mixture resembles fine breadcrumbs. Stir in sugar and sultanas. Beat egg and add to dry ingredients with sufficient milk to give a soft dough. Place on floured surface and knead lightly. Pat out to approximately $\frac{3}{4}$ in. in thickness, and cut into 2 in. rounds. Place on greased baking tins. Glaze with milk. Bake in a very hot oven, Mark 8, 450°F., 12 to 15 minutes.

Makes approx. 15.

Date Scones

8 oz. (2 cups) self raising (all purpose) flour	chopped dates
	2 oz. ($\frac{1}{4}$ cup) sugar
$\frac{1}{2}$ teaspoon salt	1 egg
2 oz. ($\frac{1}{4}$ cup) butter	approx $\frac{1}{4}$ pint ($\frac{1}{2}$ cup) milk
6 oz. ($\frac{3}{4}$ cup) finely	

Sift flour and salt, rub in butter until mixture resembles fine breadcrumbs. Stir in dates and sugar. Beat eggs and add to dry ingredients with sufficient milk to give a soft dough. Place on floured surface and knead lightly. Pat out to approximately $\frac{1}{2}$ in. thickness, and, using a 2 in. floured cutter, cut into rounds. Place on to greased baking tins. Glaze tops with milk. Bake in very hot oven, Mark 8, 450°F., 12 to 15 minutes.

Makes approx. 1 dozen.

Feather-Light Scones

1 egg	8 oz. (2 cups) self raising (all purpose) flour
1 dessertspoon sugar	
1 oz. (2 tablespoons) melted butter	$\frac{1}{2}$ teaspoon salt
about $\frac{1}{4}$ pint ($\frac{1}{2}$ cup) milk	milk for glazing

Beat egg and sugar together until thick; add melted butter to milk. Sift together flour and salt into a bowl, make a well in centre. Stir in egg mixture, then milk mixture; mix to a soft dough. Turn out on to a floured surface, knead lightly. Pat or roll to $\frac{1}{2}$ in. in thickness, cut out with a floured 2 in. cutter. Place on a lightly greased scone tray, brush tops with a little cold milk. Bake in a hot oven, Mark 7, 425°F., 10 to 12 minutes.

Makes approx. 1 dozen.

Step 3

Knead briefly, gently: *Turn mixture out from bowl on to lightly floured board; using fingertips, knead gently by turning outside edge of dough into centre, turning dough round, then turning edges in again. Repeat until dough is smooth, free from creases underneath, elastic to the touch. This kneading should be thorough, but as brief and gentle as possible, otherwise scones will be toughened.*

Step 4

Cut sharply, evenly: *Turn smooth side of dough uppermost, shape into round; using palms of hands, press out lightly to approximately ¾ in. high. Use as little flour on board as possible, to avoid floury base on scones. (Rolling pin is not necessary for small amount of scone dough; also, using rolling pin you're inclined to roll out dough too thinly.) Dip plain, sharp-edged cutter in flour; press sharply and evenly into dough, without twisting cutter. (Twisting cutter would retard rising.) One, 2, or 2½ in. diameter cutter can be used, depending on size of scone required.*

Step 5

Arrange correctly on tray: *Cut as many scones as possible from the first rolling; each successive kneading toughens dough. Shake scones out of cutter and, to obtain even cooking, place in centre of prepared tray, close together but not touching. As scones cook and rise they will be close enough to support each other, yet still retain their individual shape. If you like to have scones with soft sides, put them close together in a shallow tin as shown in pictures 4 and 5 above. Brush the top of all scones lightly with a little milk to give them a golden brown glossy appearance.*

Step 6

Bake in hot oven, cool correctly: *Bake scones in hot oven, Mark 7 to 8, 425 to 450°F., 10 to 15 minutes. Scones baked in a deeper tin may need longer cooking time. When cooked, they should be golden brown on top, sound hollow when tapped with fingertip. Remove from tray to wire cake cooler. If you prefer scones with firm, crisp top, let them stand, uncovered, on wire tray. If you prefer soft scones, wrap them, as soon as they come from oven, in clean teatowel; the trapped steam will soften the crisp top.*

And remember, never cut a scone—break it open with the fingers.

Honeyed Banana Scones

4 oz. (1 cup) self raising (all purpose) flour
4 oz. (1 cup) wholemeal self raising flour
½ teaspoon salt
1 oz. (2 tablespoons) butter
2 bananas
7 to 8 tablespoons milk
2 tablespoons honey

Sift flours and salt into basin, rub in butter until mixture resembles fine breadcrumbs. Mash bananas; combine milk, honey, and mashed bananas, add to dry ingredients and work into soft dough. Turn on to floured surface and knead lightly. Pat out to ¾ in. in thickness, cut with floured 2 in. cutter. Place on to greased baking tins, glaze tops with a little milk. Bake in very hot oven, Mark 8, 450°F., 12 to 15 minutes.

Makes 1 dozen.

Milk Scones

8 oz. (2 cups) self raising (all purpose) flour
4 dessertspoons powdered milk
pinch salt
1 teaspoon sugar
1½ oz. (3 tablespoons) butter
1½ gills (⅔ cup) water

Sift flour, powdered milk, and salt into basin. Add sugar and rub in butter until mixture resembles fine breadcrumbs. Pour nearly all the water in at once and mix to a soft dough; add extra water if necessary. Place on floured surface and knead lightly. Pat dough out to approximately ¾ in. in thickness, and, using a 2 in. cutter, cut into rounds. Place on to a greased baking tray, glaze with a little water or milk. Bake in a very hot oven, Mark 8, 450°F., for 12 to 15 minutes or until golden brown.

Makes approx. 1 dozen.

Treacle Scones

8 oz. (2 cups) flour
1 teaspoon cream of tartar
1 teaspoon bicarbonate of soda
pinch salt
1 oz. (2 tablespoons) butter
2 oz. (2 tablespoons) treacle
milk

Sieve all the dry ingredients, rub in the butter. Warm the treacle slightly, add a little milk and mix to a fairly soft dough. Turn on to a floured board, knead lightly and roll to about 1 in. thick. Cut into rounds with a 2 in. cutter and bake in a moderately hot oven, Mark 6, 400°F., for 10 to 15 minutes.

Makes 8 to 10.

Caramel Fruit Buns

4 oz. (½ cup) butter
4 oz. (⅔ cup) light brown sugar
2 oz. (⅓ cup) walnuts
12 oz. (3 cups) self raising (all purpose) flour
pinch salt
2 oz. (¼ cup) sugar
1½ oz. (3 tablespoons) butter, extra
1 egg
¼ to ½ pint (½ to 1 cup) milk
4 oz. (⅔ cup) raisins

Cream together butter and brown sugar until light and creamy. Spread half of this mixture over base of greased and greased paper lined 9 in. square slab tin. Sprinkle chopped walnuts over.

Sift flour, salt and sugar into basin. Rub in extra butter, until mixture resembles fine breadcrumbs. Beat egg lightly and add to flour mixture. Then add enough milk to mix to soft dough. Turn dough out on to floured surface and knead lightly. Roll dough into oblong 14 in. × 9 in. approximately. Spread over remaining creamed mixture, sprinkle with chopped raisins.

Roll up as for swiss roll (see page 164), cut into 16 even slices. Place slices on top of walnuts, cut side up. Bake in moderately hot oven, Mark 5, 375°F., 30 to 35 minutes.

Scones in large quantity

1½ lb. (6 cups) self raising flour
2 tablespoons sugar
½ teaspoon salt
3 oz. (⅜ cup) butter
½ pint milk
about ¼ pint water
milk for glazing

Sift flour, sugar and salt into basin. Rub butter into dry ingredients. Mix to soft dough with combined milk and water, adding extra milk, if necessary. Knead dough, roll out and fit into greased 10 in. × 11 in. baking dish. With sharp knife cut dough into approximately 36 squares. Glaze with milk, bake in hot oven, Mark 7, 425°F., 15 to 20 minutes or until golden brown.

Makes approx. 3 dozen.

For Sultana Scones Add 4 to 6 oz. sultanas to dry ingredients before adding the liquid; increase sugar to 3 oz.

Pastry

If you remember the few essentials for making perfect pastry, you will have good results every time you bake. There are just five important rules to follow.

Keep everything as cold as possible Fat should be firm; liquid should be chilled. If time permits, place mixing bowl in refrigerator for an hour before using.

Use only as much liquid as necessary Too much liquid will result in hard pastry, and will also cause pastry to shrink during baking, as the excess water evaporates in heat of oven.

If insufficient liquid is added, dough will be too crumbly for rolling.

Liquid should be added gradually, until just sufficient has been added to make pastry firm enough to be handled and rolled out without breaking.

Sift the dry ingredients Sift flour and any other dry ingredients well. This sifting helps to incorporate air into pastry mixture, as well as ensuring flour is fine, without lumps.

Fold in as much air as possible as you mix With shortcrust pastry, air is incorporated by lifting flour and butter mixture from bowl when rubbing in with fingertips.

With puff pastry, air is incorporated through the process of folding and rolling.

Roll pastry with short, jerky movements; lift rolling pin after each roll. This allows air to move about in dough. Heavy rolling will destroy air bubbles, resulting in heavy pastry.

Handle the pastry lightly Too much handling will make pastry heavy.

When rolling out pastry on a floured board, use only enough flour to prevent pastry sticking to the proof paper; this makes them easier to handle and avoids over-working the pastry.

Never stretch pastry—it will shrink back when cooking.

When rolling pastry on a floured board, use only enough flour to prevent pastry sticking to the surface. Excess flour will upset the balance of the ingredients, and could result in tough pastry. For this reason too, never turn pastry over during rolling.

How Much Pastry To Use

When a recipe calls for 8 oz. pastry it means pastry made with 8 oz. (2 cups) flour (plus the corresponding ingredients).

The exception to this is where packaged puff pastry is an ingredient; when a recipe calls for 12 oz. or 1 lb. packaged puff pastry, this is the full weight of the completed pastry in its package.

Basic pastry recipes given in this book can be reduced or increased if necessary; be sure to reduce or increase all other ingredients in proportion.

The list given below is an approximate guide to help you assess the quantity of pastry you may need.

Tarts 6 oz. pastry will line 7 in. pie plate.

8 oz. to 10 oz. pastry will line 8 in. or 9 in. pie plate.

Double-crust Pies 10 oz. pastry will give bottom and top crust for 7 in. pie.

12 oz. to 14 oz. pastry will give bottom and top crust for 8 in. or 9 in. pie.

Small Tartlets 8 oz. pastry will make approximately 2 dozen small tartlet cases.

When large tart cases with a filling require a longer cooking time than approximately 25 minutes, a double edge of pastry will prevent edges of tart case from becoming too crisp. Cut long strips of pastry, the width of the pie plate edge, from rolled out pastry. Place strips around edge of pie plate, brush strips lightly with water, line plate with pastry in usual manner. Press edges together, trim, decorate as desired.

Step 1

Cut four divisions in dough; cut only half-way through, so it is still joined at base. Pull out centre point of each division.

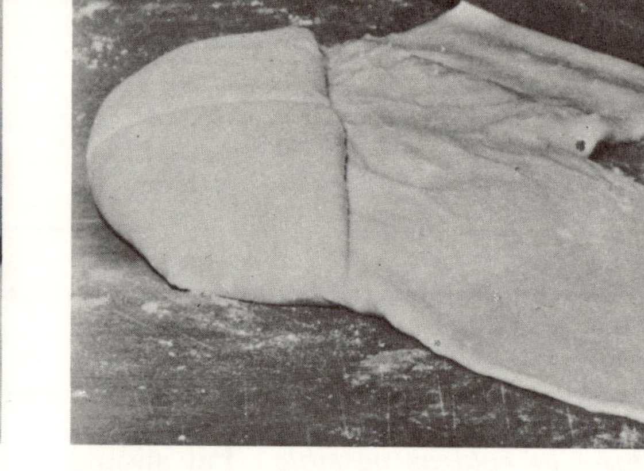

Step 2

Leaving uncut base part unrolled, roll out each of the points, as shown in picture above.

Step by Step Puff Pastry

Shortcrust Pastry

Shortcrust is probably the most widely used of all pastries, and is good for pies with sweet or savoury fillings.

Basic shortcrust uses half the amount of shortening (butter, margarine) to flour. For example, shortcrust with 8 oz. (2 cups) flour would use 4 oz. (½ cup) shortening; with 12 oz. (3 cups) flour, 6 oz. (¾ cup) shortening, etc.

½ lb. (2 cups) plain flour	4 oz. (½ cup) butter
½ teaspoon baking powder	1½ tablespoons water
pinch salt	1 teaspoon lemon juice

Sift dry ingredients, rub in butter until mixture resembles dry breadcrumbs. Mix to pliable dry dough with water and lemon juice.

The finished pastry, when it is mixed, should form a smooth ball, leaving the sides of the mixing bowl clean.

Turn on to lightly floured board, knead lightly. Roll to size and shape required.

Sweet Shortcrust Add 1 dessertspoon castor sugar for every ½ lb. flour. Dissolve sugar in the water before adding it to flour, or sift 1 dessertspoon icing sugar with dry ingredients.

Rich Shortcrust Pastry

½ lb. (2 cups) plain flour	1 egg-yolk
½ teaspoon baking powder	1 teaspoon lemon juice
pinch salt	water
4 to 6 oz. (½ to ¾ cup) butter	

Sift dry ingredients, rub in butter until mixture resembles dry breadcrumbs. Using egg-yolk, lemon juice, and little water if necessary, mix into a dry dough. Turn on to lightly floured surface and knead into a smooth round.

Biscuit Pastry

3 oz. (⅜ cup) butter	5 oz. (1¼ cups) plain flour
2 oz. (¼ cup) sugar	1 oz. (¼ cup) self raising (all purpose) flour
1 egg	

Beat butter until creamy, add sugar, beat until just combined. Add beaten egg gradually, beating well after each addition. Over-creaming at this stage will make pastry difficult to handle. Work in ⅔ of sifted flours with a wooden spoon, then remaining flour with the hand. Turn on to lightly floured board, knead lightly until smooth. (Heavy handling of pastry will toughen it and make it difficult to roll). Refrigerate 30 minutes before using.

Custard Tart

1 quantity biscuit pastry	2 tablespoons sugar
3 eggs	1 pint (2 cups) milk
1 teaspoon vanilla	nutmeg

Roll pastry on lightly floured board, carefully line a greased 8 in. tart plate. (Any breaks in the pastry could cause custard to seep through). Pinch edges decoratively.

Beat eggs, vanilla and sugar together; warm milk, gradually stir into egg mixture. Carefully spoon custard into pastry case. Bake in moderate oven, Mark 4, 350°F., 30 to 35 minutes. After 15 minutes cooking time, sprinkle with nutmeg. Do not over-cook; custard will firm as it cools.

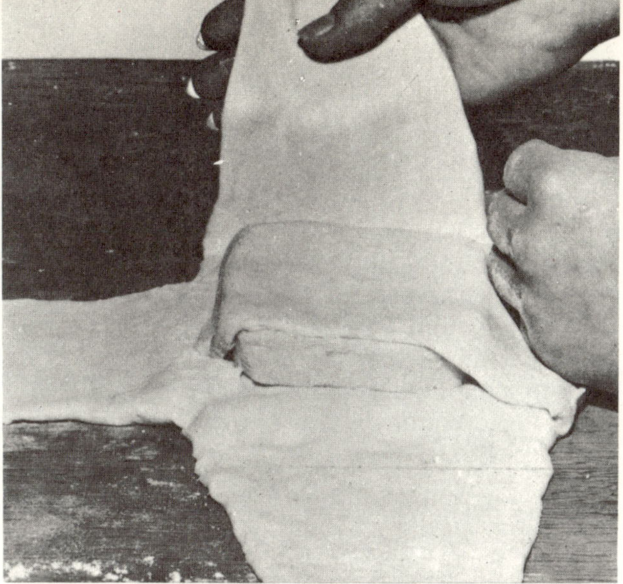

Step 3
Work butter well with spatula until soft, form into block shape. Place butter in centre of pastry. Take each individual long piece of dough, and fold it neatly over the butter.

Step 4
With rolling pin, gently press out dough; this will ease the butter through evenly, forming ridges as shown. Butter must be well distributed through dough for successful result.

Puff Pastry

Puff pastry is used as a topping for savoury pies, for vol-au-vents and for sweet pastries. Good quality puff pastry can now be bought in packaged form all ready to use—and it certainly saves a lot of time. But many housewives still prefer to make their own.

Full puff pastry uses equal amounts of flour and shortening (that is, 8 oz. (1 cup) butter and 8 oz. (2 cups) flour), but the recipe below, known as three-quarter puff (it uses three-quarters the amount of shortening to flour—8 oz. (2 cups) flour to 6 oz. ($\frac{3}{4}$ cup) butter) is more generally used. When cooked, it is easier to handle, less liable to break.

$\frac{1}{2}$ lb. (2 cups) plain flour   approx. $\frac{1}{4}$ pint ($\frac{1}{2}$ cup)
$\frac{1}{4}$ teaspoon salt   iced water
6 oz. ($\frac{3}{4}$ cup) butter

Sift flour and salt. Divide butter equally into 4 portions. Rub one portion into the flour. Mix with enough water to make a soft but pliable dough. Turn on to lightly floured board, knead 1 minute. Shape into a neat square. Put remaining butter on plate, work it well with spatula until it is soft, then shape into a block.

With sharp knife, cut down and across dough, to make 4 divisions; cut only half-way through, so dough is still joined at base. Pull out centre point of each division and press down. Leaving uncut base part unrolled, roll out each of the points, as shown in Step 2 of picture.

Place prepared butter in centre of what is now a star shape; fold each of the points over, tuck well round the butter. (At this stage depth of dough at base is approximately equal to quantity folded over top of butter.)

With rolling pin, gently press out dough, easing butter through evenly. Prominent ridges will result. Fold this into three.

Fold up bottom third, fold top third down. Seal and press edges together, give dough a half turn, so fold is on right hand side.

Repeat rolling and folding. Put pastry aside and allow to relax at least 30 minutes before continuing rolling. Roll and fold 6 times in all, with 30 minutes rest between each 2 roll-and-folds. Allow to rest another 30 minutes before using as required. When pastry is rolled and shaped as required, allow to rest another 10 minutes on oven slide before baking.

Puff pastry must always be baked in a very hot oven; baking times vary with individual recipes.

Small items (which cook quickly) cook for the required time in a very hot oven. Larger items (such as toppings for large pies, where cooking time is longer) bake for the first 15 minutes at very hot, then the temperature is reduced to hot or moderate for remainder of cooking time.

NOTE: In puff pastry, it is important to have a similar consistency of dough and shortening. If shortening is too soft, it will ooze out from between layers of dough; if too hard, it will break through when pastry is rolled, thus allowing the air to escape when pastry is cooked; this will prevent correct rising. It will also prevent even layers of shortening through pastry.

When rolling puff pastry, the ends are sealed with a rolling-pin between each rolling so air is trapped in and cannot escape, and shortening is sealed in. By the sequence of rolling and folding. the basic dough is layered with sheets of shortening in between. This process gives the 'puff' to puff pastry.

Correctly rolled and folded puff pastry will have almost 800 layers of shortening!

Dust pastry lightly with flour between each

rolling; before folding and proceeding to roll again, brush off flour gently but thoroughly. Extra flour would prevent pastry from rising well.

Rest pastry (preferably in refrigerator) for 30 minutes between each two rollings and for 30 minutes after final rolling. This enables the shortening to become firm again, and allows the pastry to relax so it does not shrink during cooking.

Do not turn pastry over during rolling. By just turning it round on the board each time it is rolled, shortening is evenly distributed throughout dough.

When rolling is completed and pastry is 'resting', cover it with a sheet of waxed paper, then a damp cloth. Waxed paper prevents pastry absorbing moisture from cloth.

Puff pastry rises considerably in baking, so roll it thinly; $\frac{1}{4}$ in. to $\frac{1}{2}$ in. is suitable for most purposes, but for large vol-au-vent cases it needs to be thicker—from $\frac{3}{4}$ in. to 1 in.

Rolled in plastic food wrap or aluminium foil, puff pastry will keep up to 4 days in refrigerator.

Flaky Pastry

Flaky pastry is often used in place of puff pastry. It is much easier to make than puff pastry, and is delightfully light.

It is often used for Continental-type pastries— thin layers of pastry sandwiched together with jam and cream.

$\frac{1}{2}$ lb. (2 cups) plain flour	approx. $\frac{1}{4}$ pint ($\frac{1}{2}$ cup)
$\frac{1}{2}$ teaspoon salt	iced water
6 oz. ($\frac{3}{4}$ cup) butter	1 teaspoon lemon juice

Sift flour and salt. Divide butter into 4 equal portions. Take one portion and rub it into flour with fingertips. Add water and lemon juice, mix to a soft dough.

Turn out on lightly floured board, knead lightly until no cracks appear in surface. Cover, let rest 15 to 20 minutes. Roll out to rectangular shape, about $\frac{1}{4}$ in. thick; shape should be about 3 times as long as it is wide.

Take second portion of butter, dot it in small pieces evenly over two-thirds of the pastry to within $\frac{1}{2}$ in. of edge. Fold up bottom third, fold top third down. Seal open edges with rolling-pin, give dough a half turn so fold is on right-hand side. Rest 10 minutes.

Repeat rolling and dotting-with-butter procedures until all butter is used. Roll dough into rectangular shape after the last of butter has been used, fold into 3, and let rest 30 minutes. Then roll to desired shape.

Rough Puff Pastry

Rolling and folding procedures for rough puff pastry are the same as those for puff and flaky pastries. Rough puff is not as rich as these two pastries and is easier to make.

Because all the shortening is incorporated into the dough, rough puff pastry should be kneaded very lightly.

$\frac{1}{2}$ lb. (2 cups) plain flour	$\frac{1}{4}$ teaspoon salt
1 teaspoon baking powder	approx. $\frac{1}{4}$ pint ($\frac{1}{2}$ cup) iced water
6 oz. ($\frac{3}{4}$ cup) butter	few drops lemon juice

Sift together dry ingredients. Cut cold, firm butter into pieces the size of a small nut and drop into the flour; stir. Mix into a fairly stiff dough with water and lemon juice, using the fingertips. Turn on to floured surface and knead very lightly.

Roll and fold as directed for puff pastry.

Although puff pastry is specified in the following recipes, rough puff or flaky pastry can be substituted with the same excellent results.

Vol-au-Vent

1 lb. puff pastry	1 egg-yolk

Roll out pastry to $\frac{3}{4}$ in. thickness, cut out two 6 in. circles. Brush baking tin with water, lay one circle on it.

Cut 4 in. circle from centre of second round; set this aside.

Moisten edge of pastry on baking tin, place over it the cut-out rim; it should fit exactly. Press rim down lightly on circle. Score rim with a knife at $\frac{1}{2}$ in. intervals in diamond pattern. Refrigerate 15 minutes. Brush top of shell with egg-yolk, beaten with 1 teaspoon of water. Make sure this glaze does not run down sides or it will prevent pastry rising evenly. Bake in very hot oven, Mark 8, 450° F., 10 minutes, reduce heat to moderately hot, Mark 5, 375°F., bake approximately 30 minutes longer, or until shell is well risen and brown.

The cut-out circle, which forms lid of vol-au-vent, should be baked separately, because it cooks much more quickly than the large puff shell. Score the cut-out circle in diamond shapes with sharp knife, brush with egg-glaze. Bake in hot oven, Mark 7, 425°F., approximately 10 to 15 minutes, or until well puffed and brown.

Vol-au-vents can be filled with creamy mixtures of chicken, fish, mushroom, etc.

Custard Tart with smooth, velvet-textured custard filling; biscuit or shortcrust pastry can be used for the pie shell.

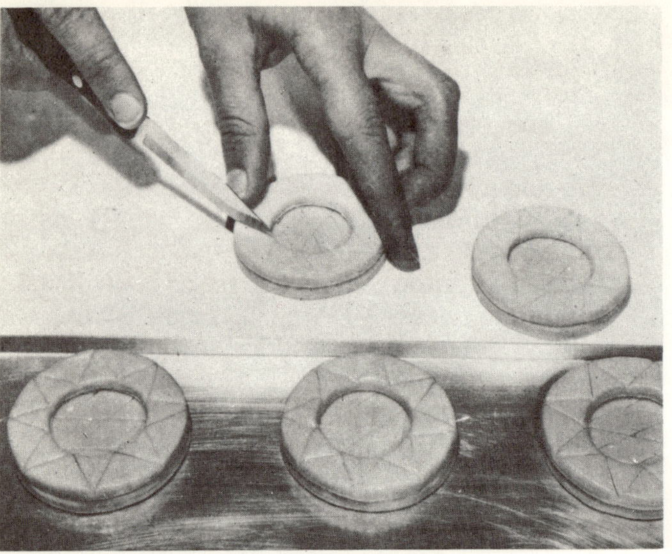

Bouchées *with back of small knife, mark top ring of pastry in V-shape, for decorative finish.*

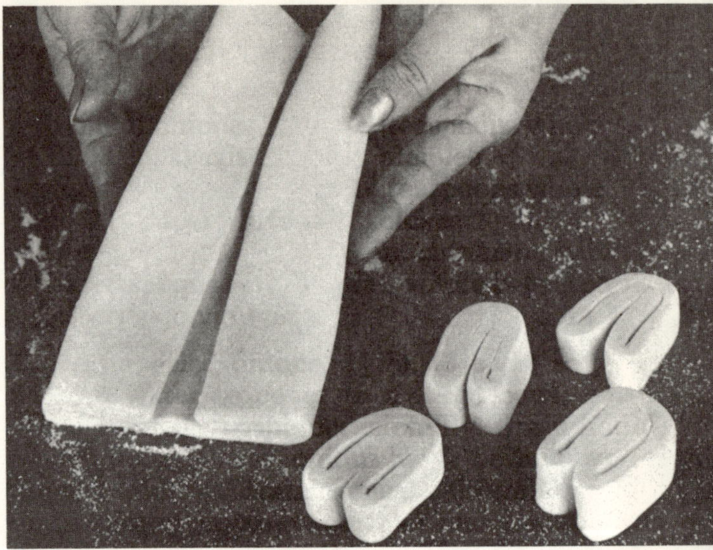

Palmiers *fold puff, rough puff or flaky pastry as shown, cut into slices with sharp knife.*

Bouchées

1 lb. puff pastry   beaten egg for glazing

Roll out pastry to $\frac{1}{4}$ in. thickness. Heat a 2 in. cutter in boiling water, cut four circles. Re-heat cutter as it cools. Using 1 in. cutter, also heated, cut a small round from centre of each alternate circle, thus making rings.

With back of small knife, mark centre of each whole circle with criss-cross pattern. Brush pattern only, with beaten egg. Brush outer rims with water. Carefully place rings into position on top of circles with patterned base. Do not stretch pastry. Press edges firmly without squashing. Again using back of small knife, mark the ring of pastry in V pattern, brush with egg.

Place well apart on baking tin which has been sprinkled with cold water. Bake in hot oven, Mark 7, 425°F., 5 minutes, cover with brown paper to prevent tops burning, reduce heat to moderately hot, Mark 5, 370°F., cook further 5 minutes.

The criss-cross part of base will rise through centre ring. When pastry cools, carefully cut out this part with a sharp knife, and use as a lid on filled bouchées.

Fill with desired filling just before serving, heat in a moderate oven until filling is piping hot. Finely chopped chicken, drained flaked salmon, oysters, chopped prawns, lobster or crab, finely chopped mushrooms, or drained chopped asparagus, can all be folded into a well-seasoned white sauce, and used as a filling.

Makes approx. $2\frac{1}{2}$ dozen.

Palmiers

On a board lightly dusted with castor sugar, roll out 12 oz. puff pastry into oblong approximately 8 in. by 14 in.; pastry should be about $\frac{1}{8}$ in. in thickness. Sprinkle lightly with castor sugar.

Fold as shown in picture, folding long sides so they meet in the centre, then bring folds over so there are four layers of pastry.

With a sharp knife, cut into $\frac{1}{2}$ in. pieces. Brush cut side of each with water, sprinkle with castor sugar. Place on greased baking tin, cut side down; allow room for expanding. Spread them open at folded ends to make a small V. Refrigerate 10 minutes.

Bake in hot oven, Mark 7, 425°F., 15 minutes or until crisp and golden. Halfway through cooking time, turn to allow second side to crisp and brown; cool.

Serve plain or dust with icing sugar.

For a delicious dessert, join two Palmiers together with whipped cream, top with icing of your own choice.

Cream Horns

Roll out puff pastry thinly, cut into strips approximately 18 in. long and $\frac{1}{2}$ in. wide (depending on size of the conical metal moulds). Moisten one side of each pastry strip with cold water.

Start at point of metal cone, wind pastry round, overlapping the dampened edge.

It may be necessary to join one or more strips of pastry, depending on size of horns required. Brush cut ends of pastry with water to join, press firmly with the finger, but do not stretch pastry.

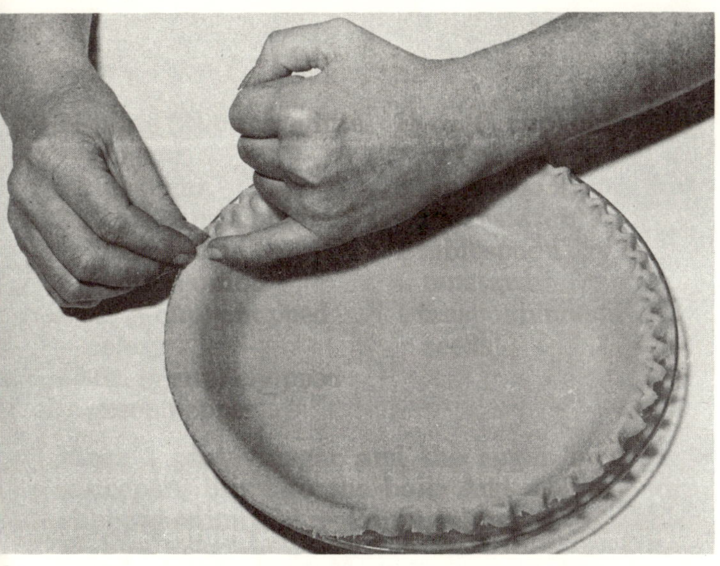 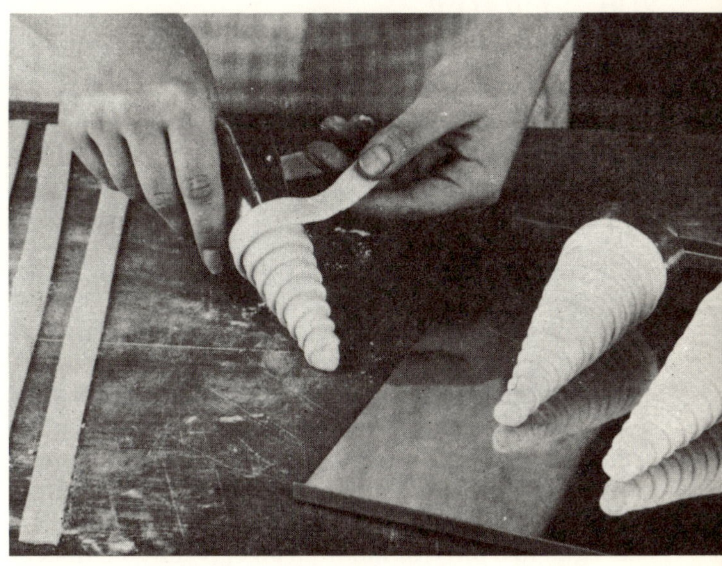

Pie edging: *pinch pastry between thumb and forefinger of right hand, pushing gently with the left little finger.*

Cream Horns: *wind pastry round metal horn, overlapping dampened edge.*

Do not bring pastry up to top end of cone; it will be difficult to remove from cone when baked.

Brush lightly with milk or beaten egg. Place on baking tin, allow room for expanding. Bake in hot oven, Mark 8, 450°F., 5 minutes, reduce heat to moderately hot, Mark 5, 375°F., cook further 10 to 15 minutes. Halfway through baking time, lift out baking tray, slip the metal moulds from the pastry horn, so pastry dries and cooks through. Cool, fill with whipped cream.

NOTE: 1 lb. puff pastry will make approx. 6 large Cream Horns.

Sausage Rolls

| 1 lb. puff pastry | egg-yolk for glazing |

Filling

1½ lb. sausage meat	water
1 onion	½ teaspoon mixed herbs
salt, pepper	2 thick slices bread

Remove crusts from bread, place into basin, barely cover with hot water. Stand for 10 minutes, drain, press out all surplus water. Combine bread, meat, grated onion, salt, pepper and herbs; mix with the hands to combine thoroughly.

Fill mixture into large piping bag, without nozzle. Roll pastry out into a rectangle, approximately 16 in. × 12 in., trim edges; cut lengthwise into three even strips. Pipe the filling lengthwise along each strip, fold one side of pastry over filling, glaze the other side with egg glazing, fold over. Do not glaze cut edges of pastry as this will prevent pastry rising well. Using back of a knife, mark the roll at ½ in. intervals. Cut rolls into 2½ to 3 in. pieces. Place on to ungreased baking tins, brush with egg glazing. Bake in hot oven, Mark 8, 450°F., 10 minutes reduce heat to moderate, Mark 4, 350° F., bake a further 15 to 20 minutes, or until golden brown and crisp.

NOTE: Some sausage meat contains a large amount of fat; it may be necessary to drain surplus fat from the trays half-way during the cooking time, to ensure rolls are crisp on base.

Choux Pastry

No wonder the French choose choux pastry to make many of the delicious pastries for which they are world-famous. It is delicate, crisp, light as a feather in the hand.

Choux pastry is leavened by steam that builds up in the batter under heat.

Once the pastry is in the oven resist the temptation to peep at it. The oven door should not be opened until cooking time is almost completed, otherwise the steam which has built up in the hot oven will escape and the puffs will fall.

To provide more steam, when baking choux puffs, sprinkle puffs and tray very lightly with water before putting into oven; the additional steam will provide bigger puffs.

However, if baking éclairs, do not sprinkle with water; they need a dry heat to preserve their shape.

If pastry shrinks when removed from the oven, generally, the simple explanation is that the pastry has not been cooked long enough.

Once the puffs are cooked and removed from the oven keep them out of draughts; a cold wind on the puffs when they are hot will also cause them to fall.

Choux Pastry

1½ gills (⅔ cup) water
3 oz. (⅜ cup) butter
pinch salt

3¾ oz. (scant cup) plain
flour
3 large eggs

Place water, butter and salt in saucepan. Bring to boil. Add sifted flour all at once. Stir vigorously with wooden spoon over heat until mixture is thick. When mixture forms a smooth ball and leaves sides of pan remove from heat. Cool slightly. Add beaten eggs a little at a time, beating thoroughly after each addition.

Beat paste well when all egg is added until it is free of lumps. Mixture should be smooth and glossy.

If eggs are only of medium size, it may be necessary to add an extra egg, or portion of egg. Beat the egg and add it gradually to the batter, adding only enough to give you batter of the desired consistency.

Then cook as directed in the individual recipes. NOTE: If making choux pastry for sweet puffs or eclairs, 1 teaspoon of sugar can be added to the basic recipe; stir it in with the sifted flour.

To Store Choux Pastry All the soft, uncooked mixture from centre of cooked puffs or eclairs must be removed before storing, otherwise pastries will soften.

Put pastries into plastic bag, fasten loosely at top; keep in refrigerator. Kept this way, pastries will stay crisp for 3 or 4 days.

Pastries may also be stored in an air-tight container.

If pastry does soften during storage, re-crispen in a moderate oven, Mark 4, 350°F., for a few minutes.

Pastries, of course, should not be filled before storing; spoon or pipe in desired filling just before serving.

Cream Puffs

Drop rounded spoonfuls of pastry on to greased baking tin, allowing about 2 in. space between puffs; they will spread during cooking. Bake in hot oven, Mark 7, 425°F., 10 minutes, reduce heat to moderate, Mark 4, 350°F., bake further 20 to 30 minutes or until puffs are golden and feel light in the hand.

Cooking time will depend on size of puffs. Allow approximate overall cooking time of 25 to 30 minutes for small puffs; approximate overall cooking time of 35 to 40 minutes for large puffs.

When cooked, remove from oven, make small slit in side to allow steam to escape; return to oven a few minutes to dry out.

When cool, puffs can be filled with whipped cream or custard; fill just before serving or the filling will soften the puffs. Sift icing sugar over top of puffs.

If serving cream puffs as dessert, ice-cream makes a delightful filling; spoon it in just before serving. Top with a rich caramel sauce.

Chocolate Eclairs

Take basic choux paste, fill into piping bag fitted with ½ in. plain tube; pipe into 2 in. lengths on very lightly greased baking tin. Leave about 2 in. between each eclair shape.

Bake in a hot oven, Mark 7, 425°F., 10 minutes, reduce heat to moderate, Mark 4, 350°F., bake further 20 minutes or until dry.

Slit each eclair open, remove any soft filling with a teaspoon, return to oven for a few minutes to dry out. Cool.

Fill with whipped cream and top with melted chocolate—you will need about 4 oz. (4 squares).

Savoury Puffs

Savoury puffs are generally made in small size; they are ideal party savouries. However, large-size puffs, filled with a savoury mixture, can also be an unusual first course, or light luncheon or supper dish.

Chicken stock (stock cubes can be used) can be used in place of the water in the basic recipe when making puffs which are to be filled with a savoury mixture.

A creamy, well-seasoned white sauce of fairly thick consistency can be used as a filling for savoury puffs; to this can be added some chopped chicken; smoked oysters; finely chopped chives; chopped prawns, crab, lobster; mayonnaise or whipped cream; curry powder; etc.

Cream Puffs, light as a feather, make a superb dessert; fill them with cream and sliced strawberries.

Hot Water Pastry

Hot-water pastry is used mainly for meat or game pies, such as the traditional favourite, Melton Mowbray Pie, given below. This is a firm, strong dough, prepared in a different way from other pastries. Boiling liquid is added to flour, and dough used while warm.

10 oz. (2½ cups) plain flour	1 egg-yolk
½ teaspoon salt	3 oz. (⅜ cup) lard
	¼ pint (½ cup) water

Sift flour and salt into bowl. Make well in centre of flour, drop in egg-yolk, cover with some of the flour. Place lard and water in saucepan. Place over gentle heat until lard melts. Increase heat, bring rapidly to the boil. Pour all boiling liquid into flour.

Water must be boiling, otherwise pastry will be difficult to mould and may crack in cooking.

Mix with wooden spoon until pastry is cool enough to handle. Continue mixing and kneading until all egg streaks are gone and dough is smooth.

This is important; insufficient kneading could cause pastry to crack during cooking.

Cover and rest in warm place 20 to 30 minutes.

Melton Mowbray Pie

1 quantity hot water pastry

Filling

2½ lb. lean boned shoulder of pork	1 onion
1 chopped knuckle of veal	salt, pepper
	water
	egg glaze

Filling Reserve bones from pork, and put these into large saucepan with veal knuckle, sliced onion, salt and pepper; add water to cover. Simmer mixture at least 2 hours to make a good stock that jells when cold; set aside.

Cut pork meat into ½ in. pieces, season with salt and pepper. Set aside.

Set aside ¼ of pastry for pie lid. Roll out remainder, line lightly greased 7 in. cake tin with pastry extended ½ in. above top. Place seasoned meat in pie shell, moisten with little stock. Roll out remaining pastry, place on top of pie, trim edges, pressing firmly together. Make rose and leaves from pastry trimmings, place on top of pie. Brush well with egg glaze. Place in hot oven, Mark 7, 425°F., cook 1 hour. Reduce heat to moderate, Mark 4, 350°F., cook approximately further 1½ hours. Brush again with glaze during cooking. Cover top with paper if too brown. Leave until cool.

Heat jelly stock. With sharp knife, carefully remove rose from centre of pie. Pour in cooled jelly, using funnel; replace decoration. Refrigerate.

The pie should be made the day before it is to be used, so jellied filling can set completely.

Veal and ham pie Substitute trimmed stewing veal for pork in recipe above; add ¼ lb. bacon, diced; one or two hard-boiled eggs can be placed in centre of meat mixture before baking.

Suet Pastry

Suet pastry—hearty, substantial, and filling—is ideal for the cold weather. It's used for old-fashioned favourite dishes, both sweet and savoury.

Be sure suet is finely chopped or grated before adding it to flour; if it tends to stick, sprinkle it with some of the measured sifted flour after grating.

Suet pastry is one of the few pastries which uses self raising flour.

½ lb. (2 cups) self raising (all purpose) flour	½ teaspoon salt
3 to 4 oz. finely grated beef suet	water to mix, approx. ¼ pint (½ cup)

Sift dry ingredients, add prepared suet, and mix well. Mix with sufficient water to give a soft but dry dough. Turn on to lightly floured board and knead well.

Steak and Kidney Pudding

12 oz. (3 cups) self raising (all purpose) flour	5 oz. suet
1 teaspoon salt	water to mix

Filling

2 lb. round steak	pepper
8 oz. ox kidney	1 large onion
2 tablespoons flour	about ¼ pint (½ cup) stock
2 teaspoons salt	

Make pastry as for basic recipe.

Dice meat and kidney into 1 in. cubes, discarding any gristle or excess fat. Toss meat in seasoned flour until well coated. Dice onion finely, add to meat.

Use ⅔ of prepared pastry to line 4 pint greased pudding basin, fill with meat; add stock. Roll out remaining pastry to form a lid. Wet edges of pudding, place top in position, sealing edges.

Cover pudding with greased aluminium foil. Steam approximately 6 to 7 hours. After this time of cooking, pudding can be turned out on to serving dish.

Watch water level in saucepan carefully during cooking time; as it evaporates, replace with boiling water.

Tartlets

Small tartlets make good eating at any time. Baked in advance, they can quickly be filled with a variety of fillings and used as a dessert or for afternoon tea. They provide a delicious treat for the family or unexpected visitors.

Biscuit or sweet shortcrust is best for tartlet cases. Four ounces of biscuit or sweet shortcrust will make 1 dozen tartlet cases. Each filling given here makes sufficient for 1 dozen tartlets.

Roll out pastry to $\frac{1}{4}$ in. thickness, cut with 3 in. floured cutter, fit into greased patty tins.

Some tartlets are baked complete with filling; some have the filling spooned into the baked, cooled cases.

When baking tartlet cases 'blind', or without a filling, prick pastry shells well with a fork, bake in moderately hot oven, Mark 5, 375°F., for approximately 10 minutes.

Apricot Cream Tarts

1 egg-yolk	1 tablespoon plain flour
1½ tablespoons castor (superfine) sugar	$\frac{1}{4}$ pint ($\frac{1}{2}$ cup) milk
$\frac{1}{2}$ teaspoon vanilla	1 dozen baked tartlet cases

Topping

15 oz. can apricot halves	2 teaspoons arrowroot

Whisk egg-yolk, sugar and vanilla until white, stir in flour. Warm milk, stir gradually into egg mixture. Place mixture in saucepan, stir until mixture boils and thickens. When filling is cold, spoon into pastry cases, level tops.
Topping Drain apricots, reserve $\frac{1}{4}$ pint syrup. Place one apricot half, cut-side down, into each pastry case. Blend arrowroot with the reserved syrup in a saucepan, stir until mixture boils and thickens, spoon over apricot halves.

Mushrooms

1 tablespoon jam	1 tablespoon milk, approx.
1 oz. (2 tablespoons) butter	$\frac{1}{2}$ teaspoon vanilla
5 oz. (scant cup) icing (confectioners') sugar	cinnamon
	1 dozen baked tartlet cases

Retail any left-over pastry to make 'stems' for mushrooms. Bake stems in a moderate oven, Mark 4, 350°F., for approximately 5 minutes or until golden brown.

Place small amount of jam into each tartlet case. Cream butter until soft and white, gradually add sifted icing sugar, and enough milk to give a smooth consistency, flavour with vanilla. Fill tart cases with the butter cream, level the tops, dust with cinnamon, place 'stems' in position.

Brandied Custard Tarts

1 egg	nutmeg
1 tablespoon sugar	1 dozen unbaked tartlet cases
$\frac{1}{4}$ pint ($\frac{1}{2}$ cup) milk	
1 tablespoon brandy	

Beat egg, sugar, milk and brandy together. Strain, spoon carefully into tartlet cases. Sprinkle with a little nutmeg. Bake in moderately hot oven, Mark 5, 375°F., for 20 minutes or until custard is set.

Butterscotch Meringue Tartlets

2 oz. ($\frac{1}{3}$ cup) dark brown sugar	1 egg-yolk
1 oz. (2 tablespoons) plain flour	1 teaspoon instant coffee powder
1½ gills ($\frac{2}{3}$ cup) milk	$\frac{1}{2}$ teaspoon vanilla
1 oz. (2 tablespoons) butter	1 dozen baked tartlet cases

Meringue

1 egg-white	2 oz. ($\frac{1}{4}$ cup) sugar

Blend brown sugar and flour with milk in a saucepan, stir until mixture boils and thickens, simmer 1 minute. Beat in butter, egg-yolk, coffee and vanilla. When cold, spoon into pastry cases. Pipe or spoon meringue on top of each tartlet, bake in moderate oven, Mark 4, 350°F., for 5 to 10 minutes, or until meringue is set and lightly browned.
Meringue Beat egg-white until foamy, gradually add sugar, beat until grains are dissolved and mixture is of meringue consistency.

Chocolate Tarts

1 oz. (1 square) plain chocolate	1 teaspoon brandy or rum
1 egg, separated	extra melted chocolate
3 to 4 tablespoons whipping cream	1 dozen baked tartlet cases

Melt chocolate in top of a double saucepan, remove from heat, blend in egg-yolk, beat until smooth and thick. Whisk cream until soft peaks form, fold into mixture with brandy or rum; lastly fold in well-beaten egg-white.

Spoon mixture into pastry cases, refrigerate until firm. Drizzle with extra melted chocolate.

Pineapple and Cream Cheese Tarts

2 oz. packaged cream
  cheese
2 teaspoons lemon
  juice

1 small can drained
  crushed pineapple
1 dozen baked tartlet
  cases

Glaze

1 teaspoon arrowroot
$\frac{1}{4}$ pint ($\frac{1}{2}$ cup) pineapple
  syrup

few drops yellow food
  colouring

Beat cream cheese until smooth, beat in lemon juice and pineapple. Spoon mixture into pastry cases, level tops. Spoon slightly cooled glaze over, refrigerate before serving.

Glaze Blend arrowroot with pineapple juice in a saucepan, stir until mixture boils and thickens. Colour as desired.

Iced Fruit Mince Tarts

1 lb. mincemeat
2 tablespoons icing
  (confectioners')
  sugar
$\frac{1}{2}$ egg-white

few drops red food
  colouring
1 dozen baked tartlet
  cases

Fill tart cases with mincemeat, making sure the top is level. Sift icing sugar, mix with the egg-white, colour pink with few drops of red food colouring. Spread icing thinly over each tartlet. Bake in moderate oven, Mark 4, 350°F., 5 to 10 minutes, or until icing sets.

Honeyed Lemon Cheese Tartlets

2 eggs
4 oz. ($\frac{1}{2}$ cup) sugar
3 oz. ($\frac{1}{4}$ cup) honey
2 oz. ($\frac{1}{4}$ cup) butter
1 dessertspoon grated
  lemon rind

3 to 4 tablespoons
  lemon juice
1 dozen tartlet cases

Beat eggs, combine with remaining ingredients in top of a double boiler, stir constantly over hot water until thickened. Allow to become cold before spooning into tartlet cases.

Maids of Honour

1 tablespoon raspberry
  jam
2 oz. ($\frac{1}{4}$ cup) butter
$\frac{1}{2}$ teaspoon vanilla
2 oz. ($\frac{1}{4}$ cup) sugar

1 egg
2 oz. ($\frac{1}{4}$ cup) self raising
  (all purpose) flour
1 dozen unbaked tartlet
  cases

Place a little jam into each pastry case. Cream butter, vanilla and sugar until light and fluffy. Add beaten egg a little at a time, beat well. Fold in sifted flour. Place a teaspoon of mixture into each pastry case, top with a pastry cross made from small strips of remaining pastry. Bake in moderate oven, Mark 4, 350°F., for 20 to 25 minutes. When cool, dust tops with icing sugar.

Nougat Tarts

1 tablespoon raspberry
  jam
1 egg-white
4 oz. ($\frac{1}{2}$ cup) sugar
2 oz. ($\frac{1}{2}$ cup) ground
  almonds
4 oz. (1 cup) coconut

1 tablespoon milk
few drops almond
  essence
glacé cherry quarters
1 dozen unbaked tartlet
  cases

Place a little jam into each pastry case. Whisk egg-white stiffly, fold in all remaining ingredients, except cherries. Place a teaspoon of mixture into each pastry case, top with a piece of glacé cherry. Bake in a moderate oven, Mark 4, 350°F., 20 to 25 minutes or until golden brown.

Jam Tartlets

raspberry or other jam
sweetened whipped
  cream

1 dozen unbaked tartlet
  cases

Fill each tartlet case with jam, bake in hot oven, Mark 7, 425°F., 10 to 15 minutes. When cold, top with dot of whipped cream.

    Tartlet cases may be pricked well with a fork, and baked in a moderately hot oven, Mark 5, 375° F., for 10 to 15 minutes or until crisp, then filled with jam.

Fresh Strawberry Tarts

$\frac{1}{2}$ lb. strawberries
2 tablespoons sugar
5 to 6 tablespoons
  water
1 teaspoon arrowroot

1 teaspoon brandy
few drops red food
  colouring
1 dozen baked tartlet
  cases

Arrange washed, hulled strawberries in pastry cases. Heat sugar and water over a low heat until sugar dissolves; remove from heat. Blend arrowroot with a little water, stir into syrup, stir over heat until mixture boils and thickens. Add brandy, colour as desired. Cool slightly, spoon over strawberries as a glaze.

Recipes for these attractive little tartlets are given on pages 209 and 210.

Desserts

Hot Desserts

Here's a choice of steamed or baked puddings; some are hearty winter foods, many are light enough to serve throughout the year. And there's a selection of other popular hot puddings.

Steamed Pudding

4 oz. (½ cup) butter
4 oz. (½ cup) sugar
2 eggs
8 oz. (2 cups) self raising (all purpose) flour
pinch salt
¼ pint (½ cup) milk
2 tablespoons jam

Beat butter and sugar together until light and fluffy; add eggs one at a time, beat well after each addition. Fold sifted dry ingredients and milk alternately into creamed mixture.

Grease 2½ pint pudding basin, cover base with jam. Spoon in pudding mixture, cover, steam 1½ hours.

Serves 4.

Ginger Pudding

2 oz. (¼ cup) butter
2 tablespoons golden syrup (cornsyrup)
1 teaspoon ground ginger
6 tablespoons warm milk
½ teaspoon bicarbonate of soda
4 oz. (1 cup) self raising (all purpose) flour
pinch salt

Beat butter, syrup and ginger until light and fluffy; add warm milk, in which soda has been dissolved. Stir in sifted flour and salt, mix well. Place mixture into 2½-pint greased pudding basin, cover, steam 1½ hours.

Serves 4.

Steamed Date Pudding

½ lb. (1¼ cups) dates
½ oz. (1 tablespoon) butter
6 tablespoons boiling water
½ teaspoon bicarbonate of soda
¼ pint (½ cup) milk
4 oz. (1 cup) plain flour
4 oz. (½ cup) sugar

Chop dates, melt butter in boiling water, dissolve soda in milk. Sift dry ingredients into basin, add dates, water and milk, stir until smooth. Pour into 2½-pint greased pudding basin, cover, steam 2 hours.

Serves 4.

Steamed Lemon Pudding

4 oz. (½ cup) butter, grated rind 2 lemons
4 oz. (½ cup) sugar
2 eggs
4 oz. (1 cup) self raising (all purpose) flour
2 oz. (¼ cup) sugar, extra
juice 2 lemons

Cream butter and lemon rind, add sugar, beat until light and fluffy. Add eggs one at a time, beating well after each addition. Fold in sifted flour, beat lightly until smooth.

Combine the 2 oz. (¼ cup) sugar with strained lemon juice, pour into greased 2½-pint pudding basin. Spoon mixture on top of liquid, cover, steam 1½ hours.

Serves 4 to 6.

Christmas Pudding

¼ lb. (⅔ cup) currants
½ lb. (1⅓ cups) raisins
½ lb. (1⅓ cups) sultanas
¼ lb. (1 cup) mixed peel
4 to 5 tablespoons brandy or ale
juice and grated rind 1 small lemon
6 oz. (¾ cup) butter
2 eggs
½ lb. (1⅓ cups) brown sugar
½ lb. (3 to 3½ cups) fresh breadcrumbs (approx. crumbs from 1 large loaf bread)
1 dessertspoon mixed spice
1 teaspoon nutmeg

Chop fruit, pour over brandy or ale, add grated lemon rind and juice; cover, leave overnight.

Cream butter, gradually add beaten eggs and brown sugar; beat well. Add remaining ingredients; stir vigorously.

To Steam Pack into greased 4½-pint pudding basin; cover with greased aluminium foil. Secure with string and steam 4 hours. For a large family pudding, double the quantities above, steam 8 hours. Steam further 2 hours on day of serving.

To Boil Place pudding in floured pudding cloth, tie securely, allowing room for pudding to expand during cooking, boil 4 hours. Reboil for 2 hours on day of serving.

NOTE: Breadcrumbs give sufficient substance to this rich pudding; flour is not used.

Apple Sponge Dessert

4 apples
4 oz. ($\frac{1}{2}$ cup) sugar
4 tablespoons water

1 teaspoon grated
  lemon rind
few whole cloves

Topping

2 eggs
$\frac{1}{2}$ teaspoon vanilla
2 oz. ($\frac{1}{4}$ cup) castor
  (superfine) sugar

2 oz. ($\frac{1}{2}$ cup) self raising
  (all purpose) flour
pinch salt
1 tablespoon sugar,
  extra

Peel, core and slice apples, combine in saucepan with sugar, water, lemon rind, and cloves, cover, cook gently until apples are tender. Place in greased pie dish; remove cloves. Spoon topping over hot apples, sprinkle with extra sugar. Bake in moderate oven, Mark 4, 350°F., 30 to 35 minutes. Serve warm with custard.
Topping Beat eggs and vanilla until thick and creamy, gradually add sugar, beat until dissolved. Fold in sifted flour and salt.
  Serves 4.

Steamed Fruit Pudding

1 teaspoon bicarbonate
  of soda
6 tablespoons cold
  water
4 oz. ($\frac{1}{2}$ cup) butter
scant $\frac{1}{2}$ pint (1 cup)
  hot water
$\frac{1}{2}$ lb. ($1\frac{1}{3}$ cups) sultanas
$\frac{1}{2}$ lb. ($1\frac{1}{3}$ cups) raisins
$\frac{1}{4}$ lb. ($\frac{2}{3}$ cup) currants

2 oz. ($\frac{1}{4}$ cup) glacé
  cherries
2 oz. ($\frac{1}{3}$ cup) mixed peel
8 oz. (2 cups) plain flour
5 oz. (scant cup) brown
  sugar
1 teaspoon mixed spice
4 to 5 tablespoons
  brandy

Dissolve bicarbonate of soda in the cold water; melt butter in the hot water. Chop fruit. Put all dry ingredients in basin and mix with the liquid; add brandy; allow to stand overnight. Mixture thickens with standing. Next day, place mixture into a greased 3 pint pudding basin, steam for 4 hours.

Lemon Delicious Pudding

3 eggs
4 oz. ($\frac{1}{2}$ cup) sugar
scant $\frac{1}{2}$ pint (1 cup)
  milk
1 tablespoon self
  raising (all purpose)
  flour

grated rind and juice
  2 large lemons
pinch salt
1 tablespoon sugar,
  extra

Separate eggs; beat yolks with sugar until light and creamy. Beat in milk, sifted flour, rind and juice of lemons, and salt. Beat egg-whites, add extra sugar gradually, continue beating until stiff but not dry. Fold into lemon mixture.
  Pour into greased deep 2-pint ovenproof dish, stand in shallow pan of cold water. Bake in moderate oven, Mark 4, 350°F., 50 to 60 minutes.
  Serves 4.

Chocolate Sauce Pudding

2 oz. ($\frac{1}{4}$ cup) butter
6 tablespoons milk
1 teaspoon vanilla
4 oz. (1 cup) self raising
  (all purpose) flour

6 oz. ($\frac{3}{4}$ cup) castor
  (superfine) sugar
1 tablespoon cocoa
good $\frac{3}{4}$ pint ($1\frac{1}{2}$ cups)
  hot water

Topping

4 oz. ($\frac{2}{3}$ cup) brown
  sugar

1 tablespoon cocoa

Heat butter and milk in saucepan, stir until butter melts, add vanilla. Sift dry ingredients into basin, add butter mixture to well in centre, stir until smooth, pour into deep, greased 2-pint ovenproof dish. Sprinkle with topping, carefully pour over hot water. Bake in moderate oven, Mark 4, 350°F., 40 to 45 minutes.
  Serves 4.
Topping   Combine ingredients well.

Caramel Dumplings

Dumplings

5 oz. ($1\frac{1}{4}$ cups) self
  raising (all purpose)
  flour
pinch salt

1 oz. (2 tablespoons)
  butter
$2\frac{1}{2}$ oz. ($\frac{1}{3}$ cup) sugar
4 to 5 tablespoons milk
1 teaspoon vanilla

Sauce

1 oz. (2 tablespoons)
  butter
8 oz. ($1\frac{1}{3}$ cups) dark
  brown sugar

pinch salt
$\frac{3}{4}$ pint ($1\frac{1}{2}$ cups) water

Dumplings Sift flour and salt into basin rub in butter, add sugar. Add combined milk and vanilla, stir well.
Sauce Combine all ingredients in large saucepan, stir constantly until boiling, reduce heat. Drop tablespoons of dumpling dough into simmering sauce, cover, simmer 20 minutes. Serve warm with whipped cream.
Serves 4.

Apple Pie

Pastry

10 oz. (2½ cups) plain flour	2 egg-yolks
pinch salt	grated rind 1 lemon
8 oz. (1 cup) butter	1 tablespoon lemon juice
2 oz. (⅓ cup) icing (confectioners') sugar	

Pastry Sift flour and salt into a basin, make a well in the centre. Slice butter, add with sifted icing sugar and remaining ingredients to well in centre of flour. Work centre ingredients to a paste with the hand, then gradually work in the flour. Form dough into a ball, cover, refrigerate 30 minutes.

Filling

5 medium cooking apples	milk
3 to 4 tablespoons apricot jam	sugar

Peel and core apples, quarter, slice finely, sprinkle with a little sugar if desired. Roll ⅔ of the pastry on a lightly floured board, large enough to line base and sides of a lightly greased 11 in. × 7 in. tin. Place apples into pastry case, dot evenly with apricot jam.

Roll remaining pastry to cover top of pie, glaze between two edges of pastry with a little milk, pinch edges together. Brush top of pie with milk, sprinkle with sugar, slit top of pie in several places, to allow steam to escape. Bake in hot oven, Mark 7, 425°F., 15 minutes, reduce heat to moderate, Mark 4, 350°F., bake further 25 to 30 minutes.

Drizzle with glace icing. Allow to cool slightly before serving. Serve with cream.

Glace Icing Sift 6 oz. (1 cup) icing (confectioners') sugar into a basin, add sufficient milk, about 1 tablespoon, to give a stiff paste.

Rum Babas

½ oz. (1 package) compressed yeast	pinch salt
1 dessertspoon sugar	3 eggs
4 tablespoons milk	5 oz. (⅝ cup) butter
8 oz. (2 cups) plain flour	1 tablespoon currants
	2 tablespoons sultanas

Syrup

¼ lb. (½ cup) sugar	squeeze lemon juice
¼ pint (½ cup) water	1 to 2 tablespoons rum
small piece lemon peel	

Dissolve the sugar in the water, add lemon rind and boil for 5 minutes. Remove rind, add lemon juice and rum.

Cream yeast and sugar, add luke-warm milk.

Sift flour and salt into basin, make well in centre, stir in yeast mixture and well-beaten eggs. Dot surface of dough with 1 oz. softened butter, cover with clean towel and set aside in warm place until doubled in bulk (about 40 minutes). When dough is well-risen, mix in the remaining softened butter and fruits. Turn out on to lightly floured board, knead well, turning edges of dough into centre. Divide mixture over eight well-greased small cups or moulds which have been stood on baking tray. Fill them not quite half-full. Cover, let rise again in warm place for 20 minutes. Bake in hot oven, Mark 7, 425°F., 15 minutes until golden. Drop Babas one at a time into the hot syrup until they are well-soaked. Babas can be made some time ahead and reheated, at serving time, in the hot syrup. Serve whipped cream separately.

Creamed Rice

2 pints (4 cups) milk	3 oz. (½ cup) rice
5 oz. (⅔ cup) sugar	½ teaspoon vanilla
½ teaspoon salt	

Combine milk, sugar and salt in saucepan, bring to boil. Gradually add rice to gently boiling milk, stirring constantly. Reduce heat, cover, simmer gently, stirring occasionally until ⅔ of liquid is absorbed and rice is tender (approx. 40 to 45 minutes). Stir in vanilla.

Serves 4 to 6.

Baked Rice Pudding

3 oz. (½ cup) rice	2 pints (4 cups) milk
2 oz. (¼ cup) sugar or brown sugar	1 oz. (2 tablespoons) butter

Place all ingredients in lightly greased ovenproof dish; stir to combine. Dot with butter. Bake in a slow oven, Mark 2, 300°F., for about 2½ hours. Stir once or twice during the first hour.

Serves 4.

Caramel Bananas

4 large ripe bananas	4 tablespoons light cream
2 oz (¼ cup) butter	thin pancakes
5 oz. (scant cup) dark brown sugar	

Peel and slice bananas. Melt butter in frying pan, add sugar, stir over low heat until sugar dissolves, bring to the boil, add sliced bananas; reduce heat, simmer until tender; stir occasionally. Stir in cream, pour over pancakes. Serve with whipped cream or ice-cream.

Serves 4.

Pears can be cooked in red or white wine. Serve them well-chilled, with the wine syrup spooned over.

Cold Desserts

Cool, elegant, quite delicious—recipes in this section range from family desserts to many of the world's classic recipes. You'll find a dessert idea here suitable for any occasion.

Banana Cream Pie

Pastry

3 oz. (⅜ cup) butter	2 tablespoons ground rice
2 oz. (¼ cup) castor (superfine) sugar	¼ teaspoon baking powder
1 egg	
6 oz. (1½ cups) plain flour	

Filling

1 oz. (2 tablespoons) butter	2 eggs
4 oz. (⅔ cup) brown sugar	¼ pint (½ cup) whipping cream
¼ pint (½ cup) water	3 to 4 bananas
½ pint (1 cup) milk	lemon juice
1 tablespoon gelatine	extra whipped cream

Pastry Cream butter and sugar, add egg, beat well. Sift flour, ground rice and baking powder, work into creamed mixture, knead well until smooth. Refrigerate 30 minutes. Roll out pastry on floured surface to fit lightly greased 9 in. pie plate. Decorate edges with trimmings, brush with water. Prick well with fork on base and round sides. Bake in hot oven, Mark 7, 425°F., approximately 15 minutes or until lightly golden; cool.

Filling Combine butter, brown sugar and half the water in saucepan; cook, stirring until sugar is dissolved (approximately 2 minutes). Cool slightly, stir in milk. Soften gelatine in remaining water, dissolve over hot water; cool. Blend into milk mixture. Separate eggs, add lightly beaten egg-yolks to milk mixture.

Allow to cool; when beginning to stiffen slightly, fold in lightly whipped cream and stiffly beaten egg-whites. Slice bananas, dip into lemon juice; reserve some slices for decoration. Arrange remainder on base of cooked pie case. Pour cream mixture over carefully; refrigerate until set.

Just before serving, decorate with extra whipped cream and reserved banana slices.

Strawberry Shortcake

2 oz. (¼ cup) butter	1 dessertspoon gelatine
4 tablespoons sugar	1 tablespoon water
2 egg-yolks	whipped cream
3 oz. (¾ cup) plain flour	red currant jelly
1 lb. strawberries	extra strawberries

Cream butter until soft, add 2 tablespoons sugar and egg-yolks, beat until light and fluffy. Work in sifted flour until well combined, place dough on to lightly floured board, knead until smooth. Press into lightly greased 8 in. sandwich tin, bake in moderate oven, Mark 4, 350°F., 15 to 20 minutes. Remove from tin, allow to cool slightly.

Wash and remove stems from half the strawberries, combine with remaining 2 tablespoons sugar, mash well with fork. Combine gelatine and water, set aside. Place strawberry mixture into saucepan, simmer until reduced by half, add gelatine mixture, stir well.

Halve remaining strawberries, arrange strawberry halves over warm shortcake, pour over the strawberry syrup. Refrigerate until set. Decorate with whipped cream and extra strawberries, which have been brushed with warmed red currant jelly.

Lemon Meringue Pie

6 oz. (¾ cup) sugar	2 oz. (¼ cup) butter
1½ oz. (⅓ cup) cornflour (cornstarch)	grated rind 2 lemons
½ pint (1 cup) water	2 egg-yolks
4 to 5 tablespoons lemon juice	9 in. baked pastry case

Meringue

2 egg-whites	2 oz. (¼ cup) sugar

Combine sugar and cornflour (cornstarch) in saucepan, blend in water and lemon juice gradually, stir until smooth. Stir constantly over medium heat until mixture boils and thickens. Remove from heat, quickly stir in butter, lemon rind and egg-yolks, beat until butter has melted. When filling is cold, spread into cooled baked pastry case. Top with meringue, bake in moderate oven, Mark 4, 350°F., 5 to 10 minutes, or until meringue is set and lightly browned.

Meringue Beat egg-whites until foamy, gradually add sugar, beat until sugar has dissolved and mixture is of thick meringue consistency.

Baked Alaska

1 layer sponge cake	6 egg-whites
1 large block neapolitan or other ice-cream	12 oz. (1½ cups) castor (superfine) sugar

Place sponge cake on heavy board, such as small bread board which has been covered with aluminium foil. If desired, moisten cake with a little fruit syrup or rum or brandy; some chopped sliced peaches can be arranged over cake, and pressed in gently. Place ice-cream on top, place in freezing compartment of refrigerator. Beat egg-whites until stiff, gradually add sugar, beat until of meringue consistency. Cover ice-cream and cake completely with meringue; rough up meringue slightly. Bake in very hot oven, Mark 8, 450°F., 3 to 5 minutes, until meringue is lightly browned. Serve at once.

NOTE: Baked Alaska is not the tricky thing to make that people imagine. Nor does it need last minute touches. The whole Alaska can be prepared, covered with meringue, baked briefly as indicated above, then returned to the freezing compartment of the refrigerator. It will stand perfectly for several hours.

Australian Apple Charlotte

4 oz. (1 cup) plain flour
2 oz. (½ cup) self raising (all purpose) flour
1 oz. (¼ cup) custard powder
1 oz. (¼ cup) cornflour (cornstarch)

2 tablespoons icing (confectioners') sugar
4 oz. (½ cup) butter
3 to 4 tablespoons water

Filling

1½ pints (3 cups) thick sweetened apple purée

1 tablespoon lemon juice
½ teaspoon grated nutmeg

Icing

6 oz. (1 cup) icing (confectioners') sugar
milk

1 oz. angelica
few drops green food colouring

Pastry. Sift all dry ingredients together. Rub in the butter until the mixture resembles fine breadcrumbs. Mix to a firm, but pliable dough with water. Turn on to a lightly floured board, knead lightly then refrigerate for 30 minutes.

Grease a 7 in. tin with removable base. Roll out two thirds of the pastry and line the base and sides of the tin.

Combine all the ingredients for the filling and put into the pastry case. Moisten the top edge of the pastry, cover with the remaining pastry and press the edges well together. Brush over with milk and make two slits in the top of the pastry. Bake in a hot oven, Mark 7, 425°F., for 10 minutes then reduce the heat to Mark 4, 350°F., for a further 20 minutes or until the pastry is golden brown. Leave to cool. Mix the icing (confectioners') sugar with enough milk to give a thick coating consistency. Add a few drops of colouring to give a pale green tint and stir in the chopped

angelica. Spread over the top of the pastry and leave until set.

Serves 6.

See illustration on Frontispiece.

Creamy Chocolate Mousse

4 eggs
4 oz. (4 squares) plain chocolate

½ pint (1 cup) whipping cream
1 tablespoon brandy

Separate eggs. Chop chocolate roughly, put into top of double saucepan; stir over hot water until melted. Remove from heat, cool a little, then blend in egg-yolks, one at a tine. Beat until mixture is smooth and thick.

Fold in whipped cream, brandy, then stiffly beaten egg-whites. Spoon into individual serving dishes, refrigerate until firm. To serve, top with a little whipped cream and grated chocolate.

Toffee Strawberries

½ lb. strawberries
1 lb. (2 cups) sugar

½ pint (1 cup) water

Wash strawberries gently, spread on absorbent paper to dry. Place sugar and water in a small saucepan and stir over a gentle heat until the sugar has dissolved. Increase heat and bring to boil. Boil syrup until it becomes a very pale gold colour. Remove from heat immediately.

Using tongs, dip strawberries by the stem into the syrup, coating the entire fruit except the stem. Place on greased baking trays and leave until toffee has hardened. Serve within an hour of making as, if kept too long, juice of the strawberries will make the toffee soft and sticky.

Toffee Grapes can be made in the same way. They're delicious to serve with after-dinner coffee.

Grape Brulée

1½ lb. seedless white grapes
½ pint (1 cup) whipping cream

3 tablespoons light brown sugar

Peel grapes; drain on absorbent paper. Place in heatproof dish, spoon over cream. Leave overnight in refrigerator. Just before serving, sift sugar over surface and place under slow grill until sugar melts. Increase heat to high, continue grilling until sugar caramelizes. Serve immediately.

Serves 6.

When grapes are out of season, other fresh or canned fruit can be used.

American Chocolate Mould

6 oz. (6 squares) plain
  chocolate
¾ pint (1½ cups) milk
3 oz. (¾ cup) digestive
  biscuit crumbs

1 egg
2 oz. (⅓ cup) nuts
cream

Melt the chocolate in a basin over hot water. Add the milk gradually and stir until well blended. Pour into a saucepan, add the biscuit crumbs and stir until the mixture thickens. Add egg-yolk, simmer 2 to 3 minutes, stirring all the time. Cool a little, then fold in stiffly beaten egg-white. Pour into an oiled 1 pint mould. Stand in a baking tin of hot water and bake in a moderately hot oven, Mark 4, 375°F., about 45 minutes. Turn out when cold. Decorate with chopped nuts and cream.
    Serves 4.

Biscotten Torte

4 oz. (½ cup) butter
4 oz. (½ cup) castor
  (superfine) sugar
2 eggs
4 oz. (¾ cup) ground
  almonds
few drops almond
  essence
¼ pint (½ cup) milk

1½ tablespoons rum
¼ pint (½ cup) extra
  milk
¾ lb. plain sweet oblong
  biscuits (24 biscuits)
½ pint (1 cup) whipping
  cream
toasted, slivered
  almonds

Cream butter and sugar until light and fluffy. Separate eggs, beat yolks into creamed mixture. Add ground almonds, almond essence and the ¼ pint (½ cup) milk. Beat egg-whites stiffly, fold in. Mix rum and extra ¼ pint (½ cup) milk together.

Arrange six biscuits lengthwise in 2 rows (3 biscuits to a row) beside each other on a sheet of greaseproof paper. Brush liberally with the rum-milk mixture. Spread with ⅓ of creamed mixture. Continue with brushed biscuits and filling, ending with row of biscuits. Wrap securely in aluminium foil, refrigerate several hours, preferably overnight.

Just before serving, arrange on serving plate, cover entire torte with whipped cream; decorate with toasted almonds. Cut in slices to serve.

Strawberries Romanoff

1 lb. fresh or 2 packets
  quick-frozen
  strawberries

6 to 8 tablespoons
  brandy or cointreau
¼ pint (½ cup) whipping
  cream

Wash and hull strawberries or allow to defrost. Pour brandy or cointreau over; cover until serving time. Arrange in individual serving dishes, top with whipped cream. Or blend whipped cream with 1 small block of vanilla ice cream which has been allowed to soften slightly. Spoon over strawberries.
    Serves 4.

Strawberries Flambé

thinly pared rind 1
  lemon
grated rind and juice
  2 oranges
4 oz. (½ cup) sugar

1 lb. strawberries
4 to 5 tablespoons
  brandy
vanilla ice-cream

Add lemon and orange rind to sugar and juice. Cook slowly in saucepan 5 minutes, pressing rind with spoon to extract all the flavour possible. Remove lemon rind, add strawberries, which have been carefully washed and dried. Spoon syrup gently over strawberries until they are coated with it. Warm brandy, pour over strawberries, set aflame. Serve spooned over vanilla ice-cream.
    Serves 6.

Crême Caramel

Caramel

4 oz. (½ cup) sugar

8 tablespoons water

Custard

3 eggs
2 egg-yolks, extra
¼ teaspoon vanilla
2 oz. (¼ cup) castor
  (superfine) sugar

½ pint (1 cup) milk
½ pint (1 cup) whipping
  cream

Caramel   Place sugar and water in saucepan. Stir over low heat until sugar dissolves. Stop stirring, turn heat up to moderate, and boil until mixture turns a caramel colour. Pour a little caramel in the base of greased, small, individual heatproof cups or mould.
Custard   Place eggs, extra yolks, vanilla and sugar in bowl. Beat lightly to combine. Combine milk and cream in a saucepan and bring to scalding point; cool slightly. Pour over egg mixture, stirring all the time. Strain into a large jug. Pour into individual moulds, over the caramel. (Makes 5 or 6, depending on size of moulds).

Place moulds in shallow baking dish containing approximately ¾ in. of cold water. Bake in moderately slow oven, Mark 2, 300°F., for approximately 30 minutes, or until custard is set. Remove moulds from water. Cool, then refrigerate a few hours. Turn out on to individual serving plates.

Biscotten Torte can be prepared the day beforehand for a wonderful party dessert.

Strawberry Bavarian Cream

1 tablespoon gelatine	4 oz. ($\frac{1}{2}$ cup) sugar
8 tablespoons cold water	16 oz. can strawberries
8 tablespoons boiling water	2 egg-whites
	1$\frac{1}{2}$ gills ($\frac{2}{3}$ cup) whipping cream

In a saucepan soak gelatine in cold water 5 minutes. Add boiling water and sugar, stir over heat until gelatine and sugar are dissolved. Place strawberries and syrup into blender; blend on high speed 1 minute, or press through sieve. Add puréed strawberries to gelatine mixture. Refrigerate until mixture is partially set.

Beat egg-whites until stiff, gradually add strawberry mixture, beat until thick and creamy. Lightly fold in whipped cream. Pour into lightly oiled 2$\frac{1}{2}$ to 3 pint mould. Refrigerate several hours or, preferably, overnight before unmoulding.
Serves 4.

Raspberry Bavarian Cream Proceed as for Strawberry Bavarian Cream, substituting raspberries for strawberries.

Caramel Bavarian Cream

1$\frac{1}{2}$ dessertspoons gelatine	1$\frac{1}{2}$ gills ($\frac{2}{3}$ cup) milk
4 tablespoons water	2 eggs, separated
6 oz. ($\frac{3}{4}$ cup) sugar	4 tablespoons milk, extra
4 tablespoons water, extra	$\frac{1}{2}$ teaspoon vanilla
	$\frac{1}{2}$ pint (1 cup) whipping cream

Soften gelatine in water and dissolve over boiling water. Place sugar and extra water in saucepan, stir over low heat until sugar has dissolved. Simmer without stirring until syrup is caramel colour. Heat milk in saucepan; when hot, add hot caramel and continue stirring over low heat until caramel is dissolved. Remove from heat. Beat egg yolks with extra milk, add to caramel; mix thoroughly. Add softened gelatine and vanilla. Refrigerate until mixture begins to set.

Fold in stiffly beaten egg-whites and whipped cream. Pour into lightly oiled 2$\frac{1}{2}$-pint mould. Refrigerate several hours or overnight before unmoulding.
Serves 4.

Crème Brulée

1 pint (2 cups) whipping cream	3 tablespoons sugar
1 in. piece vanilla bean	3 oz. ($\frac{1}{2}$ cup) light brown sugar
6 egg-yolks	crushed ice

Warm cream with vanilla bean in top of double boiler over hot water. Beat egg-yolks and sugar in basin until light and creamy. Remove vanilla bean; slowly stir warmed cream into the egg-yolk mixture. Return mixture to top of double boiler. Cook over hot, not boiling, water, stirring, until mixture coats a wooden spoon well. Pour custard into a heatproof serving dish, or into individual heatproof serving dishes.

Refrigerate until custard is firm, about 1 hour. Place dish in shallow tray filled with ice cubes. Sift a layer of brown sugar evenly over top. Place under grill at moderate heat until sugar caramelizes; watch carefully that sugar does not burn. Refrigerate again until ready to serve.

Pears in White Wine

6 medium pears	grated rind 1 lemon
8 oz. (1 cup) sugar	1 dessertspoon lemon juice
1 pint (2 cups) water	4 whole cloves
1 pint (2 cups) white wine	2 in. cinnamon stick

Peel whole pears thinly, keeping a good shape and leaving stalks in place. Place pears and remaining ingredients in saucepan. Liquid should just cover pears; if necessary add more water and wine in equal proportions. Cover, simmer gently 20 minutes, (depending on ripeness of pears), or until tender. Strain syrup, pour over pears, refrigerate. Serve with syrup spooned over.
Serves 6.

Pears in Red Wine Substitute red wine for white in the above recipe. When pears are cooked, cool then refrigerate. For jellied glaze on pears, as shown in picture, dissolve $\frac{1}{2}$ packet port wine jelly in $\frac{1}{4}$ pint ($\frac{1}{2}$ cup) boiling water; cool. Brush the jelly glaze over the cold pears. Repeat the brushing several times, if a rich glaze is desired. Serve with the strained syrup.

Cherries Jubilee

16 oz. can cherries	water
1 tablespoon sugar	4 to 6 tablespoons brandy or cherry brandy
1 in piece cinnamon stick	
2 teaspoons arrowroot	ice-cream

Drain cherries, reserving syrup. Pit cherries. Combine cherry syrup, sugar and cinnamon stick in saucepan, bring slowly to boil, simmer gently 3 minutes, strain. Blend arrowroot with a little water, stir into cherry syrup mixture, return to heat, stir until sauce boils and thickens. Add pitted cherries, heat thoroughly.

Add warmed brandy, ignite. Spoon sauce immediately over servings of vanilla ice-cream.
Serves 4.

Italian Lemon Gelato

14 oz. (1¾ cups) sugar
4 tablespoons lemon juice
2½ pints (5 cups) water
grated rind 1 lemon
½ pint (1 cup) whipping cream

In large saucepan place sugar, lemon juice, water and lemon rind. Bring slowly to the boil, stirring until sugar has dissolved. Boil 15 minutes, strain, and allow to cool. When quite cold, stir in whipped cream, pour into refrigerator trays, and freeze. When the cream is added to the lemon syrup, the mixtures do not immediately combine. However, while freezing, stir the mixture with fork frequently; the two mixtures soon blend together.

Serves 6.

Lemon Water Ice

½ pint (1 cup) hot water
6 oz. (¾ cup) sugar
8 tablespoons lemon juice
1 egg-white
grated rind 1 lemon
1 tablespoon sugar, extra

Dissolve the sugar in the hot water, add lemon juice and rind; set aside to cool; strain. Pour into refrigerator trays and freeze, stirring occasionally, until mixture is mushy; remove from trays. Beat egg-white stiffly, adding the extra sugar gradually; fold in lemon mixture. Return to freezer trays, freeze until firm.

Serves 4.

Wine Trifle

2 large cans peach halves
1 jam filled swiss roll
5 to 6 tablespoons any dessert wine or sweet sherry
2½ oz. (⅔ cup) custard powder
6 oz. (¾ cup) sugar
1½ pints (3 cups) milk
3 eggs
½ teaspoon vanilla
½ pint (2 cups) whipping cream
1 oz. (1 square) chocolate
1 teaspoon butter

Drain peaches and reserve ¼ pint of syrup. Arrange peaches on base of deep glass bowl. Slice swiss roll, stand slices round side of bowl. Dice any surplus cake, place over peaches. Combine wine and reserved peach syrup, pour over cake slices. In saucepan blend custard powder and sugar with a little milk, add remainder of milk, stir well. Cook over medium heat until mixture boils and thickens, stirring constantly. Remove from heat, add well beaten egg-yolks and vanilla; cool. Fold in stiffly beaten egg-whites. Pour over peaches, refrigerate. Before serving spoon over whipped cream, drizzle with chocolate which has been melted with butter over boiling water.

Serves 6.

Vanilla Ice-Cream

1 dessertspoon gelatine
4 oz. (½ cup) sugar
4 tablespoons water
8 oz. (1¼ cups) full cream powdered milk
2 pints (4 cups) milk
1 dessertspoon vinegar
2 teaspoons vanilla

Combine gelatine, sugar and water in saucepan, stir over low heat until sugar and gelatine are dissolved; pour into large basin. Add powdered milk, whisk until smooth, gradually beat in milk. Pour mixture into freezer trays; freeze until almost set. Spoon mixture into large basin, add vinegar and vanilla, beat until thick and creamy; this can be done in electric mixer. Return to freezer trays. Freeze until set.

This economical recipe makes approximately 5 pints (about 10 cups) of beautifully-textured ice-cream. For an even richer ice-cream, beat in ¼ pint (½ cup) cream with the milk.

Cassata

4 pints vanilla ice-cream
juice 1 lemon
1 dessertspoon sugar
1 banana
2 oz. (½ cup) glacé cherries
2 glacé apricots
1 slice glacé pineapple
2 oz. (2 squares) plain chocolate
1 oz. (¼ cup) cocoa
1 tablespoon sugar
1 tablespoon water
1 teaspoon rum
1 oz. (2 tablespoons) butter
2 oz. (¼ cup) blanched, slivered almonds
almond essence

Divide ice-cream evenly into three bowls. Keep in freezer until each is required. Combine strained lemon juice and the 1 dessertspoon sugar with sliced banana and finely chopped glacé fruits, stir into one bowl of slightly softened ice-cream. Pour into foil-lined aluminium 9 in. × 5 in. loaf tin; freeze until firm. Each layer must be firm before topping with the next.

Melt the chocolate over hot water, blend cocoa and the 1 tablespoon sugar with water, stir into melted chocolate; add rum. Stir chocolate mixture into the second bowl of ice-cream, pour over fruit layer; freeze.

Heat butter, add almonds, stir over medium heat until golden brown, drain; cool. Add almonds to remaining ice-cream, flavour to taste with few drops of almond essence, pour over chocolate layer. Cover tin with aluminium foil, freeze 4 hours or overnight. Cut into slices to serve. A little rum or brandy can be spooned over each slice.

NOTE: If desired substitute 2 oz. (⅓ cup) mixed peel for glacé apricots and pineapple.

Serves 10 to 12.

Dessert Sauces

These are easy-to-make dessert sauces, with delicious flavour. Some are to serve over hot puddings; some make a rich topping when spooned over ice-cream.

Stirred Custard

3 eggs
2 tablespoons sugar

½ teaspoon vanilla
1 pint (2 cups) milk

Beat eggs, sugar and vanilla together, place in top of double saucepan. Warm milk, stir into egg mixture. Stir constantly over simmering water until custard thickens slightly. Remove from heat immediately.

Makes 1 pint (2 cups).

Brandy Custard

2 oz. (¼ cup) sugar
¼ pint (½ cup) water
2 egg-yolks
pinch salt

2 tablespoons brandy
3 tablespoons whipped cream

Place sugar and water into saucepan; stir to dissolve sugar, bring to boil, reduce heat, simmer 10 minutes. Beat egg-yolks and salt, pour hot syrup in slowly, beating until thick and creamy. Fold in brandy and whipped cream.

Makes approx. ½ pint (1 cup).

Rich Caramel Sauce

4 oz. (½ cup) butter
12 oz. (2 cups) dark brown sugar

1½ gills (⅔ cup) liquid glucose
½ pint (1 cup) whipping cream

Combine butter, brown sugar and glucose in saucepan, stir over low heat until sugar dissolves; bring to boil, boil 5 minutes. Remove from heat, allow bubbles to subside, gradually add cream, stirring constantly. Serve warm or cold. This sauce will thicken on standing.

Makes 1¼ pints (2½ cups).

Butterscotch Sauce

1 oz. (2 tablespoons) butter
1½ oz. (¼ cup) light brown sugar

4 tablespoons condensed milk
1 dessertspoon golden syrup (cornsyrup)
¼ pint (½ cup) hot milk

Combine butter, brown sugar, condensed milk and syrup in saucepan. Cook over low heat, stirring constantly until mixture leaves sides of saucepan and is rich golden colour. Remove from heat; gradually stir in hot milk. Return to heat, cook 1 to 2 minutes.

Makes approx. ½ pint (1 cup).

Chocolate Rum Sauce

6 oz. (6 squares) plain chocolate
¼ pint (½ cup) black coffee

1 tablespoon rum

Chop chocolate roughly, add to small saucepan with hot coffee, stir constantly over low heat until chocolate melts. Remove from heat, add rum to taste. Serve warm.

Chocolate Sauce

4 oz. (4 squares) plain chocolate
good ¼ pint (½ cup) water
2 oz. (¼ cup) sugar

1 dessertspoon corn-flour (cornstarch)
1 tablespoon water, extra
½ teaspoon vanilla

Chop chocolate roughly, combine with water and sugar in small saucepan, stir over low heat until chocolate melts and sugar is dissolved; remove from heat. Blend cornflour (cornstarch) with extra water, stir into chocolate mixture, return to heat, stir until sauce boils and thickens, remove from heat, add vanilla. Serve warm or cold.

Makes 1½ gills (⅔ cup).

Mocha Sauce Add 1 dessertspoon instant coffee powder to saucepan with chocolate mixture.

Hard Sauce

4 oz. (½ cup) butter
12 oz. (2 cups) icing (confectioners') sugar

1 tablespoon brandy

Cream butter, gradually blend in sifted icing sugar and brandy. Refrigerate until firm. Serve with Christmas pudding.

Melba Sauce

Rub fresh, canned or thawed frozen raspberries through a sieve. If using fresh raspberries, a little icing sugar may be added.

Caramel Bavarian Cream has light, lovely texture. Serve with cream or with caramel sauce.

Yeast cookery

For those who haven't tried it, yeast cookery may seem involved and difficult. But, provided the simple instructions given in the recipes are followed, you'll find it easy to make beautiful bread and buns; each step of each recipe has been carefully timed.

There are just a few main points to remember when cooking with yeast.

Yeast must be fresh. If fresh yeast is not available, dried yeast can be used. Two teaspoons dried yeast is equal to $\frac{1}{2}$ oz. (1 package) fresh yeast.

Liquid added to yeast should be lukewarm, as individual recipes specify. If liquid is too cold, it will not have any effect on the yeast—the dough will not rise; if too hot, it will kill the action of the yeast. But liquid of the right temperature will bring the yeast to life.

When setting the dough to prove, leave it in a warm (but not hot) place, away from draughts.

When the dough is in the oven you will have the house filled with the fragrance of yeast cookery—which Mark Twain described as 'the very breath and perfume of home'.

White Bread

1 lb. (4 cups) plain flour
1 teaspoon salt
$\frac{1}{2}$ oz. (1 package) compressed yeast
$\frac{1}{2}$ pint (1 cup) tepid water
1 teaspoon sugar
$\frac{1}{2}$ oz. (1 tablespoon) butter

Sift flour and salt into bowl. Crumble yeast into tepid water; add sugar and butter. Stir well until yeast turns liquid and sugar dissolves. Make a well in centre of flour, pour in yeast mixture. Mix centre portion only into a soft batter, leaving walls of dry flour round edges. Knock down walls of flour to cover batter mixture. Cover with dry cloth and stand in warm place for 20 minutes. Using one hand, mix dough together, adding approximately 4 tablespoons of extra water if dough is too dry. Beat well for 5 minutes until dough is dry and springy. Place in greased bowl, reverse dough so that upper side is coated with grease. Cover with dry cloth and stand in warm place for approximately 45 minutes, until dough has doubled in bulk. Turn on to lightly floured board. Knead for approximately 5 minutes, until bubbles of gas are evenly distributed. (Check this by cutting dough in half and looking to see if gas bubbles are small and even throughout dough.) Press dough into lightly greased 8 in. × 4 in. loaf tin. Place in warm place until dough rises well above top of tin. Bake in very hot oven, Mark 8, 450°F., for 15 minutes. Reduce heat to moderate, Mark 4, 350°F., and continue baking for further 45 minutes. For last 10 minutes of cooking time, remove loaf carefully from tin and place on dry baking sheet to brown sides.

Rye Bread

$\frac{1}{2}$ pint (1 cup) water
$1\frac{1}{2}$ gills ($\frac{2}{3}$ cup) milk
8 oz. (2 cups) rye flour
4 oz. (1 cup) wholemeal plain flour
4 oz. (1 cup) plain flour
1 teaspoon ground aniseed
1 teaspoon salt
1 dessertspoon sugar
1 oz. (2 packages) compressed yeast
1 dessertspoon oil

Combine water and milk; heat to lukewarm.

Sift dry ingredients into large basin. Make a well in centre. Dissolve crumbled yeast in a little of the lukewarm water and milk mixture, add remaining water and milk mixture and oil. Pour yeast mixture into dry ingredients and beat well together. Sprinkle with a little flour, cover, and let stand in warm place until doubled in bulk. Knock down and knead a little with hand. Cover again, and let stand in warm place until doubled in bulk. Knead until smooth and elastic on floured surface. Form into bread shape and place in well-greased 8 in. × 4 in. loaf tin. Cover and leave in warm place further $\frac{1}{2}$ hour or until top rises to edge of tin. Brush with a little water, in which a little sugar has been dissolved. Bake in hot oven, Mark 7, 450°F., 40 to 45 minutes. Remove from tin, cool on wire rack.

Raisin Bread

1 lb. (4 cups) plain flour
1½ teaspoons ground
  cardamom
½ pint (1 cup) plus 4
  tablespoons milk
4 oz. (½ cup) butter

4 oz. (½ cup) sugar
1 oz. (2 packages)
  compressed yeast
4 oz. (⅔ cup) raisins
5 oz. (⅓ cup) dried
  apricots

Sift flour and cardamom into bowl. Combine milk, butter and sugar in saucepan, heat until lukewarm. Remove from heat, add yeast, stir to dissolve. Make a well in centre of flour. Pour in yeast mixture and beat well together. Cover with cloth and leave in warm place until doubled in bulk, approximately 45 minutes. Add raisins and chopped apricots, and knead on floured surface until smooth and elastic. Shape into loaf shape and place in well-greased 9 in. × 5 in. loaf tin. Cover and leave in warm place until dough has risen to just under edge of tin. Brush top with a little water, in which a little sugar has been dissolved. Bake in moderately hot oven, Mark 5, 375°F., 45 to 55 minutes. Cool on wire rack.

Cream Buns

1 oz. (2 packages)
  compressed yeast
1 lb. (4 cups) plain flour
4 oz. (½ cup) sugar
½ pint (1 cup) milk

1 teaspoon salt
2 oz. (¼ cup) butter
1½ oz. (¼ cup) sultanas
1 egg

Fluffy Mock Cream

4 oz. (½ cup) butter
1 tablespoon boiling
  milk
8 oz. (1 cup) castor
  (superfine) sugar

½ teaspoon gelatine
3 tablespoons boiling
  water
½ teaspoon vanilla

Crumble yeast into basin, mix with 1 teaspoon each of flour and sugar and all the lukewarm milk. Stand basin in warm place 15 minutes or until mixture is spongy. Sift flour and salt into large basin, rub in the butter, add sugar and sultanas, mix well. Beat egg well, add to yeast mixture, add this to flour mixture and make into soft dough. Stand in warm place 40 minutes, covered with cloth without touching dough. Turn on to floured surface. Knead well until smooth and elastic. Cut into 16 even-sized pieces, knead each into a small ball. Place on greased baking tray. Set again in warm place 15 to 20 minutes. Bake in moderately hot oven, Mark 4, 350°F., 15 to 20 minutes or until golden brown. Remove from oven, brush glaze over. Break buns apart when glaze sets, allow to cool on wire rack. When quite cold, cut small section about ¼ in. wide along top of each bun and pipe into this whipped fresh cream or mock cream, sprinkle with icing sugar, drop a little raspberry jam into centre of row of cream.
Fluffy Mock Cream Soften butter in basin with boiling milk, add sugar, beat to a cream. When mixture is creamy, dissolve gelatine in the boiling water. Add gradually to creamed mixture, beating continuously, until sugar is completely dissolved and mixture is light and fluffy. Add vanilla, beat well.
Sugar Glaze Combine 1 tablespoon gelatine, 1 tablespoon sugar and ¼ pint (½ cup) water; stir over gentle heat until sugar dissolves.
  Makes 16.

Hot Cross Buns

1 oz. (2 packages)
  compressed yeast
1 lb. (4 cups) plain flour
2 oz. (¼ cup) sugar
½ pint (1 cup) warm
  milk
1 teaspoon salt

½ teaspoon mixed spice
½ teaspoon cinnamon
2 oz. (¼ cup) butter
2 oz. (⅓ cup) sultanas
2 oz. (⅓ cup) currants
1 egg

Paste for Crosses

1 oz. (2 tablespoons)
  plain flour

little cold water

Glaze

1 tablespoon sugar
1 teaspoon gelatine

1 tablespoon hot water

Crumble yeast into basin, mix with 1 teaspoon each previously measured flour and sugar; mix in warm milk. Stand in warm place 15 minutes or until mixture is spongy. Sift flour, salt and spices into large basin. Rub in butter, add sugar and fruit. Beat egg well, add it to yeast and milk sponge. Add this to flour mixture, make into soft dough. Cover with clean cloth, stand in warm place 40 minutes; at the end of this time dough should have doubled in bulk. Turn on to lightly floured board. Knead well, turning outside edges of dough into centre. Knead until dough is smooth and elastic. Cut into 15 or 16 even-sized pieces, knead each piece into a round. Place in a shallow greased tin, space ½ in. apart. Set again in warm place 10 to 15 minutes. Make paste for crosses by mixing sifted flour to very soft paste with cold water. Using small plain nozzle, pipe crosses on each bun. Bake in hot oven, Mark 7, 450°F., 15 to 20 minutes. Remove from oven, brush with glaze made by dissolving sugar and gelatine in hot water. Cool on wire rack.
  Makes 15 to 16.

Coffee Walnut Buns

1 pint (2 cups) milk	2 lb. (8 cups) plain flour
2 oz. ($\frac{1}{4}$ cup) sugar	pinch salt
2 oz. ($\frac{1}{4}$ cup) butter	2 eggs
1 oz. (2 packages) compressed yeast	3 oz. ($\frac{1}{2}$ cup) sultanas

Warm Coffee Icing

$\frac{1}{2}$ lb. ($1\frac{1}{3}$ cups) icing (confectioners') sugar	$\frac{1}{2}$ oz. (1 tablespoon) butter
1 teaspoon instant coffee powder	milk to mix
	chopped walnuts

Place milk, sugar and butter in small saucepan, heat just to lukewarm; dissolve yeast in this mixture. Sift flour and salt, make well in centre, break in eggs. Stir in lukewarm yeast and milk mixture, beat until thoroughly combined. Mix in sultanas. Cover, stand in warm place 30 to 40 minutes to rise. Turn out on lightly floured board, knead 2 minutes; place in greased basin, stand in a warm place further 15 minutes. Turn out on floured surface, knead lightly, break off small pieces of dough about size of a lemon, roll between palms of hands to make long roll, tie this in knot. Place 1 to $1\frac{1}{2}$ in. apart on well-greased baking tray, let stand in warm place 20 to 30 minutes or until nearly double in size. Bake in moderate oven, Mark 4, 350°F., 20 to 25 minutes or until golden brown. Glaze immediately while hot with Sugar Glaze (see recipe for Cream Buns, page 225), then drizzle while still warm with warm coffee icing and sprinkle with chopped walnuts.

Makes approx. 20.

Warm Coffee Icing   Sift icing sugar and coffee into heatproof basin, add butter and enough milk to make icing of a fairly thin consistency. Place over saucepan of boiling water, stir until mixture begins to shine and butter melts. Allow to remain over water while using.

Add crumbled yeast to milk, stand 5 minutes; add egg-yolks. Beat with rotary beater 3 minutes. Add to flour mixture, mix to a soft dough. Wrap in waxed paper or aluminium foil, refrigerate overnight. Remove from refrigerator $\frac{1}{2}$ hour before dough is to be used. Roll out dough $\frac{1}{4}$ in. thick on lightly floured surface. Spread with stiffly beaten egg-whites then the walnut mixture. Roll up carefully, as for swiss roll. Cut into $1\frac{1}{2}$ in. thick slices, place close together in well-greased shallow baking tin. Let rise in warm place 30 to 40 minutes. Bake in hot oven, Mark 7, 425°F., 20 minutes, or until browned. If browned before completely cooked, reduce temperature to moderate, Mark 4, 350°F., cover with sheet of brown paper, and continue cooking. Remove from oven and brush with sugar glaze (see recipe for Cream Buns).

Makes approx. 1 dozen.

Walnut Filling   Combine walnuts, sugar, cinnamon and egg in bowl. Stiffly beat egg-whites in separate bowl.

Below is a simple alternative filling. You might like to halve filling recipes and make half the buns with walnut filling and half with sultana filling.

Cinnamon Sultana Filling

3 oz. ($\frac{1}{2}$ cup) sultanas	4 oz. ($\frac{1}{2}$ cup) butter
5 oz. (scant cup) dark brown sugar	1 dessertspoon cinnamon
3 oz. ($\frac{1}{2}$ cup) chopped almonds	

Combine sultanas, brown sugar, almonds and cinnamon in bowl. Melt butter. Brush rolled-out dough with melted butter, sprinkle with cinnamon mixture. Proceed with rolling, cutting, baking, and glazing as directed above.

Continental Cinnamon Snails

12 oz. (3 cups) plain flour	1 oz. (2 packages) compressed yeast
2 tablespoons sugar	8 tablespoons lukewarm milk
pinch salt	
8 oz. (1 cup) butter	3 egg-yolks

Walnut Filling

3 oz. ($\frac{1}{2}$ cup) ground or finely chopped walnuts	1 tablespoon cinnamon
	1 egg, beaten
	2 egg-whites
8 oz. (1 cup) sugar	

Sift flour, sugar and salt into bowl. Rub in butter.

Jams and Jellies

Jams

There's pride and pleasure in making your own good-tasting jams and jellies—when fresh fruit are in season and in good supply, or perhaps from fruit in your own garden.

Choice of Fruit

Fruit for jam-making is best used early in its season, freshly picked, dry, just ripe or slightly under ripe, when the pectin acid content is highest. As fruit ripens, the acid it contains changes pectin to sugar, so the jam does not set well.

The acid in just-ripe or slightly under-ripe fruit is necessary to draw out the pectin, improve flavour, and help to prevent sugar crystallizing. If fruit is over-ripe jam does not set; if picked during wet weather jam may ferment or mould quickly.

Equipment

The following equipment is necessary for making all types of jams.

1. Aluminium, enamel, or stainless steel preserving pan, boiler or large saucepan with wide top to allow evaporation and prevent jam frothing and bubbling over while boiling.

2. Long-handled spoon, preferably wooden, for stirring.

3. Jars free from chips and cracks.

4. Soup ladle or enamel mug for filling jars.

5. Waxed or parchment covers, paraffin wax and/or screwtops for coverings.

NOTE: Jars must be sterilised before bottling jam. To sterilise jars, wash in warm soapy water, rinse, stand upside down to drain; then stand on wooden board, place in slow oven until jars are completely dry.

Pectin Content

Rich in pectin and acid Cooking apples, black currants, plums, gooseberries, lemons, limes, grapefruit, seville oranges.

Moderately rich in pectin and acid Apricots, blackberries, greengage plums, loganberries, raspberries, sweet oranges, mandarins.

Poor in pectin and acid Late blackberries, cherries, pineapple, melon, pears, peaches, strawberries.

To overcome pectin deficiency

1. Combine fruit deficient in pectin with pectin-rich fruit (for example, apple with blackberry).

2. Add lemon juice which is rich in pectin and contains acid.

3. Add commercial pectin, following manufacturer's directions.

To test pectin content When fruit has simmered with water until soft, place 1 teaspoon of mixture into glass, add 3 teaspoons methylated spirit and leave 2 minutes to form clot.

Large, firm clot indicates fruit is rich in pectin.

Medium-size, not-so-firm clot indicates fruit moderately rich in pectin.

Weak, flabby clot indicates fruit with poor pectin content.

Use of Sugar

Correct proportion is important. For fruit with moderate to rich pectin content use 1 lb. (2 cups) sugar to 1 lb. fruit; for fruit with poor pectin content use $\frac{3}{4}$ lb. ($1\frac{1}{2}$ cups) sugar to 1 lb fruit. Sugar, warmed for quicker dissolving, is added after fruit and skins have simmered until soft.

Basic Method

1. Remove stalks, stones, and any bruised parts of fruit.

2. Place fruit in preserving pan, greased to prevent burning. Make sure the preserving pan is big enough for the quantity of jam you wish to make. It should not be more than half full when the fruit and sugar are combined, otherwise the jam may boil over when boiled rapidly.

3. Pour over small quantity of water, approximately $\frac{1}{4}$ pint ($\frac{1}{2}$ cup) to 2 lb. fruit. Juicy fruits may not require any water.

4. Cook gently over low heat until fruit is soft and pulpy. Stir frequently to prevent sticking. This cooking softens the fruit and helps extract the pectin.

5. Add warmed sugar, stir over low heat until sugar has dissolved, then bring jam to boiling point as quickly as possible and boil rapidly, uncovered. Jam must not be allowed to boil until all sugar has dissolved. *Slow cooking before the addition of sugar, and rapid, short cooking afterwards is the golden rule for jam-making.*

NOTE: Sugar can be warmed in enamel or heat-proof bowl in slow oven. It is not essential to heat sugar, but heated sugar dissolves more quickly.

In some whole-fruit jams, the sugar is added to the fruit and the mixture allowed to stand overnight. In this case the mixture should be heated very slowly until the sugar has dissolved.

6. Boil jam rapidly, stirring occasionally, until it jells when tested.

To test   Spoon a little on cold saucer (place saucer in refrigerator 30 minutes before testing), refrigerate 2 or 3 minutes. If it jells, glazes on surface, and crinkles when touched, jam is cooked. If no skin forms, further boiling is necessary to evaporate more liquid. Remove jam from heat while testing.

7. Just before bottling, skim jam well to remove any scum on top.

8. Fill into sterilised jars. (For some whole-fruit jams or marmalades, allow to cool in pan until a thin skin begins to form on top, then stir gently and pour into jars. The liquid thickens on cooling and holds the fruit in suspension—this means it will not rise to the top when put into jars).

9. Fill jars to the brim.

10. Cover with disc of waxed paper, then with metal or plastic airtight lid.

11. Label jars, mark them with date of bottling. Store in cool, dry place.

Covering Jam   If there is condensation between jam and its cover, mould will form on top. To avoid this, cover jam when hot or when completely cold; never cover jam when it is warm.

Strawberry Conserve

1 lb. strawberries	finely grated rind and
1 lb. (2 cups) sugar	juice $\frac{1}{2}$ lemon

Wash and hull strawberries, place in a saucepan with sugar and lemon. Stir over low heat until sugar dissolves. Increase heat, boil gently 10 minutes, or until conserve jells when tested on a cold saucer. Skim, turn on to a large plate; stand overnight, turning over several times so that berries become plump and well mixed with juice. Pack into hot sterilized jars, seal.

Makes 1½ lb.

Blackberry Jelly Jam

1 lb. blackberries	1 lb (2 cups) sugar
(including some red	juice $\frac{1}{2}$ lemon
ones)	

Wash blackberries, place in large saucepan, crush well. Bring to the boil, reduce heat, simmer 30 minutes. Add lemon juice and warmed sugar, stir until dissolved, bring quickly to the boil, boil rapidly for approximately 10 minutes, or until jam jells when tested on cold saucer. Pour into hot sterilised jars, seal.

Makes approx. 1½ lb.

Blackberry and Apple Jam

8 lb. blackberries	3 lb. sour apples
1 pint (2 cups) water	sugar

Wash and remove stalks from blackberries and put into pan with $\frac{1}{4}$ pint water. Simmer slowly until fruit is soft then pass all through a sieve. Peel, core and slice apples, add remaining water and cook until tender. Mash with a spoon, add the blackberry juice. Weigh the pulp and add an equal quantity of sugar. Stir, bring to the boil and simmer until jam sets when tested on a cold plate. Pot and cover at once.

If the pan is weighed before cooking is begun, the weight of pulp can easily be calculated.

Morello Cherry Jam

2 lb. morello cherries	$\frac{1}{2}$ pint (1 cup) water
juice 2 lemons	$1\frac{1}{4}$ lb. ($2\frac{1}{2}$ cups) sugar

Wash cherries, remove stones, (stones can be removed with a special cherry pitter); tie stones in a piece of muslin. Place strained lemon juice and water in large bowl. Place layer of sugar in bowl and layer of cherries, continue until all sugar and cherries are used. Cover and stand overnight.

Next day, strain syrup into saucepan, place over medium heat, stir until sugar dissolves. When syrup is boiling, add cherries and muslin bag, boil 15 minutes. Start testing jam after 15 minutes, or boil until jam jells when tested on a cold saucer. Remove jam from heat while testing, as it is very easy to overcook cherry jam, and spoil both flavour and colour. Discard muslin bag.

Remove any scum from jam, (but avoid stirring) before bottling into hot sterilised jars, seal.

Makes about 2 lb.

Sweet Orange Jam

2 oranges	2 pints (4 cups) water
1 lemon	3 lb. (6 cups) sugar

Wash oranges and lemon, slice very thinly, remove pips. Place fruit in a basin, add water, cover and stand 2 days.

Place fruit and water in a large saucepan; boil 1 hour. Add warmed sugar, stir until dissolved. Boil rapidly for approximately 40 to 50 minutes, or until jam jells when tested on a cold saucer. Pour into hot sterilised jars, seal.

Makes about 2½ lb.

Tomato Jam

9 lb. ripe tomatoes	6 lb. (12 cups) sugar
lemon juice	

Pour boiling water over the tomatoes and remove the skins. Put the fruit, sugar and a little lemon juice into a pan and bring slowly to boiling point when the sugar should have dissolved. Boil until the fruit is transparent and the syrup thick. Skim if necessary. Leave the jam to get cold, then pour into jars and cover.

Makes about 10 lb.

Fresh Apricot Jam

4 lb. fresh apricots	juice of 1 lemon
¾ pint (1½ cups) water	4 lb. (8 cups) sugar

Wash the fruit, cut in halves and remove stones. Crack these to remove kernels and blanch. Put the fruit in a pan with the water, lemon juice and blanched kernels. Simmer until tender and contents of pan reduced a little. Add warm sugar, stir until dissolved then boil briskly about 15 minutes. Test for setting, then pot and cover at once.

Makes about 6½ lb.

Dried Apricot Jam

1 lb. dried apricots	3 lb (6 cups) sugar
3 pints (6 cups) water	2 to 3 oz. almonds
juice of 1 lemon	

Wash apricots well, put into a basin with the water, cover, and soak for at least 24 hours. Put the contents of the basin into a pan, add lemon juice and boil gently for ½ hour stirring now and then. Add sugar and blanched almonds and boil until the jam sets when tested. (Stir frequently after the sugar has been added.)

Pot and cover at once.

Makes about 5 lb.

Plum Jam

3 lb. plums	3 lb. (6 cups) sugar
½ pint (1 cup) water	juice 1½ lemons

Wash plums, cut in halves, remove stones. Place in large saucepan with the water and ¾ lb. (1½ cups) sugar. Cook gently until plums are tender, stirring occasionally. Add remaining sugar, stir over low heat until sugar dissolves; add lemon juice. Boil rapidly until jam jells when tested on a cold saucer. Pour into hot sterilised jars, seal.

Makes 5 lb.

Damson Jam

4 lb. damsons	4 lb. (8 cups) sugar
1¼ pints (2½ cups) water	

Wash the fruit, put into a pan with water and bring to the boil. Simmer until the fruit is cooked.

Add sugar, stir until dissolved then boil quickly, removing the stones as they rise to the surface. Test after about 10 minutes boiling. When ready, pot and cover at once.

Makes about 6½ lb.

Apricot and Pineapple Jam

½ lb. dried apricots	2 lb. (4 cups) sugar
¾ pint (1½ cups) water	grated rind 1 lemon
15 oz. can crushed pineapple	juice 2 lemons
3 oz. (¾ cup) grated carrot	

Soak apricots in the water overnight.

Put into a pan with undrained pineapple and carrot, bring slowly to the boil, cover, simmer until apricots are tender, (approximately 20 minutes). Add sugar, lemon rind and juice, stir over a low heat until sugar dissolves. Increase heat, boil rapidly until jam jells when tested on a cold saucer; start testing after 10 minutes. Pour into hot sterilized jars, seal.

Makes approx. 3½ lb.

Recipes in this section for jams and jellies enable you to make the most of fresh fruits in season. Even three or four pieces of fruit will give several jars of jam with orchard-fresh flavour.

Apple Ginger

4 lb apples	3 lemons
1 pint (2 cups) water	3 teaspoons ginger
8 oz. preserved ginger	syrup
	3 lb. (6 cups) sugar

Peel apples and slice thinly. Tie the cores, pips and peel in a piece of muslin. Add water, cover and simmer until apples are soft. Remove muslin bag and mash apples with a spoon. Add chopped ginger, grated rind and juice of the lemons, ginger syrup and sugar. Stir until boiling, boil for 10 minutes then test for setting. Pot and cover at once.

Makes about 5 lb.

Japonica Jam

4 lb. japonica fruit or	2 teaspoons powdered
quince	cloves
6 pints (12 cups) water	
sugar	

Wash and slice the fruit, put into a pan with the water, boil until tender. Sieve, then weigh the pulp and add an equal amount of sugar. Stir until boiling. Add spice and boil for 10 minutes. Test for setting and when ready, pot and cover at once.

Three Fruit Marmalade

1 large orange	3¼ pints (6½ cups) water
1 large grapefruit	sugar (approx. 4½ lb.)
1 large lemon	(approx. 9 cups)

Wash fruit, slice orange and grapefruit finely; using skin, pith and flesh; discard seeds. Roll lemon well with the palm of the hand until skin is soft, halve lemon and extract juice, discard seeds. Place fruit (including the lemon halves) into large saucepan with the water, cover, bring to boil, add lemon juice, simmer 30 minutes, cool. Pour mixture into large crockery basin, cover, stand 36 hours. Remove lemon skins, measure fruit mixture, allow ½ lb. (1 cup) sugar to each ½ pint (1 cup) of fruit, add 1 extra ½ lb. (1 cup) of sugar. Heat fruit mixture, add warmed sugar, stir over low heat until sugar dissolves. Increase heat, boil rapidly until marmalade jells when tested on a cold saucer, approximately 30 minutes. Allow to stand 5 minutes before pouring into hot sterilised jars; seal.

Makes approx. 3 lb.

Blender Marmalade

1 large carrot	1 pint (2 cups) cold
1 orange	water
2 lemons	2 lb. (4 cups) sugar

Wash and coarsely chop carrot and unpeeled orange and lemons. Place in electric blender and blend on low speed until very finely chopped (about 30 seconds). Pour into large saucepan, add sugar and water. Heat gently, stirring constantly, until sugar dissolves. Bring to the boil, reduce heat, simmer 30 minutes; increase heat, boil rapidly 30 minutes, or until jam jells when tested on a cold saucer, pour into hot sterilised jars, seal.

Makes about 2½ lb.

If you haven't an electric blender, wash and roughly chop carrot, orange and lemons and put through a hand mincer, or an electric mincer.

Lemon Curd

4 lemons	4 oz. (½ cup) fresh
5 eggs	butter
	1 lb. (2 cups) sugar

Wash the lemons and grate the rind thinly. Beat the eggs and put with the lemon rind, juice and butter into the top of a double boiler. Stir over low heat until the sugar has dissolved and the mixture thickens. Strain into small sterilised pots and cover immediately.

This preserve is best made in small quantities as it will only keep for a short time.

Grapefruit Jam

1 large grapefruit	2 lb. (4 cups) sugar
2 pints (4 cups) boiling	
water	

Wash grapefruit, slice finely, removing seeds. Place in a basin, add boiling water, cover, stand overnight. Place fruit and liquid in a large saucepan, simmer over a low heat for approximately 30 minutes or until rind is tender. Add warmed sugar; stir over low heat until sugar dissolves. Bring quickly to the boil, boil rapidly until jam jells when tested on a cold saucer, approximately 40 minutes. Allow to cool for 10 minutes before pouring into hot sterilised jars, seal.

Makes 1½ lb.

Jellies

The perfect jelly is bright, clear and slightly a-quiver; it should have the true flavour of fruit used. Here are hints for turning out perfect jellies.

To Prepare Fruit

Hard or firm fruits Leave unpeeled and uncored, cut into small pieces.
Soft fruits or berries Wash and allow to drain.

Basic Method

1. Place prepared fruit in greased preserving pan with water to cover. Cook gently until fruit is quite tender—usually $\frac{1}{2}$ to $\frac{3}{4}$ hour. Overcooking destroys jelling properties. It is not necessary to add water to berry fruits; they generally contain enough liquid. However, if berries are not very soft, a little water may need to be added to prevent fruit sticking to pan.
2. Test for pectin. (See Jams.)
3. Prepare quantity of sugar, amount depending on result of pectin test: For fruit rich in pectin allow 1 lb. (2 cups) sugar to 1 pint (2 cups) syrup; for fruits moderately rich in pectin allow $\frac{3}{4}$ lb ($1\frac{1}{2}$ cups) sugar to 1 pint (2 cups) syrup.
4. Strain fruit through layers of cheese-cloth tied to legs of stool or chair inverted on table; place basin under centre of cloth.

   Pour boiling water through cloth, then pour fruit pulp through. Leave to drip overnight. Do not squeeze bag, as it can cause cloudiness in jelly.
5. Measure syrup, place in pan with correct proportion of warmed sugar, stir until dissolved.
6. Boil rapidly until jelly sets when tested.
7. Skim; bottle immediately.

Cranberry and Apple Jelly

3 lb. apples	water
2 lb. cranberries	sugar

Wash the apples and cut into thick slices without peeling or coring. Wash the cranberries and put all the fruit into a pan with sufficient water to cover. Simmer gently until the fruit is quite tender and mashed. Strain through a jelly cloth, allowing it to drip overnight. Weigh the extract, put into a pan and bring to the boil. Add an equal quantity of sugar, stir until dissolved and then boil briskly for about 10 minutes. Test for setting and when ready pour into hot jars and cover at once.

Crab-Apple Jelly

crab-apples	sugar
water	

Remove stalks from crab-apples, wash fruit, cut in halves. Place fruit into large saucepan, cover with water. Bring to the boil, reduce heat, simmer gently 30 to 45 minutes, or until fruit is soft. Strain through cloth; measure liquid, bring to boil. For every pint (2 cups) of liquid allow $\frac{3}{4}$ lb. ($1\frac{1}{2}$ cups) sugar; boil for approximately 45 minutes, or until mixture jells when tested on a cold saucer. Pour into hot sterilised jars, seal.

Pickles and Chutneys

Hot or cold meals gain extra flavour when you add the zesty taste of a good pickle, or richly flavoured chutney or relish. For best results use good quality ingredients and the right equipment, as outlined below.

Ingredients

Vegetables, Fruit Fresh, crisp, in season, barely ripe, in good condition.

Vegetables of inferior quality do not keep; if wilted, will not absorb pickling solution well.

Vinegar Essential ingredient, used plain or spiced; use good-quality brewed malt vinegar; for light-coloured vegetables use white, wine, or cider vinegar.

Only the best vinegar should be used for pickling, i.e., vinegar containing an acetic acid content of at least 4 percent. Bulk vinegar usually contains less than this and is therefore not as satisfactory.

Equipment

Aluminium or enamel-lined vessels; wooden spoon for stirring and mixing flavouring and thickening ingredients.

NOTE: Do not use unlined copper pans, metal tops for jars or bottles, or pans which are used for jam-making.

Bottling and Sealing

Fill pickles and chutneys into clean, dry, sterilised, wide-necked jars.

Make jars completely airtight with plastic (not metal) screw-tops, wax, or use patent jars.

Sweet Fruit Chutney

2 lb. tomatoes
3 large onions
2 large cooking apples
1½ lb. (3 cups) sugar
4 oz. (⅔ cup) sultanas
4 oz. (⅔ cup) currants
1 tablespoon salt
1 tablespoon whole cloves
pinch cayenne pepper
2 pints (4 cups) brown malt vinegar

Skin tomatoes, chop roughly. Peel and chop onions; peel, core and chop apples. Combine all ingredients in large pan, stir over low heat until sugar is dissolved. Simmer, uncovered, approximately 2½ hours or until chutney is thick. Pour into hot sterilised jars, seal.

Makes about 3 lb.

Mango Chutney

3 large ripe mangoes
1 small onion
1 chilli
1 teaspoon mustard seeds
1 teaspoon celery seeds
2 oz. (⅓ cup) raisins
2 oz. (⅓ cup) currants
1 tablespoon chopped mixed peel
1 teaspoon finely chopped green ginger
1 clove garlic, crushed
1 teaspoon salt
½ teaspoon cinnamon
½ teaspoon nutmeg
½ teaspoon allspice
2 oz. (⅓ cup) brown sugar
6 tablespoons brown malt vinegar
6 tablespoons lemon juice

Peel mangoes, roughly chop flesh, discard skin and seeds. Chop onion and chilli; tie mustard and celery seeds in a muslin bag. Combine all ingredients, cover, stand overnight. Place mixture in a large saucepan, boil steadily for 30 minutes, or until thickened. Remove muslin bag, pour chutney into hot sterilised jars, seal.

Makes approx. 1½ lb.

Apple Chutney

6 lb. peeled and cored apples
3 lb. shallots
4½ lb. light brown sugar
4½ pints vinegar
3 lb. sultanas
3 oz. mustard seed
1 tablespoon salt
¾ oz. cayenne pepper

The apples should be weighed after they have been peeled and cored.

Put the chopped apples and peeled and chopped shallots into a pan with all the other ingredients and boil until thick. This will take about 2 hours. Pour into warm dry jars and seal at once.

Piccalilli

cauliflower	1 oz. (1 tablespoon)
cucumber	mustard
button onions	1 quart (4 cups) vinegar
French beans	1 oz. (2 tablespoons)
salt	turmeric
1 oz. (2 tablespoons)	4 chillies
flour	2 oz. loaf (or $\frac{1}{4}$ cup
	granulated) sugar

Prepare 4 lb. of the vegetables. Divide cauliflower into small flowerettes, peel cucumber and cut into pieces, peel onions and leave whole. Choose small beans and string them. Spread all the vegetables out on to a large dish, sprinkle with salt and leave for 24 hours. Drain well and leave to dry. Mix the flour and mustard to a smooth paste with a little cold vinegar. Put the rest on to boil with the turmeric, chillies, sugar and mustard paste. Stir all well together and bring to the boil. Add the vegetables and boil gently for 15 minutes. Leave to cool, then pot and tie down when cold.

Marrow Chutney

8 lb. ripe marrow	8 chillies
salt	12 shallots
2 quarts vinegar	1 teaspoon ground
12 oz. loaf (or 1$\frac{1}{2}$ cups	ginger
granulated) sugar	2 oz. (2 tablespoons)
2 oz. (4 tablespoons)	mustard
turmeric	

Peel and cut the marrow into small cubes. Cover with salt and leave overnight. Boil the vinegar, sugar, turmeric, chillies and shallots for 15 minutes. Add the drained marrow and boil until very soft. Add ginger and mustard mixed smoothly with a little cold vinegar. Pour into warm dry jars and seal at once.

Green Gooseberry Chutney

2 pints gooseberries	2 pints (4 cups) vinegar
3 medium sized onions	$\frac{1}{2}$ lb. (1$\frac{1}{3}$ cups) light
12 oz. (1$\frac{1}{2}$ cups) raisins	brown sugar
1 saltspoon red pepper	2 tablespoons ground
little salt	ginger
	little mustard seed

Top, tail and chop gooseberries, chop onions and raisins. Put into a pan with all the other ingredients. Mix well and simmer for about 1 hour. Pour into warm dry jars and seal at once.

Quince and Lemon Chutney

3 lb. quince	2 blades mace
1 large lemon	1 stick cinnamon
1 teaspoon each—	small piece root ginger
allspice, coriander,	1 onion
salt	1 clove garlic
3 to 4 cloves	$\frac{1}{2}$ lb. (1$\frac{1}{3}$ cups) sultanas
6 peppercorns	$\frac{1}{4}$ lb. stem ginger

Peel and core quince, chop lemon and remove seeds. Tie all spices in a piece of muslin. Peel and chop onion, crush garlic. Put all ingredients into a large pan, bring slowly to the boil, simmer until fruit is soft and the volume reduced by half— about 45 minutes. Pour into warm jars and seal at once.

Apricot and Orange Relish

1 lb dried apricots	1 teaspoon salt
2 chillies	1 lb. (2$\frac{2}{3}$ cups) light
2 cloves garlic	brown sugar
2 shallots	1 orange
$\frac{1}{2}$ oz. preserved ginger	6 almonds
$\frac{1}{2}$ pint (1 cup) white	
wine vinegar	

Wash the apricots, cover with cold water and leave to soak overnight. Simmer until soft in the same water. Cut the chillies—all seeds removed— garlic, shallots and ginger into small slivers and put into a heavy pan with the vinegar, salt, sugar and grated rind and juice of orange. Bring to the boil then add cooked apricots cut into pieces. Simmer for 20 to 30 minutes stirring frequently. About 5 minutes before the end of the cooking add blanched and shredded almonds. Pour into warm jars and seal at once.

Spiced Peaches

1 lb. peaches	$\frac{1}{2}$ teaspoon cloves
$\frac{1}{2}$ lb. (1 cup) sugar	$\frac{1}{4}$ of a nutmeg, grated
1 teaspoon each—	$\frac{3}{4}$ gill (6 tablespoons)
cinnamon, allspice,	cider
coriander	

Plunge the peaches into boiling water and remove the skins. Cut in half, remove stones and put peaches into a pan. Mix the sugar with the spices and sprinkle over the fruit then add cider. Heat very slowly until the sugar has dissolved then bring to the boil. Simmer 2 to 3 minutes. Using a slotted spoon, put the peaches into wide necked jars. Continue to boil the syrup until it starts to thicken (5 to 10 minutes) then pour over the peaches. Seal at once.

Spiced peaches are very good with ham, bacon, pork, cold duck or pheasant.

Green Tomato Pickle

2 lb. green tomatoes
½ cauliflower
1½ lb. onions
2 oz. (¼ cup) salt
water
2½ pints (5 cups) brown
    malt vinegar
2½ lb. (6½ cups) light
    brown sugar
5 oz. (1¼ cups) plain
    flour

1 dessertspoon
    turmeric
1 dessertspoon dry
    mustard
1 dessertspoon curry
    powder
½ teaspoon nutmeg
½ teaspoon ground
    cloves
½ teaspoon ginger

Wash vegetables well, chop skinned tomatoes into small pieces, break cauliflower into small flower-ettes. Peel and chop onions, place all vegetables into a large bowl, sprinkle with salt, cover with water, stand overnight. Drain, rinse well in cold water. Place 2 pints (4 cups) of the vinegar into a large pan with brown sugar, stir over a low heat until sugar is dissolved. Bring to boil. Add vege-tables, bring to boil again. Blend all dry ingredi-ents with remaining ½ pint (1 cup) vinegar, gradually add to vegetable mixture, stir until mixture boils and thickens, reduce heat, simmer 10 minutes, stirring occasionally. Pour into hot sterilised jars, seal.

Makes approx. 7½ to 8 lb.

Clear Mixed Pickles

1 cauliflower
1 large carrot
2 cucumbers
½ cabbage
4 green peppers

12 oz. (1½ cups) sugar
2½ pints (5 cups) white
    vinegar
1 dessertspoon salt
2 chillies

Wash all vegetables well. Cut cauliflower into small flowerets, peel carrot, cut into thick strips. Place cauliflower and carrot in saucepan, cover with water, boil until just tender; drain. Cut cucumbers into quarters lengthwise, remove seeds, chop roughly. Cut cabbage into coarse pieces; remove seeds from peppers, cut into 1 in. pieces.

Place prepared vegetables into a large bowl. Combine sugar, vinegar and salt in a saucepan, bring to the boil, pour over vegetables, cover, stand overnight. Pour into hot sterilised jars. Remove seeds from chillies, add 1 or 2 chilli strips to each jar, seal.

Makes 6 to 6½ lb.

For a Chinese-style of mixed pickle, 4 sticks of celery, 5 to 6 spring onions (scallions) (use white part only) and 1 in. piece of green ginger can be added. Cut celery and spring onions (scallions) into 2 in. pieces, peel ginger, cut into thin slices. Cook these in boiling water 2 minutes, drain then add to other vegetables.

Pickled Onions

4 lb. small onions
1½ lb. (3 cups) salt
water
2 pints (4 cups) white
    vinegar
2 dessertspoons salt
1 dessertspoon ginger

1½ teaspoons whole
    allspice
1½ teaspoons whole
    cloves
1 in. cinnamon stick
few whole peppercorns

Place unpeeled onions, 1½ lb. (3 cups) salt and enough water to cover in a large bowl; cover, stand 2 days, stirring occasionally. Drain liquid, peel onions. Cover onions with boiling water, stand 3 minutes, drain. Repeat this boiling water and draining process two more times. Pack onions into hot sterilised jars. Combine all remaining ingredients in a saucepan, bring slowly to boil, reduce heat, simmer 10 minutes. Cool slightly, strain, pour over onions, seal.

Oriental Chutney

2½ lb. dried apricots
1½ lb. dried peaches
1½ lb. stoned dates
2 lb. sultanas
1½ lb. seedless raisins
1½ lb. currants
6½ lb. light brown
    sugar
2 oz. (¼ cup) salt

¼ lb. garlic
1 oz. (1 tablespoon)
    ground cloves
1 oz. (1 tablespoon)
    cinnamon
1 teaspoon cayenne
    pepper
2 pints (4 cups) vinegar

Cut the apricots, peaches and dates into very small pieces. Wash all the dried fruits. Cover with water and simmer until tender and thick. Add the rest of the ingredients and boil rapidly, stirring well, for about ½ hour or until the contents of the pan are thick. Add extra salt if necessary. Pour at once into hot jars, seal and store for 6 months before using.

Pickled Beetroot

3 to 4 medium sized
    beetroot
salt
water
½ pint (1 cup) brown
    malt vinegar

¼ pint (½ cup) water
4 oz. (½ cup) sugar
¼ teaspoon cinnamon
1 bayleaf
2 whole cloves
4 peppercorns

Wash beetroot well, cook in boiling salted water until tender, or until skins are easily removed. Combine remaining ingredients in separate sauce-pan, bring to boil, lower heat, simmer 5 minutes. Cool.

Peel and slice beetroots, pack into hot sterilised jars. Strain vinegar, pour over beetroot. Seal.
NOTE: Beetroot, because of its high sugar content, ferments easily, so this type of pickle is best made in small quantities, and used as soon as possible.

Corn Relish

1¼ pints (2½ cups) white vinegar
1 cup sugar
2 10 oz. cans whole kernel corn
1 medium onion
2 oz. (¼ cup) chopped celery
1½ oz. (¼ cup) chopped green pepper
1½ oz. (¼ cup) chopped red pepper
3 tablespoons cornflour (cornstarch)
1 tablespoon dry mustard
1 teaspoon mustard seeds

Place 1 pint vinegar and the sugar in a large saucepan, bring to the boil. Add drained corn, chopped onion and remaining chopped vegetables. Reduce heat, simmer 20 minutes. Blend cornflour (cornstarch) and mustard with remaining ¼ pint vinegar, add with mustard seeds to vegetable mixture. Stir until mixture boils and thickens; reduce heat, simmer further 5 minutes, stirring constantly. Pour into hot sterilised jars, seal.

Makes 1½ to 2 lb.

Bread and Butter Pickles

4 large cucumbers
salt
1 pint (2 cups) cider vinegar
¼ pint (½ cup) hot water
3 dessertspoons sugar
1 dessertspoon mustard seeds
1 teaspoon salt
4 strips pimento or red pepper

Wash cucumbers well, slice very thinly. Arrange in layers in large shallow dish, sprinkling a little salt between each layer (about 2 oz. (¼ cup) salt in all). Cover, stand overnight.

Wash cucumbers well in cold water, drain, set aside. In a large saucepan, combine vinegar, hot water, sugar, mustard seeds and salt, bring to boil; reduce heat, simmer, uncovered, 5 minutes. Add cucumbers, bring just to boiling point, remove from heat. Using tongs, and working quickly, pack cucumbers tightly into hot sterilised jars. Add a pimento strip to each jar. Fill with vinegar mixture to within ½ in. of top, seal at once.

Makes 4 to 4½ lb.

Crisp Cucumber Sticks

These are prepared exactly as Bread and Butter Pickles, but instead of cutting cucumbers into thin slices, cut them lengthwise into thick sticks. If cucumbers are long, cut sticks to convenient size to fit into jars. Then proceed as for Bread and Butter Pickles.

Cucumber Relish

4 cucumbers (approx. 4 lb.)
2 oz. (¼ cup) salt
1 red pepper
1 green pepper
½ lb. onions
3 sticks celery
½ oz. (1 dessertspoon) mustard seeds
¾ lb. (1½ cups) sugar
¾ pint (1½ cups) white vinegar

Peel and dice cucumbers, sprinkle with salt. Stand 3 hours, or overnight; drain liquid from cucumbers. Seed and dice peppers, peel and chop onion, chop celery. Chop all vegetables finely. Add cucumbers and prepared vegetables with remaining ingredients to large saucepan.

Stir over low heat until sugar dissolves, increase heat, boil 30 minutes uncovered. Pour into hot sterilised jars, seal.

Makes 2½ to 3 lb.

Pimentos

2 lb. red peppers
boiling water
iced water
1 pint (2 cups) vinegar
1 pint (2 cups) oil

Wash peppers, cut in half, remove seeds and stems. Place in basin, pour over enough boiling water to cover, allow to stand 2 minutes. Drain, cover with iced water; drain again, pack firmly into hot sterilised jars.

Boil vinegar in saucepan for 2 minutes, add oil. When it boils again, pour over peppers, making sure they are covered with liquid. Seal.

Makes approx. 2½ lb.

Pickled Red Cabbage

1 red cabbage
salt
4 pints (8 cups) white vinegar
½ oz. (1 tablespoon) whole cloves
½ oz. (1 tablespoon) whole allspice
½ oz. (or 1 in.) cinnamon stick
few peppercorns
¼ teaspoon nutmeg

Remove discoloured outer leaves from cabbage, cut in quarters, remove thick core. Shred cabbage finely; place in large china basin in layers, sprinkling each layer well with salt. Cover, stand overnight. Drain well. Combine remaining ingredients in heatproof basin, cover with a plate, stand over a saucepan of water; bring water slowly to boil, remove saucepan from heat. Allow vinegar and spices to steep over the warm water for 2 hours; strain through fine cloth. Pack drained cabbage into hot sterilised jars, pour vinegar over, seal.

Confectionery

A tempting assortment of home-made sweets is irresistible and, if you have some cooking to do for a school or church fête, you'll find the sweets made from these recipes are always fast-sellers with the children at the confectionary stall.

A sweets or candy thermometer is a good investment if you plan to make a large quantity of sweets; it helps to take the guesswork and uncertainty out of cooking times and temperatures. Some of the recipes given here use a sweets thermometer; below are directions for its correct use and care.

But if you have not got a thermometer, use the following temperature table and the cold water test as guides.

Soft ball   236 to 240° Fahrenheit. A small quantity of syrup dropped in cold water moulds easily with the fingers into a soft ball.

Firm or hard ball   250 to 260°F. Test as for soft ball. The syrup should mould into firm ball.

Small crack   265 to 290°F. Syrup is clear, but when dropped into cold water cracks and breaks if crushed with fingers.

Hard crack   295 to 315°F. Syrup is golden in colour, snaps and crackles when a little is dropped into cold water.

The cold water test   Spoon a little syrup into cold water and mould with fingers; a shallow bowl makes it easier to see and manipulate syrup; if desired consistency is not reached, cook further and test again. Use fresh cold water for each test, because as water becomes warm the test is less accurate.

Use and care of sweets thermometer   Do not place cold thermometer in boiling syrup. First immerse in cold water and bring to the boil, then check the reading on the thermometer for accuracy (water boils at 212°F., use this reading to check accuracy). If thermometer is not the type that clings to side of pan, return to hot water after each test. When immersing in syrup, cover bulb completely and gently change position of thermometer occasionally in syrup. With thermometer upright, take reading as near eye level as possible.

Toffees

1½ lb. (3 cups) sugar	4 tablespoons brown
½ pint (1 cup) water	malt vinegar

Combine sugar, water and vinegar in saucepan, stir over a low heat until sugar has dissolved. Increase heat, boil rapidly for approximately 15 minutes, or until a small amount of mixture will crack when tested in cold water. Remove toffee from heat, allow bubbles to subside, pour into paper patty cases. Leave for 5 minutes before decorating with chopped nuts, hundreds-and-thousands, coconut etc.

Makes 1 dozen.

Cooked Fondant

1 lb. (2⅔ cups) icing (confectioners') sugar	¼ pint (½ cup) water flavouring food colouring
2 dessertspoons liquid glucose	

Place sugar, glucose and water in saucepan, stir over low heat until sugar has thoroughly dissolved; increase heat, bring to boil, and, using sweets thermometer, boil to 240°F. Remove immediately from heat, allow bubbles to settle, then pour into basin, allow to cool.

When syrup is cool, beat with a wooden spoon until thick, then knead with hands until firm enough to handle.

If required, use a little sifted icing sugar when kneading. Colour and flavour and use as desired.
Peppermint Creams   Colour green, flavour with peppermint essence, roll into balls, flatten slightly.
Prune or Date Creams   Remove stone from fruit, press into canoe-shape, fill recess with coloured and flavoured fondant.

Ever popular Toffees, with an assortment of colourful toppings, are always fast sellers at school or church fêtes.

Peanut Brittle

¾ lb. loaf (or 1½ cups granulated) sugar
¼ pint (½ cup) water
½ lb. (¾ cup) golden syrup (cornsyrup)
2 teaspoons glucose
1 oz. (2 tablespoons) butter
3 oz. (½ cup) peanuts
½ teaspoon lemon essence
1 teaspoon bicarbonate of soda

Put the sugar, water, syrup and glucose into a pan. Stir over gentle heat until sugar has dissolved then boil to 300°F. Add butter, peanuts and essence. Stir until butter has melted then add bicarbonate. Pour on to a well oiled slab. Roll out at once with an oiled rolling pin and break up when firm and brittle.

Honeycomb

6 oz. (¾ cup) sugar
2 tablespoons honey
2 tablespoons golden syrup (cornsyrup)
2 tablespoons water
1½ teaspoons bicarbonate of soda

Place sugar, honey, syrup, and water into saucepan, dissolve over low heat, stirring occasionally. When sugar has dissolved, bring to boil, then reduce heat to low; heat should be just sufficient to keep mixture gently boiling. Cook approximately 12 to 15 minutes or until syrup is brittle when a little is dropped in cold water; cooking time will vary slightly, depending on size and thickness of saucepan.

Be careful syrup does not burn. Remove from heat, stir in bicarbonate of soda quickly. Pour immediately into greased 6 in. sandwich tin. When cold, break into pieces.

Buttered Rum and Brazil Nuts

12 oz. (1½ cups) sugar
2 dessertspoons liquid glucose
¼ pint (½ cup) water
1 oz. (2 tablespoons) butter
4 dessertspoons rum
1 lb. shelled brazil nuts

Place sugar and glucose in saucepan, add the water, stir until sugar dissolves; do not stir after mixture reaches boiling point. Boil steadily to 238°F. on sweets thermometer, (or soft ball stage), then add butter and rum. Boil again until mixture is light honey colour or when a little dropped into cold water forms a hard ball and snaps and crackles. Remove from heat, drop in nuts, lift out one at a time, place on greased paper to set.

Coconut Ice

1 lb. (2⅔ cups) icing (confectioners') sugar
½ lb. (2 cups) desiccated coconut
1 teaspoon vanilla
½ teaspoon lemon juice
2 egg-whites
4 oz. (½ cup) vegetable shortening
pink or green food colouring

Put sifted icing sugar, coconut, vanilla, lemon juice and slightly beaten egg-whites into large basin. Melt shortening over gentle heat. Allow to cool slightly, pour on to ingredients in basin. Combine thoroughly. Press half the mixture into greased bar tin lined with greaseproof paper. Add pink or green colouring to remaining mixture. Press firmly on top of white mixture.

NOTE: If a third layer is desired, divide mixture into three parts. Add 1 dessertspoon sifted cocoa, blended to a smooth paste with a little milk, to one part; blend well, press on top of pink or green layer in tin.

Butterscotch

1 lb. (2 cups) white sugar
3 oz. (½ cup) brown sugar
4 dessertspoons liquid glucose
2 oz. (¼ cup) butter
¼ pint (½ cup) water
½ teaspoon cream of tartar

Place in saucepan the sugars, glucose, butter, and water in which cream of tartar has been dissolved; stir over low heat until sugar has thoroughly dissolved. Increase heat, bring to the boil, using sweets thermometer, boil to 290°F. Remove immediately from heat, allow bubbles to settle, then pour into greased tin about 8 in. square, or on to oiled slab. Mark into squares with oiled knife before it becomes cold.

Rocky Road

2½ tablespoons gelatine
1½ gills (⅔ cup) cold water
1 lb. (2 cups) sugar
¼ pint (½ cup) boiling water
1 dessertspoon lemon juice
1 teaspoon vanilla
pink and green food colouring
3 oz. (½ cup) chopped nuts
6 oz. (1⅓ cups) chopped glacé cherries
4 oz. (4 squares) plain chocolate
2 oz. (¼ cup) solid white vegetable shortening

Soak gelatine in cold water, place sugar and boiling water in large saucepan, bring slowly to the boil. Add the soaked gelatine, boil steadily 10 minutes. Pour into two large basins; cool. Add lemon juice and vanilla. Colour one pink and one green. Beat each colour until very thick, then pour into greased, shallow tins. When quite cold and set, remove from tins, and cut into irregular pieces. Fill roughly into large container, sprinkle nuts and cherries through marshmallows. Melt chopped chocolate and shortening together over hot water, set aside to thicken slightly. Trickle chocolate mixture thickly through and over marshmallows.

Cut into pieces when set.

Marzipan Fruits

1 lb. (2⅔ cups) icing (confectioners') sugar	4 dessertspoons sherry squeeze of orange or lemon juice
4 oz. (1 cup) ground almonds	few drops almond essence, if desired
2 egg-yolks	

Sift icing sugar and ground almonds, mix well. Stir in egg-yolks beaten with sherry, fruit juice, and almond essence. Mix into stiff paste, adding a little more fruit juice, if required. Knead slightly on board.

Apple Shape from round of marzipan. Push clove in each end, with pointed end out for stalk and clubbed end for blossom.

Orange Roll a round of marzipan on fine grater to get indented skin effect. Push in clove for stalk.

Strawberry Roll small amount of marzipan to slight point at one end; paint with food colouring, then roll in red sugar (coloured with food colouring).

Banana Shape from cylinder of marzipan. Point ends and slightly curve banana.

Pear Shape from round of marzipan, bring one end to a point. Press clove in pointed end for stalk.

Paint fruit with appropriate food colouring.

Toffee Apples

½ pint (1 cup) water	½ teaspoon cream of tartar
1½ lb. (3 cups) sugar	
1 dessertspoon white vinegar	apples red food colouring

Combine water, sugar, vinegar, and cream of tartar in saucepan. Heat over low heat, stirring to dissolve sugar completely. Use small brush dipped in cold water to wash down sugar grains from the sides of the saucepan. Undissolved sugar in the syrup or on sides of saucepan could cause mixture to 'candy' instead of remaining clear.

When sugar has dissolved, stop stirring. (Stirring after mixture has boiled will cause candied toffee). Bring mixture to the boil. Boil steadily approximately 5 to 8 minutes. This time will depend on degree of heat under saucepan and also on size and type of saucepan used. A small saucepan will take longer, because there will be less quick evaporation of mixture; also a heavy based saucepan will take longer to cook the mixture than a thin based one.

Begin testing syrup by dropping small teaspoons of syrup into small bowl of cold water. Use fresh water after each test. First test; the mixture will probably be like syrup and will dissolve in the cold water. A few minutes later the mixture will be thick and sticky. Then the mixture will form a soft ball when rolled between the fingers in the testing water. At this stage mixture will begin to bubble thickly. Test again; mixture should form a hard ball when rolled between fingers.

Quickly add red food colouring to give a rich colour. If obtainable, burgundy red food colouring gives best colour. Don't stir; the boiling movement will evenly mix the colouring through toffee. (Stirring the colouring in after the toffee has reached right temperature can cause candying).

Test mixture as before; it should form thin threads of toffee in the water. Test again a few minutes later. Listen carefully as toffee hits the water; it should give quite a loud, sharp crack. Remove pan from heat immediately.

Stand saucepan about 10 to 15 minutes until all bubbling has completely stopped and toffee has cooled.

Have apples prepared: Wash apples well, pat dry; do not rub or polish. Pierce each apple through centre with a butcher's wooden skewer, set aside. Do not refrigerate.

All varieties of apples can be used, but the best results are obtained by using green Granny Smith apples.

The natural oils on the skin of some varieties of red apples can affect toffee coating. The oils tend to prevent toffee clinging to apples, and as toffee drains away, bubbles form under toffee.

Tip pan on its side until there is a deep pool of toffee in the base. Gently lower apples one at a time, at a slight angle, into toffee. Slowly turn apples once round in toffee until completely coated. Lift apple from toffee. Do not hold apple upright, but keep at the angle. Twist round once or twice, allowing excess toffee to run around apple. Then stand apple upright on greased greaseproof paper to set.

If using red apples and bubbles begin to form during coating, plunge toffee coated apples in basin of cold water. This sets toffee and arrests the forming of further bubbles.

Turkish Delight

4 dessertspoons
  gelatine
$\frac{1}{4}$ pint ($\frac{1}{2}$ cup) cold
  water
8 oz. (1 cup) sugar
grated rind of 1 orange
grated rind of 1 lemon

$\frac{1}{4}$ pint ($\frac{1}{2}$ cup) hot water
5 tablespoons orange
  juice
5 tablespoons lemon
  juice
pink food colouring

Softed gelatine in cold water. Make syrup from sugar, rinds and hot water; when boiling add softened gelatine. Boil gently 20 minutes. Remove from heat, add fruit juices; strain mixture. Colour with a few drops of pink food colouring.

Pour into wetted 8 in. tin, allow to set. When firm cut into squares, using knife dipped in hot water. Roll in sifted icing sugar mixed with a little cornflour.

Marshmallows

2 oz. (8 tablespoons)
  gelatine
$\frac{1}{2}$ pint (1 cup) cold
  water
2 lb. (4 cups) sugar

$\frac{3}{4}$ pint (1$\frac{1}{2}$ cups) boiling
  water
2 teaspoons vanilla
1 dessertspoon lemon
  juice

Soften gelatine in cold water. Add sugar to boiling water. Stir to dissolve sugar, bring back to the boil. Add soaked gelatine, boil steadily 20 minutes. Allow to cool to lukewarm. Flavour with vanilla and lemon juice. Beat until very thick and white. Pour into tins which have been rinsed out with cold water. Allow to set. Cut into squares, roll in icing sugar or toasted coconut.

To Toast Coconut Spread coconut on baking trays, bake in moderate oven, Mark 4, 350°F., 10 to 15 minutes. Shake trays occasionally. Alternatively, the coconut can be put into large, heavy frypan and toasted over moderate heat. Shake pan continually so coconut does not burn.

Chocolate Ginger Sticks

2 oz. crystallized
  ginger
3 oz. ($\frac{1}{2}$ cup) finely
  chopped dates

3 oz. (3 squares) plain
  chocolate

Put ginger and dates through fine mincer or chop very finely. Shape into sticks approximately 2 in. in length and $\frac{1}{4}$ in. wide. Place chocolate in top of double boiler, melt over hot water.

Place date and ginger sticks on wire rack, spoon chocolate over. Refrigerate until set.

Makes approx. 1$\frac{1}{2}$ dozen.

Sherried Chocolate Dates

grated rind of 1 orange
2 dozen dessert dates
5 to 6 tablespoons
  sweet sherry

4 oz. (4 squares) plain
  chocolate
1 oz. (2 tablespoons)
  white vegetable
  shortening

Grate rind from orange, taking care not to remove any white pith. Place rind in saucepan, cover with water, simmer 5 minutes. Drain.

Pit dates, fill with small amount of orange rind, press together. Place sherry in basin, add dates, cover; leave overnight or at least 1 hour.

Chop chocolate and shortening, melt in top of double saucepan over hot water. Drain dates slightly. Using tongs, dip dates in melted chocolate; place on waxed paper until chocolate has set.

Coconut Roughs

1 oz. (2 tablespoons)
  melted butter
1$\frac{1}{2}$ oz. ($\frac{1}{3}$ cup) hot
  mashed potato
8 oz. (1$\frac{1}{3}$ cups) icing
  (confectioners')
  sugar

pinch salt
1$\frac{1}{4}$ tablespoons cocoa
10 oz. (2 cups) coconut
1 teaspoon vanilla

Beat butter into hot potato, gradually beat in sifted icing (confectioners') sugar, salt and cocoa. Add coconut and vanilla, mix well. Spoon teaspoons on to greaseproof paper, refrigerate until firm.

Old Fashioned Fudge

1$\frac{1}{2}$ lb. (3 cups) sugar
pinch salt
2 oz. ($\frac{1}{2}$ cup) cocoa
$\frac{1}{2}$ pint (1 cup) milk

2 tablespoons liquid
  glucose
1$\frac{1}{2}$ oz. (3 tablespoons)
  butter
1 teaspoon vanilla

The right degree of heat is essential for success in this economical delicious fudge; a sweets thermometer is necessary.

Combine sugar, salt, cocoa, milk and glucose in saucepan, stir over low heat until sugar dissolves. Increase heat, boil rapidly until mixture reaches 234°F. Remove from heat, add butter, allow to cool to 110°F. Add vanilla, beat until fudge loses its gloss and starts to change colour. Immediately pour into greased and lined 8 in. sandwich tin, cut into squares when cold.

Sherried Chocolate Dates, with fresh orange-flavoured filling, are delicious to serve with after-dinner coffee.

Drinks and Punches

There's a selection of well-blended punch recipes here for every occasion—weddings, engagements, birthday parties; plus thirst-quenching drinks for summer, and hot drinks to warm when the weather is cold.

Iced Tea

freshly brewed tea — lemon slices
ice cubes — mint sprigs
sugar

Allow tea to cool at room temperature. (Chilling tea too rapidly will make it cloudy.) Sweeten to taste if desired, strain. Place ice cubes in glasses, add tea. Garnish each glass with lemon slice and mint sprig.

Delicious Iced Coffee

$2\frac{1}{2}$ tablespoons instant coffee powder — vanilla ice-cream
$\frac{1}{2}$ pint (1 cup) hot water — whipped cream
$1\frac{1}{2}$ pints (3 cups) cold water — grated chocolate — glacé cherries

Dissolve coffee in hot water, add cold water; sweeten if desired; refrigerate until ready to serve. Place a generous scoop of ice-cream into each glass, fill with iced coffee. Top with whipped cream, grated chocolate and a glacé cherry.

Serves approx. 4.

Lemon Cordial

1 lb. 10 oz. ($3\frac{1}{4}$ cups) sugar — $\frac{1}{4}$ oz. (1 dessertspoon) epsom salts
$1\frac{1}{2}$ oz. ($1\frac{1}{2}$ tablespoons) tartaric acid — $1\frac{1}{2}$ pints (3 cups) boiling water — 2 large lemons

Combine sugar, tartaric acid and epsom salts in a large bowl, add boiling water, stir until sugar is dissolved. Cool. Finely grate the rind of 2 lemons, squeeze juice, add to liquid, allow to become cold. Pour into bottles, cork, or cover with screw caps, store in refrigerator. Mixture will keep for 2 to 3 weeks.

Makes $2\frac{3}{4}$ pints of concentrated lemon cordial. To drink, dilute with iced water.

Blender Lemonade

1 large lemon — 1 pint (2 cups) iced water
2 oz. ($\frac{1}{4}$ cup) sugar

Wash lemon, cut off thick ends, cut lemon into 8 pieces. Place all ingredients into electric blender, blend on high speed until lemon is finely shredded. Strain. Use soon after blending.

Makes approx. 1 pint.

Home Style Ginger Beer

Ginger Beer Plant

$\frac{1}{2}$ pint (1 cup) cold water — 1 teaspoon sugar
1 teaspoon ground ginger — $\frac{1}{2}$ teaspoon instant coffee powder — 1 teaspoon honey

Combine all ingredients in a screw top jar. Feed plant each day for 7 days with additional 1 teaspoon sugar, 1 teaspoon ginger, 1 teaspoon honey and $\frac{1}{2}$ teaspoon instant coffee powder.

To Make up Ginger Beer Dissolve $1\frac{1}{2}$ lb. (3 cups) sugar in 2 pints (4 cups) hot water. Add 7 pints cold water and strained juice of 3 lemons. Add to this the strained liquid from screw-top jar (strain through fine muslin cloth). Pour into clean, dry, airtight bottles; seal tops. The best bottles to use have special clamp tops. Keep 3 to 4 weeks before using.

Makes approx. 10 pints.

To Keep Plant Alive Halve the residue strained into muslin, return to jar with $\frac{1}{2}$ pint water (1 cup); let stand 1 week, feeding each day as before.

Irish Coffee

1 tablespoon Irish whiskey — strong black coffee — unwhipped cream
1 teaspoon sugar

Place whiskey into small, warmed goblet, add sugar. Fill to within $\frac{1}{2}$ in. of top with black coffee.

Stir quickly to dissolve sugar. Top with $\frac{1}{4}$ in. layer of cream. The best way to do this is to hold a spoon over coffee, and gently pour cream over back of spoon bowl so that cream floats on top. Do not stir.
Gaelic Coffee   Use Scotch whisky instead of Irish whiskey.

Mulled Wine

1 bottle claret
2 cinnamon sticks
6 cloves
1 tablespoon sugar

$\frac{1}{2}$ pint (1 cup) brandy
1 piece lemon rind
nutmeg

Combine claret, crushed cinnamon sticks, cloves, sugar, brandy and lemon rind in saucepan, heat slowly, do not boil. Strain wine through a fine strainer. Serve hot in mugs, sprinkle with a little nutmeg.
Makes approx. $1\frac{1}{2}$ pints.

Gluehwein

1 bottle claret
6 whole cloves
1 cinnamon stick

6 lemon slices
6 orange slices
2 tablespoons sugar

Place all ingredients in saucepan, heat slowly but do not allow to boil. Strain wine through a fine strainer, serve hot. Garnish with extra lemon and orange slices.
Makes approx. $1\frac{1}{2}$ pints.
NOTE: 1 tablespoon brandy may be added to each glass before adding the hot Gluehwein.

Glogg

1 bottle port wine
1 bottle Burgundy
1 bottle Aquavit
1 cinnamon stick

1 tablespoon whole
   cloves
raisins
blanched almonds

Combine port, burgundy and aquavit in a saucepan, heat slowly, simmer 3 minutes. Tie cinnamon and cloves in a muslin bag, dip into simmering wine mixture for 1 minute. Place a few raisins and almonds in each glass, top with the Glogg, serve hot in coffee mugs.
Makes approx. 4 pints.

Apple Cider

4 lb. over-ripe, bruised
   or spotted apples

6 pints (12 cups) cold
   water
$\frac{1}{2}$ lb. (1 cup) sugar

Wash and dry apples. Cut into $\frac{1}{2}$ in. slices; place in large crockery basin, cover with the cold water. Cover with cloth and allow to stand 10 days, stirring daily. The mixture will ferment and bubble.

After 10 days, drain apples and discard, reserve liquid. Stir in sugar, stirring until dissolved. Strain through several thicknesses of fine muslin; do not squeeze muslin. Bottle into clean dry bottles and allow to stand, uncorked but covered with cloth, for 14 days. The cider will continue to bubble in the bottle, the bubbles becoming smaller and less frequent toward the end of this period. If necessary, re-strain into clean dry bottles to remove sediment. Cork securely, label and date. Keep for three months before using.
Makes 3 pints.

Port Sangria

1 bottle claret
$\frac{1}{2}$ bottle port
$\frac{1}{2}$ pint (1 cup) marsala

4 tablespoons orange
   juice
1 tablespoon lemon
   juice

Combine all ingredients, mix well. Sliced strawberries can also be added. Pour into jugs. Garnish with orange and lemon juice.
Makes about $2\frac{1}{2}$ pints.

Wine Sangria

2 bottles red wine
$\frac{1}{4}$ pint ($\frac{1}{2}$ cup) brandy
$1\frac{1}{4}$ pints ($2\frac{1}{2}$ cups)
   lemonade

oranges, strawberries
   or other fruit

Combine wine and brandy, add a few orange or lemon slices and whole strawberries, pour over crushed ice. Just before serving add chilled lemonade. Garnish with spirals of orange rind.
Makes approx. 4 pints.

Buckingham Palace Punch

This recipe comes from Monsieur René Poussin, a former Chef at Buckingham Palace.

juice and grated rind
of three lemons
pinch of cinnamon
pinch of cloves
$\frac{1}{2}$ grated nutmeg

$2\frac{1}{2}$ oz. lump or granulated sugar
3 pints (6 cups) water
1 bottle dark Jamaica
   brandy
1 bottle brandy

Put lemon rind, juice, spices, sugar and water into a pan and boil for 5 minutes. Add rum and brandy. As soon as it is hot, strain through muslin and serve.
Makes 5 pints.

Party Punch

½ lb. (1 cup) sugar
2 pints (4 cups) water
⅛ pint (¼ cup) strong
  black tea
4 oranges
4 lemons
15 oz. can light grape
  juice

15 oz. can crushed
  pineapple
1¼ pints ginger ale
orange slices
maraschino cherries
strawberries

Combine sugar and water in saucepan, stir over low heat until sugar dissolves, bring to boil; reduce heat, simmer 5 minutes. Add strained tea, refrigerate. Squeeze juice from oranges and lemons. Add strained fruit juices, grape juice and undrained pineapple to syrup; refrigerate. Pour into punch bowl; just before serving, add ginger ale, garnish with orange slices, cherries and hulled and sliced strawberries.

Makes approx. 6 pints.

White Wine Punch

3 bottles white wine
¼ pint (½ cup) brandy

juice ½ lemon
melon

With melon baller, cut balls from melon. Put into bowl, cover, refrigerate.

Have the wine well chilled; Moselle is a good wine to use for this punch.

At serving time, pour wine into punch bowl, add lemon juice, brandy and melon balls. Ice cubes can also be added. If water melon is available, this will add colour to the punch.

Makes approx. 4 pints.

Champagne Fruit Punch

½ lemon
1 orange
15 oz. can pineapple
  pieces
¼ pint (½ cup) brandy

2 tablespoons sugar
1 bottle Moselle
1 bottle champagne
1¼ pints soda water

Slice the lemon and orange finely, drain pineapple pieces, discard syrup. Combine fruit, brandy and sugar in punch bowl; refrigerate. Before serving, add remaining ingredients.

Makes approx. 4 pints.

Superb Party Punch

2 lb. peaches
sugar
4 pints dry white wine
½ bottle red wine

⅛ pint (¼ cup) Cointreau
⅛ pint (¼ cup) brandy
1 bottle champagne

Peel peaches, slice into punch bowl, sprinkle lightly with sugar. Add chilled white wine, red wine, Cointreau and brandy. Just before serving, stir in chilled champagne.

Makes approx. 1¼ gallons.

Pineapple Punch

1½ pints (3 cups) strong
  tea
1½ gills (⅔ cup) lemon
  juice
1 pint (2 cups) pine-
  apple juice

½ pint (1 cup) fresh
  orange juice
½ lb. (1 cup) sugar
2½ pints lemonade
1¼ pints ginger ale
lemon slices

Strain tea, combine with fruit juices and sugar, refrigerate. Just before serving, add chilled lemonade, ginger ale and ice. Place half a lemon slice in each glass before pouring in punch.

Makes approx. 7 pints.

Tahitian Rum Punch

1 bottle white wine
¼ pint (½ cup) canned
  pineapple juice
1½ gills (⅔ cup) fresh
  orange juice

1½ gills (⅔ cup) lime or
  lemon juice
2½ pints ginger ale
sugar
fresh fruit slices

Chill all ingredients well; combine rum, strained fruit juices and sugar to taste, in a punch bowl. Just before serving, add ice and ginger ale. Garnish with fresh fruit slices.

Makes approx. 5 pints.

West Indian Punch

This is the famous rum punch of the West Indies. It is compiled in the following proportions:

1 bitter   (1 measure of lemon juice)
2 sweet   (2 measures of sugar syrup)
3 strong   (3 measures of rum)
4 weak   (4 measures of water)

With 1 bottle of rum as the base, the punch is prepared as follows:

½ pint (1 cup) lemon
  juice
1 pint (2 cups) sugar
  syrup (made from
  1 lb. (2 cups) sugar
  and 1½ gills (⅔ cup)
  water)

1¼ pints rum
2 pints (4 cups) water,
  extra
grated nutmeg
angostura bitters

Make syrup; combine water and sugar in saucepan. Bring to boil, stir to dissolve sugar; cool.

Mix all ingredients together lightly. Add a few drops of angostura bitters to give a light pink tint. Refrigerate until well chilled.

Put a spoonful of crushed ice in each glass, pour in punch. Top each glass with grated nutmeg. A maraschino cherry can be added.

Makes approx. 5 pints.

White Wine Punch, served sparkling cold, has colourful balls of watermelon added just before serving.

Index

Index

American Weights and measures

American measurements

If you are to get consistently good results when cooking it is necessary to weigh or measure the ingredients very accurately. All recipes in this book are based on Imperial weights and measures, (see pages 8-9) with American cup equivalents given in parenthesis. Measures in weight in the Imperial and American systems are the same but measures in volume are slightly different. The following table shows the equivalents:

Spoon measurements

U.S.	Imperial
1¼ teaspoons	1 teaspoon
1¼ tablespoons	1 tablespoon
1 tablespoon	1 dessertspoon
16 tablespoons (1 cup)	20 tablespoons
48 teaspoons (1 cup)	60 teaspoons

Liquid measurements

U.S.	Imperial
1 gill	5/6 English gill
1 pint	5/6 ,, pint
1 quart	5/6 ,, quart
1 gallon	5/6 ,, gallon

Level spoon measurements are used in all recipes in this book.

American cup measures

The standard eight liquid ounce measuring cup is used for recipes in this book.

The jug shown in the sketch measures up to 10 fluid ounces. The 8 fluid ounce, or 1 cup measure, is clearly shown, together with fractions of cup measures. Millilitre (ml.) measures are also shown.

To measure dry ingredients with a cup, spoon ingredient lightly into cup until it reaches required mark. Hold glass measure at eye level to make sure of measurement. Never pack ingredients tightly into cup, unless recipe specifies this.

When measuring a liquid ingredient, the cup should be on level surface.

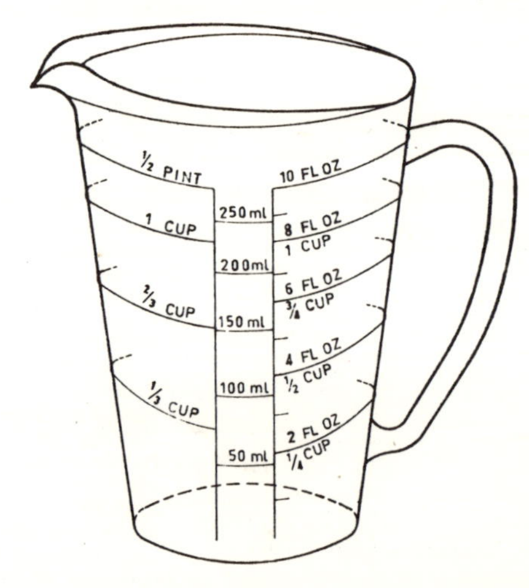